WELL-PRESERVED

WELL-PRESERVED

THE ONTARIO HERITAGE FOUNDATION'S
MANUAL
OF PRINCIPLES AND PRACTICE
FOR **ARCHITECTURAL
CONSERVATION**

MARK FRAM

THE BOSTON MILLS PRESS

Canadian Cataloguing in Publication Data

Fram, Mark.
   Well-preserved : the Ontario Heritage Foundation's manual
of principles and practice for architectural conservation

Includes index.
ISBN 0-919783-42-2

1. Historic buildings — Conservation and restoration.
2. Historic buildings — Ontario — Conservation and
restoration.   3. Architecture — Conservation and
restoration.   4. Architecture — Ontario — Conservation and
restoration.   I. Ontario Heritage Foundation.   II. Title.

NA109.C3F72 1988   363.6′9′09713   C88-094139-1

Published by:
THE BOSTON MILLS PRESS
132 Main Street
Erin, Ontario, Canada
N0B 1T0
(519) 833-2407
Fax (519) 833-2195

American Association
for State and Local History
Award of Merit

Winners of the
Heritage Canada
Communications Award

Edited by John Parry
Designed by Mark Fram
Cover design by Gill Stead
Printed by Ampersand, Guelph

The publisher wishes to acknowledge the financial assistance
of The Canada Council, the Ontario Arts Council, and the
Office of the Secretary of State.

To understand a place one must know its memories.

Richard England

. . . spirit always adheres to forms. *That is why forms survive.* Because even when specifics are forgotten, a form can retain an aura of what originated it and so pass on not the doctrine but the sense of life.

Michael Ventura, "Hear That Long Snake Moan", *Whole Earth Review*, Spring 1987

A builder will probably point out that a cheaper material will show a useful saving. This may be true, but it is at this point that we must summon up all our powers of resistance to temptation, because nine times out of ten the economics are going to be wrong. Not only in the long term will the inferior material add to maintenance costs or deteriorate sooner, but in the short term also will reflect the loss of intrinsic value in the house.

Beverley Pike, *The Good Looking House*, 1980

Foreword

Until a very few years ago, the task facing the conservation-minded was straightforward: to rescue landmark properties under threat of destruction and prevent their demolition. Once the bulldozers had been fought off, the struggle moved to the next threatened property. Conservation was a black-and-white, yes-or-no business. "Rescue" was the catch-phrase. Subsequent rehabilitation or restoration was usually left to take care of itself.

Rescue is still the first step when a heritage property is at risk. But simple rescue is no longer sufficient.

Every building has productive uses — even if only symbolic — but buildings do not last unless maintained against the relentless forces of age, weather and decay. And, as many individuals and conservation organizations have discovered, a building of historical or architectural importance does not maintain its quality and distinction if left to take care of itself.

Long-term success of any conservation treatment or strategy depends on the *quality* of the work — on proper care of the old and proper fit of the new. Many fine old buildings have lost their special look and feel, and much of their historic and landmark significance, in being modernized for new or extended use. Though many rescued structures have new leases on life, few are exemplary — quality of new work and attention to detail vary greatly, from excellent to very bad. Good old work has far too often been destroyed or trivialized by new work of little sensitivity and less skill.

The conservation field has blossomed and matured, with many knowledgeable professionals, much useful information in print, and many keen and concerned owners and custodians of heritage properties. But there has been little sharing of knowledge of successes and failures and of lessons to be learned from both. There are no widely accepted national or provincial standards for quality in conservation work. Professional training is specialized and fragmented, and few practitioners are knowledgeable outside their area of expertise. Useful published information is scattered in many sources, few of them Canadian. And many useful specialized publications leave out essential parts of the conservation process.

To meet this challenge, the Ontario Heritage Foundation considers it vital that everyone involved in conserving built heritage — owners, communities, public agencies, interest groups, practitioners — have ready access to a common base of knowledge and principles about heritage conservation. Thus this guide to good conservation practice.

Richard M. Alway, Chairman
Ontario Heritage Foundation

Preface and acknowledgements

You can find many "how-to" books dealing with old buildings. This is much more a book about *what* to do. And why to do it.

The book is about architecture, both old and new, in its most generous sense — not just the picture-postcard views of monuments but the landscapes and streets in which buildings sit and the small details of their forms, too. And not only monuments, but also commonplaces, or what some call vernacular architecture. This book is about recognizing the important qualities of all these places, and about conserving both place and quality, for now and for the future.

It isn't enough to simply preserve those qualities without attending to the quality of conservation work itself. This book encourages both recognition of "heritage", wherever you may find it in your own environment, and recognition of the difference between good work that respects that heritage, and bad work that detracts from it. It's essential to do the work well. Thus the title, "*Well*-preserved".

Along with many others, I enjoy looking at and learning about architecture and towns and countrysides. These are endlessly fascinating places. I trained, graduated and worked as an architect, though I've never registered formally as one. My not-so-private joke about my interest in these places is that I like architecture too much to actually *do* it — at least not to help produce new buildings that destroy or disfigure what exists.

You may have noticed that few practitioners in architecture, planning, engineering or building are able to build for others anything like the places they really care for or even the places where they work or live. Rarely does a new building live up to its promised comfort or durability, and even more rare is the opportunity to make adjustments and improvements. Though the product is meant to last a long time, and often seems to take a long time to construct, during its actual production there never seems to be enough time to make it well.

Once out of school, most practitioners leave behind the study or understanding of either historic or contemporary architecture and building — even simple and basic qualities such as bodily comfort or pleasing sound and light get attention only when something goes terribly wrong. And most new buildings, even those that do not tower over their neighbours or sprawl over the landscape, grow old with very little grace. The clients, users and neighbours of buildings seem to be represented better by other groups — historians, geographers, even journalists — in appreciating and promoting improved quality in human environments.

Recent publications about the traditional qualities of buildings and places (books that we may both admire and shake our heads over) expose the yawning gulf between the quantitative "standard of living" and the quality of where and how we live. Seeing the inadequacies of the new, we look back at what came before. Old buildings and settled landscapes offer opportunities to store and recapture our nostalgia for simpler times. Many people maintain an impossible but touching belief that the simplicity of the past (or is it just the *appearance* of simplicity?) must be preferable to the complex present. Our grandparents would tell us otherwise — the past, however it looks, remains in the past. To respect both past and present, we must acknowledge which is which. Conservation — what this book is about — means being honest and truthful, not merely romantic, about the past.

Conservation of places and objects is neither art nor science, but rather *craft*. Conservation, well done, ought to bring together intelligence, eye and hand to work on places and things — to protect them, to keep them alive and to pass them down to the next generation. We no longer make buildings and streets and landscapes the way we once did. So we should try to maintain some of these places, and to keep alive the qualities of craft they embody. Perhaps, then, craft itself will reawaken to modern needs and help produce the next generation's inheritance.

In conservation, it is possible to identify and recommend appropriate treatments for almost any problem with relatively little effort. It is possible to carry out almost any responsible repair on the job with satisfactory results, again with relatively little effort. And it is possible to isolate and deal with the extraordinary exceptions responsibly and efficiently with the help of expert problem-solvers. But, unhappily, these possibilities come together all too rarely.

There's hardly anything *new* in this book. After all, conserving buildings, places and environments is by no means new. In each of the several subdivisions of heritage conservation — architecture, historical research, archaeology, museology, and so on — a wealth of data, experience and advice awaits the patient observer and practitioner. But the information is specialized, fragmented and sometimes even contradictory. Though there is a lot of common sense in conservation, it is unfortunately seldom followed. Too much is misinterpreted, too little learned. So I tried to put this information together in a way that would make it easy for you to find out just enough to let you do what needed doing, or to find out more about it before you went ahead, or to find someone to help you do it.

One very strong impetus for this book has been the growing number of inquiries to people like me at public agencies or private offices about what to do about old buildings and properties (and how to do it), and the lack of enough people to answer them, either in public or private practice. So the reasoning among my colleagues went like this: let's put down in one find-it-yourself resource enough guidance to take care of most of the questions, and turn the experts loose on the really difficult problems. Since there are few experts at hand, the book tries to give answers to most of the regular questions while giving some direction toward solving the more difficult problems, while waiting for the professionals to arrive (and, one hopes, save the day).

Accordingly, this book is what you might call an "expert system" — or at least the prelude to one. Computers are being put to work to compile and analyze and regurgitate not only huge databases of information, but also the rules for making decisions from that information, attempting to harness not only the expert's data but also his or her methods of understanding and making decisions. Such expert systems are useful where there are many fairly standard diagnostic techniques and solutions, and where human expertise is hard to get and more urgently required for the non-standard situations.

At the beginning of this book's development in late 1986, the idea was to construct just such a computer-based system, with a book as a byproduct. Though some of the tools to construct such a system existed then, it would have taken a few extra years to get the book done. Technology was not quite ready for such a modest effort as this. So we did it backwards. Here's the book. The system should be catching up soon.

This book owes a great deal to a great many people, though as compiler and author I bear the usual responsibility for the gaps and inadequacies of the finished product. I was very fortunate to have had the counsel of conservation professionals in Toronto, Ottawa, Montreal, New York, Washington, London, Edinburgh, York and Paris as I assembled this material. I am especially grateful for the time and attention given my early efforts by the following people, each of whom provided verbal or written comments, both critical and supportive. I hope the final product fairly respects their advice:

Laurie Beckelman, New York Landmarks Conservancy
Heather Broadbent, Ontario Heritage Foundation
Margaret Carter, Consultant, Ottawa
Lynne DiStefano, Brescia College, London, Ontario
Neil Einarson, Manitoba Historic Resources Branch, Winnipeg
Jane Fawcett, UK ICOMOS and Architectural Association, London, England
Anne M. de Fort-Menares, Architectural Historian, Toronto
Wesley Haynes, New York Landmarks Conservancy
Desmond Hodges and others, Edinburgh New Town Conservation Committee
Donald W. Insall, Donald Insall & Associates Ltd., London, England
Alistair Kerr, B.C. Heritage Trust, Victoria
H. Ward Jandl, Preservation Assistance Division, U.S. National Park Service
Frank G. Matero, Center for Preservation Research, Columbia University
Michael McClelland, Toronto Historical Board
Marilyn Miller, Heritage Branch, Ministry of Culture and Communications
Richard Moorhouse, Heritage Branch, Ministry of Culture and Communications
Susann Myers, Heritage Branch, Ministry of Culture and Communications
Lee H. Nelson, Preservation Assistance Division, U.S. National Park Service
Bonnie Parsekian, RESTORE, New York City
Matthew Saunders, Ancient Monuments Society, London, England
Jean Simonton, Heritage Branch, Ministry of Culture and Communications

Peter H. Smeallie, Building Research Board, U.S.
    National Research Council
Rod Stewart, Rod Stewart Construction Ltd., Port
    Hope
Herb Stovel, Heritage Canada, Ottawa
Ted Teshima, Ontario Heritage Foundation
Christopher Tossell, Ontario Heritage Foundation
Martin Weaver, Heritage Canada, Ottawa
Anna M. Young, Ontario Heritage Foundation

Lee Nelson very kindly allowed me to adapt his unpublished paper, "A methodology for identifying historic character" (12 December 1986).

Others who encouraged and helped include: Liz Addison, Jim Anderson, David Bouse, Melissa Gordon, Christine Gutierrez, Denis Heroux, Diana Jervis-Read, Dana Johnson, Harold Kalman, Ray and Cindy Kipfer, Mark London, Carol Priamo, Jeff Stinson, Margo Teasdale, John Weiler and Phillip Wright, together with my many professional colleagues from the Ontario Ministry of Culture and Communications, some of whom have joined the growing ranks of heritage specialists outside government.

The ministry was sufficiently generous to have given me the opportunity to do much of this work as a special assignment, and for that I am very thankful. The ministry's motivation came in large part from the directors of the Ontario Heritage Foundation who have served on its Architectural Conservation Committee, especially Lynne DiStefano and Anna M. Young, who, in chairing the Committee, made it impossible for either the ministry or me to let this project slip away.

Over the years I (and my colleagues) have dealt with all sorts of requests, comments, complaints and cries for help from hundreds of individuals and communities in Ontario. I am grateful for both the challenges these people have thrown at us and the help they have given us too, sometimes simultaneously. They are far too numerous to name, so I thank them all by offering this book by way of compensation for their energy and interest in heritage conservation.

It is customary to thank the legions of researchers and typists normally responsible for books of this magnitude, but I must confess that it is almost all my own doing (or should that be "fault"?). Though the data is not computerized, the book itself *is* — drafted, composed, laid out and typeset on a microcomputer (almost entirely with a program called JustText, running on an Apple Macintosh). But I still needed help. I am especially grateful for the hospitality and encouragement of Henry Sears, Catharine Tanner and David Hollands of Sears & Russell Architects, and for the assistance of Scott Kerr who shared the daunting task of whipping the drawings into shape and onto these pages. John Parry did an excellent job in editing my sometimes wayward prose, and John Denison of The Boston Mills Press enthusiastically helped me to help him get this book out in good order.

In the end, I am grateful most of all to two somewhat irregular muses: tolerance and patience. Especially patience. Her kindness has gone well beyond the call of duty, and I owe her a great debt. I intend to pay her back, very soon.

MF

INTRODUCTION

Architecture is what you do to a
building when you look at it.

Walt Whitman

What this book is

A commitment to conserving historical memories and patterns adds immeasurably to our lives and the arguments for their demolition on the grounds of "progress" are quite indefensible; if technology is to add to our lives, then a route via destruction cannot be justified because it impoverishes us.

Terry Farrell, "British Architecture After Modernism" (1984)

A tool for conservation

WELL-PRESERVED is three rather different things. It is a narrative, arranged to reflect how heritage conservation ought to take place, from understanding to planning to doing to maintaining. It is a compendium that can be read in almost any order, offering pieces of information about many topics, from general to specific. It is a catalogue, providing access to other more detailed sources.

Though this book, like a building, has to do many jobs at the same time, its basic purpose is to tie together principle and practice. The principles come from diligent research and international charters; the practice comes from many how-to guides, technical publications, and the shared experience of many trained professionals.

Before now there has been no comprehensive reference available that bridges principle and practice. In conservation, there are sometimes cases where principle and practice seem to conflict. WELL-PRESERVED tries its best to show the difference between good practice based on principles and bad practice based on expediency. It tries to show how good practice, in the end, can be more efficient than bad, once the full value of the building or site is understood and factors of time and durability are taken seriously.

The key to the connection of principle and practice is to understand that heritage resources are irreplaceable. Each building or tool or document represents or embodies a specific event or moment or episode or trend in human life. Even something mass-produced may merit special attention for having been used in a unique way. This uniqueness is not replaceable or reproducible by any means, even by copying or counterfeiting. It may not be valuable in a monetary sense but may be culturally important, because people are *attached* to things and places — they feel their lives lessened by the deterioration or disappearance of a heritage resource. This basic message runs throughout the book, from general to particular.

A guide for decision-making

WELL-PRESERVED stresses that heritage resources are precious, irreplaceable, and deserving of every effort to retain and maintain them.

Heritage resources run from collections of small objects in museums to entire landscapes and regions displaying the legacy of past generations. They have essential and tangible everyday uses yet are important symbols of cultural values and aspirations. Heritage conservation mirrors this duality — it is of growing importance as an economic activity and as a cultural pursuit.

Conserving the material legacy of the past under a wide range of conditions requires people with many different skills and interests. They must co-ordinate their decisions to keep heritage resources intact as connections to the past and as assets for the future.

This book focuses on the immovable resources of lands, buildings and structures, not as isolated features but as places with contexts in time and place. Though conservation must pay great attention to myriad details, a property's surroundings and wider community interests must not be forgotten.

A directory of information sources

WELL-PRESERVED is a catalogue to other sources of guidance in print. Topical references are given in the form of a simple code: a four-letter abbreviation of the author's or editor's name and two digits indicating year of publication. The codes are compiled alphabetically in the bibliography at the end of the book. The bibliography attempts to be comprehensive and up-to-date, though many useful items do not appear for reasons of space. In some cases, there may be a more recent edition of a listed book.

Ontario has no single easily accessible public repository of information about heritage conservation, though some government agencies, universities and public libraries have excellent collections of books and articles on specific topics. With patience, one can find any item through public libraries, by inter-library loan.

Who should use it

Building owners should find here the basic questions and concerns they will need to address in relating their contemporary needs to the architectural heritage of their buildings. Most of the answers should be here, too. For small projects and capable owners, the advice may be taken straight, but the book should be equally useful as a reference to aid in understanding and evaluating the advice of consultants, specialists and contractors. Since it concentrates on both details and their larger contexts, the guide's advice can be used for conservation projects from the very small to the very large.

Architects and engineers should find the guide a vehicle for communicating with their clients and an outline of criteria for building evaluation and remedial work that emphasizes the value (both aesthetic and pragmatic) of retaining as much as possible of the architectural distinction of an older building in the course of extending its useful life. Architects must recognize the many differences between new construction and conservation work in old-building projects and take them into careful account in meeting the needs of both client and building.

Heritage organizations, such as local architectural conservation advisory committees (LACACs), historical societies, museums, and even libraries, will be able to use this guide as a sourcebook of advice and information resources to respond to requests for conservation assistance. Published material is not always readily available and what is at hand may not satisfy immediate needs.

Municipal officials and LACAC advisers can use this guide to help owners of properties designated or eligible for designation under the Ontario Heritage Act decide how best to (and how not to) rehabilitate, restore or modernize in order to maintain historical and architectural character.

Builders, contractors and construction trades should find here explicit guidance on the special care and techniques needed to maintain the aesthetic and functional integrity of older buildings. The guide will give builders a sense of how to integrate individual trades, and how owners and their consultants will assess ongoing work and overall results. Much of the manual's advice is directed toward improving workmanship by pre-planning and careful monitoring.

Specialized building consultants, such as energy retrofit consultants, will find here the full context within which to modify new-building or energy-conserving techniques to suit real conditions and constraints. Retrofit measures that achieve sharp short-term efficiencies are seldom suitable for older buildings, and the unmistakeable look and feel of some retrofit techniques do not suit landmark buildings or even modest residences.

Heritage consultants, such as architectural historians, researchers, archaeologists and conservators, will find here the context for their special work within the project as a whole. Skilled reconnaissance of a building often supplies many answers about appropriate treatment and technique, but only when done at the right time and with practical application in mind.

Enthusiasts and volunteers can use this book as a guide to the finer points of old buildings, structures and sites, and as a point of departure for local surveys and inventories of notable buildings, structures and districts. Much valuable information about heritage resources is gathered, recorded and maintained by a growing number of informed and public-spirited individuals and specialist groups interested in archaeology, history, architecture, agriculture, industry and landscapes.

How to use it

ACCESS TO INFORMATION

Throughout the book, look for bibliographic and other information in this column, as well as for the underlying principles of the "Good practice" guidelines. See the diagram opposite for help in navigation.

Organization

WELL-PRESERVED has four main parts.

"The inheritance" looks at the material heritage of building and environment built up in Ontario over the past two centuries and more. It outlines forces and influences that determined the look of buildings, communities and landscapes. It concludes with a guide to help define the value and demonstrate the importance and use of this built heritage for the future.

"Careful conservation" defines the terms and principles governing conservation of buildings and their environments. The principles collect and connect the experience of international organizations and local builders, and stand at the heart of the book's guidelines on good practice. They should also guide conservation decisions and activities beyond this book's limitations.

"Good practice" is filled with practical applications for these conservation principles on the job. Numerous brief case studies and illustrations bring to life the principles within the context of practical guidelines based on a great deal of experience. Some information and advice is repeated, to make each section self-contained, with cross-references to other topics and other resources. Every job, from archival research to mixing mortar, is traced to specific principles of careful conservation.

"Ways and means" surveys the human and material resources available to promote and guide heritage conservation. The information is current for 1988, but may become dated as professionals, organizations, legislation, and funding programs develop in response to economic and environmental changes, to the increasing age of buildings, and to the evolution of conservation techniques.

Appendices provide background information on charters, codes and organizations that aid or govern conservation work. The extensive references list many published sources for further information.

Applying the advice

Though the book is in a particular order, conservation seldom proceeds so neatly. Good conservation work involves stepping back from the job at hand to see a larger picture, that of the building or site over many generations, from past to future. Every building project, old or new, involves many sideways and even backward steps. No simple diagrams of process can easily explain this "shuffling". The maxim "look before you leap" covers much of the advice in this book. Sometimes that may mean pausing deliberately when circumstances otherwise press for completion.

This book presumes basic understanding of elementary building principles. Its advice is abridged, but offers directions to more detailed technical information from a wide range of sources. Both novices and experts should find extra help through the book's topical references.

Other books, magazines, and even television offer a rapidly growing body of information on practical matters of heritage conservation, but often ignore many useful *connections* between specialties. Good conservation practice involves many different skills and levels of skill, tied together by strong bonds of communication and co-operation. Though much of the finest construction and conservation work may be the legacy of one person, a successful project requires collaboration among many.

Where to find things on the page

1. Section heading.

2. Conservation principles on which the advice is based (elaborated in pages 44 to 55).

4. Topic title.

5. Background information and explanation.

6. Technical or other supplementary information.

7. Guidelines offering advice about what to do or not to do in a specific situation, based on the conservation principles for the topic (marked by a ❖).

Principles ❷

2.3 Work in order
2.4 Work at right pace
2.5 Appropriate skills
4.1 Respect for (natural) aging process
4.4 Respect for uniqueness (pattern, ensemble, detail)
4.6 Minimal conjecture/informed invention
5.1 Priorities of features, priorities of work
6.2 Maximum retention
6.3 Patina preserved
6.5 Safe working conditions
7.1 Traditional repair (proven technology)
7.2 Replacement in kind/recycled materials
7.4 Reversible repair
7.4 Cautious high-tech repair
7.5 Recipes tested before application

References ❸

For general information on all types of roofing on stone buildings, especially houses, see BOWY80, CUNN84, DAVE80/86, FINE86, HANS83, HUTC80, KAPL78/86, KIRK84, KITC83, LABI80, LITC82, LONDB4, LYNC82, MELV73, POOR83, READ73, READ82 and STLOnda. For larger and more complex buildings see FEIL82 and STAH84.

For examples of appropriate materials and styles for early residences, see MACR63, MACR75 and MCAL84. See MACE98, RADF83 and POWY29 for early specifications and drawings of roof construction. The special problems of metal roofing are covered in GAYL80, INSA72, PETE76 and TIMM76. Of the small-building sources noted above, LABI80 and POOR83 have useful advice on repairs to slate roofing, while DAVE80/86 and LITC82 cover chimney repairs for old houses (see also WILL83).

Types and materials

The roof is the most exposed part of a building; it often dominates a building's visual character, but is also the single element most vulnerable to weathering and thus to periodic change. Even when well maintained (and inaccessibility makes maintenance difficult) roofing materials do not last as long as other parts of the exterior. Much deterioration throughout a building is caused by too much moisture in the wrong place over a period of time — and much of this moisture gets in through gaps or weaknesses in the roofing, especially at junctions or edges. At some points in a building's life an owner will face a crucial decision whether to continue repairs or to replace the roofing entirely. In these cases, where conservation may mean renewal rather than repair, the craft, durability and visual impact of the old must be recalled very carefully by the new.

Roofing materials in 19th-century Ontario included shingles in wood, slate, and metal, as well as continuous seamed sheets of metal. Metals for roofing included copper, tin-plated iron, terne-plated iron (terne is a lead/tin alloy), and (very rarely) lead. The early 20th century added asphalt shingles and clay and concrete tiles to the repertoire. With few exceptions, the general lightness of structures (compared to European precedents) was echoed in lightweight roofing materials — copper rather than lead, thin slates rather than heavy stone flags. Even lowly asphalt has had a long career on roofs, tested by the Royal Engineers as waterproof roofing in Kingston as early as 1840.

Roofing techniques distinguish between flat or very shallow roofs where water-*proofing* is needed to resist moisture penetration from standing or slowly evaporating water and snow, and more or less steep roofs which emphasize rapid water-*shedding*.

In Ontario, flat and shallow roofs are usually covered with continuous sealed membranes of tar or bitumen (usually laid with gravel to protect the membrane) on a built-up base of paper and felt over a wooden substructure of joists and roof boards. Much rarer for low-pitch roofs is sheet metal (copper or terne-plate) with interlocking flat seams — extremes of temperature make metal roofs especially vulnerable to creeping, curling and punctures.

A flat roof must retain its integrity despite accumulations of rain and snow as well as tremendous variations in temperature from day to day — even hour to hour. Many tar-and-gravel roofs on quite old buildings sit on top of worn-out metal. Few built-up roofs last long without leaking, though the effective life of a well-maintained flat roof range from 10 years to perhaps 30.

On sloping roofs, metal roll or sheet roof ❺ provides a smooth, relatively impervious surface, but can fail at seams and joints as well as at punctures. Thermal expansion and contraction tax every part of a metal roof — most deterioration comes at folds or standing seams that cannot move enough to relieve strains. The use of standing seams or even wooden battens at seams gives metal roofs a characteristic vertical emphasis and also offers the metal considerable room to expand and contract.

Repairing metal roofing is expensive and requires experienced experts; poor short-term repairs will accelerate deterioration. Shingle roofing in any material is more vulnerable to leaks between units and at flashings, but it is more amenable to bit-by-bit repairs; a roof's overall life can be extended by those repairs, but only to a point. The flashing and drainage of all sloped roofs are critical, for any water build-up can back up underneath shingles or sheets by capillary action, as if the roof were sucking on a straw. Locating sources of leaks may not be so easy as looking for obvious dampness; much moisture may be coming via capillary action from the side or even from below.

❖ Carefully assess the remaining life expectancy of a roof before deciding to repair or replace part or all of its surface — especially slate roofs, where many slates may or may not be reusable (see "Replacement", below).

❖ Look and feel very carefully in attic spaces for subtle signs of damp or rot that may not be apparent from above. Inspect the roof in wet weather to see it at its worst.

❖ Ensure that the space beneath the roof is properly ventilated, so that any moisture can readily evaporate without damage to structure or materials and to dissipate summertime heat build-up.

DURABILITY

Ontario's climatic extremes take their toll on roofing. Slate and copper are the most durable of the historic materials, lasting up to 100 years without needing major repairs or replacement. Properly installed, wooden shingles may be good for 40 years or more; asphalt shingles may last 15 to 25 years. Each material has advantages and disadvantages. Slate is heavy and brittle, but durable. Metals are light, but prone to punctures and buckling. Wood is light, but vulnerable to rot unless treated, and even more vulnerable to fire. Asphalt shingles are light — and relatively cheap — but not so durable as more traditional coverings. Newfangled lightweight composition materials try to imitate the texture and colour of slate, with more durability than asphalt, but their lifespan is uncertain. ❻

❖ Make certain the roofing is properly anchored and that the anchors are not corroded or broken.

❖ Make vents, skylights and other new elements fit as discreetly as possible, both visually and materially. Flash and seal any openings fully and inspect them regularly. There are many traditional ways to conceal or incorporate such elements, as part of the roofing itself or in conjunction with gables, dormers or chimneys (see VISUAL HARMONY AND GOOD FIT).

❖ Make sure there is proper protection against damage by lightning, especially for high buildings in rural areas. Lightning rods on barns and churches may or may not be properly grounded; if not, they will be worse than nothing in the event of storms.

Repairs

❖ Arrest deterioration and repair problems in the roof *structure* before final repairs on the roof *surface*. Remove wood damaged by infestation or rot and replace with sound material. If replacing roof boards with plywood sheathing, provide sufficient ventilation between roofing and sheathing. Make sure that the roof has temporary covering while it is open for repairs.

❖ Be especially careful about safety on sloped roofs. Work in cool weather. Take special precautions when working on brittle slate roofs (soft-soled shoes, wooden planks or ladders to obviate walking on slates, and so on) — sloppy repair work may break more slates than it fixes.

❖ *Never* use bituminous (tar) patches on metal or shingle roofs. Such patches do not cure a leak; they only postpone its damage for a short while. They are almost completely irreversible and often cannot be fixed without complete replacement of the underlying material.

❖ Match the colour, dimensions, texture and material of surrounding roofing when replacing individual units or sheets. In the case of slates, maintain any polychrome patterns that may exist. Ensure that substitute units are fastened in a way and with materials that will not hasten

deterioration around them. Do not artificially age the appearance of new sections of copper — in time, they will fit into the general appearance of the roof without assistance.

❖ Ensure chemical and physical compatibility between roofing, fastenings and flashings. Do not use copper with cedar shingles. Do not use different together — fasten copper with copper, terne-plate with lead-coated nails, and so on. Decorative iron cresting designed for slate roofing will not go with a copper replacement roof. Watch for signs of corrosion of metal flashings and drains from stone particles eroded from slate roofs and replace deteriorated troughs and downspouts.

Replacement

❖ Wherever possible, replace worn-out roofing with the same materials. Where there is sufficient documentary or archaeological information, consider replacing modern short-life roofing with the more durable covering of the building's earlier years. Do not presume that the original material was necessarily wood shingles or copper sheeting. Consider a conjectural "period" substitution only when it proves impossible to determine the authentic materials and techniques used for the roofing (or when the historic technology is no longer available), and then only treatments commonly used in the region during the period of construction.

❖ Do not lay new roofing over top of existing roofing. Ensure that roofing can expand and contract without losing its integrity.

❖ Consider the choice between repair or replacement of slate roofing with the following in mind: ❽

❑ Soundness of the slates in general
❑ Integrity and durability of existing flashing
❑ Capacity of existing roof structure
❑ Percentage of slates that can be re-used — thickness, brittleness, sound nail-holes, cracking
❑ Estimated life of sound slates

❾

---

3. References, in a shorthand code: the first four letters of the author's or editor's name (or the book title if there is no author), plus two digits for the year of publication (or "nd" if no date is available), and in a few cases an extra "a" or "b" to distinguish otherwise identical codes for two different books. The codes and their complete references are listed alphabetically in the bibliography, pages 225 to 231. The bibliography is limited almost entirely to books; though it is comprehensive and very current, it is by no means a complete listing of what is available. There are also many helpful magazine and journal articles, but these would be far too many to list and generally less accessible than books.

8. Checklists of elements, decision-making criteria or actions (marked by a ❑).

9. Photographs or drawings that supplement the text, giving examples of good, questionable or bad practice.

THE INHERITANCE

Ever since its founding by William Morris in 1877 the Society for the Protection of Ancient Buildings has had a particular philosophy. This can be summed up in the words "conservative repair" and is the antithesis of "conjectural restoration".

The basic idea is that ancient fabric should be disturbed as little as possible, the patina of age left on unscraped surfaces, and history not falsified by moving buildings to other sites or completing unfinished portions. When repairs are necessary they should be done with materials sympathetic to the existing structure but not concealed by artificial tooling, ageing, or staining.

We should only approach old buildings humbly, being, as Morris said, "only the Trustees for those who come after us". Indeed the best attention we may pay them is to "stave off decay with daily care". Simple operations like keeping gutters clean, pointing sound, and woodwork painted, will maintain buildings at minimum expense for generations.

David Pearce, in introduction to 1981 reprint of A. R. Powys, "Repair of Ancient Buildings", 1929.

The architect may be disappointed that the advice given is not more precise, and the layman may complain that it is too technical. If that is so I would remind the first of these critics that each case must be treated as a separate problem, that he can expect to find nothing in the text of this book which will completely apply to any actual case. The advice is intended to be helpful in suggesting a right treatment, and not as providing dogmatic instructions as to the only way to proceed; and if the layman learns from the following pages that the difficulties are greater and the alternative methods more in number than he had thought, and therefore comes to realise what an infinity of care must be exercised in arranging for, and carrying out, such works, my two objects will be fulfilled.

A. R. Powys, in preface to "Repair of Ancient Buildings", 1929.

The built environment — an irreplaceable legacy

It is easy nowadays (much easier than a decade ago) to argue for the protection of great monumental buildings, seats of government, former mansions of the rich, even the more humble architecture of the picturesque village. These places are rare and are intimately connected to both history and the tales we embroider onto history. They are not, however, typical of the myriad buildings more closely woven into everyday existence — houses, shops, factories, schools, farms.

We have inherited a great stock of more or less commonplace building that appears in statistical accounts as a pool of capital investment, aging and needing constant maintenance and repair. But each item in this stock, each building, is an individual worth careful consideration. Though most are ordinary working parts of the environment, each may be worth as much to our cultural inheritance as the grandest edifice, if only we look carefully and understand what we see.

Every old building or structure has distinctive qualities that may make it worthy of attention when advanced age and other factors force an irreversible decision about its fate.

Giving the inheritance its names

Several different terms — "historic architecture", "historic buildings", "built heritage", "architectural heritage", and so on — refer to much the same thing. Each includes the inherited stock of old buildings and properties constructed and maintained by human activity. In this context, one should think of "architecture" very generally, for very few older buildings can be traced to any single person, much less one called "architect". "Buildings" include not only houses and other forms of shelter, but also structures such as bridges and factories, even roads and fencelines. All of this together is the "built environment".

Geographers call this combination of building, site and environment "cultural landscape". An even broader concept — "cultural heritage" — covers the entire spectrum of artifacts produced by a culture, including fixed places, portable items, oral traditions, even systems of belief. Museum professionals refer to the "material culture" of artifacts in collections, but often include the outside world of buildings and environments. Environmentalists and planners consider every element of the environment a potential "resource" available for use or deserving of protection — thus, "heritage resources".

Clearly, these related concepts overlap, and distinctions may be subtle. They are specialized terms for similar concepts, calling attention to the character of individual places and objects, particular contexts and common threads. They recognize and name creations that fulfil human needs and protect important values.

Understanding the inheritance

The value of any portion of this inheritance is its importance to those with economic resources or authority to decide on its future. The worth of the past is its worth for the future. Though a site or building may be deemed important enough to be saved, it cannot be saved without the means to sustain its future. Revealing a building's importance as a heritage resource can help affirm its value for future use.

The past is a collection of memories, individual and shared. The built environment is an essential part of the achievements of the society that constructed it. An individual building may be important for what it embodies of its builders or for what it represents of those builders. The way it looks, the irreplaceable craftsmanship of its construction, the skill evident in its component parts and their combination on a distinctive piece of ground are visual and tactile evidence of the style and quality of construction of a specific era, now gone forever. These factors comprise a building's

Classics is good stuff. Anything that gives you a foot in the past is good stuff. Can't understand the present if you don't know the past, what?

> Robertson Davies, "What's Bred in the Bone", 1985

Interpretive and commemorative markers explain the value and importance of many heritage resources, be they buildings, sites or landscapes.

Conserving buildings may involve difficult situations and choices. In this case, the three-storey façade is submerged beneath a new office block as an outcome of high land values and development pressures, but the result does not respect the scale, detail and character of what little survives of the historic building.

The built environment is an ensemble made up of many parts; it loses most of its cultural value when its parts are taken apart and taken away.

perceptible "architectural" value. The building is also associated to people and events in the past, to individual and shared memories. This "historic" or "historical" value is less tangible, yet more powerful: reverence for history has a longer and broader tradition than appreciation of architecture and it is more easily communicated. Some remarkably ugly and graceless buildings are nevertheless cherished by their communities. Conversely, some delightful treasures in built form are unprotected and decaying because no one has yet appreciated their excellence, because an entire area has been given up for lost, or because they are threatened with ill-considered "modern improvements".

Coping with change

This threat of modern improvement is the darker side of heritage conservation. The world has been transformed during this century, in both quantity and quality. In many ways, the modernism of previous generations has failed to live up to its promise, and our environment has been despoiled in the name of progress. Many towns and cities have been disfigured by huge office and apartment blocks and by empty sites awaiting development. Even individually well-designed buildings intrude into neighbourhoods, casting deep shadows, funnelling high winds, introducing more and more disruptive traffic and pushing out the people who had once taken pride in their surroundings. There are few guarantees that

new development will be more livable than the old, and there is a lot of evidence to demonstrate the opposite. The conservation of buildings and communities has often seemed at war with change, with "progress".

The other side of "improvement" is the abandonment of properties as priorities and economic activities change and even migrate across the landscape. Though development may pass by a community or region and thus lessen the pressure for dramatic change, such circumstances may remove the impetus to maintain properties and thus threaten heritage resources by slow neglect. Clearly, a balance of old and new, of repair and development, must be achieved.

Conservation depends on the future. The importance of the past depends on resources to maintain it into the future, on the very agents of change that threaten it. The value of the built environment must be demonstrated within a context of change. Valuing and evaluating historic architecture is an essential part of planning for the future.

Deciding to conserve

Most publications on heritage conservation take it for granted that the decision about the importance of a property and the need for conservation has already been made. But because conserving a place depends on why and how it has been selected, and by whom, this guide starts from the beginning, that first decision.

The following pages surveying "the inheritance" lay out the background to discovering how all or part of an old building or site may merit care and conservation. They survey the many dimensions of architecture and landscape: their development over time, extraordinary variety, stylistic and artistic character, and variation from region to region. They show how to evaluate the importance of specific places and the reasons for their conservation. Is the place important enough to save? Very often the answer is "yes". But that "yes" raises many other questions, most beginning with "how", whose answers must be sought in the conservation principles and practices that follow.

Building as an historical activity in Ontario

The first question usually asked about an old building is, "When was it built?" But no historical factor is so potentially misleading as mere age. The value of history lies only incidentally in dates; it is far more important to fit a place into its time and circumstances. A construction date is only a first step in evaluation, not a goal. And antiquity may not be a place's only important historical attribute. The oldest surviving house in a neighbourhood may not be the most valuable to the neighbourhood's history. Chronology is far more complex.

Construction or development of a building or landscape is invariably part of a larger story, tied into the development of community, region and nation. The year of construction must be seen in context of technology of the time, strength or weakness of the local and wider economies, stylistic fashions of the day, social status of the builder, and other contemporary structures (even those yet to come). Though very early buildings are generally rare, construction has always been subject to multi-year cycles and a building from a slow construction period may well be "rarer" than one put up during an earlier boom.

No single comprehensive information source can assign a place its historical distinction. There are wide and deep national and provincial influences and more singular influences of region and neighbourhood. Names, dates and politics have little direct effect on the development and look of land and building. By themselves, historical documents seldom offer conclusive evidence about what appeared on the ground at any time.

The following sketch leaves out prehistoric native occupation of the land, which left no permanent buildings and only fragmentary material traces.

Early European settlement

The economic formation of Ontario was not a smooth rise from early trading through colonization of land and resources to the variegated agricultural and industrial force of today . Business growth was cyclical, adoption of new technologies was uncertain, and the flow of people in and out varied with events in the wider world.

Until after the American Revolution, Ontario's only regular European inhabitants were fur traders, and the only establishments with any permanence were their posts and small fortifications. When occupation of Upper Canada's land became necessary for political and defensive reasons after 1784, settlement proceeded in fits and starts with the immediate arrival of Loyalists, followed later by many more American and British immigrants.

The earliest buildings appeared very basic and elemental, with only a rare flash of the Georgian elegance of the mother country or the former colonies to the south. Only after the War of 1812 did local production of some goods become more than mere subsistence. In the early 1820s came rough manufacturing and more-than-rough building, to accommodate a post-war boom in immigration and the large-scale export of timber, the colony's primary staple good. The best of the surviving early residences come from this first period of Upper Canadian prosperity.

Waves of growth

Economic depression coincided with the 1837 rebellions and halted colonial growth. Slow recovery accompanied political reform in the early 1840s, but development then slowed once more. Only when the Reciprocity Treaty of 1854 permitted liberalization of trade and access to the American market for staple resources did the provincial economy come alive in a spurt of railway- and town-building. The grand Italianate mansions, railway stations and main-street blocks of this period defined the character of many towns in the south; prosperity could be seen as well in new dwellings that replaced the first humble farmsteads. This boom, based on trade in wheat and lumber and on government action, ground to a halt in 1866, when the Reciprocity Treaty was abrogated. The recession coincided with Confederation and deepened into depression in 1873.

Expansion of the railways to the prairies improved central Canada's financial state, and the early 1880s saw a renewal of the earlier

---

The fatal metaphor of progress, which means leaving things behind us, has utterly obscured the real idea of growth, which means leaving things inside us.

> *G.K. Chesterton, "Fancies Versus Fads", 1923*

There are many sources for the economic and social history of the province (some rather dry and academic), but few examine architecture and building as part of that history. A good general survey with regional coverage is CURR63; it provides many useful basic references for both economic and social history. The standard source for economic references is EAST67. The Ontario Ministry of Natural Resources published TOPI75 as a planning aid for a proposed system of historical parks; though the parks were never built, the report offers a useful potted historical geography of the province that describes and maps what activities were happening where, and when.

commercial expansion and growing importance for Ontario's towns and cities in the national economy. Though Canada had hardly begun to capitalize on its western resources, the landscape of southern Ontario was maturing, and the character and scale of many of its main streets were fixed in the brick, metal, glass, and stone that still survive. The large factory joined the earlier small workshop; the farm began to produce more varieties of food for nearby communities, supplanting its earlier dependence on exports of wheat. Though northern Ontario had been economically important for the fur trade long before 1800, permanent settlement became possible only as railway construction opened it to logging and mining. But the boom turned to bust in the 1890s, reaching its nadir in a world-wide depression of 1896, to which Canada's trade was especially vulnerable.

Fortunes changed rapidly, and despite a brief slowdown around 1908, the period from 1897 to well into the First World War was one of great expansion and great building in Ontario, based largely on servicing western expansion. Some older centres of the south were transformed by new factories, commerce and utilities, while the north was opened up by railway-based mining, lumbering and eventually agriculture. By 1920, a post-war lull had slowed development, but the booming late 1920s produced new transformations: paved roads, middle-class subdivisons, even modest skyscrapers. The more successful cities and towns experienced diverse and continuous growth, becoming less susceptible to cycles of boom and bust, but towns based on natural resources or single industries bore the badges of abrupt growth and the scars of equally abrupt decline.

The Depression which followed 1929 reached its deepest point around 1933. After partial recoveries in 1935 and again in 1938, the wartime economy of 1939–45 finally reaffirmed Ontario's economic growth. By this time, though, the "frontier" was essentially closed, even in the north. New building appeared in the gaps of an already filled-out landscape or in complete redevelopments. After some difficult post-war adjustments, the cycles continued: down in the early 1950s, up in the 1960s and '70s, down in the energy crunch of the early 1980s, up again afterwards. Each peak brought a construction boom, and it

is now possible to distinguish characteristics unique to each period.

The modern-day character of many Ontario towns can be traced to one or another of these peak building periods — the 1820s, the 1850s, the late 1880s, the 1900s and 1910s, the late 1920s — so that building during slow times, comparatively rare, may well be more valuable than representatives of the peaks; yet the overall character of a neighbourhood or town relies heavily on those peaks.

Timing and the built environment

These economic cycles and their associated social and cultural forces cannot in themselves explain the many local variations. Specific events and episodes place a building in its local time. When the railway came or did not come, when a certain pattern book showed up in town, when a prominent local family visited a big city for the first time, when a certain colour of brick became available, when a branch bank failed, when a charismatic preacher arrived — all these are part of the detective puzzle of chronology.

Improvements in transportation are crucial, both directly and indirectly. The railway allowed importation of new materials and tools as well as new people, and consequent differences in woodwork, for example, between buildings before and after the railway can help determine their dates and their influences on other local buildings of the period. A five-year difference between the railway's coming to one town and then another may account for a considerable difference in the look of their buildings. Many towns owe their special character to the coming of the railway at a particular time, and many also owe survival of much of that character to inertia when the railway was abandoned.

Later, the automobile's need for paved roads changed the landscape of entire regions, as well as the design of buildings to better attract the attention of drivers and passengers. Buildings of the 1920s that reflect these changes often stand next to other buildings of the 1920s built in the spirit of the 1890s, or even the 1860s.

The role of government (from local to federal) has also varied from place to place, and from

Waves and cycles in building appear most conspicuously on "main street". Few commercial streets display uniform architecture, because few were built up continuously in a few years. Buildings of several eras and unbuilt lots punctuate every Ontario townscape, giving each its distinctive character and rhythm by echoing the pace of building over many years.

time to time. Public construction often took over when economic slowdowns halted private construction — many courthouses appeared during slow periods throughout the 19th century, and many provincial highways and bridges were built during the Depression. Social and cultural institutions have also filled in gaps in private construction. Some churches preceded development of surrounding residential areas, while others appeared only after their neighbourhoods and congregations had attained stability — few were built *during* a boom.

As towns and rural areas matured from one rush of building to the next, the quality of construction and detail may have generally improved. With community maturity, a building can more likely be attributed to a known architect, builder or contractor.

Among the most lasting effects of the ups-and-downs of building is the movement of population from place to place. Economic disparities have pushed people out of declining regions and lured them to prosperous areas. Regions long since passed over by new developments have often been very stable. Residents of town and countryside often establish strong ties to buildings and land over generations, continuously using and maintaining their built heritage — though lack of resources for maintenance has sometimes led to deterioration. In busier areas, especially around cities and in prime recreational zones, people seem more mobile. In these places, conservation of built heritage relies on the search for and recovery of a community's earlier identity to distinguish among the generic look-alike developments that obscure the traces of that past.

Diversity in the built environment

The "architectural heritage" consists not merely of grand public buildings or the mansions of the rich. Such monumental places are in any case much less evident in today's rapidly developing towns and cities. More modest material reminders of the past, from industrial sites to main streets to working farmsteads, have become far more valuable as vital elements of present and future plans. Even the most humble place or building has potential for continued or enhanced use in a new context.

Nevertheless, it is difficult to decide if a generating station is more historically important or practically reusable than a theatre or a row of workers' cottages. Each type of place must be considered on its own merits, with its own problems and potentials. As every historical activity has contributed to the distinction of a town or rural area, types of building or landscape associated with those activities deserve attention.

There are many ways to classify built features, and the following breakdown is by no means definitive. Each type has characteristics of its own yet each overlaps with other types. Every town or district has a particular combination of "standard" elements that may well exist individually in other places. Nevertheless, even houses built from a pattern book widely available during a given era are different because of their particular contexts of time, place and people. Seemingly similar wildlands may differ based on the history of their logging and their abandoned relics.

The knotty questions of style and importance must respect the type of building or district: commercial versions of a style may vary from residential treatments, and may be comparable with one another only detail by detail (see ELEMENTS AND STYLES).

A catalogue of types

Waterways

Roads and bridges

Railways and stations

Communications

Abandoned lands

Woodlands

Mines

Mills

Fields

Farmsteads

Dwellings

Churches and cemeteries

Schools

Community initiatives

Parks and gardens

Public works and utilities

Social institutions

Industries

Commerce and main street

Hotels and entertainment

When you know how to look, you can discover the spirit of an age and the physiognomy of a king even in a door-knocker.

Victor Hugo, "Notre Dame de Paris"

Texts on the types of buildings and environments found in Ontario are increasing rapidly in number. These include several volumes by Macrae and Adamson, newer regional studies that examine architecture or landscape by type, and research studies published by federal and provincial heritage agencies, some of which are hard to find but worth the search. An excellent series of sources for rural southern Ontario houses and mills are Blake's historical studies in the conservation authority reports of the 1950s, generalized in BLAK69. A useful digest of the types on which this section is based is in FRAM84a.

See, in general, BLAK69, CHAP66, GREE74, HUMP80 and RICHnd; for waterways, LEGG76; for road bridges, CUMI84; for wildlands, HILT86 as well as early conservation authority reports; for farms, ARTH72; for mills, PRIA76; for dwellings, MACR63 and REMP80; for churches, MACR75 and REMP80; for courthouses and town halls, CART83b, MACR83 and DECA87; for parks and gardens, VONB84; for commerce, PRIA78, HOLD85 and LONG87.

WATERWAYS

Most of the province was first settled via its watercourses, and many in the south were improved with canals, locks and harbours to make navigation easier and more reliable. At first, such improvements were both commercial and military. The Rideau waterway is the oldest of this type still in use. There are traces, both relic and operating, of many other navigation improvements, in wood and stone, and later concrete. Locks, docks, wharves, warehouses, lighthouses, elevators and shipyards may have been taken for granted in the past, but where they have survived have become attractions for residents and visitors. Many are no-nonsense products of basic engineering, modest but well built; some have been embellished with architectural detail of great charm and interest. Some waterfronts, attractive for tourism and recreation because of their historic interest, have difficulty maintaining that distinction in the face of out-of-key new developments.

ROADS AND BRIDGES

Only in this century have roads and streets been paved as a matter of course; until the era of bicycles and automobiles, road travel in country and even town was unreliable. Yet even the most primitive early roads were vital, providing access and defining the present-day network of land ownership. Most modern highways follow the routes of the first settlers or the even earlier native peoples. The frequent roadside rows of trees in both town and country are human additions of the last century, to shelter fields and improve neighbourhoods. The unspectacular but lumpy topography of Ontario has required bridges of all types since its earliest settlement, from modest wooden, metal and concrete structures to the great arches and suspension spans at the province's borders. Each bridge is an important visual and historical landmark, and many embody engineering and design innovations unique to their era.

RAILWAYS AND STATIONS

Waterways and muddy tracks may have colonized Ontario, but railways enriched and industrialized it. Agriculture, lumbering and mining were all transformed and modernized by the railway. On occasion railway companies built entire settlements. Tracks, with their embankments, trestles and bridges, transformed the landscape and have massive traces even where abandoned. Stations were and in a few cases still are magnificent gateways for the traveller, built in grand style to rival any public building. Though passenger travel is no longer what it was, many stations remain, sometimes recycled to new commercial or public uses. There are northern communities whose sole land access is by rail, and whose look and livelihood depend on trains. Every southern community owes its character, even its building materials, to some 19th-century decision by a railway to pass through, or pass by.

COMMUNICATIONS

Though often consisting of little more than towers and wires, or even less substantial lines of sight between towers, the routes and terminals of energy and communication are vital components of the contemporary landscape. Their origins lie in the earliest hydroelectric developments of the late 19th century. Some of these were bold architectural monuments to a new industrial age, and some still produce power. The lacy towers of electric transmission are seldom considered visual assets, though the oldest lines near the oldest stations have historical importance as engineering structures. Few early communication features have outlasted rapid technological change, though some early aircraft hangars and communication towers of unusual or innovative design survive; their protection must be based on their intrinsic historic importance, since their visual interest is admittedly unconventional.

ABANDONED LANDS

Very little of what we regard as wilderness is really untamed. Much of Ontario that looks wild is second- or third-generation forest growth that contains relics of prehistoric occupation or of later efforts to trade in its furs or to log or mine its resources. Yet this landscape, now much used for recreation, has its own history and relics of recreational use, back as early as the first retired officers going to the hunt in the 1820s. The railways opened many such opportunities in the north, creating and selling the wilderness idea as a tourist draw. Where "virgin" unharvested land does survive, it is a rare reminder of pre-settlement Ontario. Other wild-looking places may be evidence of settlement gone sour, of the land exhausted. They often hold traces of their past almost undisturbed, but newly vulnerable to destruction if made accessible again.

WOODLANDS

Almost all of Ontario has been at one time productive woodland, complete with shanties, loggers, sawmills and itinerant camps. Lumbering is dynamic, moving into the wilderness and leaving in its wake new communities and farmland, but also much wasteland. Regeneration is very slow in Ontario's climate, and most producing woodlands are in the north. But small mills, some even able to run under a head of water, still survive in southern woodlots, reminders of the wholesale harvesting of the great hardwood and pine forests by early loggers and settlers.

MINES

Isolated minesites exist throughout the province from the nation's earliest oilfields in the southwest, to the latest gold strikes in the north. Many sites have been abandoned, and they offer evidence, often in decaying condition, of the fortunes of a risky business: headframes, ore houses, workshops, underground works and open pits. Though Sudbury's metal mines are important to the world, Ontario's most conspicuous mining is not for precious ores, but for building materials: shale, clay, sand, gravel. Their huge pits are both gross disfigurements of the rural landscape and impressive monuments of industrial growth. Technical experimentation and innovation has been important in mining, and many structures central to that history survive, deteriorating and almost forgotten, in remote locations.

MILLS

Mills are the scattered, water-powered, small-scale precursors to the modern industries of Ontario. Among the first permanent non-military buildings were British-built gristmills that gave early settlers some self-sufficiency. Almost every early settlement was based on mills that ground flour, sawed lumber, processed wool into cloth, distilled alcohol, tanned leather or forged metal. Built of heavy timber, sometimes encased in stone, these structures have often survived while their communities disappeared. A few still operate as mills. Their landmark character comes from their size, simple yet refined architectural details and well-thought proportioning. Sawmills were often built of their own products as a form of advertising, though fire or rot has claimed many. The stone grist- or fulling-mill survives in many small communities, sometimes recycled to new use, but often still vulnerable to continued neglect.

FIELDS

Southern rural landscapes, whether flat or rolling, are framed and given their characteristic form by rows of fences, trees and bush. The field-landscape is a vital reminder of both early settlement and maturing agricultural practice in the 19th century. There remain occasional reminders, in more remote and hard-to-farm areas, of the stony and stump-strewn fields of the pioneers. More productive areas in the south still present semblances of the rolling terrain of wheat that dominated the early railway era and the smaller variegated fields that followed, but recent tendencies to much larger fields and to neglect or demolition of the tree-lined drives and traditional field patterns have exposed the land to erosion and removed many of its prettiest views. Orchards in Niagara and market gardens near southern cities are overrun by urban development; only rarely does any feature but the road grid survive urbanization.

FARMSTEADS

The heart of the agricultural industry, and the social forces that go with it, is in the huddle of farmhouse, barns, sheds, cribs and windbreaks that lies at the heart of every farm. The growth and emerging prosperity of many farms are often visible in the sequence of houses built on the same property by succeeding generations; even the oldest cabin sometimes survives as a shed. The house grows larger, becomes more stylish and comfortable; the barn gets bigger, housing more equipment, more livestock, more grain. The most prosperous farms acquire canneries or tanneries. But others never prosper, never get beyond the first or second house on account of poor soil or poor management, and these survive next to the successes, presenting a vivid cross-section of history. The big barn is key to this historic assemblage — it can no longer be built in traditional form or materials, and it is vulnerable to decay at the hands of both natural elements and barnboard thieves.

DWELLINGS

Every residence from the rural cottage to the city mansion displays both the stylistic interests and social status of builders and occupants in traces both subtle and conspicuous. In numbers, this is the most ubiquitous type; in character, the most variable. Covered in almost any durable material, in almost any conceivable style, most Ontario houses have skeletons of wood, with windows and decoration in wood. Where original forms and details survive, external styling and internal planning can date a house almost as surely as a cornerstone. Dwellings may also display an entire history of use and change, and conservation often involves a delicate balance of preservation and use. In this sense, a modest house may be a no less important and valuable artifact than a grand residence. Multiple housing, especially urban apartment blocks, is not common in Ontario; the rarity of early examples gives them special importance.

CHURCHES AND CEMETERIES

The characteristic skyline of Ontario towns and villages punctures the horizon with steeples. Just as for farm residences, church-building becomes more and more ambitious with the prosperity of congregations. Ontario's traditionally multiform Christianity has bequeathed several churches to even the smallest 19th-century towns, and most have been well kept. They express both deep attachment to the faith of the old country and the drive and ambition of the new. Denominations other than Protestantism have built places of worship at once similar to the main Protestant streams and distinct from them in both plan and detail. The characteristic greenery of Ontario communities is enriched by the burial grounds adjacent to these churches, with finely cut and carved stones and sculptures that are both artistic and informative. But church and cemetery face their advancing age, and its toll on their fabric, with dwindling resources.

SCHOOLS

School-building has been at the boundary between private and public responsibilities since the first lessons in private homes, and schools have both domestic and public aspects. Ontario's 19th-century educational reforms in curriculum and construction produced many well-built and even innovative designs. Many communities still have a one-room schoolhouse, though few are still in educational use. Larger schools have become community landmarks, clothed in modest versions of the grand public-building styles of the day. Some may survive with their original layout more or less intact. University education began early in Ontario; University College in Toronto is recognized as one of the world's finest Gothic Revival college buildings. Even some recent educational buildings have architectural distinction, expressing continued aspirations to academic excellence; but older structures face uncertain futures on account of age, changing requirements, and tightening budgets.

COMMUNITY INITIATIVES

Although Ontario society's chief traditional institutions were home, church and school, public life became more open and secular as prosperity permitted, and then demanded. Public parks, community halls, fraternal organizations, public libraries and other philanthropic facilities are features of most communities, though their presence did and does vary considerably from place to place. Their architecture ranges from modest to ornate, clearly related to the community's prosperity, or its lack, at the time of construction. Some buildings emulated the commercial street (fraternal halls often let their ground floors for rent); some followed the more official architecture of government (Carnegie libraries could be richer-looking than the town hall). The most conspicuous local community initiative seems now to be the hockey arena, though national centennial and provincial bicentennial have contributed to rehabilitation and renewal of many earlier facilities.

PARKS AND GARDENS

Early aesthetic improvements to the landscape came as farmers began to replant rows of trees as windbreaks, and as horticulture matured into a widespread social pursuit, from railway-station gardens to agricultural colleges. Private estates and their gardens became important badges of prosperity in late Victorian times, though formal gardens had always been part of the intentions, if not achievements, of early settlers in the extreme climates of Ontario. Public gardens, conservatories, bandshells and street beautification became popular at the turn of the century, and the most reform-minded towns of the era inherited a legacy of handsome parks and streets as a result. Public recreation became a watchword for mid-20th-century towns and even for "wilderness", as public bodies began to reserve lands to satisfy burgeoning leisure demands. The look of designed landscapes still oscillates between deliberate formality and (even more deliberate) "naturalness".

PUBLIC WORKS AND UTILITIES

While community initiatives sprang from local pride and prosperity, public works emerged from more pragmatic local needs and from the programs of provincial and national governments. The first public works were defensive, including forts and other works along the U.S. border; much later the military became more concerned with facilities for enemies further distant. The second agenda for government was to construct administrative and judicial facilities, from legislative buildings to courthouses, gaols and post offices. With increasing population and urbanization came demands for clean water, waste disposal, firefighting and police protection, and many of these produced architecture of quality and distinction. Provincial and federal buildings often followed standard designs with only small modifications for local conditions, thus enabling ready identification from place to place. Still, many local variants survive.

SOCIAL INSTITUTIONS

The construction of hospitals, asylums and other social service facilities from the mid-19th century tried to satisfy both the political demands of communities and the moral demands of professionals and their clients and patients. The provincial government recognized early an obligation to build facilities for the very ill, from tuberculosis sanatoriums to "insane asylums", and many such complexes are still in use, albeit with different functions and treatments. The first asylums paved the way for more humane convalescent facilities for the war-wounded. The earliest gaols paved the way for massive prison complexes, whose architectural elegance may be quite different from their real character. Early pride of community and government in such constructions has faded to more quiet discomfort — newer institutions seem to seek anonymity in forms little different from, say, suburban schools.

INDUSTRIES

While hydraulic power drove the early rural mills, capital and labour powered the industrial expansion of Ontario communities into this century, producing a legacy of building that ranges from rough back-lane workshops to huge factories. The most ambitious or prosperous industries erected buildings of substance and up-to-the-minute style, emulating the tastes of their bankers and shareholders. Even simple urban warehouses could wear the stylish ornament of main-street commerce. Resource- or energy-dependent operations such as distilleries could build entire settlements. But even modest factories had to be substantial buildings to withstand the forces of their machinery. These began to be reused for a variety of non-industrial purposes once technology began to demand the sprawling single-storey plants typical of today's large-scale industry.

COMMERCE AND MAIN STREET

Community prosperity is readily visible in the activities and buildings of its markets, shops and banks and their aggregations on its main streets. Some public markets evolved from an open lot by the town hall into a large covered building. Shops evolved from the parlour of the merchant's house into huge glazed fronts of multi-storey mixed-use buildings. Though shops and fronts have changed greatly, much of an original façade may survive above, usually because of costs rather than conservation-mindedness. The suburban mall has left many main streets vulnerable to decay but has also freed them from some of the pressures to deface themselves. Much government assistance has gone toward main-street rehabilitation in order to help conserve the wider community; this has sometimes imposed standard street treatments and furnishings on towns that were once quite different in appearance.

HOTELS AND ENTERTAINMENT

Because early travel was so slow, inns and taverns popped up everywhere, often augmenting simple houses with enlarged porches and outlying stables. Though temperance legislation altered their forms later, full-blown hotels became essential parts of main-street commerce. The railway and later the automobile permitted lodge and resort development throughout Ontario's well-watered "wilderness"; the motel is merely their modern descendant. Urban recreation in the form of opera house, theatre or cinema was housed in both modest storefronts and grand halls. Many communities still possess auditoriums that echo with the memories of performances far grander than could be put on today. Even the once-condemned drive-in is now a rare historic artifact of the pre-video era.

Styles and labels

Much of Ontario's built environment can be sorted and catalogued not only by type and function but also by appearance. While every building is a unique response to the needs of its builders and occupants, characteristics shared from building to building and place to place add up to a recognizable look for a given era. These shared characteristics are often called a building's "style". Strictly speaking, style refers to the way something is described, so that styles should offer a straightforward system of classification. But "style" has other very subjective connotations: something may have style, something else may have *no* style. In considering the value of the built environment, there is no such distinction. Style is *always* present. It is the visible character of a place, the other side of the coin of function, yet equal in value.

Style must be taken seriously. However, while the conventional idea of style offers a convenient set of labels to recognize and compare buildings of a given era and locality, the label itself is never sufficient to understand the importance of the style. *Real* style is the result of countless decisions about design, about arrangement of function, about the way in which builder and occupant wish to "display" themselves. The importance of these factors cannot be packaged neatly and labelled definitively. The label is poor shorthand for the much fuller visual description.

Dimensions of style

Architectural character is composed of elements that may contribute to an overall impression of a building or add variety and drama within the whole. These elements include the profile or skyline of a building, massing, balance, dimensions and proportions of its parts, use of or preference for certain materials (for both physical and visual properties), colours, and workmanship of details. A brief style-label can seldom do justice to the complexities of a single building, though the effort of assigning the label may permit some comparison to other similar buildings or features.

There are few sharp boundaries between styles, and modern labels for historical styles have frequently been invented after the fact. In the 19th century, most architecture was called "modern"; today we call the same buildings "Victorian". The desire to tag fashions of style with special labels seems to have been a 19th century invention. The 20th century's modern movements have not stopped this penchant for identifying new fashions and coining names for them.

A label such as "Victorian" is close to meaningless unless part of a longer phrase. It is important to distinguish the specialized usage of a name for architectural description from its more generalized use. It is also important to distinguish building types — the characteristics of any style will depend on functional attributes of entrances, windows, floor heights and visibility that are very different in residential, commercial or institutional architecture. An Art Deco office can be compared with an Art Deco bridge, but only after taking into account their functions.

Many buildings do not fit into conventional categories of style. They may be eccentric or innovative. A given structure may have been built "between" two styles, in a gray area which, even if named, might be the only one of its kind. Any attempt to drag a building of unusual distinction into a general category may abuse both building and label. Though every style (even the most "modern") has precursors, accurately describing revival styles can be difficult, if the original's influence is visible only in applied decoration.

For instance, Tudor Revival residences often consisted of fake half-timbering on a conventional structure and layout. Though "Tudor Revival" would be accurate so far as it goes, it would be far from complete without further definition and would obscure differences in the style over time. Dimensions and functions of rooms and spaces in a given type of structure built during one period tend to be remarkably consistent, even where style-labels are quite different, but over time these basic plans and functions tend to change. A 1910s Tudor Revival house might at first glance look like a 1940s Tudor Revival house, but the room sizes and ceiling heights of the 1910s version will have much more in common with those of other styles of the 1910s than with what comes later.

Historical periods don't die — they are just reinterpreted.
Charles Gwathmey

There are many "style" books: chronological listings and descriptions of features of generally accepted style labels. Some are visual glossaries, while others are more analytical. Most are concerned with residential styles, though LONG87 is a notable exception dealing with commercial forms. There is no guide specific to Ontario at this writing. For general guides to Canadian and North American styles, see WHIF69, BLUM77, GEBH77, WALK81, POPP83, or MCAL84. An excellent regional visual reference to architectural details is found at the end of CRUI84. One of the rare examples that does not restrict its coverage to residences is in MCHU85, covering central Toronto. The building-type studies by Macrae and Adamson (MACR63, MACR75, and MACR83) explore styles as well, each in a different way; the variation among their treatments reflect not only typological differences, but also more than two decades of reassessing what the labels actually mean.

Glossaries of architectural and building terminology are also common; FLEM80 and HARR75 seem the most thorough and readily useful for old-building terminology. See also Appendix 8, "A note on glossaries of technical and specialized terms".

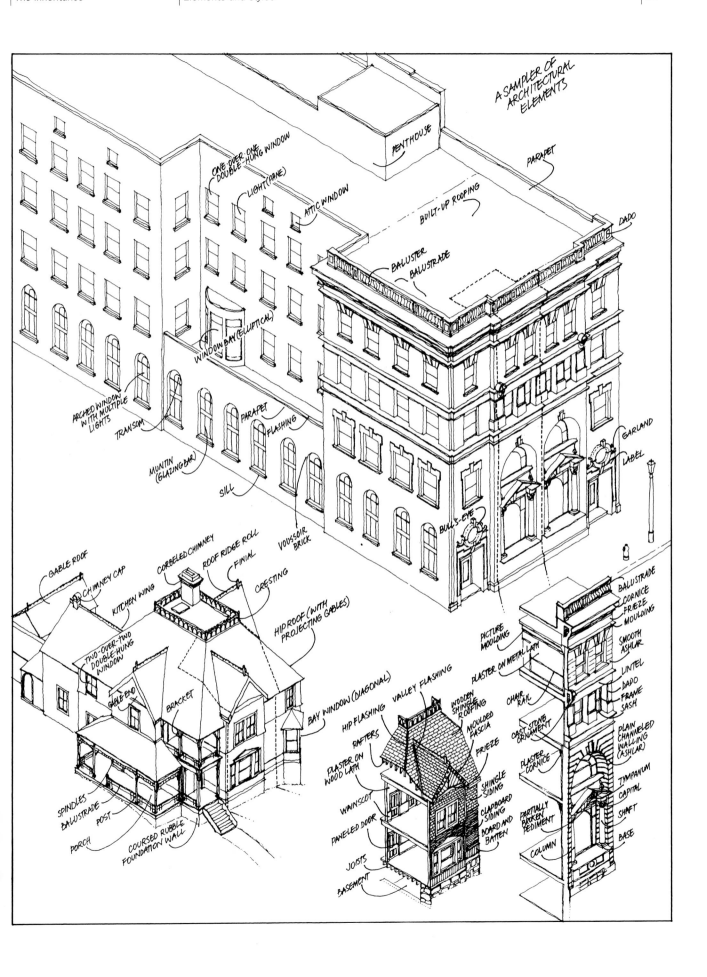

A SAMPLER OF ARCHITECTURAL ELEMENTS

Origins and transformations of style

Almost always, style labels come from buildings of the wealthy — from mansions or from main streets. These were the buildings first and most frequently written about in early accounts. In colonial settlements the difference between wealthy and modest examples of style was a matter of degree. Basic proportional systems and functional characteristics were often common to every building; these affected building cost very little. What distinguished wealth from modest means was size and scale of building and elaborateness of ornament and finish. In this respect, "Georgian" describes not only a specific style, but as well a more fundamental *approach* to matters of style that was to change quite radically soon after Upper Canada came to be.

Early in the 19th century the wealthy of the English-speaking world (first in Britain and the United States, eventually in Canada and other colonies) adopted a vogue for "the new", for changing style to keep ahead of more modest emulations. Hence the "battles" of styles and the tremendous eclecticism we now associate with the 19th century. This was not new to architectural history, which can be interpreted as constant oscillation between simple and ornate from one period to the next, as constant re-evaluation of the visual "density" of spaces and details. But in the "Victorian era", coincident with tremendous industrial growth and population movements, the pace of oscillation accelerated dramatically. New decorative elements and materials appeared first in mansions, cathedrals and commercial buildings. When these tastes moved later to more modest houses, local churches and even industrial structures, the wealthy and powerful tried to move on to something "new".

These currents of change were greatly enhanced by the adoption of Gothic antecedents. Forms of Gothic inspiration permitted great variation within the overall profile and mass of a building, instead of the much more disciplined regularity of earlier (Georgian) Classicism. This movement was so strong that by the end of the century even Classical elements had been grafted into the wild variety of eclectic forms. Much has been written about the change in social ideology and economic structure that coincided with these new architectural fashions. But the basic, materialistic impulse to "keep ahead of the Joneses" may have been the factor most responsible for the overwhelming variety of historic styles in architecture in Ontario, as elsewhere in North America.

Ontario style-labels from the 1780s to the 1940s

The following is by no means a definitive breakdown; it has obvious overlaps, and equally obvious gaps. Its purpose is to point out things to look for. For many architectural observers, assigning labels has its own recreational value, apart from its utility in comparing buildings. There is no agreement about the breaks between styles or even about some of the names themselves. A label for Ontario may describe something differently from its usage elsewhere. The cautions noted above apply to this catalogue as well as every other such listing — and the better guides will say this quite clearly in their own introductions.

This catalogue omits pre-Loyalist constructions and leaves off just before the mid-20th century. This is not to say that very recent buildings have no heritage value, merely that labels for them will be much too tentative to be of lasting use. The ranges of dates are quite generalized, and a good example of a style may have been built well after its period, especially in remote areas of both south and north. An excellent example of a labelled style may not be the best building of its era or locale (see EVALUATION AND DECISION-MAKING).

"Sources" refers to the influences or roots that best account for the genesis of a style. Sometimes the origin is geographic, part of a set of cultural fashions imported by a group of immigrants. Sometimes the source is one or more publications, particularly commercial pattern-books, and even popular magazines. Occasionally a specific building or architect is responsible for a host of subsequent imitators: for instance, the names of Robert Adam and H. H. Richardson are integral to the labels for the styles that followed their work.

"Composition" refers to the overall character, proportions, symmetry and planning of a building as an ensemble. Since composition varies so much from building to building even within a style, many of the words used to describe similarities within a style are subjective and open to many interpretations. Nevertheless, this overall character is seldom reproducible in modern dress and is an essential part of the justification for our "attachments" to older buildings.

"Details" such as materials, windows or woodwork are much more consistent among buildings of the same style-label and are more readily distinguishable and describable identifiers of a style — which means they are usually the most crucial items to conserve. Comments on the specific application of style-labels to types of heritage features are split between "Residences" and "Others", since most of these labels came from studies of residential types and were only later applied to commercial, public or even engineering structures.

This brief catalogue offers but a few indications of what distinguishes one style-label from another. Further information should be mined from one of the many comprehensive surveys, though most of these confine themselves to residential forms.

The inclusion of a category of "mixtures and others" acknowledges the difficulty of pinning down a label for buildings that may be not simply impure representatives of conventional styles, but isolated cases that resemble no conventional style at all. Sometimes idiosyncrasy is quite deliberate, as in the case of oriental influences, but more often represents unconventional, even naïve, personal tastes.

Whenever it is difficult to apply a conventional label, good conservation practice demands that the place be described fully and carefully; the shorthand label can come later.

A catalogue of styles

Log houses and shanties (1780s–1980s)

Loyalist/Georgian (1780s–1860s)

Neoclassical/Adamesque (1810s–1830s)

Regency/Picturesque (1820s–1840s)

Greek Revival (1830s–1860s)

Gothic Revival (1840s–1870s)

Italianate/Italian Villa (1840s–1870s)

Octagon (1850s–1870s)

High Victorian Gothic (1860s–1890s)

Second Empire (1860s–1880s)

Stick Style/Carpenter Gothic (1870s–1890s)

Queen Anne (1880s–1910s)

Richardsonian Romanesque (1880s–1900s)

Chateauesque (1880s–1930s)

Beaux Arts/Classical Revival (1880s–1940s)

Colonial/Georgian Revival (1890s–1940s)

Late Gothic Revival (1890s–1940s)

Industrial/Functional (1900s–1930s)

Prairie/Craftsman (1900s–1930s)

Tudor Revival (1900s–1940s)

Mission/Spanish Revival (1910s–1930s)

Art Deco/Art Moderne (1920s–1950s)

International (1930s–1960s)

Mixtures and others

LOG HOUSES AND SHANTIES (1780s–1980s)

ORIGINS — expediency, haste and the need for temporary shelter, based on earlier American and Québecois practice. Northern European ethnic practices added later refinements. Though the form died out with sawn lumber and lightweight framing, it became "rustic style" in the late 19th century, especially in the north and parklands, for cottages and lodges. It is still considered "style"-ish for rural owner-builders and houses made from kits.

COMPOSITION — as a shanty or first homestead, usually one large box, sometimes subdivided by partitions. The basic building had a shed or simple gable roof, rubble stone chimney and tiny windows. Later versions were better proportioned and roomier, sometimes with summer-kitchen tails of log or frame.

DETAILS — horizontal logs, keyed at corners, more or less rough, with moss or dirt chinking. Corner-keying techniques often followed ethnic traditions; *pisé* (vertical timbers) was rare in Ontario. Proper windows and frames were uncommon at first, but simple Georgian mouldings appeared later around enlarged windows to "civilize" the exterior. Later hewn-log constructions were usually covered with clapboard or brick cladding.

RESIDENCES — primarily a residential and farmstead form. Some large barns survive.

OTHERS — lodges and resorts on Canadian Shield used log construction and rustic "ornaments" as tourist attractions, though modelled more on western or American forms rather than local precedents.

LOYALIST/GEORGIAN (1780s–1860s)

ORIGINS — from English Palladian and Scottish Georgian styles, derived in turn from the Italian Renaissance through style books. The fashions arrived with the merchant-class elites of Upper Canadian Loyalists and later British immigrants.

COMPOSITION — generally box-like, symmetrical elevations, with Classical (via Renaissance) proportions. Five-bay fronts, with two windows on each side of a central doorway, were most characteristic. Structures were from one to three storeys, but usually two, with centre-hall plans. Larger compositions comprised a central block with symmetrical wings. The typically side-gabled roof was often pitched high enough to allow a half-floor in the attic.

DETAILS — simple cornices with returns at gable ends, sometimes with dentils. Other typical features included panelled doors, small-paned double-hung windows (often 12 panes over 12, 4 panes wide), and simple classical mouldings in modest pediments and arches. Flat-topped or shallow-arched fanlights, transoms, and sidelights marked the central entry, sometimes with a Palladian window centered in the storey above. At first plainly clad with clapboard, the style was adapted to stone and brick; corners were sometimes embellished as contrasting quoins.

RESIDENCES — mostly detached houses, though there were urban rows or terraces, usually with three-bay fronts and side-hall plans.

OTHERS — public buildings emulating large-house compositions, stretched into multiple bays. The style's simplicity suited it to non-conformist churches.

NEOCLASSICAL/ADAMESQUE (1810s–1830s)

ORIGINS — refinement of Georgian details in Britain (Robert Adam) through closer study of Classical originals, especially Roman (though *thought* to be Greek). The forms were spread through influential pattern books, and popularized through the extensive use of the similar Federal style in the U.S.

COMPOSITION — much the same as its Georgian precursors but somewhat different in detail, including a somewhat lower roof pitch.

DETAILS — departed from its Georgian predecessors, with less robust, thinner and sharper mouldings. Its applied pilasters or arches punctuated plain Georgian wall surfaces,with semi-elliptical entryway fanlights and more elaborate Palladian windows. The style's more ornately decorated surfaces often featured ornamented panels on elevations, with carved garlands and swags, and semi-circular louvred vents in gable ends. Corners were emphasized with pilasters, and cornices punctuated with elaborate dentils.

RESIDENCES — popularly felt to be a fashionable refinement, and thus an improvement, of the earlier Georgian look. Neoclassicism appealed as an "advanced" style, especially for town-house interiors aspiring to elegance.

OTHERS — primarily a residential style, though it influenced churches. Some details appeared in Anglican churches, especially in their interior proportions and elaborate multi-paned windows.

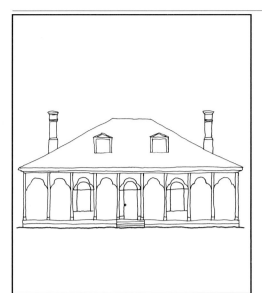

REGENCY/PICTURESQUE (1820s–1840s)

ORIGINS — influenced by English taste for the picturesque in painting and gardens, and by architectural forms in other British colonies. This period saw a new appreciation of setting and landscape and romanticized rusticity in garden design.

COMPOSITION — symmetrical plans and elevations, and occasionally four-square symmetry. Single or one-and-a-half storey structures typically featured hipped or gabled roofs with broad eaves. Verandahs and porches made their first appearance, adapted from both Québecois porches and bungalows in British India. Deep verandahs were constructed on one or two fronts but seldom wrapped around fully as in tropical British colonies.

DETAILS — mouldings, windows and entrances still Classically-based. Large windows and even French doors opened from several rooms to the verandah. Wooden treillage supported the sometimes upswept-curved ("bell-cast") verandah roof, often with decoratively exposed rafter-ends. While stucco walls were considered most stylish, brick walls were as common.

RESIDENCES — primarily a residential style characteristic of southern Ontario, but quite uncommon in adjacent U.S. states.

OTHERS — churches began to show Gothic and picturesque features, including pointed windows with trellis-like glazing, mock castellations and ornamental woodwork.

GREEK REVIVAL (1830s–1860s)

ORIGINS — resurgence in Europe of the recording and emulation of Classical originals leading to the bolder "correct" usage of Classical elements. Further influenced by American republican ideology (which in turn emulated ancient Greek democratic tradition), Classical architectural forms were spread through pattern books, especially those by U.S. architect Asher Benjamin.

COMPOSITION — symmetrical plans, similar to earlier classical styles. Narrow-lot adaptations featured side-hall plans disguised by symmetrical elevations. Gabled "temple" fronts were fashioned from either pedimented porticos or gable ends. Double-height porches were supported by monumental, usually Doric, columns, echoed by pilasters.

DETAILS — reversion to very simple ornamentation, if any. Larger windows and panes (9 over 9, or 6 over 6) were retained. Doorways became heavier and deeper, but still featured sidelights and transoms. Beneath the cornice were plain, sometimes continuous entablatures; gable ends had deep returns. Walls were typically clad with clapboard or ashlar (finely dressed stone) or with stucco scored to imitate ashlar.

RESIDENCES — in Ontario, primarily a residential style (as distinct from the U.S.). Non-standard improvisations derived from pattern books were especially common away from towns.

OTHERS — occasional temple fronts on churches; public buildings featured wide, shallow mouldings and entablatures surrounding doors and windows.

GOTHIC REVIVAL (1840s–1870s)

ORIGINS — from England, championed by A.W.N. Pugin. Building on picturesque tastes, the style revived specific mediaeval Gothic forms in a manner similar to the earlier revival of correct Classical precedents. It spread rapidly via pattern books, most notably those by U.S. architects A.J. Downing and A.J. Davis.

COMPOSITION — generally symmetrical in organization from part to part, though independently symmetrical parts might be assembled irregularly. Both roof pitches and gables were steep. Wall continuity was broken up by projecting or recessed bays.

DETAILS — verticality emphasized wherever possible, with features such as board and batten cladding, crenellations, extra gables, and pointed arches for windows and entrances. Porches with split posts and shallow roofs were built across the front. The style is notable for its profusion of carved and turned woodwork featured on finials, decorated verge boards, verandahs and entrances. Polychrome brickwork heightened the decorative effects.

RESIDENCES — best known is the ubiquitous Ontario Gothic centre-gabled farmhouse, often possessing a "tail" with its own central gable and a second porch. There were also larger mansions in the style, with irregular plans and elevations.

OTHERS — beginning of the "true" ecclesiological church styles, for all denominations, featuring pointed arches and ornate carvings.

ITALIANATE/ITALIAN VILLA (1840s–1870s)

ORIGINS — from the English picturesque tradition and its constant search for new forms of rusticity. This form was inspired by informal Italian farmhouses with characteristic square towers, combined with Classical Italian Renaissance townhouse features. Indirect influences came from American pattern books (A.J. Downing and Samuel Sloan).

COMPOSITION — more controlled irregularity than the Gothic, but still variable. Despite marked horizontal features — low-pitched hipped rooflines and wide overhanging eaves — the style maintains vertical emphasis with square-plan towers or belvederes and angular bays.

DETAILS — tall, heavily moulded openings; deeply panelled double doors; paired or triplet windows with round or shallow semi-elliptical arches; deep mouldings in wood or stone. The Italianate is sometimes called "bracketed", from its numerous heavily carved wooden brackets under broad eaves and bracketed mouldings over windows or doors. Corners were often emphasized by quoins.

RESIDENCES — encompasses a wide range of variation (even different style-labels), from farm to city. This style offered new distinction to row housing, with its emphasis on articulating windows and doors.

OTHERS — first distinctive commercial storefront style, with deep recesses, very large plate-glass windows, cast-iron posts and pressed-metal cornices.

OCTAGON (1850s–1870s)

ORIGINS — an oddity based on American phrenologist Orson Fowler's 1849 theory of healthy and economical construction through the "efficient" geometry of an octagonal plan. Spread through pattern books, this building type was confined to upstate New York, southern Ontario and the near American midwest.

COMPOSITION — octagonal floor plan, usually two storeys, often with belvedere and surrounding porch. A shallow hipped roof was typical.

DETAILS — Fowler's prescriptions were austere. Most octagon buildings followed Italianate styling and featured deep bracketed eaves and Classical designs for spindles and porch posts. Structures were typically of frame construction with wood or stucco cladding.

RESIDENCES — primarily a residential phenomenon. Though few in number, they were invariably well-known landmarks and remain so.

OTHERS — some barns built as octagons or polygons for the sake of efficiency, though survivors are rare. A few early town plans (e.g. Goderich) were based on the same geometry (predating Fowler).

HIGH VICTORIAN GOTHIC (1860s–1890s)

ORIGINS — derived from the earlier domestic and ecclesiastical Gothic Revival, adding variations from both ancient and recent examples. Promoted by John Ruskin and new professional publications like "The Builder", it gained acceptance as a suitable secular style for British public buildings (Houses of Parliament), and was adopted subsequently for Canada's own Parliament buildings.

COMPOSITION — characterized by steep roof pitches, steep gables, turrets, crenellations, castellations, deep recesses, reveals, bays and rambling porches. Massing was irregular, though assembled from symmetrical parts.

DETAILS — polychrome brick and stonework, often rusticated. Heavily carved wood or stone surrounded doors and windows. Roofs were of slate, sometimes polychrome, rather than wood, and ornamental ironwork was applied to finials and cresting. Tall, narrow openings were marked by pointed arches and lancet windows, though at its most ornate this style even accommodated such Classical details as round arches.

RESIDENCES — much decorative brickwork, especially contrasting red and yellow. Bargeboards and finials on gables were very ornate. Large panes of glass (2 over 2, even 1 over 1) were generally used.

OTHERS — used extensively for churches, courthouses, government buildings and colleges. Residential motifs were greatly expanded in scale, "domesticating" the appearance of these institutions.

SECOND EMPIRE (1860s–1880s)

ORIGINS — direct rival to High Victorian Gothic. Imported from France (the Second Empire was that of Napoleon III, 1852–70) via both England and the U.S., the fashion was transmitted more by personal "high-style" contacts, architects and professional journals than by pattern books.

COMPOSITION — most conspicuously the mansard roofline, which provided a fully usable attic storey. Roofs were straight-sided, concave or convex, with dormers. Mansard-roofed towers were occasionally featured. Vertical massing was more generally symmetrical than other contemporary styles, though still somewhat irregular.

DETAILS — heavy bracketing, similar to Italianate though eaves not so broad. Deep Classical window and door mouldings encasing large panes of glass emphasized the vertical. Roofs were often of polychrome slate with iron cresting. Dormers were universally used as part of the style rather than as add-ons. Dormer windows took on many different shapes including pediment and even round styles. Favoured materials were brick and ashlar. Pressed metal ornament sometimes replaced and emulated stonecarving.

RESIDENCES — much used for urban row housing and small town lots due to the added floor space afforded by the mansard roof.

OTHERS — important main-street commercial style, with decorated upper storeys atop fully glazed ground floor. Many public buildings and even factories carried mansard rooflines.

STICK STYLE/CARPENTER GOTHIC (1870s–1890s)

ORIGINS — revival of the earlier Gothic Revival, spread by pattern books and lumber and hardware mills. These styles were a transitional stage leading to the Queen Anne and eventually to the Tudor Revival.

COMPOSITION — rather subdued from earlier Gothic forms, with a less steeply pitched roof and rectilinear rather than angular volumes and projections. Many examples featured gables with deep overhanging eaves and sometimes cross gables at the same height as the main roof.

DETAILS — often Tudor-like raised "sticks" against clapboard or shingled walls and gables to "express" the underlying structure. Angular supports and decoration, chamfered braces and exposed rafter ends were typical. Simplified lancet or flat-topped windows were set in shallow frames and mouldings.

RESIDENCES — most frequently used in central and "near-northern" Shield communities as the first large-house style, though many examples were built in suburbs near larger towns.

OTHERS — motifs used by lodges and lumber mills to impart a "woodlands" character. The fire hazard presented by the exposed wooden construction precluded its use in urban settings. Its lancet windows and pointed spires graced many early northern churches.

QUEEN ANNE (1880s–1910s)

ORIGINS — zenith of 19th century picturesque, created by R.N. Shaw in England and spread through Canada via American architectural magazines. Primarily based on rural, rustic Elizabethan and Jacobean forms, the style also incorporated some Classical motifs in vogue during Queen Anne's reign (1702-14).

COMPOSITION — irregular plans, elevations and silhouettes with both hipped and gabled roofs. Structures built in this style featured projecting polygonal bays, turrets, towers and chimneys.

DETAILS — distinguished by tremendous variety and complexity of detail. Spindlework and other intricate woodwork adorned porch supports and gable ends. Unrestricted by convention, Classical features such as Palladian windows appeared in gables, with decorated pediments. Eclectic wall surfaces typically featured "half-timbering" of stucco around exposed sticks, or mixed shingles, tiles, brick and stone. Windows often contained coloured glass, often as small panes surrounding a large clear pane.

RESIDENCES — primarily a residential style. A wood-clad version of this style was used extensively in large-lot suburban or small-town settings. However, large numbers of narrow-lot versions in terra cotta, masonry and wood were built in Toronto, Ottawa, London and other cities of the era.

OTHERS — some use in public buildings and urban churches, with Classical details muting the flamboyance of High Victorian Gothic. Though its commercial use was minimal, it pointed to a subsequent revival of Classical motifs for main streets.

RICHARDSONIAN ROMANESQUE (1880s–1900s)

ORIGINS — based on 11th-century French and English forms. Recorded by H.H. Richardson during his French Beaux-Arts training, Romanesque features were applied as a masonry-based variant of the Queen Anne style. Diffused through journals, Richardson's designs were widely emulated, especially for public buildings, in cities where codes required (fireproof) masonry exteriors.

COMPOSITION — much the same as Queen Anne (see above) but with a more massive profile and masonry walls replacing wood cladding. Projections were less dramatic, and more rounded than polygonal; recesses were deeper and darker.

DETAILS — dominated by round arches, both Romanesque (sitting on piers or walls) and Syrian (springing almost from ground level). Heavily rusticated masonry, especially sandstone, contrasted with smooth brickwork in both texture and colour. Ornately carved stone ornament was common. There was much use of unglazed terra cotta. This style also featured deeply recessed windows and doorways with stone mullions and gabled dormers.

RESIDENCES — only mansions could afford expensive stone masonry. Many large houses in this style were built on relatively small city lots, especially in Toronto.

OTHERS — primarily a public building style, the successor to High Victorian Gothic, for post offices, government buildings and town halls. It was seldom used for commercial buildings.

CHATEAUESQUE (1880s–1930s)

ORIGINS — based on châteaux of the era of François 1 (1515-1547), mixing Italian Renaissance with French Gothic. The form was championed by R.M. Hunt, the first American architect to study at the École des Beaux Arts. It was diffused via American journals as a residential style for the very wealthy.

COMPOSITION — steeply pitched hipped roofs, round or rectilinear bays, multiple dormers. Symmetrical parts were combined within an asymmetrical whole. Turrets, towers and chimneys emphasized verticality, while bands of classical mouldings defined the horizontal.

DETAILS — predominantly stone facades (usually gray limestone) featuring finely cut ashlar walls or mildly rusticated coursed stone, classical mouldings, stone window mullions and carved pinnacles. Carved motifs were both Classical and Gothic. Cast iron was used for roof cresting and other ornamentation. Roofscapes were punctuated with small "attic" dormers next to gabled and wall dormers. Early taste for plain slate roofs gave way to copper.

RESIDENCES — primarily mansions for the wealthy. The style was too expensive for wide emulation. Cast stone was substituted for some carving and moulding on less costly structures.

OTHERS — notable as the railway-hotel style across Canada. It was also used for federal government buildings, well into the 20th century.

BEAUX ARTS/CLASSICAL REVIVAL (1880s–1930s)

ORIGINS — last of several styles brought back by American architects trained at the École des Beaux Arts. Diffused through office apprentices and magazines, revived Classical forms were championed by urban reformers and popularized at the 1893 Chicago World's Fair.

COMPOSITION — based on "correct" Classicism, directly from Greek and Roman precedents. Symmetrical structures featured flat or low-hipped roofs with cornices, balustraded parapets, colonnades, arcades, temple fronts and rectilinear bays. "Beaux Arts" was distinguished from the more "refined" (restrained) Classical Revival by grandiose compositions, dramatic scale, statuary, and Roman orders and arches.

DETAILS — predominantly stone facades (usually gray limestone, sometimes cast-stone substitutions) featuring finely cut ashlar walls and elaborate mouldings. Measured orders, especially Ionic and Corinthian, were often used for coupled columns or pilasters. Carved stone balustrades, cartouches, swags and other Classical details were conspicuous. Entrances and windows were often very large openings.

RESIDENCES — used primarily for mansions for the wealthy, but forms and materials were too expensive for wide emulation. Cost savings were sometimes achieved by substituting cast stone for carved ornament.

OTHERS — primarily a public and commercial style, particularly identified with banks. This style was also used in many planning schemes for park layouts and civic squares, very few of which were ever executed.

COLONIAL/GEORGIAN REVIVAL (1890s–1940s)

ORIGINS — first revival style based on North American models (themselves revivals of still earlier forms). It marked a return to "roots", and to more simplified forms from the eclecticism of the recent past. It was popularized through consumer magazines, professional journals and textbooks as the "style" in which to clothe modern functional homes.

COMPOSITION — simple rectangular volumes with shallow gabled or hipped roofs and symmetrical window and door arrangements. Small dormers were hipped or gabled.

DETAILS — self-conscious but inaccurate emulation of earlier styles, mixing American Colonial with Upper Canadian Georgian. Clad in shingle, clapboard or brick, these revivals featured restrained Classical detailing in columns, engaged piers and cornices. Windows were shuttered and sometimes small-paned.

RESIDENCES — most often used for detached houses in middle-class suburbs of the 1920s, but still in common use today. The search for local precedents to emulate motivated early survey and preservation activity in the 1930s.

OTHERS — very much a domestic style. American suburban commercial variants were not popular here.

LATE GOTHIC REVIVAL (1890s–1940s)

ORIGINS — return to more accurate, sober renditions of Gothic style derived primarily from English precedents and inspired by published illustrations of English Gothic country-house revivals.

COMPOSITION — low, long, rectangular, generally symmetrical masses, but following site irregularities. Gabled roofs featured gable-end dormers. Occasional low towers or subsidiary bays were tucked into inside corners in courtyards.

DETAILS — use of stone both inside and out. Walls displayed simple but irregular rough coursing. Openings were framed by cut stone. Leaded and stained glass windows, often elaborate, were supported by stone mullions. Bay windows with window seats were sometimes incorporated into the design. Exterior walls were occasionally inhanced with panels of stucco or half-timbering (seguing into Tudor Revival).

RESIDENCES — one of several middle-class suburban styles whose popularity peaked in the 1920s. The boxy plans used for these suburban houses differed little from those of other revival styles used in similar contexts.

OTHERS — primarily a public building style. Often called "Collegiate" Gothic, elements of this style are found in early skyscrapers, college buildings, institutions and even hydro-electric stations.

INDUSTRIAL/FUNCTIONAL (1900s–1930s)

ORIGINS — a long tradition of increasingly massive engineering structures was marked not by style-labels but by function, form and size: grain elevators, bridges, gasworks. New construction techniques and materials helped to create forms that were important in the establishment of "modern" style-labels later on. While engineering tradition evolved apart from architectural currents, engineering innovations greatly affected subsequent architectural styles.

COMPOSITION — geometric forms based on structural and functional requirements: silos for bulk storage, open frames for factory-building, arches and trusses for bridges.

DETAILS — dependent on materials and functions, seldom applying decoration, except when in the public view. Abstract geometric decoration were occasionally used. Reinforced concrete was introduced for both structure and surface, with occasional attention to coloured or patterned aggregate.

RESIDENCES — not a residential style, though it eventually inspired "modern" houses.

OTHERS — multi-storey factory buildings with concrete or steel frames and large expanses of steel-framed multi-pane glazing, sometimes with brick infill panels and exposed concrete frames. Numerous concrete truss and arch bridges were constructed during this period.

PRAIRIE/CRAFTSMAN (1900s–1930s)

ORIGINS — two threads from the same skein. Prairie styling arose from the U.S. mid-west, where the extensive works of Sullivan and Wright were based on structural clarity and expression tied to natural forms of decoration. Craftsman styling, based on similar arts and crafts movements in England and the U.S., was diffused through popular magazines as a "modern" house style.

COMPOSITION — low, broad "bungaloid" massing responding more to the dictates of the site than to formal planning. The Prairie style tended to hipped roofs, the Craftsman to gables. Both styles favoured broad eaves and horizontal emphasis. Boxy Sullivanesque variants featured flat roofs, modulated brick and tile or terra cotta surfaces.

DETAILS — exposed structural members, especially rafter ends (sometimes faked). Angular geometric designs were used for doors and leaded windowpanes, while simple coloured glazing served as accents. Deep porches were supported by chunky wood or masonry piers. Stucco, shingle or brick sheathing often had timber stick accents.

RESIDENCES — Craftsman was the principal small-house style through the 1910s and 1920s, especially in big-city suburbs and new towns in the north. This style was even promoted as the "provincial" style in planned resource communities.

OTHERS — used for rural institutions (convalescent hospitals and sanatoriums) and for "wilderness"-based tourist lodges and cottages. Commercial examples can be found in suburbs or in the north where the American influence was more direct.

TUDOR REVIVAL (1900s–1940s)

ORIGINS — no single source. Like the Queen Anne, it came from England, out of Late Gothic Revival and the Arts and Crafts movement, and was popularized through U.S. magazines. Tudor Revival followed the trend to more faithful emulations of historical styles. Often called "Jacobethan", its intrinsic eclecticism satisfied contemporary eclectic tastes.

COMPOSITION — boxy, though often contrived to appear L-shaped, with steeply pitched roofs, prominent gable ends and elaborate chimneys. Roofs were typically shingled in slate or wood, occasionally curved in to resemble thatch.

DETAILS — chiefly distinguished by false half-timbered wall surfaces with stucco infill between dark-stained or painted wood. Later variants were partly stone-faced with cast-stone trim. Windows were tall, narrow and small-paned, often grouped. The entry was often recessed, sometimes in a very small porch projection. Wrought iron ornament and hardware were typical.

RESIDENCES — very popular in most suburbs, peaking in the 1920s and again in the 1940s. Elements of the style remain in common use today.

OTHERS — almost completely a residential style (see Late Gothic Revival as public and educational version).

MISSION/SPANISH REVIVAL (1910s–1930s)

ORIGINS — derived from Mediterranean/Spanish Baroque via Mexico and the U.S. southwest, and popularized through magazines. Along the way, the original style was simplified, idealized and mixed in with southwestern U.S. adobe vernacular, sometimes with Islamic overtones.

COMPOSITION — shallow pitched clay-tile roofs, and multiple-curved parapets on wall-gables. Broad eaves in earlier versions retreated to a more boxy form later on. Structures were generally one or two storeys high.

DETAILS — smooth and shaped stucco walls; recessed, arcaded entries; small recessed windows; and rose windows set in gables. Rounded arches were used for windows and ground-floor arcaded porches. Terra cotta, wrought iron and even pressed metal were used for ornament and hardware. Details often used forms taken from other styles, including both Tudor Revival and Deco.

RESIDENCES — mostly used for detached houses, but also garden apartments and small residential blocks. The style was often used for residential garages, regardless of the house style, reflecting the 1920s boom in car ownership.

OTHERS — commonly used for public garages and filling stations, suburban commercial areas, and urban park structures.

Ethnic patterns and their historic effects on Ontario architecture can be inferred in some ways from furniture design; see PAIN78. The contributions of specific ethnic groups to the look of North American architecture is treated in UPTO86. Photographic archives are often good sources of raw material for local architecture and its variation from place to place. Major collections exist at the Archives of Ontario (Toronto), the National Archives of Canada (Ottawa), Queen's University (Kingston), the University of Western Ontario (London), and the University of Toronto. Local photographic collections, and the photographs that may be reproduced in local histories, will also offer useful references for the distinguishing characteristics of communities in the past. There may well have been university studies of the local architecture of a specific area; check with departments of geography, history or "Canadian studies" at nearby universities.

In some areas a particular culture may show itself in its uses of material, proportion and detailed workmanship. Polish settlements along the colonization roads of Renfrew County have architectural woodwork no less traceable in style to European antecedents than that of their furniture. Mennonite areas of Wellington and Waterloo counties have Pennsylvania-German barns and simple farmhouses similar in form to neighbouring Scottish houses but with subtly different proportion and detail (again, much like their respective differences in furniture-making).

Surviving buildings from the early 19th century in such places as Prince Edward County and along the shore of Lake Erie display differences between Loyalist architectural taste and that of later American arrivals, even in houses built at the same time.

Each group shared the other's cultural traditions, but one favoured Georgian features and proportions imported directly from Britain while the other preferred its Georgian "filtered" through American examples. Many such "stories" are legible in the architecture of specific areas, but studies documenting them are unfortunately few in number.

Historical maps can give some rough indications of regional influences and identifiable variations in older architecture across the province. But in practice, only individual investigations and close observation will reveal patterns and relationships in local architecture and landscape. Despite its difficulty, recognition of subtle differences between communities and regions is vital to conserving their character.

Only subtle variation in colour of brick or profile of moulding may distinguish buildings of the same era in different regions. More conspicuous variants, such as the cobblestone walls of Paris (top) or the robust limestone houses along the Rideau waterway (bottom), are relatively rare. Formal styles tended to appear in many places simultaneously, especially after the railway booms of the 19th century that permitted not only rapid communication of ideas, but transportation of manufactured building products as well.

Evaluation and decision-making

Asking the right questions

Assigning importance to a building or site — determining its value as "historic" or "architectural" or "cultural" resource — is primarily a matter of knowledgeable opinion. Often, the requisite knowledge belongs to an expert or specialist. But because non-specialists often decide what to do about a heritage resource, they must learn how to understand a resource's importance and what that means in practice.

A systematic approach to evaluation may be contentious. No matter how many objective factors are identified, the ultimate decision relies heavily on the relative weight of each factor, and weighting is often very subjective. Some evaluation schemes are based more or less on connoisseurship and emphasize well-known architects, or the "best" of a kind, excluding modest places without such pedigree. In contrast, environmental evaluation schemes describe places without pre-judging them, giving them benefit of any doubt and permitting flexible responses tailored to actual or potential threats. Ideally, any heritage evaluation scheme should combine the best qualities of both, and emphasize making and directing arguments for importance to the right audience.

Evaluation schemes must correspond to the types of resources they work with — no single "master" evaluation scheme fits every type of heritage property. A principal criterion of value is how well a resource relates to others of its type, and many features of, say, a bridge cannot be compared with a house or a factory. So the questions that follow do not comprise an evaluation scheme for all heritage resources, but a framework that may be used to develop a program for research, inspection, and reporting — even scoring — for a community, or a set of comparable properties or even a single old building.

The questions follow a sequence from intrinsic character to outside threat and, given sufficient time, it makes sense to try to answer them in that order. But when there is some immediate threat or urgency, it may make better sense to ask them in *reverse* order. (For guidance on gathering information to answer these questions, see HISTORICAL RESEARCH, INSPECTION and RECORDING.)

What is it?

Is it a house, a bridge, a village, a farm, a street? Is it an earthwork made by human hands or a product of natural erosion? Is it an office that was once a mansion, a house that was once an inn, a cottage that was once a mill? Before anything else, look carefully at what it is, what it's used for, what it may have been before, what it was or might have been when built. Identify its use, describe its physical characteristics, note its surroundings, and record these observations in a comprehensible form.

How is it tied to the past?

Is the place associated with specific events or notable people? Does it more generally represent broader themes of economic change and social development? Or does it merely look old and arouse nostalgic feelings for "the past" in a general, impressionistic way? Answering these questions requires research into documents and other objects that may not be located at the place.

How does it compare with others of its type?

Is it the best of its kind? the first? the last? Did it influence later examples? Is it quite different from other examples or an ideal representative for all of its kind? Answers may require general expertise about the type of feature and research into other fields of knowledge as well.

How is it unique, and special in its surroundings?

What are its physical qualities, inside and out? Is it well crafted, by hand or by machine? Are its parts artistically arranged? How does it suit its setting? Is it a recognized landmark? Are its surroundings enhanced — or devalued — by its presence? These questions can be answered only through very careful looking, not necessarily the preserve of experts. Anyone who is willing to learn the discipline of observation can see and record these qualities.

One of these days two young people are going to stumble across a ruined farmhouse and leave it alone. . . . Well, what are you sitting there gaping at?

S.J. Perelman, "Down with the Restoration!", 1938

Most of the literature about evaluation methods and systems is in specialized professional journals; see especially the publications of the Association for Preservation Technology (APT). Provincial and federal heritage agencies have done much work in this area and may be able to offer useful general advice, though they have not published much advisory material for wider use. See KALM80 (or KALM80a), SYKE84, and MADD85. For environmental evaluation techniques that go beyond the art-historical models used in most heritage inventories, see NEWC79 and MCAL80.

What knowledge may be created by its conservation?

Are there physical remains of other cultures or other times hidden inside a structure or buried in its environs? Can the knowledge compiled and recorded for this project be useful elsewhere? Will this knowledge be useful to experts? to the wider public? Even the most specialized knowledge can be applied in unanticipated ways. But the brokers of this knowledge are most likely to be scholars and teachers, in history, geography, archaeology, and so on.

To whom is it important?

Who has — or may have — a stake or investment in the continued existence of a place? Do individuals or groups have attachments to a place? Are there individuals or groups with general interest in conserving architecture or landscape or artifacts? Can these people influence others? Will they act? Do they know they can — and should? Though often embroiled in conservation, "the community" or "the government" does not actually conserve heritage. Only real and identifiable people do.

For what purpose is it important?

Is it useful for science, for the advancement of understanding and knowledge? Is it a resource for community education and recreation? Is it a vehicle or focus for expressing a community's pride and ambition? Will it attract visitors and tourists? Does it perform any of these roles now? Will it in the future? These are questions for the most part about planning, and answers may be contradictory: for instance, scholarly research may not mesh well with busloads of tourists.

In how large an area is its importance felt?

Does it attract attention within its neighbourhood? the wider community? the county or region? Ontario? Canada? the continent and beyond? Breadth of importance is as large as the organization that recognizes it. Municipalities list and designate properties within their boundaries; UNESCO maintains a World Heritage list. Between lie many compilations, general or specialized, of recognized resources. Though relied on heavily, such lists are seldom complete or even sufficient, and recognition of an important place is not automatic.

Is it threatened?

Has a place been left to rot? Is it not being maintained? Is it no longer useful for its original purpose? Is its original purpose no longer useful? Is it being overwhelmed by its use? Is it in the way of some "improvement"? These are questions of planning, of the future. They often have no clear-cut answers, as they involve many external influences. Conservation is almost always a response to these influences, rather than a strong influence of its own — though that may be changing.

Finding the right answers

Answering questions about a heritage resource is primarily a matter of diligent applied research. An investigator must look into records of the past and plans for the future. And he or she must be most attentive to the present state of the thing itself.

Research into the past requires the use of books, correspondence, drawings, deeds and photographs and any other existing records of the building or site. Some of these may be as old or even older than the subject of the research, while some may be quite recent. Such documents may exist within a building under examination, but quite often research demands a thorough look through libraries, archives, museums, municipal files and personal papers. Research also can make use of material artifacts associated with a property, be they furnishings or archaeological finds and other items of material culture that may survive in the hands of an individual or in local museums.

Historical research for the evaluation of buildings and landscapes requires accurately locating a place in its particular context of time and events. There are many scales of time, and many ways a building can be associated with time. And there are many ways this association can be made meaningful for purposes of protecting the building itself. A building or site or entire community may be most important in relation to one specific person at one specific time: for instance, its founding or construction by a notable person. A place may be important chiefly for its association with a long-term development — for instance, a characteristic pattern of fields and farmsteads peculiar to a specialized form of agriculture in one area over several decades.

Research into the future may be no less important for many buildings and sites. Documents such as comprehensive municipal plans, zoning by-laws, redevelopment and improvement plans, feasibility studies and even newspaper accounts provide information that can suggest what sort of future is faced by one or many heritage resources. Determining the likelihood of change in the surroundings of a place will permit reasoned assessment of its long-term usefulness. Finding information about such change is as much a job of detection as the archival prowling for data about the past — though municipal planners and their consultants are likely to have most of the information. Other levels of government are less readily accessible and must sometimes be actively pursued for information, especially about large-scale environmental projects that will affect communities and countrysides.

The hinge between past and future is the present state of the place, its use and condition, and its special, irreplaceable character. Considered as an artifact, a heritage resource is a special kind of document, linking past with potential. The place must answer many of the most practical questions. It must be assessed by knowledgeable eyes and hands, and the data thus gathered properly collated and interpreted by knowledgeable heads. There are many aids for this work of inspection and understanding: sketches, measured drawings, photographs, notes, interviews. Though these are prepared by people at the site for their own use, they can help others who may not see the place at all, but who may be instrumental in making decisions.

The answers that support evaluations and decisions become important documents whose care and protection is also a concern for conservationists. Our principal means of communication about heritage is on paper, in text and pictures. Documents enable us to compare places, tie pre-existing information to a place, and relate a place to the knowledge that will permit its fullest possible understanding. Each added documentary record is a vital and useful expansion of that knowledge.

From evaluation to action: keeping principles in mind

An existing building limits the possibilities for satisfying the needs of clients and future users. But it can offer a dividend in return, an added set of qualities, spaces and details that no new construction can match. It offers a different balance of past to future, and the designer's approach must respect that balance. A new-building design approach cannot deal with the realities of a building often much older than the new-building designer.

Though new buildings are supposed to be have higher standards of structure and safety than older ones, an old building may actually be far sturdier. Though much less regulated by legal standards, historic practice often used more generous margins for structural safety and strength than modern codes. Traditional building techniques have proved reliable for centuries. Many modern practices and materials are disappointing, requiring expensive repairs within a few years. Much deterioration now suffered by historic buildings has been caused by quite recent repairs.

No matter how un-modern and un-standard an old building may be, it embodies and displays quality and distinction that have lasting value. It deserves the utmost respect in making decisions about extending its useful life. It can be just as or even more durable, safe and solid than new, if conserved with care and understanding. There is no single best way to conserve every building or site for the future. Many courses of action may have to be explored. The keys to successful conservation are careful choice of a plan of action, and implementation in the most responsible, and principled, way.

Evaluating heritage resources is becoming more reasoned and scientific as demands on those resources have diversified. Worthy exemplars of a given style may be modest or grand, but each has an equal claim to recognition and protection. With greater public appreciation of built heritage the view of importance has broadened so that "value" is a function of several factors rather than just one.

CAREFUL CONSERVATION

It is better to preserve than to repair, better to repair than to restore, better to restore than to reconstruct.

A. N. Didron, 1839

Conservation activities

The wide range of conservation

The many types, styles and places of heritage value present many different opportunities and problems — and demand many different solutions, each one tailor-made. Accordingly, conservation has as many dimensions as heritage itself. "Conservation" is used in this book as the most generally accepted and inclusive term to cover the breadth of activities aimed at safeguarding heritage for the future. Conservation means acting to prevent decay. Two characteristics distinguish conservation: wise use and intervention. Wise use means making use of and caring for resources intelligently and conscientiously, recognizing their qualities, vulnerabilities and importance, and protecting them as a matter of course. Intervention means acting deliberately to make changes, or to resist changes, in order to remove or obviate threats to those resources. Successful conservation requires both.

Every definition is dangerous.
Erasmus, "Adagio", 1500

In this book, "conservation" refers generally to many activities at a number of levels. It must be understood in context — if it appears vague in a given context, it should be taken to apply as generally as possible. (American publications may use "preservation" as synonym for this sense of "conservation".)

Because conservation is not an especially strict science or discipline, its terms are used differently by different writers and practitioners. This guide is hardly likely to bring order out of this chaos; critical readers may grind their teeth. As much as possible, the following definitions of activities are based on a consensus from published sources, and they will be followed as faithfully as possible throughout this guide.

Several other old-building activities are not included in this list because they are either subsidiary to these categories or are simply not conservation. Though many "re-" words are used within conservation practice, others may be questionable: redevelopment, retrofit, remodelling, and so on (see "modernization", below). These are not necessarily hostile to heritage conservation, but they are not part of it. Some of the following activities can be considered conservation only under very special circumstances.

Survey

A survey is a reconnaissance, a necessarily superficial overview of possibilities. Whether at the scale of region or single building, it is a cursory examination to determine if there are heritage resources deserving attention and possibly conservation. A survey may be an unguided exploration seeking clues. It may also be a guided, even touristic, activity meant less for initial discovery than for the education of those who follow.

Inventory

Taking inventory of a stock of resources, counting them up, is often the first concerted conservation activity. Conservation requires at some point that specific resources be selected from a larger stock. Thorough inventory will provide vital information on the dimensions and numbers of heritage resources, as well as the scale of problems threatening those resources. Inventory is not a one-time-only activity; since the environment changes constantly, stock must be taken on a regular basis.

Inspection

Careful observation is perhaps the central and most important conservation activity. Every intervention starts with inspection. The full value of any heritage resource cannot be understood without it, and its value depends on the inspector's knowledge and attentiveness. An inspector's ability to see, to understand, and to communicate that understanding is absolutely essential. Inasmuch as conservation may be considered a science, inspection is its scientific foundation. Its importance cannot be overestimated.

Recording

Recording or documenting a heritage resource is integral to conservation's scientific mandate. Some of the information represented by a building or site or artifact can be put on paper and separated from the resource itself, without in any way damaging the resource, and this information may assist a variety of further activities. Much of our understanding of places we have not visited or cannot visit is based on written or pictorial descriptions, and our ability to compare resources is almost always based on such records.

Research — archaeology, history, architecture

Research is detective work that aims to put together a comprehensive understanding of a heritage resource from its component parts and disciplines. Though it is often a specialized activity, its larger goal must be to establish the whole worth of a resource or collection of resources. Research evidence may be in the form of documents, portable artifacts or the very fabric of a building and its setting. In integrating this evidence, research adds value to the resource, revealing it to be more than the sum of its parts. Publication of research results is an important conservation activity that aids the growth of knowledge and expansion of other conservation activities.

Planning

Planning — making decisions in advance in a rational and strategic fashion — is not exclusive to heritage conservation. Conservation planning consists in marshalling financial and organizational resources to support all the other conserving activities. But in every other aspect of urban, rural, regional or strategic planning there is scope and need to plan for heritage conservation. Indeed, these other more comprehensive vehicles often provide the most effective means of planning for conservation. In Ontario, much of the legal framework that can protect heritage resources is contained not in specific heritage legislation but in environmental and planning laws. Through preparation of municipal plans and environmental assessments a great deal of survey and inventory of heritage resources is carried out.

Financing

Lining up the fiscal resources does not require special conservation knowledge, but it is essential nonetheless. Because heritage conservation has been recognized as having great public benefits, direct and indirect, public funds are available from several sources, even for certain private projects. Some of these programs are earmarked for

property conservation; others subsidize the uses for which a property can be conserved. Proving that a conserved heritage resource will be a viable community asset can encourage private and commercial funding, despite the bias of conventional lenders and the tax structure toward new construction.

Acquisition

Since it is the owner's responsibility to maintain and conserve property, it is essential that a heritage resource has a conservation-minded owner. When a property ceases to have a viable use, its ownership and its fate often become vulnerable. Acquiring an endangered building or property may be the first tangible intervention toward long-term protection, but should be undertaken only after careful consideration to maintenance requirements, physical suitability for the intended use, and financial feasibility.

Maintenance

Regular and frequent maintenance of the material and features of a building or site is the most productive and least damaging of all tangible conservation activities. Maintenance *is* wise use. Good property maintenance prevents or obviates the need for more radical intervention, and dramatically extends the useful life of a place. This is demonstrated in reverse, unhappily, by the rapid deterioration of any property not well maintained.

Protection and stabilization

When a heritage resource has already suffered from deterioration, the first priority is to rescue it from further decay and stabilize its condition while longer-term remedies are sought. Sometimes a temporary custodian may take charge of this work while making preparations for more permanent repairs. This aspect of conservation may demand speedy work, with insufficient time to consider alternatives; accordingly, rescue measures must be temporary and reversible without damage.

Cleaning

Removal of dirt and grime is only partly a conservation treatment; its other purpose is almost emotional, appealing to our desire for newness by "revealing" the "original" look of the building. Unfortunately, aggressive cleaning to serve the latter purpose is not conservation at all, and even may be an agent of erosion and further deterioration. Cleaning, especially removal of dirt or old paint from exterior walls, must be considered very carefully — cleaning for conservation should remove only those pollutants and grime that will attack those surfaces if left unattended and leave in place the protective patina or skin that age has left behind.

Preservation

In its specific rather than general sense, preservation consists of stopping (as permanently as possible) processes contributing to deterioration of a building or site and making essential repairs to keep it in its existing state. Certain types of new work may be considered part of preservation in this restricted sense: structural reinforcement, drainage repairs, and so on. Indeed, preservation is primarily hidden work, to keep a property as it was found, but permanently stabilized.

Rehabilitation

Rehabilitation returns or upgrades a property to a useful state through repair (and in many cases alteration), combining an efficient use for the future while preserving and maintaining its important historical and architectural attributes. Though the preferred use for conservation purposes is normally the original one, rehabilitation often provides for change or adaptation of uses and spaces. In combining intervention and wise use, it often allows conservation of properties whose original uses are no longer viable. Some properties are more adaptable than others, and rehabilitation may require less-than-ideal compromises.

Recycling/conversion

Recycling is a rehabilitative strategy that involves changing the use of a place; indeed, the change in use may motivate a project even where the existing building is in good repair. Particularly in towns and cities, the property market may suggest changing the use and

economic base of perfectly sound older buildings, perhaps "threatening" them by virtue of their speculative potential as "empty" space. Recycling is conservation only inasmuch as it preserves and maintains important historical and architectural attributes. Special caution is needed to prevent unacceptable destruction or removal of valuable heritage features. Careful juxtaposition of skilled new work with heritage features may enhance both old and new.

Restoration

Restoration is the recovery of the forms and details of a property as it appeared (or may have appeared) at a particular time by removing work of intervening periods and, where necessary, replacing or reproducing missing elements. Restoration can be especially controversial because it is supposed to respect original materials as well as archaeological and authentic documentary evidence, and these may be incomplete, requiring informed conjecture about the gaps. Though it may be possible to reproduce an original feature exactly, restoration is often (and should be) distinguishable from the original so as not to falsify history, architecture or archaeology.

Modernization

Most of the "re-" words are types of modernization: "retrofit" for energy conservation, "remodelling" for new interior fashions, "redevelopment" for completely new buildings, and so on. Installing modern appliances and utilities, improving the comfort of a building's interior, and making modifications to conform to legal requirements are not conservation treatments as such, but rather treatments requiring conservation responses. Modernization is part and parcel of rehabilitation and enhancement of use — it is essential, but should proceed in a conservation project only under the most careful control and with the greatest respect for the heritage values of the property.

Reconstruction

Reconstruction involves the re-creation of a vanished building or feature on its original site, based on evidence from historical and literary documents, pictorial records and archaeological evidence. Faithfulness to a vanished original may include even the use of traditional building techniques, but often a reconstruction will be built on a modern framework of structure and utilities. Reconstruction poses the same difficulties as restoration, and though exact replication may be possible, the final result is often (and should be) distinguishable from a genuine work of the period so as not to falsify history, architecture or archaeology.

Interpretation

Interpretation is an educational process intended to reveal to an observer or visitor a heritage resource's information and value, sometimes accessible only to very knowledgeable people who must interpret to a wider audience. The art requires both understanding and the ability to communicate that understanding. Interpretive devices include publications, site markers, commemorative plaques, films and professionally guided tours. Though interpretation may exist apart from the heritage resource it uses, it can spark direct action to safeguard that and similar or nearby resources.

Relocation

Relocation involves moving and re-erecting a building or feature on a new site. Because siting and community context are so vital to a heritage resource's value, moving can be considered conservation only when the alternative is complete destruction. It is difficult and expensive to move a building, and, once moved, an old building may be unstable and subject to even more deterioration. Relocation has been used with some success to re–create the impression of pioneering settlements in artificial parks — a useful interpretive roles — but replicas may be far better suited to such settings than devalued and damaged originals wheeled into place.

Taking notes — a mundane but essential part of just about every activity in every conservation project.

Caring for the past using lessons from the past

In the Western world, conservation of architectural remains was a concern as early as Roman times, when imperial regimes sought legitimation by adapting earlier Greek forms and their symbolism. The grandest Greek and Roman monuments were relatively durable works of stone, and we can see how both the forms and their symbolic associations were preserved and used. During the Renaissance, these Classical models inspired renewed appreciation and adaptation of earlier forms, and raised the issue of the conserving old and unstable originals to facilitate this "borrowing". But, until the late 18th century, it proved difficult to repair and restore ancient monuments, even if there was the will to do so. European building technology had barely advanced from Roman times (despite the innovations of the Gothic cathedral construction) and Classical sites had often been pillaged for building stone.

Technical advances in the 19th century, especially the development of structural iron and steel, and the mechanization of the building process pioneered in North America, offered means to rescue and prevent further deterioration of ancient monuments. Widespread popularization of the past followed from the increasing and spreading wealth of the industrial revolution. New popular tastes included growing "romantic" attachments to more recent and modest relics, and many Europeans began to restore or reconstruct churches, castles, and even humble cottages. But romantic and inaccurate restorations and reconstructions defaced genuine (if aged and deteriorated) parts of buildings and entire structures, and replaced them with "better" invented Gothic or Classical features.

Conjectural restoration and its falsification of historical evidence so enraged those concerned with preserving traditions in the face of industrialization that William Morris and others in England formed the Society for the Protection of Ancient Buildings in 1877. SPAB considered erasure of genuine historic material far more sinister than any other threat to historic buildings. But its most enduring legacy, born from its curious combination of romantic attachment to

historical artifacts and crafts and its scientific approaches to problem-solving and repair, is the idea that building conservation, preservation and restoration should be *principled*. This stance has developed far beyond SPAB's original mission to prevent "improvers" from despoiling English Gothic cathedrals. The doctrine of "repair rather than replace" that lies at the heart of every national and international charter for conservation comes from SPAB's struggles of more than a century ago.

The first international charter on architectural conservation emerged from the 1931 Athens Conference on the restoration of historic buildings. That document was supplanted in 1964 by the Venice Charter, the basis for every set of statements directing or encouraging conservation and maintenance of historic buildings.

The following conservation principles are founded on these published documents. The principles apply the philosophy embodied in the international charters and in the mandate of the Ontario Heritage Foundation. They reflect ongoing efforts to develop a charter for conserving old buildings and properties to suit the variety of conditions across Canada.

The principles often overlap and refer to each other. They are more comprehensive and more specific than the charters from which they derive, but they remain generally applicable to all heritage properties and their surroundings. They explain and elaborate the "why" of every conservation activity. "Good practice" presents the "what" and "how" of conservation by referring back to these principles as the foundation for its advice.

The principles are presented in a sequence from "beginning" to "end". But conservation is more cyclical than linear, a large loop that circles back on itself, with many smaller loops and connections within the sequence. Some of the more important links are noted on the chart opposite. Those facing especially difficult problems with few reliable precedents should examine these links as they consider potential solutions.

... the architects' moral charter, as it were, includes the duty to work with the real world and its inherited content. It is better to recycle what exists, to avoid mortgaging a workable past to a non-existent future, and to think small. In the life of cities, only conservatism is sanity. It has taken almost a century of modernist claims and counterclaims to arrive at such a point. But perhaps it was worth the trouble.

> Robert Hughes, "The Shock of the New" (1980)

The growth and development of architectural conservation in Britain is charted most thoroughly in FAWC76 and MADS76. Information about the American "preservation" movement may be tracked through MADD85; good summaries of its history may be found in NATI76a or KEUN84. The Canadian experience is more fragmented; see FALK77 and DENH78.

There is no single published collection of all international conservation charters and guides, though see CONV83 for UNESCO conventions and recommendations. The Venice Charter, the Appleton Charter (ICOMOS Canada), and the Ontario Heritage Foundation's grant-aid standards for building conservation projects are reproduced as Appendix 2, Appendix 3 and Appendix 4, respectively.

The format of the principles is based on the "pattern languages" devised by Christopher Alexander and his colleagues (see ALEX77).

TASK	PRINCIPLE	Associated principles
PLANNING	1.1 Planned conservation	*1.2 - 2.1 - 3.2 - 3.3 - 4.5 - 9.6*
	1.2 Comprehensive understanding	*1.1 - 2.1 - 3.2 - 3.3*
	1.3 Balance of use and preservation (cautious conversion)	*1.1 - 1.2 - 4.2 - 4.3 - 4.4 - 4.5 - 5.2 - 8.5*
	1.4 Viable use	*1.1 - 1.2 - 1.3 - 4.5 - 5.2 - 8.6 - 9.2*
ORGANIZING	2.1 Co-ordinated work	*1.1 - 2.2 - 2.3 - 2.4*
	2.2 Co-operation among specialties	*2.1 - 2.3 - 2.4 - 5.5 - 6.4 - 6.5*
	2.3 Work in order	*1.1 - 3.2 - 3.3 - 3.4 - 4.3 - 6.4 - 6.5*
	2.4 Work at right pace	*2.2 - 2.3 - 3.3 - 6.4 - 6.5*
	2.5 Appropriate skills	*2.1 - 4.6 - 6.4 - 6.5*
	2.6 Second opinions when in doubt	*1.2 - 2.5 - 4.6 - 6.2 - 6.4 - 7.4*
ASSESSING	3.1 Record of found state	*2.3 - 2.4 - 4.1 - 4.3 - 4.4 - 6.1 - 9.1*
	3.2 Thorough and documented research	*2.1 - 2.3 - 2.5 - 4.2 - 5.2*
	3.3 Informed reconnaissance/inspection	*2.2 - 2.3 - 3.1 - 3.2 - 4.1 - 4.2 - 4.3 - 4.4*
	3.4 Archaeology (site & structure) for reconnaissance	*1.2 - 2.2 - 2.5 - 5.4 - 5.5*
	3.5 Specifics of uniqueness (pattern, ensemble, detail)	*1.2 - 3.1 - 3.2 - 3.3 - 4.4 - 6.4*
	3.6 Maximum information content/conservation of complexity	*1.2 - 3.1 - 3.2 - 5.6 - 6.2 - 9.6*
	3.7 Benefit of doubt in evaluation	*3.2 - 3.5 - 4.2 - 4.4 - 4.6*
DESIGNING	4.1 Respect for (natural) aging process	*1.3 - 3.2 - 3.3 - 6.3 - 8.1*
	4.2 Respect for period/historic continuity, sequence	*1.2 - 3.2 - 3.3 - 3.5 - 4.3 - 6.4 - 8.1*
	4.3 Respect for accumulations	*3.1 - 3.2 - 3.3 - 5.3 - 5.6*
	4.4 Respect for uniqueness (pattern, ensemble, detail)	*3.3 - 3.5 - 6.3 - 6.4*
	4.5 Respect for setting/context in community	*1.1 - 1.2 - 1.3 - 1.4 - 3.3 - 4.4*
	4.6 Minimal conjecture/informed invention	*3.1 - 3.2 - 3.3 - 3.4 - 5.6 - 6.1 - 6.2 - 7.3 - 9.1*
SPECIFYING	5.1 Priorities of features, priorities of work	*2.3 - 2.4 - 5.5 - 5.6 - 6.4*
	5.2 Fitting use of existing spaces	*1.1 - 1.3 - 1.4 - 3.2 - 3.3 - 8.3 - 8.6 - 9.3*
	5.3 Minimal alteration, minimal intrusiveness	*2.6 - 3.6 - 5.6 - 6.2 - 6.4 - 8.6*
	5.4 Archaeology (site & structure) for rescue of artifacts	*2.2 - 2.5 - 3.2 - 3.4 - 9.4 - 9.6*
	5.5 Minimal emergency action/stabilization to buy time	*1.1 - 2.1 - 2.2 - 2.4 - 2.6 - 5.4 - 5.8 - 5.9 - 6.1 - 7.3*
	5.6 Minimal removals	*4.1 - 4.3 - 6.1 - 7.1*
	5.7 Reconstruction for wholeness	*2.6 - 4.1 - 4.2 - 4.3 - 4.6 - 8.1 - 8.2 - 9.1*
	5.8 Moving as last resort	*2.6 - 4.4 - 4.5 - 6.1 - 9.1*
	5.9 Façadism as last resort	*2.6 - 4.4 - 4.5 - 6.1 - 9.1*
PROTECTING	6.1 Record of changes during project	*3.1 - 3.3 - 4.4 - 9.1 - 9.5*
	6.2 Maximum retention	*3.6 - 5.6 - 7.1 - 8.1 - 8.2*
	6.3 Patina preserved	*3.3 - 4.1 - 7.7 - 9.2*
	6.4 Respect for craft	*1.2 - 3.3 - 4.4 - 7.1 - 7.2 - 9.2*
	6.5 Safe working conditions	*2.1 - 2.2 - 2.3 - 2.4 - 5.1 - 7.7 - 9.2 - 9.3*
REPAIRING	7.1 Traditional repair (proven technology)	*1.2 - 2.5 - 3.2 - 6.4 - 7.6*
	7.2 Replacement in kind/recycled materials	*3.3 - 7.1 - 7.3 - 7.4 - 7.6*
	7.3 Reversible repair	*5.5 - 6.4 - 7.1 - 7.4 - 9.2*
	7.4 Cautious high-tech repair	*2.6 - 6.5 - 7.3 - 7.5 - 7.6 - 9.2*
	7.5 Recipes tested before application	*6.5 - 7.1 - 7.3 - 7.4*
	7.6 Maintainable repairs	*4.1 - 7.1 - 9.2*
	7.7 Gentle cleaning	*2.3 - 6.3 - 7.4 - 7.5*
ENHANCING	8.1 Distinctive new work	*4.1 - 4.2 - 4.3 - 9.4*
	8.2 Added value (high quality) in new work	*1.3 - 3.5 - 4.4 - 6.4*
	8.3 Complementary additions	*1.3 - 1.4 - 4.2 - 4.3 - 4.4*
	8.4 Independent additions	*1.4 - 4.3 - 4.4 - 6.4 - 7.4*
	8.5 Energy conservation	*1.3 - 1.4 - 7.1 - 7.3 - 7.4 - 9.2*
	8.6 Aided access	*1.1 - 1.3 - 1.4 - 4.4 - 5.3 - 5.6 - 8.2 - 8.3 - 9.3 - 9.6*
KEEPING	9.1 Record of altered state	*3.1 - 6.1 - 9.4 - 9.5 - 9.6*
	9.2 Faithful maintenance	*1.1 - 1.3 - 1.4 - 5.1 - 5.3 - 6.3*
	9.3 Emergency plan	*5.2 - 9.2 - 9.5 - 9.6*
	9.4 Conservation commemorated	*9.1 - 9.5 - 9.6*
	9.5 Records maintained and accessible	*1.1 - 1.2 - 3.1 - 5.4 - 6.1 - 9.1 - 9.6*
	9.6 Knowledge shared	*1.1 - 1.2 - 3.2 - 9.4 - 9.5*

Planning: Co-ordinate and integrate conservation work with other developments and activities; keep a solid sense of the longer term and the larger picture.

1.1 Planned conservation

Treatment must be planned in advance, and decisions made as much as possible before any irreversible work (which most capital work is). Conservation and planning are both forward-looking activities and need to be co-ordinated. Planning decisions may be taken many years before deliberate physical changes; conservation decisions can and must be taken well in advance of the necessity to conserve.

1.2 Comprehensive understanding

Many skills, trades, materials and techniques are involved in every building project, old or new, and conservation decisions must acknowledge their interrelations. Though detailed knowledge of components and details of a project is essential, so is an overview of how parts of a building fit together, how the building fits into its surroundings physically and functionally, and how the building is important in its larger community, past, present and future.

1.3 Balance of use and preservation (cautious conversion)

Buildings often outlive the function for which they were created, and subsequent adaptation must be balanced with (not necessarily against) their material and symbolic heritage values. Though aspects of a building may need modification to suit new use, the new program or use should be adjusted as much as possible to suit the existing spaces and details. Building programs can be remarkably flexible in adapting functions to non-standard spaces, just as non-standard (old) buildings can add extraordinary delight to the satisfaction of current and future functional requirements.

1.4 Viable use

Every building, historic or not, must serve a viable social or economic use that will ensure maintenance of its physical fabric into the future. Even the most economically "useless" monument must have a role to play (even symbolic) and requires care to mitigate or prevent deterioration caused by time and human activities. Some person or persons must take personal custody and care of the resource. Complex decisions about such a complex thing as a building must be taken frequently, and custodial responsibility must be clear and inseparable from day-to-day and long-term use of the place.

Organizing: Harness the skills and talents of many people, and make the best use of their time and energy.

2.1 Co-ordinated work

Because buildings are complex, care and conservation can be complex and must be co-ordinated in a skilled, knowledgeable manner. Some person or persons need to take personal responsibility for co-ordinating interdependent work, before and during a project. For historic buildings, project co-ordination must take into account not only work to be done, but also the building itself and its vulnerability to inadvertent damage.

2.2 Co-operation among specialties

Every building and conservation project requires the contributions of several disciplines and trades, specialists able and willing to share their knowledge with people in other specialties. Individual workers must acknowledge colleagues' contributions and aid one another, both in understanding specialized languages and techniques and in assisting each other's work.

2.3 Work in order

For any conservation work, planning must precede assessment, which must precede the design and specification, and so on, acknowledging the peculiarity of a specific situation. In general, research comes before design, and rough work before finishing, but this sequence may repeat itself over and over as work on individual portions proceeds.

2.4 Work at right pace

Conservation work must not be unduly rushed. Outdoor work must not be undertaken during inappropriate seasons or without complete protection during weather that would jeopardize ultimate durability of treatment. Some remedies and repairs require curing time which cannot be accelerated. Though "fast-track" techniques may have their place in new construction, repair work cannot be rushed and must follow thorough understanding of the problem and potential solutions; often the most appropriate treatment is the most traditional — quite possibly the slowest.

2.5 Appropriate skills

The range of conservation problems necessitates a corresponding variety of skills. The right skill must be matched to the job, from research to maintenance. Many skills are not specialties and can be learned by anyone with care and patience. But where special expertise (based on experience and training) is warranted, it must be recruited and given resources to do the work properly.

2.6 Second opinions when in doubt

Since solutions to some types of conservation problems require the diagnosis of a situation from partial or vague information, and each project has its own peculiarities, for which previous experience may or may provide useful precedents, more than one person's opinion or expertise must be sought in doubtful or difficult cases. When there is doubt, having more than one qualified opinion will permit a rational decision, based on broad experience and technique, rather than an expedient one based on authority without understanding.

Assessing: Understand fully the things and places to be conserved; make that knowledge useful for immediate needs and the longer term.

3.1 Record of found state

There must be a complete record collected or created for a property, site and buildings that are to be conserved or modified in any way. It should document the state of the place before work begins and, as much as possible, its history. It can include drawings, notes, photographs and any other appropriate form of documentation, and must be good enough to provide the basis for designs, specifications and repairs. Ideally, such a record should be in at least two places — the original with those responsible for custody and care of the project, and a copy in a public repository or archive.

3.2 Thorough and documented research

Whatever the scope of a conservation project, from repair of damaged woodwork to planning a conservation district, research must be thorough, within the requirements of that specific situation. Enough information must be at hand to facilitate the correct decisions. Though every case is different, research must reveal enough background to enable someone other than the researcher to reach similar conclusions based on the same evidence.

3.3 Informed reconnaissance/inspection

Every building or property must be understood fully as a physical artifact and be properly inspected as such. The most aspect is accurate knowledge of physical condition — siting, dimensions, arrangements, details, and the often subtle traces of previous uses and modifications. Inspection and recording are specialties that improve with education and experience The sophistication required for a given reconnaissance must be tied to its purpose — cursory inspection may be suitable for community inventories, while major rehabilitation will require inspections and reports from several professional perspectives.

3.4 Archaeology (site and structure) for reconnaissance

Archaeological exploration (irreversible testing for hidden artifacts or clues), where warranted, aids the understanding of the building as an artifact. Direct and indirect evidence of previous occupancies can corroborate doubtful visible evidence. Hidden spaces that are likely to conceal stuctural or other elements of historical importance (as well as present and future utility) should be opened up only in the most careful and delicate manner possible, so that they can be made good without undue long-term damage or loss of historical evidence.

3.5 Specifics of uniqueness (pattern, ensemble, detail)

The uniqueness of any building or site — characteristics that set it apart from others of similar type and configuration — must be analyzed and made explicit in order to evaluate its importance in its community and beyond and to judge the effect of repairs or modifications. For a tract of land, the topography must be assessed and described, according to conventions of geographical and landscape description. For a building, uniqueness must be considered as its combination of individual details, the assembly of those details into simple or decorated surfaces and spaces, and the pattern or rhythm of all the building's features (the most obvious example being symmetry). Only in such a systematic manner can places be compared and relative merits established.

Designing: Match carefully the qualities of what is to be conserved with the needs of the place and the people who will conserve, maintain and use it.

3.6 Maximum information content/conservation of complexity

A building has many secrets to yield, both in material, architectural terms and in associative, historical terms. Conservation must strive to capture and maintain as much of this information as possible, both for the project at hand and for wider goals and other projects. In archaeological excavations, even the most elementary fragment can tell the expert witness a great deal, by virtue of its material, how it may have been broken off from another piece, where it lies in relation to other pieces and to surrounding layers of soil, and so on. A building can yield just as many clues through careful examination, recording, and expert analysis. The complexity of this architectural and historical information is one of the most important differences between the old and the much simpler new.

3.7 Benefit of doubt in evaluation

Because it is often difficult to guarantee that all relevant historical information will ever be available to back up an estimation of a property's heritage value, it is vital to give the property benefit of doubt in assessing its importance. Seldom is it known just who was responsible for the original construction of most buildings, so that those with any sort of biography attached tend to be valued more highly than others with as much intrinsic merit, if not more. Benefit of doubt should be given to properties with high material and architectural value, even where historical associations are generalized rather than specific.

4.1 Respect for (natural) aging process

Every conservation activity must respect the natural aging and change that affect every building. Weathering and other natural processes and human activities produce tangible evidence of the passage of time which cannot and must not be replaced once effaced. In judging what can be left in its aged appearance, one should give benefit of doubt to leaving signs of age alone, either in whole or in detail.

4.2 Respect for period/historic continuity, sequence

Every building, though built to unique requirements in a specific place, more or less represents the fashion of its day and locale. Conservation and modification must not violate this characteristic by giving the impression of periods earlier than the original construction. Where the building is itself a revival of an earlier fashion (not uncommon), conservation must respect it as characteristic of its own period, rather than that of its inspiration.

4.3 Respect for accumulations

Where additions and modifications have altered original appearance, these should be retained as much as possible, as evidence of the passage of time and the contribution of subsequent users. Re-creating an impression of the period of original construction, where appropriate and feasible, must not destroy evidence of intervening modifications that have acquired their own heritage values.

Specifying: **Make clear instructions for translating design intentions into results and understand the tangible requirements of conservation work.**

4.4 Respect for uniqueness (pattern, ensemble, detail)

All conservation and modification activities must follow from a thorough understanding of existing details, ensembles and patterns of a building or site, and that understanding must inform both spirit and substance of the proposed work. No standard design recipes must be applied without being filtered through this understanding of existing unique characteristics.

4.5 Respect for setting/context in community

Since much of the present-day and future heritage value of a building or site consists in its distinctive physical presence in its community, conservation and modification must protect this spatial relationship. This requirement applies both to the building or site and to surrounding properties and public roads and spaces; it includes environmental factors such as building height, bulk (density), traffic, noise and greenery, which should be dealt with so as to that minimize alteration of the "fit" of a property in its setting.

4.6 Minimal conjecture/informed invention

There must be no attempt to falsify the historical evidence of a building by reconstructing features in a manner that pretends that they existed despite lack of evidence. But, given our own eclectic tastes and those of much of our architectural inheritance, one may construct features (clearly evident as revivals and not originals) that may have existed in a conjectured past, so long as they are based on an understanding of the history of that community and its characteristic forms.

5.1 Priorities of features, priorities of work

Conservation work should proceed in a logical order that deals with serious deterioration, structural weakness, and other high-priority items before less urgent repairs or finish work. Work should also be ordered according to availability of resources and people and to the relative visibility of features requiring work.

5.2 Fitting use of existing spaces

Existing or new uses for historic buildings or site should be tailored as far as possible to the existing arrangements and dimensions of spaces. This includes rooms as well as means of access — halls, stairs, entrances — together with exterior spaces and access to the overall site. The historic use of the building's spaces should be maintained as much as possible, even if the function behind that use may have changed.

5.3 Minimal alteration, minimal intrusiveness

Conservation should alter as little as possible the existing look and feel of historic buildings. Materials and finishes should be retained wherever modification is not absolutely required. Addition or replacement of damaged materials and features should be unobtrusive and fit in to the existing character both visually and functionally.

5.4 Archaeology (site and structure) for rescue of artifacts

Archaeological exploration to salvage or rescue artifacts must be undertaken if they may be damaged or destroyed in the course of conservation work. Building and surroundings may yield previously hidden materials of importance to the value of the building or artifacts of importance on their own. Such archaeology must be undertaken before phases of irreversible work begin, and the project's resources and personnel must be correspondingly co-ordinated.

5.5 Minimal emergency action/stabilization to buy time

In emergencies, where there is danger of immediate building damage or collapse, one must stabilize the situation so as to provide time to carry out proper systematic conservation. Stabilization may include structural props, temporary weatherproofing and any other measure necessary to protect both the building and those at work within it; all measures must be essentially reversible and cause no further damage.

5.6 Minimal removals

Only materials of relatively little intrinsic interest that conceal more valuable features should be considered removable, and only where underlying features are in relatively good repair. Any material removed must be thoroughly documented in the project's records, and should be made available for re-use as repair materials elsewhere in the project.

5.7 Reconstruction for wholeness

Where the original ensemble or pattern of a building has been disfigured by previous removal of some details, reconstitution of missing details to re-establish the whole should be acceptable so long as originals and copies are distinguishable and there is corroborating evidence of the earlier undamaged appearance or configuration. Where missing material is lost and cannot be replaced in kind, it should be replicated only by techniques and materials of equivalent durability that will not damage surviving building elements.

5.8 Moving as last resort

Removal of all or part of a building to another location destroys much of a building's uniqueness and all relation to setting; it can be accepted only as an alternative to total destruction. Where a building must be moved, its existing location must be recorded in detail; its new location should as much as possible evoke its historic setting but should clearly indicate its former site. Removal and display of building fragments should be similarly constrained.

5.9 Façadism as last resort

Removal of the structural and interior fabric of a building and retention of all or part of its façade as a decorative component in a new development violate much of the material value of a building, reducing it to an artifact without context. Such destruction of a building's uniqueness and setting can be accepted only as an alternative to total destruction.

Protecting: Work carefully and respectfully, aware always that historic places and materials are fragile and irreplaceable.

6.1 Record of changes during project

All changes made to a building in the course of conservation or modification must be clearly documented in relation to the record of its previous condition, in drawn, written or photographic form, as appropriate. This record must be maintained and updated regularly as work proceeds and compiled at the end of a project.

6.2 Maximum retention

Repairs ought to retain as much historic material as possible in sound condition, for its symbolic or visual heritage values and for its functional utility. Where diagnosis requires partial removal or damage of historic material, this should be done to the most limited extent possible, unobtrusively, and in a manner amenable to repair in kind without further damage or removal.

6.3 Patina preserved

Signs of wear and age evident on the surfaces of exposed materials and features should be retained wherever they do not cause hazards for contemporary uses, except surfaces whose maintenance in polished or cleaned condition is essential to historic authenticity. Surface patina of many materials indicates their true age, prevents environmental deterioration and should not be removed simply to give a "new" appearance.

6.4 Respect for craft

Elegance of forms, marks of tools, slight irregularities of surface and dimension, variation among ostensibly identical features, and any other signs of craftsmanship must be respected in repair work, and damage avoided at all costs. Repairs must employ skills and techniques of a quality no less than those used on the original work. Handwork must be employed to repair handwork. Where possible, these qualities of craft should be revealed to view where previously obscured.

6.5 Safe working conditions

All safety regulations must be followed in conservation work, and hazardous materials and techniques suitably supervised and controlled. Because much conservation work is not standardized, special care must be taken in advance to ensure safe working environments while protecting the historic fabric. Every project should be assessed for unusual hazards, and every worker made responsible for individual safety precautions.

Repairing: Do what is necessary to prolong the life and quality of a place and regard that work as its own legacy for the future.

7.1 Traditional repair (proven technology)

As far as possible, long-lasting repairs to a building or site should employ materials, techniques and formulations used at construction or during its early life. The primary tests of a repair technique are its efficacy over time and its independence from effects on adjacent features. Experience with similar situations over time should guide the selection of appropriate techniques and skills.

7.2 Replacement in kind/recycled materials

Where materials or features have deteriorated beyond repair, they should be replaced in kind, using similar materials and techniques. Where possible, removed materials in sound condition should be recycled within the project. Replicas must be based on surviving features or on incontrovertible documentary evidence (normally photographic) of their earlier existence, form and colour. Replicas must be visibly distinguishable from originals, even where matching is accurate.

7.3 Reversible repair

Where a repair is to be deliberately temporary, whether part of emergency treatment or a longer-term program of progressive actions, it should be removable or replaceable without damage to surrounding historic material. Such a repair must be reasonably accessible for such subsequent work and must not be concealed by more permanent work.

7.4 Cautious high-tech repair

When considering alternatives to traditional repair techniques, use great caution. Modern formulations must be compatible with the physical and chemical properties of surrounding materials and must not cause or promote further deterioration. They must not be used for permanent repairs unless proven durable and fitting.

7.5 Recipes tested before application

A generic repair technique whose effectiveness depends conditions of use on a project must be tested under those conditions, especially when its effects cannot be easily reversed. Tests should be done in inconspicuous locations that simulate overall conditions, especially visibility. All recipes or techniques must be tested as they are actually mixed or used on site.

7.6 Maintainable repairs

Wherever possible, repair techniques should be easily maintainable or adjustable to accommodate movements in the building or changes in environmental conditions. Repair locations must be accessible for subsequent maintenance or adjustment, because all buildings change subtly after construction or repair. There should be some unobtrusive means of access to hidden or difficult-to-reach spaces. Long-term maintenance must be specified as part of every repair treatment.

7.7 Gentle cleaning

Surfaces should be cleaned just enough to remove agents of deterioration, not eroded to a new-looking appearance. Removal of patina inevitably takes away surface material. This is acceptable only when underlying material is deep, strong and coherent enough to stand in for the removed surface. Where periodic cleaning is required, it should be done relatively frequently and gently rather than at long intervals with more radical treatments.

Enhancing: Make any new contributions in full recognition of the spirit and substance of the old, with full regard for sequence and continuity in time and space.

8.1 Distinctive new work

New work should be clearly distinguishable from old in a manner that gives both dignity while not impairing the building's historic fabric. This distinction may be bold or subtle, even perceptible only by a trained or attentive observer, but it must be there and demonstrable in the long term.

8.2 Added value (high quality) in new work

New work should be of high quality, a positive contribution of its own period, and enhance the heritage value of the property. It must be of a standard at least as high as the historic fabric it adjoins, in terms of quality of materials, craft and visual appeal. Even where it is designed to be unobtrusive setting for the old, it must demonstrate the best qualities of its own time: direct comparability between old and new requires more care than in an isolated new building. The combination of old and new should be of more lasting value than either on its own.

8.3 Complementary additions

Whether its relation to the old is deferential or assertive, new work must deliberately and intelligently acknowledge the old. Historic details, ensembles and patterns must be explicitly addressed in the design of new work, and no new elements or configurations should clash with or trivialize the old. No addition should be designed by a recipe approach without deferring to the uniqueness of what is already there.

8.4 Independent additions

Additions should be as much as possible structurally and mechanically independent of the historic fabric, so as to permit removal should circumstances warrant. Even where removal is unlikely, physical independence is vital to protect the environment, structure and durability of the historic fabric from less proven and secure aspects of new construction. Stability and integrity of an existing building must not be compromised by additions.

8.5 Energy conservation

No measure that will cause material damage or deterioration should be undertaken simply to conserve fuel. Measures to insulate thermally or alter humidity must be taken only with extreme care, and the equilibrium of internal environment should not be altered unless it can be shown that there will be no subsequent damage due to trapped moisture or other agents of deterioration. Measures to improve comfort should be flexible and reversible, and wherever possible traditional means of energy conservation should be used. The lifespan of energy conservation techniques must not compromise that of historic material.

8.6 Aided access

Where conservation includes expansion of public use, measures to enhance access by wheelchair or other ambulatory aids must avoid destruction of historic material and offer access in a manner similar to its traditional pattern. Ramps, elevators and similar aids must be inserted or added with great care and respect for the building, and its users. Aided access must not overwhelm unique features of the building. It must be considered as adding to the building and its overall value, not as taking away from the existing fabric.

Keeping: Take proper care of old and new and use the place and the knowledge it contains fully and wisely.

9.1 Record of altered state

There must be a complete record compiled for a property, site or building conserved or modified in any way, documenting its state at the completion of work in relation to its pre-existing state. Such a record, including drawings, notes, photographs and any other appropriate documentation, will provide the basis for any future designs, specifications or repairs, and its standard of documentation must be good enough for these purposes. Ideally, it should be in at least two places — the original with those responsible for custody and care of the place, and a copy in a public repository or archive.

9.2 Faithful maintenance

There should be explicit maintenance and housekeeping specifications and schedules compiled and resources available to execute them in the long term. They should prescribe periodic treatments and inspections and should be assigned to the responsibility of specific people. Maintenance must provide for monitoring and control of environmental factors (primarily humidity and temperature) on daily, weekly and seasonal bases, in a manner best suited to the continued life of the building's fabric, inside and out.

9.3 Emergency plan

Those charged with custody and care should prepare a plan of response to the threat of fire or natural disaster that will minimize damage, safeguard as much as possible of the fabric, and protect its occupants. Fire warning and suppression techniques should be incorporated unobtrusively into major modifications or additions. Environmental monitoring systems should have devices to warn users of changes that may indicate impending problems.

9.4 Conservation commemorated

The work required to conserve a building or site and extend its useful life should be recognized alongside any commemoration of its origin and early life. Every building should be marked in some manner with the year or years when conservation was undertaken, to indicate the historic importance of that effort and to alert observers that there may be old and new work to be distinguished. The marker itself should not detract from what it marks.

9.5 Records maintained and accessible

Records of a building or site before, during and after conservation work, together with more general documentary records of inventory and research, ought to be maintained in a public repository and made available to anyone engaged in conservation work, and to the wider public as well.

9.6 Knowledge shared

There ought to be no restraints on the sharing and circulation of knowledge about heritage conservation. Information for public education, advancement of technical knowledge, and encouragement of good practice must be circulated as widely as possible and should inform efforts at every level to seek out and conserve buildings and sites of heritage value.

GOOD PRACTICE

To take up . . . an 18th-century brick floor, once considered a sign of poverty, but whose surface, reinforced by innumerable layers of wax and polished by use, is infinitely more dignified and durable than the glazed tiles which takes its place, merely to install wiring and plumbing beneath the floor, is nothing but technical incompetence. It is a sign of the incapacity to grasp and to handle the complexity of a building.

It is necessary to find ways in which the deterioration of individual parts of the construction can be arrested, ways which in any case involve modifying the appearance and composition of materials. It is necessary to replace irreparably damaged components, or those elements that have been lost, where their absence makes preservation or use impossible — from a collapsed roof to a missing window or door. And finally it is necessary to add what was never there but which has become indispensable, like electric lighting or heating. But, like the building trade, architects also seem to have lost the ability to repair. Repairing means adding on without eliminating, increasing the complexity and density of the construction, just as a layer of stucco or plaster finish for frescoes was added to many German or Austrian Gothic churches in the 18th century.

. . . there is a forgotten tradition of additions as minute as they were significant; not many people remember that when Etienne Louis Boullée was working on the boiseries and rocaille of the Hôtel d'Evreux, the modern Elysée, he knew how to limit himself to supplementing the decoration of a mirror, or the trabeation of a transom. All the more reason that today, when existing structures are recognized as resources and testimonies of the past, attention should be turned to the detail, to a section of plaster, a fixture, a floor. . . The building is a stratification and a palimpsest, in which the requirements of use and the effects of deterioration are laid down at differing rates. The project is built up out of distinct parts, those which are new of necessity and those which already exist. It is not a unitary design that brings them together, but the attempt to attain a level of quality in keeping with what is already there.

Alberto Grimoldi, "Architecture as reparation", 1985.

Using the good practice guidelines

The guidance on the following pages combines principles of careful conservation with the experience of hundreds of conservation professionals and thousands of conservation projects. It is not, however, an encyclopaedia of conservation practice — merely a digest. Each topic offers a brief outline of do's and don'ts (mostly do's), together with underlying principles and references on which the guidelines are based and which contain much more detailed advice.

These guidelines concentrate on the differences between standardized renovation and the more comprehensive task of conserving fully the heritage values of what is renovated. They offer advice about what to do much more than how to do it. They fit with and offer access to the many readily available sources of technical advice.

Together, the guidelines and the sources offer a kit of tools for conservation, to fine-tune the quality of all forms of "re-" work, from the details of mouldings to the planning of regions.

The guidelines presume a certain amount of background knowledge about buildings and their materials and familiarity with some of the terms used in architecture, planning and construction. The guidelines themselves are very brief. Detailed information that expands on these very brief points will be found in references noted in the margins of each topic.

The guidelines themselves are just that — guidelines. They mean to guide work, not dictate it. Their purpose is to enable co-operation among all the participants in the conservation process and to facilitate the best use of the many skills needed to achieve the best and most durable results — visually, functionally, economically, and truthfully.

Learning from cases: the varieties of successful conservation

If you multiply the number of types of properties that can be thought of as heritage resources by the varieties of chronology, style and region, and then further multiply by the different conservation treatments that any one of them might receive . . . it becomes clear that no two cases will be quite alike. Hundreds of structures have been conserved with respect and care, largely (whether witting or not) according to the philosophy that underlies the conservation principles in this book. Thousands of others have been far less thoughtfully repaired and modernized, their heritage values ignored and often completely destroyed. Further thousands that lie somewhere in between. Every project can teach some useful lessons about conservation work.

Completed conservation projects, whether good or bad (or both), should be assessed with the principles of careful conservation in mind. It isn't necessary to fill out a checklist of all 56 principles to rate a project. But it *is* necessary to look critically at work done in relation both to surviving historical materials and features and present and future uses of the property.

Looking for good ideas

In looking at any building or site for ideas to use for other places, examine its overall form, profile and silhouette, and then look at it detail by detail. Note what looks like original or historic work and what appears to be recent or new. Assess how old and new join, visually and physically. Ask how things were done and how they might have been done better. And be especially attentive to differences between that case and your own, even where there are apparently similar details or general conditions. Underlying causes of deterioration may differ and may call for quite different repairs, even where the final appearance may be similar. Above all, be sensitive to the craft evident in old work, in subsequent repairs, and even in very modern work that adjoins the old. Sloppiness not only looks bad; it may also betray poor work hidden behind, which will soon cause problems for both old and new elements.

The following pages offer many examples of the various facets of heritage conservation well done. Though even the most exemplary project may have weak points, each guideline offers some demonstrates how principles of careful conservation are useful in practice. The true test for good principles, good practice and good advice is a well-preserved result.

Conservation in progress, detail by detail.

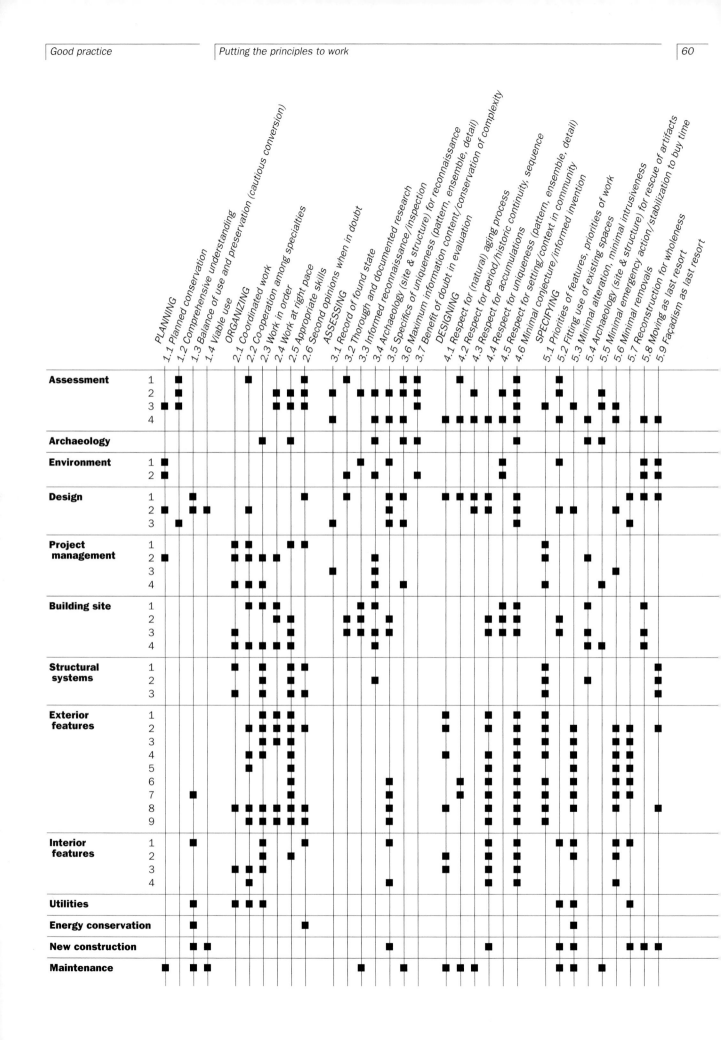

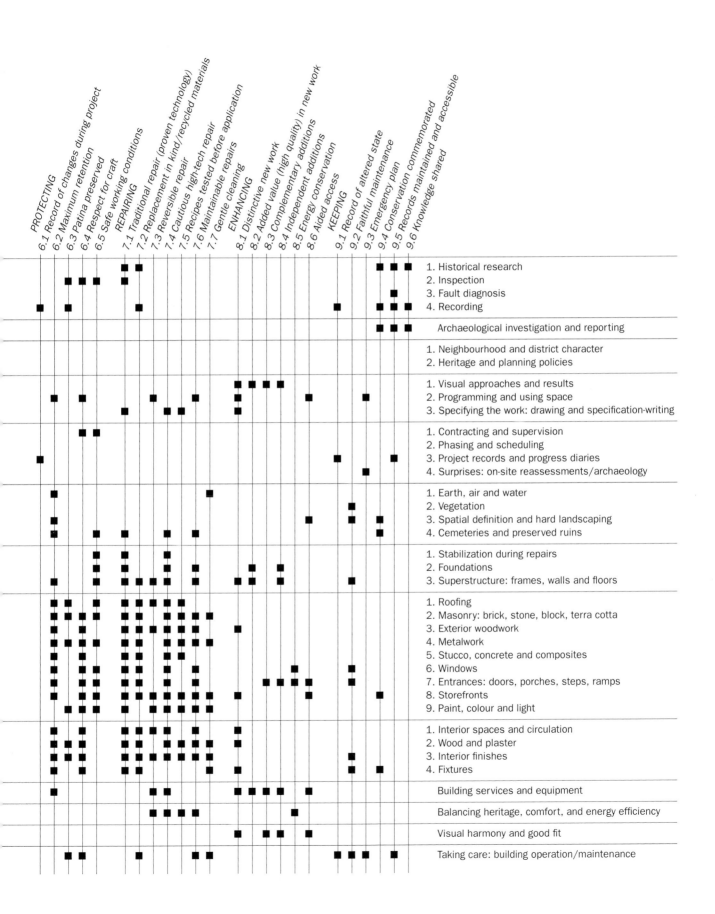

Historical research

References

General guides to methods and goals for researching buildings and environments include KING77, KIRK84, KITC83, LYNC72, LYNC76, NATI76a, SEAL79, SYKE84 and TECH86. Items offering directions to research sources in Canada and Ontario include CART83/83a, CUMI84, FRAM84, KALM80 and PARK79.

Good general sources for Ontario architecture and towns are BLAK69, FRAM84a, GREE74 and TAUS86. Some sources that provide useful context for research into Ontario architecture are BLUM77, GEBH77, HUMP80, MCAL84, MUTH79, POPP83, WALK81 and WHIF69. See also the sources for individual building types in "Types and varieties", page 14.

For general reference purposes, see CHAM80, MADD85, RICHnd and WHER82. See also the reference works listed in "Professional advice for free (and almost free)", page 200.

Research to suit the problem

Research is the basis for every conservation activity, from detailed work on an individual property to planning environmental changes affecting entire communities and regions. Research for conservation must usefully answer specific questions (see EVALUATION AND DECISION-MAKING). The search for data to help give those answers must be careful and methodical, no matter how small the resource.

Before anything else, write out the questions to be answered as explicitly as possible; many clues to their answers are contained in the questions themselves. Most often, research is a detective search for documents, whether primary sources directly connected to a place or secondary sources one or more times removed from those primary documents.

Primary sources normally stand on their own as evidence, but they can be inaccurate and should be relied on only very cautiously in the event of any doubt. Such documents may include deeds and other property records, wills, personal accounts, correspondence, diaries, personal interviews, business papers, historical drawings and old photographs.

Secondary sources are based on and abstracted from primary sources and often require corroboration by primary evidence or by a consistent pattern in other secondary sources, such as directories, published histories and guidebooks.

The balance between primary and secondary information depends on the purpose of the investigation. To evaluate an individual property — and decide on the appropriateness of restoring some missing features, for example — documentary evidence of the appearance to be restored is absolutely essential, and secondary information about other buildings is less important. But in planning for a district or studying an environmental project, the need to look at many properties simultaneously will increase reliance on secondary information such as directories, assessment records, and other sources of compiled data that allow broad comparisons.

Research should take advantage of and make links to historical context, beyond the individual project. Much of the original physical context of every heritage property

has disappeared. Though it is impossible to recover or restore those missing surroundings, research may establish a good deal about what used to exist and how it related to a place, together with pieces of the story of its original development. Research can and should produce a sense of this context strong enough to guide planning and conservation.

Tracking down sources

❖ Local libraries have much valuable information (local histories, clipping files, old directories and atlases, etc.), are used as informal archives by many communities, are where other researchers start (giving opportunities to share information), and have lists and indexes of other sources locally and beyond. Librarians can get almost any item through interlibrary loan, and often know who is doing similar research.

❖ Local museums collect information to explain and interpret collections of artifacts and they often have copies of locally useful sources from larger archives. Curators usually know who may be knowledgeable about a given building or area.

❖ Local archives are growing in number, often as offshoots of local or county museums. Collections vary, but personal papers and photographs can be helpful, and archivists can direct you to other sources, even private ones. Wills can help one understand the history of a property's residents, but may be of little direct assistance with buildings. Minutes of local council meetings going back to the 19th century can document early development in urban and suburban areas, especially construction of public places, roads and utilities.

❖ For specific properties, use land title or registry offices to trace deeds to the original grant or patent. These offices also have maps showing original dates of subdivision.

❖ For one or more properties, use assessment rolls where available. They show successions of owners and tenants, and abrupt changes in building valuation may represent major construction, of new

Knowing when a building was built or modified will locate it in time and permit understanding of its community context. Even if nothing is known about the builders, secondary sources and other indirect information may tell much about what sort of people built a place, their social and economic status, and so on. For instance, knowing if a building was built before or after construction of a railway connection will help set it in its economic context and thus permit its comparison to those in other communities. In studying areas or districts, it is crucial to establish the sequence of buildings as they appeared, in order to determine who may have influenced whom or which buildings influenced which within the district.

buildings or additions. Most are on microfilm at the Archives of Ontario, in Toronto; some copies are on file at local museums or archives.

❖ For notable buildings in southern Ontario, consult "Archindont" at the Metropolitan Toronto Central Reference Library, which compiles newspaper and journal references to many buildings by address, back to the mid-19th century.

❖ For larger municipalities, check building department records; some cities have permit information and even drawings on file.

❖ Picture collections with historic photos are widespread, but few are well indexed and there is no co-ordinated index for collections in the province; check the National Archives of Canada in Ottawa, the Archives of Ontario, and local libraries, museums and archives; the local newspaper office may have a long history and thus (maybe) an extensive photo collection.

❖ Bird's-eye views, insurance atlases, and old aerial photos have been compiled in major collections at the National Archives, and at some university libraries (especially the University of Western Ontario in London).

❖ Major collections of architectural drawings at National Archives and the Archives of Ontario have design or working drawings of some historic buildings, but coverage is spotty.

❖ University libraries and archives often have important holdings useful to their communities; even relatively new universities such as York and Brock have collections of historical documents and images for their regions.

General guidelines

❖ Keep faithful notes; write as neatly as you can. Others may need to refer to your research, and you might have trouble with your own rough scratching after a while. Everyone has a favourite tool: index cards, notepads, bound books, portable computers.

❖ Cite sources carefully and accurately; you

may have to return them long after initial contact.

❖ Keep notes about even the most mundane, indirect bits of data: they may well provide a crucial link in a chain of information that offers conclusive evidence of a building's importance.

❖ Distil explicit answers to specific questions (see EVALUATION AND DECISION-MAKING); where possible, tie these findings to a uniform evaluation scheme or nomination form (some municipalities use standard forms for heritage designation background reports). If you have no standard form, invent one, but base it on an accepted reference (see RECORDING).

❖ Try to relate a building to a specific year, both for original construction and for major additions. This advice is often hard to follow in practice.

❖ File a copy of your research at your local library, archives or LACAC (Local architectural conservation advisory committee); it will help other researchers (you would certainly appreciate having others' work to help your own project).

Relating research to other activities

❖ Where research is directed toward conservation of a specific property, include summary historical information on the property and its surroundings in the record of the conservation project, together with clear copies of visual documents that may help design, specify and execute the work.

❖ Do not rely completely on historic architectural drawings as records of what was built; changes during construction were frequent, sometimes radical: extra wings and floors may have been added or taken away, and designs for ornate details not executed fully.

References

For some background to the understanding of the character of a place impressionistic approach to assessing the character of a place, see ALEX77, LYNC72 and LYNC76.

Detailed inspection guides and checklists for residential buildings include BOWY79, CARS82, HERI87a/87b, HOW86, KIRK84, MELV74, OXLE83, POOR83 and READ82. For other types, see HOLL86, KEMP81, MEAD86, PICH84/84a, SEEL85 and STAH84.

For heritage districts, see CUMI85, LYNC76 and WRIG76.

Photography is an essential part of inspection; see BORC78, CHAMnd and MCKE70, as well as other sources in "Recording", page 74.

The contexts for inspection

Inspection of a single property, or a larger area with many elements, may have several objectives. The following guidelines provide a common denominator for these several ways of looking.

Two primary forms of investigation are in order for an individual building and site. First, the building's distinctive character must be identified and recorded to permit evaluation of its importance, both overall and in detail. Second, its physical state and need for repairs must be identified and recorded to enable specification of repair or preservation work. These two ways of looking permit judgment of the appropriate form for repairs or new work.

Looking at a wider area, from a potential heritage conservation district to an entire region, clearly requires a planned and selective approach. Such extensive inspection must concentrate on the identifying type of building or feature in a comprehensive or even statistical way but should be based on something of the approach suggested for individual buildings. The broad-brush survey of neighbourhood and community complements understanding of an individual building's character, by giving it context.

Identifying architectural character

Before assigning stylistic labels or other categories to a building, look at it as a piece of architecture with perceptible features of design, setting, materials, workmanship and feeling. Consider how much of what you see appears integral to its history and what seems to have been added or taken away from the original. Note these impressions carefully for comparison with corroborating documentation (especially historic photographs and drawings). Distinctive character may reside in a building's overall form and shape, particular features or apparent "appendages", such as porches or chimneys, details of wooden trim or window-glazing, craftsmanship apparent in the shape and surface of details or overall composition, and arrangement and sequence of interior spaces and their own details.

Look at the building from a distance, at its overall view from the street or from neighbouring properties. Find, and photograph, the most comprehensive view, the one that would be the picture postcard. Consider and note which aspects seem most striking, which aspects define the uniqueness of the building — in other words, the features that would be most missed if removed or changed:

❑ Overall shape — is there something distinctive about the size, form, massing, skyline or profile of the building against its background?

❑ Openings — is there a special rhythm or pattern to the arrangement of wall and roof to windows and other recesses or voids?

❑ Roof — does the roof's slopes and materials contribute positively to the building's character? Or are they simply background to walls and other elements?

❑ Projections — are there building parts projecting from the overall mass that are distinctive or special: chimneys, porches, balconies, cupolas, towers, window bays?

❑ Trim — are there special or conspicuous secondary features removal of which would devalue the building: bargeboard, shutters, decorative stucco or terra cotta?

❑ Materials — is there something distinctive about the brick, timber or other exterior materials, their colour, pattern or texture, the way they appear in different lighting conditions or different seasons?

❑ Setting — does the building fit well on its site; are its features and orientation tailored to the surroundings so that building and site are inseparable?

Look at the building much closer, at arm's length. Find, and photograph, several distinctive elements as if they were an artist's still-life compositions of light, form, colour and texture. View these as you would if you were about to pick up tools to do work on them; look for the signs of their making:

❑ Texture — do the materials' surfaces, smooth or rough, contribute to the overall impression of the building; do they show their age by virtue of a patina, and is that patina superficial dirt or intrinsic to the material; or is the texture a combination of underlying material and a different coating, such as paint?

- Assembly — are the joints between elements of one material or between different materials interesting in themselves; are they of rare or unrepeatable design and execution?

- Handcraft — are there signs of workshop or on-site hand-tooling that make plain or decorated elements one-of-a-kind; do forms and handwork visibly demonstrate care and skill in their combination?

- Close-up v. distant — are there important aspects that can be seen only close up?

Look inside the building, where its historic character, often out of public view and more easily modified, may have been most altered. Again, try to appreciate and photograph a "postcard" view of every major space, in a way that emulates your entry into that space. Examine interiors as spaces and details together, because of their more intimate and frequent use.

- Rooms and spaces — are there spaces of unusual size, height, proportion, or function particular to this building or building type: parlours, church naves, banking halls, proscenium stages, and so on?

- Sequence of spaces — do entrances, hallways and stairways offer carefully formal or informal access to rooms, in a designed order and with arranged views inside or out?

It is absolutely vital to move around, into and through a building and its site — carefully recording impressions and observations — in order to appreciate the character and potential importance of the place.

- Sound — do sounds carry clearly within a space or are they muffled (taking into account existing furnishings); does the acoustic quality fit the publicness or intimacy of the space; do interior and exterior walls keep sounds out or let them through?

- Light — does natural window light reach all or any of the space; is there borrowed light from adjacent spaces; do the quality and direction of the light enhance or detract from the proportions and details of the space; if the windows and spaces seem to have been altered, is there still a sense of the original daylighting?

- Features — are there fixed three-dimensional features that add distinction: balustrades, railings, mantelpieces, interior shutters, built-up cornices, doors and windows, doorframes and windowframes, and so on?

- Finishes — are there two-dimensional or modestly textured features that give interiors their close-up interest: decorative painting, marbling or stencilling, wallpapers, wood colour and grain, plasterwork, pressed metalwork and trim, and so on?

- Exposed structure — are there posts, beams, trusses, nogging and other structural elements exposed to view that give a space added visual interest?

- Fittings and furnishings — are there removable or portable elements that nevertheless survive from any of the building's earlier phases, that give clues to the historic quality and use of its spaces?

In answering these questions, assign priority to vital items, then to those that support these first-ranked items, next to items that are neither assets nor liabilities, and last to those that clash with important aspects. Make no value judgments about oldness or newness but look for intrinsic craft and quality of design and execution. Then compare these assessments with the results of historical research, which should establish associations of these features to past events and people. Together, architectural character and historic association will add up to a comprehensive value for the place as heritage resource and indicate directions for its conservation.

Assessing a building's condition

The following checklist summarizes aspects that must be examined for purposes of conserving visible architectural features and their supporting structure (there are several excellent guides to old-building inspection that provide more details).

For all but the smallest properties, it may well pay to retain someone experienced in surveying and inspecting old buildings, to ensure that the job is done to the right level of detail and to ascertain hidden or disguised faults (see FAULT DIAGNOSIS). It makes good sense to inspect a building in wet weather, despite the discomforts, as well as dry, in order to see how water runs off — or through — a building. The best season for major inspections is spring, when moisture-related deterioration is most visible and when several months lie ahead for urgent repair and preservation work.

Ideally, at least two people should undertake inspection and recording together, to aid each other and to consult in the case of puzzling evidence. They must take appropriate safety precautions, especially where the structure may be weak or where poor ventilation and infestations may produce and harbour hazardous organisms.

Building site

❒ Boundaries in relation to building; general orientation; survey markers

❒ Slopes to and from building; drainage from building to site, away from site; soil conditions; liability to flooding, erosion, subsidence

❒ Vegetation (trees, climbers, etc.) — species, root types, health, proximity to buildings

❒ Walls, fences, gates, outbuildings — materials, dimensions, state of repair

❒ Services and service access — telephone, electricity, gas, water, sewer connections; meters; septic tanks

Roofs

❒ Shape: hipped, gabled, flat — are there sags, low spots?

❒ Complexities: ridges, valleys, dormers — are junctions sound, flashings intact?

❒ Materials: slate, metal, asphalt, wood; combinations and patterns — are elements missing, worn, cracked, discoloured, lifting; are there signs of another roofing beneath?

❒ Eaves: troughs, gutters, vents, parapets, brackets, rafter ends, bargeboard — are gutters missing, cracked, sagging, peeling; are vents or gutters blocked; is painted trim cracked, broken, peeling; are parapets properly flashed, stable, with sound masonry and pointing?

❒ Chimneys: materials, flashing — are flashings and caps secure; are masonry and mortar sound, or decayed; are chimneys stable, vertical?

Walls

❒ Structure — is it solid masonry, combined masonry and rubble, wood frame, post and beam, masonry veneer; are there cracks evident, long or short, recent or old; are features out of alignment, walls bulging or out of plumb?

❒ Masonry: brick, stone surfaces; mortar and pointing — are surfaces sound, joints tight; are units cracked, broken, missing, efflorescing, pitted?

❒ Wood cladding — are boards cracked, peeling, warped, discoloured, dented, rotting?

❒ Trim and ornament: stone, terra cotta, artificial stone, wood, metal — is it sound, securely attached; is it cracked, crazed, rusted, peeling, discoloured; missing; are there rust stains beneath or below?

Foundations

❒ Grade and exposure — which way does the ground slope; do downspouts drain completely away; is water pooled against or near the building; are there signs of the ground around the building having been raised or lowered?

❒ Materials — is masonry cracked, discoloured, spalling, stained; is wood cracked, peeling, rotting; does it appear wet when surroundings are dry; are there signs of crumbling mortar or rotten wood immediately adjacent; is wood in direct contact with ground; are there signs of insect infestation?

❒ Integrity — are foundations even, level, settling, buckling, and in which locations; are cracks recent or old?

Windows and doors

❒ Materials and dimensions: metal, wood, plastic, glass, paint — are they sound, or cracked, peeling or rusted; do they appear to be original or later replacements?

❒ Assembly — are openings properly aligned, gaps properly covered by moulding or weatherstripping; are frames secure and square; do they show recent movements in cracked paint or crooked joints; do doors swing freely, or fall open or closed due to being out of plumb?

❒ Moisture — is there condensation inside windows, or between double glazing; are there stains or other evidence of wetness beneath windows, inside or out?

Porches and extensions

❒ Materials and dimensions: metal, stone, wood, plastic, glass, paint — are they sound, or cracked, peeling or rusted; do they appear original or later replacements?

❒ Attachment — are porches, steps, fire escapes, cornices, porticos, etc. securely connected to building; are their foundations independent or attached; are there subsurface foundations at all; are there signs of such features having been removed?

Basements

❒ Material — is masonry cracked, discoloured, spalling, stained; is wood cracked, peeling, rotting; does it appear wet when surroundings are dry; are there signs of crumbling mortar or rotten wood immediately adjacent; are there signs of insect infestation?

❒ Integrity — are walls even, level, settling, buckling, and in which locations; are cracks recent or old; is the floor heaved, cracked, damp? is there any floor at all?

❒ Structure — are structural supports directly beneath what they are supporting; do joists and floors sag noticeably; have structural members been cut for utilities; have cut areas been reinforced?

❒ Moisture — are there signs of past flooding, of leaks from floor above, near utilities?

Living and working spaces

❒ Structure — which partitions are load-bearing?

❒ Materials: plaster, wood, metal, masonry — are they sound, or uneven, cracked, out of plumb or alignment; is there evidence (discoloration, holes covered over, seams of paint, etc.) of previous features having been removed; are there signs of settlement, old or recent (bulging walls, long cracks, etc.)?

❒ Finishes: paints, stains, etc. — are they dirty, peeling, stained, cracked, crazed; has recent painting covered earlier deterioration; has paint buildup obscured details?

❒ Stairs and floors — are they springy, uneven, sloping, noisy to walk over; is wood spongy, decayed, splintering; are there signs of rot, infestation?

Attics, shafts and concealed spaces

❒ Integrity and ventilation — is light visible though walls, to the outside or to another space; are there ventilators for windowless spaces, of suffcient capacity; do pipes or exhausts pass through concealed spaces without leaks?

❒ Structure — do rafters, sheathing and other elements sag noticeably; have structural members been cut for utilities; have cut areas been reinforced; are wooden elements soft, damp, cracked; are metals rusted, paint peeling or off altogether?

❒ Moisture/insulation — is there a vapour barrier, and which side of any insulation is it on; are there signs of condensation on insulated areas, near openings; are there signs of leaks at corners or near flashed areas at chimneys or parapets?

❒ Infestations — are there signs of birds, bats, insects, rodents, past or present; are precautions such as facemasks being taken during inspection?

See WRIG76 for considerations in defining districts and CUMI85 for legal aspects of districts under the Ontario Heritage Act.

Heritage districts

The character of areas or districts of heritage value is based on recognizable correspondences among buildings and properties, together with differences between that aggregation and its surroundings. A district's character is comprised of many ingredients. Consider the following as a basic outline of what to look for and assess:

☐ Historical associations (with individuals, groups, events)

☐ Architectural value (compared to others of their type, era, architects)

☐ Vernacular design (modest buildings no less valuable than grand ones)

☐ Integrity (state of preservation of earlier conditions)

☐ Architectural details (quality and craft of construction)

☐ Landmark status or group value (relation to surroundings, either standing out or providing context for others)

☐ Open spaces (as context for existing structures and as neighbourhood amenity)

☐ Vacant land and contemporary structures (as context for existing structures and as sites for fitting new developments)

The boundaries of districts are also important, because public perception and appreciation of their character are based on a geographical definition (and because heritage and planning laws require it). Boundaries are based on a combination of factors, including physical situation, visual perceptions, patterns of historical evolution, and various legal definitions of property and land use regulations.

See NEIGHBOURHOOD AND DISTRICT CHARACTER, HERITAGE AND PLANNING POLICIES, and VISUAL APPROACHES AND RESULTS.

Periodic inspections

Buildings and sites should be inspected regularly, at half-yearly and yearly intervals for some items and features, at longer intervals for others. Such inspections should be part and parcel of maintenance programs for those places.

See TAKING CARE.

Relating inspections to documents and to other activities

Thorough inspection is the foundation for any physical work on the building, as well as for its understanding and interpretation as a heritage resource in its setting.

❖ Keep thorough records of visits, including date, time of day, and weather conditions.

❖ Use photographic film generously. Photograph from many angles and under different lighting conditions. Take plenty of photographs of details. Consider what historical photographs you would want or need to reconstruct features accurately, and make your own photographs accordingly.

❖ Ensure that photographic locations and directions of views are noted; other people will have to use these data, and they may not have seen the building or site themselves.

See RECORDING.

Defining a district of architectural or historical value requires transforming the three dimensions of space onto a two-dimensional map — and then transforming the map into policies that will maintain the values deemed important. This requires great skill at the very beginning, in observing, appreciating and noting how individual elements combine to make a whole that is more than its parts.

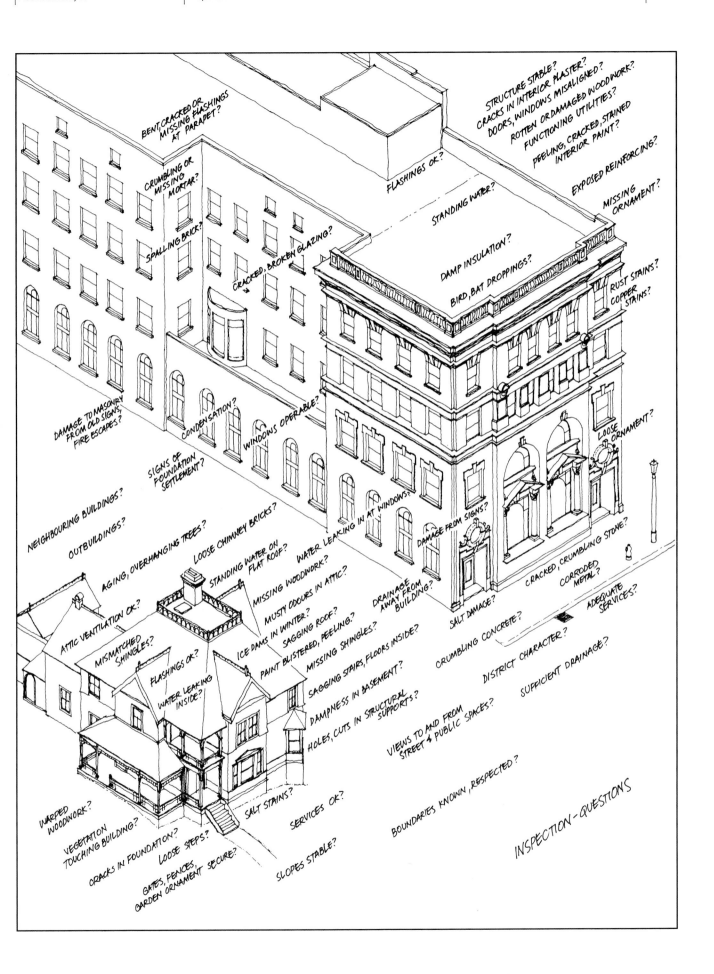

BENT, CRACKED OR MISSING FLASHINGS AT PARAPET?

CRUMBLING OR MISSING MORTAR?

SPALLING BRICK?

CRACKED, BROKEN GLAZING?

FLASHINGS OK?

STRUCTURE STABLE?
CRACKS IN INTERIOR PLASTER?
DOORS, WINDOWS MISALIGNED?
ROTTEN OR DAMAGED WOODWORK?
FUNCTIONING UTILITIES?
PEELING, CRACKED, STAINED INTERIOR PAINT?

EXPOSED REINFORCING?

MISSING ORNAMENT?

STANDING WATER?

DAMP INSULATION?

BIRD, BAT DROPPINGS?

RUST STAINS? COPPER STAINS?

DAMAGE TO MASONRY FROM OLD SIGNS, FIRE ESCAPES?

CONDENSATION?

WINDOWS OPERABLE?

SIGNS OF FOUNDATION SETTLEMENT?

NEIGHBOURING BUILDINGS?

OUTBUILDINGS?

LOOSE ORNAMENT?

AGING, OVERHANGING TREES?

LOOSE CHIMNEY BRICKS?

STANDING WATER ON FLAT ROOF?

WATER LEAKING IN AT WINDOWS?

MISSING WOODWORK?

MUSTY ODOURS IN ATTIC?

DAMAGE FROM SIGNS?

DRAINAGE AWAY FROM BUILDING?

CRACKED, CRUMBLING STONE?
CORRODED METAL?

ATTIC VENTILATION OK?

MISMATCHED SHINGLES?

ICE DAMS IN WINTER?

SAGGING ROOF?

PAINT BLISTERED, PEELING?

MISSING SHINGLES?

SAGGING STAIRS, FLOORS INSIDE?

SALT DAMAGE?

CRUMBLING CONCRETE?

ADEQUATE SERVICES?

FLASHINGS OK?

WATER LEAKING INSIDE?

DAMPNESS IN BASEMENT?

HOLES, CUTS IN STRUCTURAL SUPPORTS?

VIEWS TO AND FROM STREET & PUBLIC SPACES?

DISTRICT CHARACTER?

SUFFICIENT DRAINAGE?

WARPED WOODWORK?

VEGETATION TOUCHING BUILDING?

LOOSE STEPS?

SALT STAINS?

SERVICES OK?

BOUNDARIES KNOWN, RESPECTED?

CRACKS IN FOUNDATION?

GATES, FENCES, GARDEN ORNAMENT SECURE?

SLOPES STABLE?

INSPECTION - QUESTIONS

Fault diagnosis

References

See FEIL82 and especially HOLL86 for details on building-fault analysis and diagnosis. See TIMM76 for explanations of how many historic materials age and decay, and TRIL72/73 for problems of poor workmanship. Though focused on problems of acid rain, WEAV87 is an excellent survey of many other physical and chemical agents of building-material deterioration.

See also the sources listed in "Inspection" (page 64).

Basic tools for inspection and diagnosis.

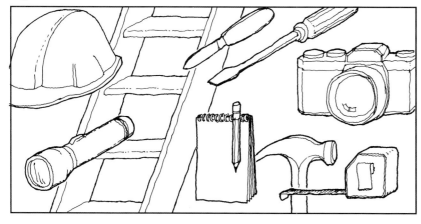

The need for experienced expertise

Diagnosing a building's ills from its apparent deterioration is an acquired skill, based on training in architecture and building science and proved by experience with many types of buildings and conditions. But even the most expert diagnostician often cannot determine with absolute certainty the cause of a crack or stain or the more serious symptoms that may lie beneath. Most conclusions are more or less probable, based on previous experience and careful reading and understanding of the case. Specialized instruments can be used to assess tricky situations, including moisture meters, strain gauges, thermographs, and even portable X-ray devices, but these may not be readily available.

It *is* necessary to have simpler devices in hand during inspections: binoculars, mirror, flexible flashlight or endoscope (for looking around corners in the dark — inside walls, for instance), measuring tape, pocket-knife, screwdriver, ladder, and so on. It is crucial to make as accurate a diagnosis as possible, without causing damage to the building by peeling away layers of material that cannot be replaced; as far as possible, building-fault diagnosis must be non-destructive.

Much of the information relating symptoms to likely causes appears under descriptions of individual materials or building elements.

Symptoms

❖ Generally, look for stains, discolorations, cracks, breaks, misalignments, discontinuities, bulges, traces of sloppy repairs, and so on. *Feel* and poke around for dampness, uneven or crumbling surfaces, and unusual sponginess. *Smell* for odours of decay, unusual yeasty odours, and so on (though take full precautions against inhaling dangerous organic substances associated with bird and bat droppings). *Listen* for hollow or dull sounds when a supposedly solid surface is struck.

❖ If there is an opportunity to monitor a building for a period of time, check cracks and other discontinuities for recent movement.

❖ Watch for signs of deterioration, changes in cracks, and so on, during early stages of work.

❖ Identify priorities for remedial action immediately and make sure that designs and specifications treat the most urgent work first.

❖ Record all symptoms thoroughly with notes, photos and sketches, especially where what is wrong is not immediately evident.

Confirmation on the job

❖ As things are discovered and diagnoses confirmed or revised, notes about these changes must become part of the project record, so as to build up a body of experience and improve diagnosis the next time. This is as true for work from one day to the next on a single project as for work from project to project.

❖ Monitor site work extremely carefully to avoid incorporating new flaws that will contribute to future problems.

Interdependent causes

Opposite is a chart of causes of building deterioration and the places where they are most likely to cause problems. Their effects are often cumulative and interrelated. Weigh this checklist against evidence from thorough inspection. Some faults can be fought directly with preservation treatments, but others are environmental and thus harder to control.

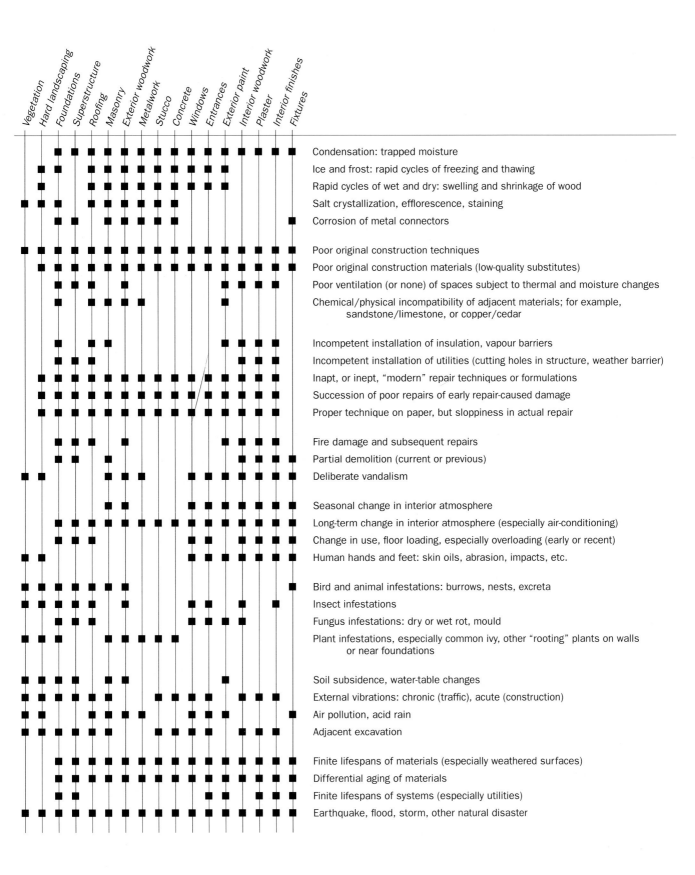

Column headers (left to right):
Vegetation, Hard landscaping, Foundations, Superstructure, Roofing, Masonry, Exterior woodwork, Metalwork, Stucco, Concrete, Windows, Entrances, Exterior paint, Interior woodwork, Plaster, Interior finishes, Fixtures

Condensation: trapped moisture

Ice and frost: rapid cycles of freezing and thawing

Rapid cycles of wet and dry: swelling and shrinkage of wood

Salt crystallization, efflorescence, staining

Corrosion of metal connectors

Poor original construction techniques

Poor original construction materials (low-quality substitutes)

Poor ventilation (or none) of spaces subject to thermal and moisture changes

Chemical/physical incompatibility of adjacent materials; for example, sandstone/limestone, or copper/cedar

Incompetent installation of insulation, vapour barriers

Incompetent installation of utilities (cutting holes in structure, weather barrier)

Inapt, or inept, "modern" repair techniques or formulations

Succession of poor repairs of early repair-caused damage

Proper technique on paper, but sloppiness in actual repair

Fire damage and subsequent repairs

Partial demolition (current or previous)

Deliberate vandalism

Seasonal change in interior atmosphere

Long-term change in interior atmosphere (especially air-conditioning)

Change in use, floor loading, especially overloading (early or recent)

Human hands and feet: skin oils, abrasion, impacts, etc.

Bird and animal infestations: burrows, nests, excreta

Insect infestations

Fungus infestations: dry or wet rot, mould

Plant infestations, especially common ivy, other "rooting" plants on walls or near foundations

Soil subsidence, water-table changes

External vibrations: chronic (traffic), acute (construction)

Air pollution, acid rain

Adjacent excavation

Finite lifespans of materials (especially weathered surfaces)

Differential aging of materials

Finite lifespans of systems (especially utilities)

Earthquake, flood, storm, other natural disaster

Buildings deteriorate in many ways, and in many places, but most problems will be found at the top and at the bottom. At the roof, the building is most exposed and least looked after. Near the ground, simple symptoms like salt stains on brick may have many potential causes, and each must be checked out before corrective action can be taken.

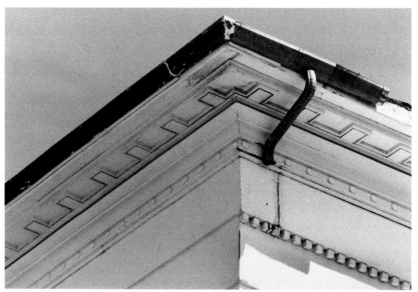

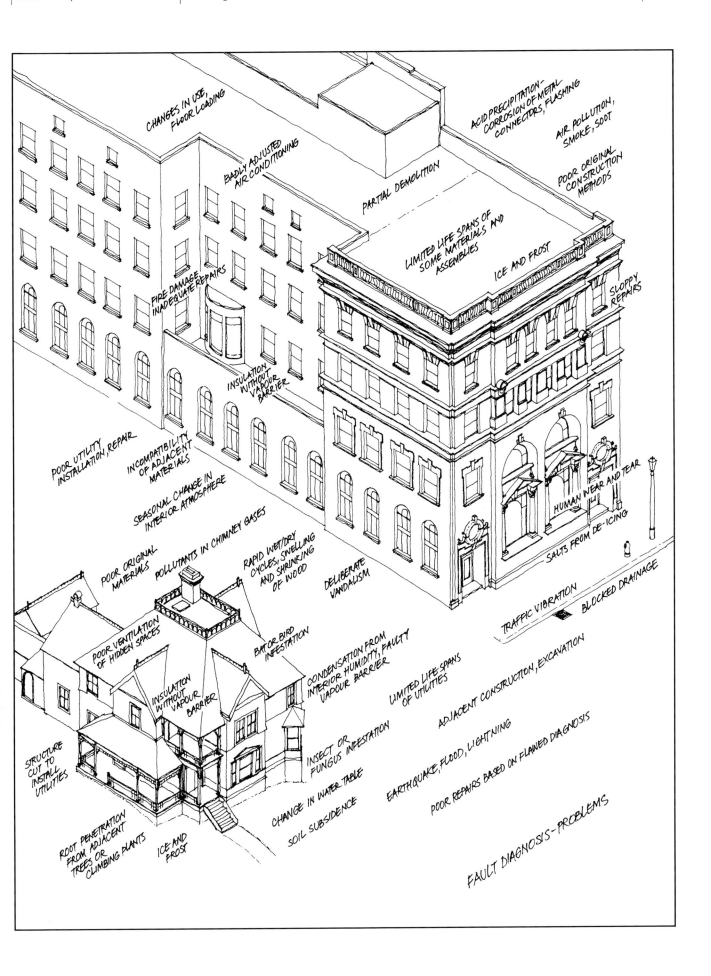

CHANGES IN USE, FLOOR LOADING

BADLY ADJUSTED AIR CONDITIONING

PARTIAL DEMOLITION

ACID PRECIPITATION- CORROSION OF METAL CONNECTORS, FLASHING

AIR POLLUTION, SMOKE, SOOT

POOR ORIGINAL CONSTRUCTION METHODS

LIMITED LIFE SPANS OF SOME MATERIALS AND ASSEMBLIES

ICE AND FROST

SLOPPY REPAIRS

FIRE DAMAGE INADEQUATE REPAIRS

INSULATION WITHOUT VAPOUR BARRIER

POOR UTILITY INSTALLATION, REPAIR

INCOMPATIBILITY OF ADJACENT MATERIALS

SEASONAL CHANGE IN INTERIOR ATMOSPHERE

HUMAN WEAR AND TEAR

SALTS FROM DE-ICING

POOR ORIGINAL MATERIALS

POLLUTANTS IN CHIMNEY GASES

RAPID WET/DRY CYCLES, SWELLING AND SHRINKING OF WOOD

DELIBERATE VANDALISM

TRAFFIC VIBRATION

BLOCKED DRAINAGE

POOR VENTILATION OF HIDDEN SPACES

BAT OR BIRD INFESTATION

CONDENSATION FROM INTERIOR HUMIDITY, FAULTY VAPOUR BARRIER

LIMITED LIFE SPANS OF UTILITIES

ADJACENT CONSTRUCTION, EXCAVATION

INSULATION WITHOUT VAPOUR BARRIER

INSECT OR FUNGUS INFESTATION

EARTHQUAKE, FLOOD, LIGHTNING

POOR REPAIRS BASED ON FLAWED DIAGNOSIS

STRUCTURE CUT TO INSTALL UTILITIES

CHANGE IN WATER TABLE

SOIL SUBSIDENCE

ROOT PENETRATION FROM ADJACENT TREES OR CLIMBING PLANTS

ICE AND FROST

FAULT DIAGNOSIS-PROBLEMS

Recording

Principles *for* recording

3.1 Record of found state

3.4 Archaeology (site & structure) for reconnaissance

3.5 Specifics of uniqueness (pattern, ensemble, detail)

3.6 Maximum information content/conservation of complexity

5.4 Archaeology (site & structure) for rescue of artifacts

6.1 Record of changes during project

9.1 Record of altered state

9.5 Records maintained and accessible

9.6 Knowledge shared

Principles *based on* recording

4.1 Respect for (natural) aging process

4.2 Respect for period/historic continuity, sequence

4.3 Respect for accumulations

4.4 Respect for uniqueness (pattern, ensemble, detail)

4.5 Respect for setting/context in community

4.6 Minimal conjecture/informed invention

5.2 Fitting use of existing spaces

5.6 Minimal removals

5.8 Moving as last resort

5.9 Façadism as last resort

6.3 Patina preserved

7.2 Replacement in kind/ recycled materials

9.4 Conservation commemorated

References

See CHIT80, PATT82 and MCKE70 on graphic recording techniques and drawing standards for buildings; FLAD78 is an excellent informal guide to field recording for archaeology. Photographic recording is covered in BUCH83, MCKE70, CHAM73, CHAMnd and BORC78; special attention is given in HECK79 to photographs as on-the-job documents. A good background work for architectural photography in general is BUSC87.

The requirements of recording for comprehensive inventories are examined in BRAY80, SYKE84 and TECH86.

Making records

A complete record of a property consists of a compilation of research, inspection and fault-diagnosis notes. Others evaluating the property and planning its conservation can make full sense and use of each of these components only if they are combined as a full and comprehensive record. The records of a heritage resource are the essential links between its past and its future.

❖ Keep and cultivate records of research, planning and conservation work during the project, not as an afterthought; keep track of new information, as well as changes in plans and executed work.

❖ Conservation records will often have legal importance, as a basis for heritage designation and/or grant aid, or as a record of workmanship and/or liability.

Texts

❖ There is no particular "best" format for compiling text material, but use chosen formats consistently — whether cards, looseleaf pages, hardbound notebooks, computer disks. Use a format that meshes well with supporting visual materials.

❖ Back up information all the time and keep spare copies of texts at separate, secure locations.

❖ Ensure that all copies are consistent with their originals. Put current dates on originals and copies to keep track of changes and ensure that copies are up to date.

❖ Building inspection and fault-diagnosis information should be directly tied to specification-writing. Use standard construction indexing where possible (not so easy in conservation; repair specifications may appear in many sections of standard new-construction formats).

❖ For designation and other purposes, convert research and evaluation notes into a formal summary of specific reasons for building importance, noting features of greater or lesser priority for recognition, preservation, and so on.

Site sketches and measured drawings

❖ Keep annotated field sketches from surveys and inspections together with their texts; it will be difficult to understand either if they are separated.

❖ Never presume that spaces and dimensions are perfectly rectilinear, or that there is a perfect match between original drawings/dimensions and finished work, even in relatively new construction.

❖ Double-check long runs of cumulative dimensions.

❖ Use sketches and photographs together: use field notes and drawings as keys to locations and directions of photographs and photographs as keys to locate sketches and notes.

❖ Final measured or record drawings must depict as fully as possible not only regularities and symmetries of the original design and intent but also irregularities and imperfections. Such drawings must never "neaten up" angles and dimensions.

❖ Follow consistent and standardized recording and drawing practices.

❖ In cases where there may be new construction following the metric (SI) system, record existing dimensions in both imperial (foot/inch) and metric units, and translate any standard modules or other consistent historic measurements into metric units consistently. Measured drawings done to metric scale should note dimensions in feet and inches, and should always include a graphic scale showing units in both systems.

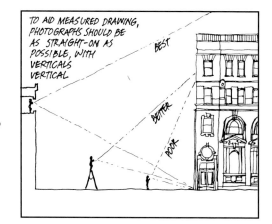

TO AID MEASURED DRAWING, PHOTOGRAPHS SHOULD BE AS STRAIGHT-ON AS POSSIBLE, WITH VERTICALS VERTICAL. BEST BETTER POOR

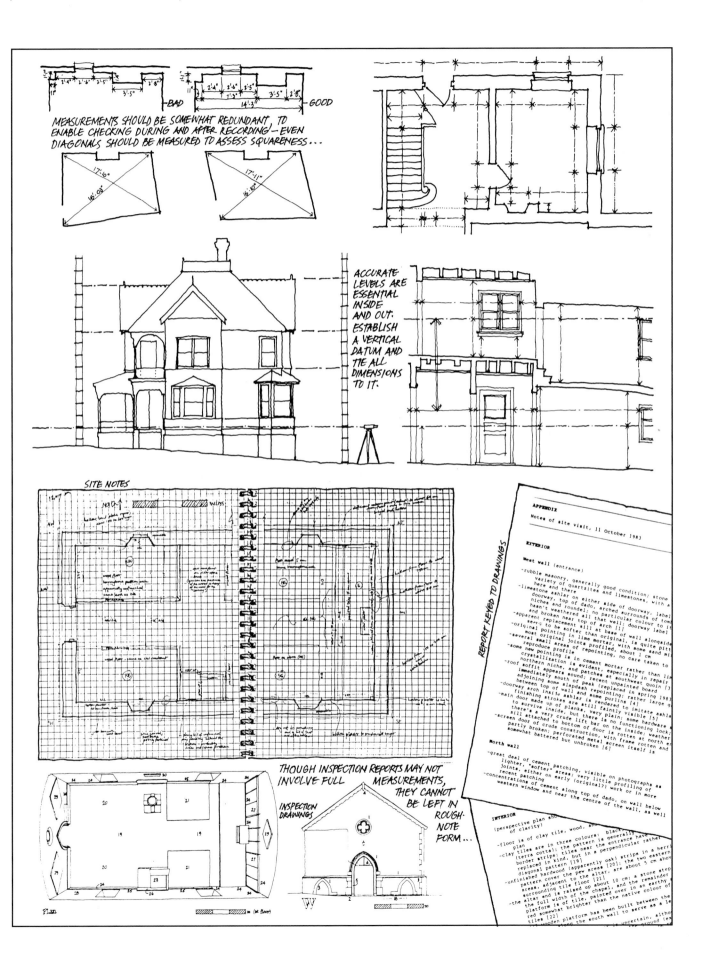

MEASUREMENTS SHOULD BE SOMEWHAT REDUNDANT, TO
ENABLE CHECKING DURING AND AFTER RECORDING — EVEN
DIAGONALS SHOULD BE MEASURED TO ASSESS SQUARENESS...

ACCURATE
LEVELS ARE
ESSENTIAL
INSIDE
AND OUT.
ESTABLISH
A VERTICAL
DATUM AND
TIE ALL
DIMENSIONS
TO IT.

SITE NOTES

REPORT KEYED TO DRAWINGS

THOUGH INSPECTION REPORTS MAY NOT
INVOLVE FULL   MEASUREMENTS,
            THEY CANNOT
INSPECTION   BE LEFT IN
DRAWINGS   ROUGH·
                NOTE
                FORM...

In general, cloudy days are preferable
to clear weather for making
permanent photographic records. The
shadows of sunny days obscure
important details. But the shadows
do help reveal the three dimensions of
the building and site. Ideally, a
photographic record should include
similar views taken in different
conditions of light.

Photographs of buildings should
focus in on details and materials, but
the record is not complete without a
depiction of the building's context in
town or countryside (below and
bottom right).

Photographs

❖ Don't be stingy with film; in relation to other costs of conservation, film is very cheap. Use a variety of angles, perspectives, lighting conditions (see INSPECTION).

❖ Use both black-and-white and colour films. Black-and-white is important for comparison with historic photographs and as a base for drawings and specifications; colour slides are useful for presentations; colour slides and prints, properly calibrated, are useful for colour-matching and analysis.

❖ Consider annotated Polaroid prints as useful aids for site note-taking, but use 35 mm or larger-format negatives for permanent records and larger prints.

❖ Keep copies of black-and-white contact sheets with text records, keyed to notes and sketches.

❖ Use clear prints, annotated, as part of text, with a view to their incorporation in specifications; such photos should include a graphic scale to permit rough measurements.

Photogrammetry/rectified photography

Terrestrial photogrammetry can be very expensive (precision cameras and stereoscopic plotters cost tens of thousands of dollars) but may save money and time over extensive recording by hand. It may be the only way to get accurate measurements from inaccessible or dangerous features. Though firms experienced with aerial photogrammetry can do accurate plots from stereoscopic photographs, few can do ground-based work. New microcomputer-based systems that can use photographs from small-format cameras under suitably controlled conditions are now becoming available; for the current state of the art, contact ICOMOS Canada (see Appendix).

❖ For photographs that can be used for approximate dimensions, follow photogrammetric practice in taking clear, straight-on elevation photos in cloudy-bright lighting (minimal shadows) with a graphic scale in view, even if not shooting for photogrammetry. Such rectified photos can be used for approximate dimensioning if the wall or floor planes to be measured (and the scaling device itself) are parallel to the plane of the film, that is, to the back of the camera.

Video, audio and micro

❖ Use portable videotape equipment as an adjunct to other techniques when recording processes in motion or as a travelling camera through sequences of spaces. Combining a videographic record with a soundtrack of oral interviews or narrations can add a vital aura to other depictions of the life in and of a building.

❖ Use small dictation tape units as an aid to notetaking on site but be sure to transcribe such audio notes immediately afterward.

❖ If a conservation project anticipates use of computer data storage and graphic devices, it may be possible and effective to compile an electronic record of the existing building from the information gathered on site, to generate dimensions, material quantities and architectural drawings. This is a rapidly developing area, and is likely to become more affordable and expeditious in the very near future. In any case, do not use a system that cannot store and cope with the numerous irregularities (of dimensions and materials) in existing buildings and sites. This is especially important in computer-generated drawings.

KEEPING records

❖ Use consistent formats for filing.

❖ Make summary information easily copyable and available to others involved in the project and to researchers on other projects.

❖ File a duplicate copy of the complete records in the local archives or other suitable repository.

References

Archaeology comprises both intellectual study of the past and practical craft; few texts treat both together. To understand how the study underlies the craft, see KING77 and TECH86. Guidelines for responsible archaeological conservation and fieldwork include FLAD78, KEUN84 and TREA80. For archaeological aspects of building investigation, see FEIL82 and SEEL85; for southern Ontario physiography, see CHAP66.

Archaeology and building

Archaeology concerns itself with artifacts and other material evidence of the past — tools, weapons, domestic utensils, art objects, industrial machinery, human or animal remains, rock art or structures, fragments or traces of building materials, foundations and ruins of former structures — any object or place modified by human activity. Analysis and understanding of this material and its context give us valuable and irreplaceable information, unavailable in any other way, about human interaction with the environment over a long period.

Because archaeological evidence lies hidden from view — underwater, underground, or inside walls and hidden places of buildings — it seldom comes to light in a predictable way. During rehabilitation or restoration, chance discoveries are not unusual. Some material may have direct connection to the history of the building, but some may be much older, relics of earlier, even prehistoric occupation of the same site. Even areas developed and redeveloped over the last two centuries may have buried evidence of prehistory.

Particularly sensitive are shorelines of lakes and rivers and former shorelines, such as sand and gravel pits and other post-glacial physiography. Prehistoric cultures used these zones intensively. More recently many waterfronts have witnessed initial settlement and early industrial development. Long-used agricultural landscapes often have similarly rich archaeological potential.

There is also a more localized archaeology of the building itself, its hidden spaces and immediate surroundings. Careful exploration may reveal material evidence of construction and early occupation, through broken or throwaway items in pits and privies and in material hidden or simply forgotten in an attic or basement or even between two walls.

Conserving the value of this evidence requires very careful recording of location, condition and context of artifacts as well as care in their retrieval and storage. Because the location of an object in a particular context offers as much information to a knowledgeable observer as the object itself, it is essential to record an object *before* it is removed, if it is to be removed at all. This can be done through notes, drawings, or photographs, but it must be done (see INSPECTION and RECORDING).

It is often worthwhile to bring in an expert to assist — someone trained in the uses and values of artifacts, with skills in archaeology and/or museology. On larger projects, where there is a strong likelihood of chance discoveries, it is vital to have someone with such skill as part of the regular working team. In other cases, arrangements for a quick response to a chance find might be made with a local museum or a provincial archaeologist.

Buildings as archaeological sites.

For information about licensing and its requirements, contact one of the Ministry of Culture and Communications' archaeological field offices; see Appendix 6, "Heritage organizations and information resources". There are offices in London, Ottawa, Sault Ste. Marie, Thunder Bay and Kenora, in addition to the main ministry office in Toronto.

Archaeology and the law in Ontario

Most archaeological exploration anticipates some disturbance of the ground, and any activity of this sort is regulated by the Ontario Heritage Act. Such exploration requires a provincial licence. Sites of great importance may be designated by the province, and no work of any kind undertaken there without express permission. Licensing procedures are set out in sections 48-51 and 65-66 of the Act; regulation of the sites themselves is covered in sections 52-64.

The archaeological report

Archaeological evidence is similar to other information gathered in the investigation of a property. It must be properly compiled with other records of research and inspection to form a base for planning conservation work. Licensed archaeological exploration normally requires submission of an archaeological report, identifying in detail the reasons for exploration, methods used, details of the location and nature of artifacts recovered, inferences based on these discoveries, and action based on the discoveries and inferences.

A copy of the report must be filed with the Ministry of Culture and Communications at the conclusion of the work. The report can then be used by others exploring similar properties or assembling data on many sites in order to broaden knowledge of general historical trends within a region or between regions.

Ongoing monitoring

In general, for archaeological purposes it would be ideal to have every potential "hiding place" explored before conservation work begins, but in practice this is seldom the case. A strategy for dealing with chance finds during work should be included in the overall management scheme for the project (see PHASING AND SCHEDULING and SURPRISES), and should be included in the archaeological report.

❖ Use caution in opening up any hidden space, for health and safety reasons and to minimize damage to artifacts.

❖ No object should be moved or disturbed in any way until its state and location are accurately recorded, and this must be made clear to every worker on the job.

❖ Information about any archaeological findings must be included in the final record of the property's conservation.

Landscapes as archaeological sites.

Neighbourhood and district character

Principles

1.1 Planned conservation

3.3 Informed reconnaissance/ inspection

3.5 Specifics of uniqueness (pattern, ensemble, detail)

4.5 Respect for setting/context in community

5.2 Fitting use of existing spaces

5.8 Moving as last resort

5.9 Façadism as last resort

References

There is a considerable literature on the subject of context and compatibility between old and new. See especially CUMI85, EDWA46, GOON80, LANG78, NATI80 and WRIG76 for criteria for districts as a whole and for the fit of individual buildings.

Broader treatments of the subject of environmental fit include ALEX77, FRAM84a, LYNC72, LYNC76, NEWC79, PERC79 and ZEIS84; see LENC82 and PRIZ75 for particular attention to the colours of buildings and landscapes. Detailed aspects of the fit of buildings into existing streets are covered in BROW80, CAPP86, DUTO85, HILL82 and RESE85.

The administrative niceties of heritage conservation districts in Ontario are covered in CUMI85.

Though these are all features with heritage value, it is their combination with one another that offers this town its special distinction.

The importance of context

Much of the motivation for heritage conservation comes from a general concern that future construction will not fit as well into a neighbourhood as existing structures. The public has a growing sense that conservation is essential to neighbourhood or district planning, beyond preservation of single buildings. The character of an area, with its buildings, landscapes and streets, has become of considerable value, even though no single person owns or controls this amenity — and even though its boundaries may be difficult to determine.

A district of particular heritage importance may be a collection of pleasant residential streets with solid Victorian houses, a main street lined with commercial blocks of many eras, a collection of mill and factory buildings along a waterfront, or even a rural landscape of scenic interest. Such areas are more than the sum of their parts and are demonstrably unique. They may be amenities for local people as well as attractions to visitors from near and far. They serve as a tangible focus for community pride.

Buildings have been described as having good or bad manners toward their neighbours. If there really is such a choice, then both old and new must strive to present the best manners possible. And the neighbourhood itself should support that.

Preserving context

❖ Maintain existing principal views into and out of property; do not obstruct prominent building features with new construction that violates the symmetry or other aspects of the historical planning of the property, especially on façades that face major public ways.

❖ Continue to use historic means of access — paths, drives, etc.

❖ Maintain, or if necessary redefine, the property's edges with their historic features — fences, vegetation, and so on — in a way that frames views into the property. Use visual documents and archaeological evidence to locate these features.

❖ New construction should correspond to and complement buildings on adjacent properties.

❖ New or repair work should not confuse the historic character of an area by creating an impression of greater age or of a different region or even country — revivals should be clearly identifiable as revivals, not "originals".

❖ Keep new site features such as parking and utilities inconspicuous, separate from the principal public faces of a building, located preferably in areas used historically as service zones (side or rear yards, and so on).

❖ Heritage structures of any sort should not be removed from their sites, not even within a property, unless there is overwhelming evidence that the only alternative would be demolition. Relocations should maintain as much as possible the pattern of visibility and access of the original siting.

See INSPECTION, RECORDING, HERITAGE AND PLANNING POLICIES, and VISUAL APPROACHES AND RESULTS.

Buildings and landscapes come
together in many different ways —
as linear streetscapes, as public
spaces defined by greenery and
surrounding buildings, as
rhythmical aggregations of buildings
with similar forms and materials, as
collections of relics of former
activities, and so on.

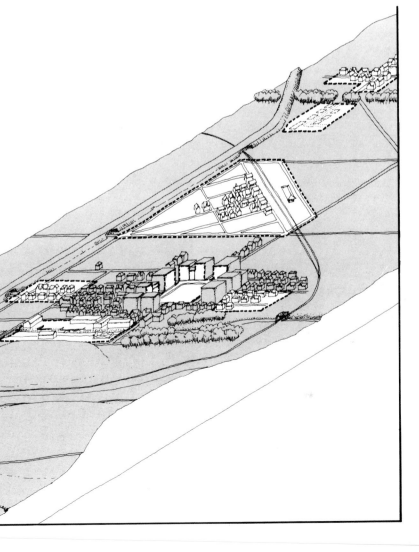

References

Preparation of designating by-laws and planning statements are covered for Ontario in FRAM84 and CUMI85; for further help contact the Ministry of Culture and Communications (see Appendix 6, "Heritage organizations and information resources"). Other jurisdictions' publications may also be helpful in preparing plans and by-laws; see, for instance, GLAS83, KEUN84 and RODD83.

For examples of other planning issues and strategies that may affect heritage resources, see FLEM82, STIP80, THUR83 and WILL78. An interesting guide to the development of arguments and cases for defending and promoting conservation at public hearings is SPAR71.

See also the sources listed in "Neighbourhood and district character" (page 80).

Promoting conservation, with caution

Promoting heritage conservation on a large scale can sometimes create its own problems, both for conservation of built heritage and for other community goals. Massive investment in tourist-oriented development or rapid inflation of property prices in an area being "gentrified" by higher-income groups may overwhelm and even wipe out the heritage values that attracted such interest in the first place. Such rapid change and economic pressure create the temptation to "over-renew" heritage properties, to make ill-advised changes that will reduce their heritage value and quite often their life expectancy, in the effort to make their appearance "like new".

❖ Develop, publish and maintain high standards for neighbourhood and building conservation, in order to temper this rush to modernize and "clean".

❖ Enumerate and assess all the social costs of planning policies that promote community renewal before such policies are implemented. Such costs may include displacement of population and of traditional uses and habits, increased vehicular traffic and noise, and narrowing of the economic base.

❖ Tourism can be a valuable community industry but must be treated with care. Develop "gentle", low-key strategies to promote visits by local residents and others. Promote tourism through guidebooks, selective building conservation and progressive small improvements in public amenities.

❖ Avoid massive capital investments that eradicate or severely damage the character of a place, such as standardized street furniture and paving, insertion of shopping malls out of scale with local needs, or renovation of waterfronts by obliterating traces of their working history.

Fitting the past to future plans

Heritage conservation cannot be completely isolated as a separate section of a municipal plan. It should be part and parcel of planning for land uses and activities. Whether or not they mention "heritage" by name, many land-use policies have direct and indirect implications for conserving heritage properties — often their effects are more potent than overt "heritage" policies.

❖ Local area plans should be based on thorough research and analysis of the historical background of the area, including an inventory of properties whose character is directly tied to that history.

❖ Planning policies should make clear that their implementation through zoning by-laws, business improvement areas, renewal plans and so on will take heritage conservation into account and ensure that no expenditure of public funds causes destruction of any identified heritage resource.

❖ Every legal instrument with planning aspects should be reviewed and its effect on heritage determined. Where possible each should promote conservation or at least not penalize it. For example, policies for eventual removal of non-conforming uses should be tempered by retention of the area's historic architectural character and provide that new uses will adapt to that character.

Tourist development may enhance the appreciation of a place's heritage — but tourists may also overwhelm the heritage they come to see.

Dealing with neighbourhood change

❖ Municipal plans should declare openly and publicly the municipality's desire and commitment to preserve its heritage on the ground; such declarations are invaluable advertisements and encouragements even where they lack tools to "enforce" compliance. If such policies are lacking, efforts should be made to have them adopted as a matter of high priority.

❖ New construction should follow a sort of environmental "golden rule" (do unto others as you would have them do unto you): new building should cause no impact that would not be welcomed by that same building if it already existed.

❖ Ensure that all applicable laws are followed by new construction adjacent to heritage properties, with special care to avoid environmental hazards.

❖ Proposals for new work on properties both within and adjacent to heritage sites and districts should be assessed at the earliest possible stages of planning. This analysis should cover traffic, microclimate, demography, noise and other factors that would reduce (or enhance) the heritage value of properties adjacent to new buildings, roads or other projects.

❖ Where Ontario's Environmental Assessment Act covers a new project, assessment of impact should consider heritage resources of all types, and any negative effects should be mitigated as part of the project.

❖ Development control and zoning by-laws should ensure that new development does not damage heritage properties. Consideration of such laws should be at least as systematic as the investigations required for environmental assessments.

Establishing heritage districts

❖ Areas of consistent architectural character that are distinctive collections of private properties and public spaces should be designated heritage conservation districts and woven onto other plans and policies.

❖ Ensure full public participation in planning and establishing heritage districts, whether as formal heritage conservation districts under part V of the Ontario Heritage Act, or as special areas for other planning purposes: business improvement areas, community renewal areas, waterfront districts, scenic routes, and so on.

❖ Establish clear and well-publicized policies and programs as early as possible in the process of district planning to direct development on a consistent basis, with guidance for making new developments good neighbours with what exists.

❖ Ensure that research and assessment of the district and its edges are comprehensive, and present those findings clearly.

❖ Provide for diversity as well as consistency in assessing and planning districts. Include vacant lands within district boundaries where their development offers opportunities that may either enhance or damage the character of the district, and make explicit criteria for the quality of development on such lands — especially on frontages facing heritage properties.

❖ Make heritage districts part and parcel of comprehensive local planning, not separate add-ons.

❖ Build on locally distinct historical and physical characteristics, with careful attention to historical documents, especially photographs, rather than adopting standard street "beautification" designs and hardware.

A major environmental project may overwhelm the scale and activity of not only towns but countrysides as well. These impacts must be anticipated and mitigated as well as possible, and may even raise doubts about the merits of the project itself.

References

For general principles of integrating or contrasting old and new, see EDWA46, ICOM86, LYNC72, LYNC76, NATI80, PYE78, RENY86, SCHO82, TECH82 and ZEIS84. More specific attention to townscape is given in BENT85, CUMI85, GOON80, HILL82, LENC82, NATI80, HOLD85, PRE70, PRIZ75 and WORS69.

The individual fit or neighbourliness of additions or adjacent buildings is discussed in varying aspects in DIBN85, DUTO85, ICOM86, HOLD85, HOW86, NATI80, SHOP86, STEP72, TECH82 and THOR84. For guides to historic styles and features see, for instance, BLUM77, CHIT85 and POPP83, as well as other sources noted in "Elements and styles" (page 20).

A visible respect for history

For every conservation project, from the smallest to the largest in scale and expense, there must be consistent and conscientious design, maintaining architectural character in the face of change and respectfully relating old to new. Among the great dangers of conservation treatments is over-enthusiasm — replacing too much, cleaning too well, making a falsely historic appearance in an attempt to recover the feeling rather than the truth of the past. This cavet applies to whole projects, not simply new additions inside or out (see VISUAL HARMONY AND GOOD FIT).

❖ Base all designs for replacement or restoration of former features on dependable documentary evidence, distinguishing clearly between features demonstrably part of the building's history, and those that informed experts think existed in that place in the past, but cannot be fully substantiated.

❖ Generally, assemble research and inspection information and develop approaches to conservation and existing or new use that aim at a specific and well-crafted final appearance for the job. This means taking a respectful approach to past work combined with intelligent, high-quality new work. The final look should reflect history as a continuum that includes original material and craft, worthy past modifications, and the new work. This entire ensemble will be the future's inheritance.

❖ Consider design approaches and existing components according to features of the old and the planned:

  ❏ Space: the arrangements of rooms, their linkages to interior circulation and exterior views

  ❏ Mass: profiles, skylines, shades and shadows

  ❏ Colour: hues and shades as perceived, together with evidence of historic colours

  ❏ Material/texture: visual, tactile, thermal, acoustic, both historic and contemporary

  ❏ Light/lighting: natural and artificial, historic and modern, comfort and utility

  ❏ Furnishings and fixtures

  ❏ Architectural details

  ❏ Signs

  ❏ Mechanical equipment

❖ Pay close attention to junctions of old and new, to whether joining will pay most respect to one or the other.

❖ Consider carefully the relative independence of old and new portions of the work, especially how they are visually dependent or independent.

❖ Be especially careful not to obscure signs of age and irregularities found in the dimensions and materials of older work.

Modes of historical respect

Adopt a mode of respect that is unambiguous, whether clearly contrasting or clearly "snuggling up". The following approaches are part of a continuum of possible ways to design successfully with the old and so should not be considered exhaustive. But the approach used should be generally consistent throughout a project.

❖ Take into account the robustness or delicacy of historic style and use — whether by matching or contrast, the historic character must not be overwhelmed by repair, modification or addition. For instance, buildings with relatively robust exterior wooden mouldings and carvings can be made to look lacy and delicate by inserting heavy new elements; this would distort the character of the existing work and should not be done.

❖ Examine historic precedents for clues to appropriate conservation strategies and the mating of old and new. Needs to modify, expand, or build next to existing buildings are by no means new, and there are many examples, both good and bad, of how these have been satisfied. Most common is the service wing or "kitchen tail" of older dwellings — the tail may be a simple box, or a reduced but decorated version of the main building, or it may be the original house itself, with the larger front portion being the true addition.

Reconstitution/period reproduction:
 Integral respect for the old; choice of
 new colours, materials, etc.
 subordinated to the historic
 architectural character; new functions
 adapted rigorously to existing and
 former spaces and details

❖ Conjectured restoration must not be
 confused with accurate reproduction of
 missing features. Handling of details or
 materials may evoke a period but must not
 masquerade as that period. This requires
 informed judgement on the part of
 designer and observer.

❖ Specify and use wherever possible the
 same materials and techniques used for
 original or early repair work.

❖ Do not artificially age (chemically or
 physically) reproduced or restored
 features. Patina and apparent age
 distinguish old and new; the new
 materials will age gracefully in their own
 time, as did the originals.

❖ Be faithful to the dimensional modules of
 the original; these are seldom exact,
 according to modern practice, and
 certainly not metric.

Approximation/complement:
 Identification with the essential *genius*
 ***loci* of the place, using its unique**
 patterns of profile, massing and form
 as design cues; a more integrative
 meshing rather than a detail-by-detail
 matching

❖ Understand and use the place's overall
 patterns — symmetries, framed views,
 hard v. soft textures, arrangements of
 natural lighting, and so on — to guide
 design for missing features or new
 additions.

❖ On those rare occasions where the original
 design was only partly completed and
 plans exist for a completed version,
 consider completion of the original design
 only as filling in an overall pattern; do not
 allow the final look of the project to
 confuse the true historic building with a
 new extension or infill.

Cautious contrast/self-effacement:
 Departure of the new from the
 existing, from an analysis of existing
 spaces and materials, implying old and
 new are correlated, in context with
 each other

❖ New, contrasting work should clearly defer
 to the old, in scale, colour and detail. The
 new should be sympathetic and
 harmonious, taking its cues from good
 work already there.

❖ Where new work will appear greater in
 quantity overall, it should be designed as
 backdrop to the old, through judicious use
 of axes and viewpoints and through the
 patterns of access to and within the
 completed project.

❖ Consider contrasts as matters of degree;
 there should be correspondence even in
 contrasting details. For instance, where
 new or replacement trim is not to be as
 ornate as surviving originals, perhaps
 evoke the originals through painted colour,
 shades or patterns, even artificial lighting.

Radical contrast:
 Affirmation of the new vis-à-vis the old,
 as more or less equal partners, but
 with due respect to the old

❖ Whatever design strategies are used to
 contrast old and new, the new must not
 trivialize the look of the old.

❖ Even the most radical contrast should
 acknowledge the feature of the old to
 which it should be related; new elements
 or new substitutions for missing elements
 must line up properly, obey patterns or
 rules that guided the original, and emerge
 from what exists rather than ignoring it.

When existing buildings are more or less free-standing within a larger space, it is especially important to respect their fundamental forms (especially how they are seen against the backdrop of sky and surrounding landscape) when repairing, adding on, or building adjacent — whether by conscientious mimicry, approximation, or cautious contrast (right).

There are many historic examples of matching or filling in street frontages that managed to accommodate additional storeys without trivializing adjacent buildings or the façade beneath.

In built-up urban areas where buildings are generally consistent in overall form, it is possible to work with what exists with more deliberate contrast. Each of these projects introduced new elements — some cautiously, some dramatically — while maintaining the scale and rhythm of their surroundings.

Principles

1.1 Planned conservation
1.3 Balance of use and preservation (cautious conversion)
1.4 Viable use
2.2 Co-operation among specialties
3.5 Specifics of uniqueness (pattern, ensemble, detail)
4.3 Respect for accumulations
4.4 Respect for uniqueness (pattern, ensemble, detail)
4.6 Minimal conjecture/informed invention
5.2 Fitting use of existing spaces
5.3 Minimal alteration, minimal intrusiveness
5.6 Minimal removals
6.2 Maximum retention
6.4 Respect for craft
7.3 Reversible repair
7.6 Maintainable repairs
8.1 Distinctive new work
8.6 Aided access
9.3 Emergency plan

References

For general considerations of reconciling the character of the old with the performance requirements of the new, see BENT85, ICOM86, LYNC72 and STAH84. Technical aspects of programming and re-use are covered in different ways in BUIL85, BUIL86, MARK79, NATI76, NIBS80, PARNnd, REAL81, SHOP86, STAH84, STEP72, VILA81 and WILL78.

Some explicit guidance for the tailoring of new functions to existing spaces may be found in BALL83, DIBN85, KAPL78/86, STAH84 and TECH82. There are case studies of good and not so good recycling in AUST88, BINN82, DIBN85, ELEY84, HOW86, ICOM86, KIRK84, MARK79, NATI76, NATI80, SHOP86, VILA81 and WARN78.

Matching needs and spaces

Architectural programming is the craft of determining the characteristics of the physical spaces required for the functions to be accommodated in a building. At its minimum, a program is a list of functions and the dimensions of the spaces needed to hold them. But there are many other needs besides "raw" space; a good program will describe lighting, access, acoustics, and other performance requirements that a designer must satisfy, for individual spaces and the overall result.

For conservation, the program for future use must be laid out with the existing building and its spaces in mind. The architectural program for continued or new use must be based on the assessment of architectural character (see INSPECTION). Some combinations of old and new cannot work without destroying the old, but that is rare; there are degrees of fit and adjustment, and these should be worked out to maximize the contribution and continued use of existing spaces.

❖ As much as possible, maintain existing uses and/or users, or restore the original use.

❖ As much as possible, use existing spaces and access patterns without modification. There should be more flexibility in the use-program for an existing building than for a new one.

❖ Allocate new uses to existing rooms and spaces so as to incorporate and preserve existing finishes and fixtures. Keep in mind long-term maintenance and durability of historic finishes in new use. As much as possible, concentrate service spaces and areas requiring new finishes or considerable mechanical upgrading in one area.

❖ Take advantage of "happy accidents" and peculiarities of the existing plan to enhance the program; for instance, should rooms in large old houses be converted to offices, use built-in storage for electronic equipment or file storage.

❖ Decide which existing spaces can best accommodate physical change. Rank them according to distinctiveness, public accessibility and view, functional requirements for upgrading services, and so on. For instance, public entrances, lobbies, hallways and major public rooms with heritage value may be much less tolerant of changes than areas such as rented offices and service zones (see INSPECTION).

❖ If the use-program cannot be suited to existing spaces without severe compromises (of program or architecture) add new spaces outside the existing structure.

❖ Make sure that dimensions of new furnishings and fixtures will let them fit through non-standard doors and corridors and into non-standard room shapes and sizes.

Old building, new performance?

❖ Upgrade existing structure, utilities, and so on as discreetly as possible, consistent with the chosen approach to fitting new into old (see VISUAL APPROACHES AND RESULTS).

❖ Maintain existing uses as much as possible; this will help restrict upgrading to repair or replacement of worn-out components.

❖ Locate new uses demanding structural capacity or occupancies beyond existing capacities on lower floors or in areas that can be upgraded without compromising or upgrading the entire structure.

❖ In upgrading or recycling do not follow a formula but look at existing conditions and the underlying rationale for upgrading. For instance, do not follow standard approaches to fire safety retrofit but carry out a life-safety study to customize retrofit requirements to the existing building (see CONSERVATION AT LAW).

Each of these places "recycles" yet maintains its historic attributes in different ways, from the addition of new housing in the rear yard of a former mansion, to the conversion of a service yard to a public space serving new offices and shops, to the "planting" of a combined sculpture and observation deck atop the piers of a former bridge (right). The conversion of a mill to an inn even manages to take advantage of the water power available by virtue of its location (below).

Recycling a railway station — as a railway station. An integrated bus/train and local transport terminal allowed the rehabilitation of a historic structure for current and future requirements. Many other apparently redundant stations could be similarly rejuvenated, if the needs of several users can be co-ordinated.

A SALUTE TO THE GRAVENHURST STATION

A community success story for Gravenhurst

Reflections on the past, direction for the future
Official opening: Oct. 4, 1986 at 2:30 p.m.

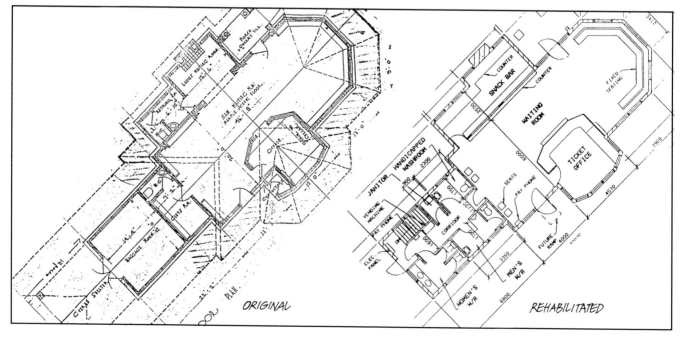

ORIGINAL

REHABILITATED

Using carefully fitted additions to provide new space, modern services and better public access, especially for the disabled.

Aided accessibility

❖ Plan for added handicapped accessibility without removing historic fabric.

❖ Insert wider doorways, elevators, chair-lifts or ramps adjacent to but not impinging on valuable historic fabric or make such access part of distinct additions.

❖ Where possible, use elevators that do not require rooftop additions; use centrally located elevators, rather than internal ramps, to connect uneven levels in the existing building or between old building and new addition.

❖ Use internal ramps only when space permits a sufficiently safe shallow slope.

❖ Where staff is constantly in attendance, consider portable ramps.

❖ Provide wheelchair-accessible entrances as close as possible to existing floor levels with external ramps and where possible, to minmize their visual impact, make them slope down from ground level to a lower-level entrance rather than up.

❖ Where new external ramps are unavoidable, place them so as not to disturb the formal symmetry or balance of the building and design them to fit discreetly into the overall look of the place. In practice, this may mean using a side or rear elevation as a new major entrance. Small adjustments to external grade levels may reduce or eliminate the need for ramps outside the building or for level changes inside (see SPATIAL DEFINITION AND HARD LANDSCAPING).

Specifying the work: drawing and specification-writing

Principles

1.2 Comprehensive understanding

3.1 Record of found state

3.5 Specifics of uniqueness (pattern, ensemble, detail)

3.6 Maximum information content/conservation of complexity

4.6 Minimal conjecture/informed invention

5.7 Reconstruction for wholeness

7.1 Traditional repair (proven technology)

7.4 Cautious high-tech repair

7.5 Recipes tested before application

8.1 Distinctive new work

References

General instructions that can be used as models for dealing with some aspects of conservation work may be found in DAVE80/86, KIRK84, MULL81, POWY29, REID84 and SHOP86. More specific professional and technical advice is in FEIL82, FERG86, LEVI78, MEAD86, STAH84 and TIMM76. Some books provide sample specifications in outline form; for instance, see BOWY80, HIGG85 and INSA72.

Old pattern books and construction texts can offer very useful guidance on earlier construction practice. Some have reappeared in reprint form, but one exceptionally useful text on specifications, MACE98, can be found only in the odd library or old-book store.

Specifying quality: making good work easier to do

Specifying and getting results of high quality are difficult for any construction project, old or new, but have special importance for conservation, where it is seldom possible to recover from damage due to poor work. It is necessary to instruct properly those doing work, telling them what to do and in some cases how to do it. In general, specifications are documents — drawings, photographs, written and verbal descriptions of procedures, general instructions on packages, legal requirements in building codes, and so on. Among these may be a formal "construction specification", a written set of instructions that forms part of a legal contract to carry out construction work.

Getting the best results requires the attention and care of everyone, from owner to worker, and clear communication at every stage. Because conservation involves taking records of the existing building and transforming them into plans and specifications for work, there may be shortcuts from the standard new-building sequence — program to design to working drawing (and specification) to contracting to supervision. For instance, on modest conservation jobs, documents generated by inspection and recording may provide sufficient instructions for repairs or replacements, by the addition of clear notes to drawings and photographs.

Nevertheless, this informal approach must be used with caution — it may lead to problems itself. It will produce good results only if both specifier and worker are fluent in that method of communication and have the appropriate skills. For a conservation job to go well, everyone involved must understand clearly where it might go wrong.

Specifications (both written and drawn) thus act as the bridge between the documentary record and the work itself. Every activity in heritage conservation requires written and graphic instructions. But since much repair work is not reversible, written instructions — in the construction specification, on working drawings, and in memoranda and change orders — must be right, because they direct the quality of the work. They will provide the reference against which success or failure is judged, including matters of liability.

Documentation: informal specs to contract documents

❖ Every conservation project should be specified on the basis of a full inspection record; there should be enough graphic and verbal information to enable specifier or designer to make instructions for the necessary work without having to redo those instructions during the work (unless "surprises" cause new problems).

❖ Drawn, photographic, written and verbal communications should all comprehensive and consistent (common sense, but not so common practice). Drawings and written instructions should reflect the irregularities and uniqueness of the existing building.

❖ As far as possible, develop specifications and drawings on the standard construction specification model but ensure that preservation and repair prescriptions are located throughout the documents in the appropriate places, not just under general "Requirements".

❖ As far as possible, use accepted conservation specifications or specifications modelled after a project widely recognized as successful, rather than inventing new prescriptions. Shared experience makes conservation work more efficient and effective. (Unfortunately, there are few models available at present.)

❖ Instructions should be in forms and styles appropriate to the type of work and the audience:

❏ Sketch drawings and annotated photographs for client and public agency approvals should be accompanied by written descriptions of the pertinent general quality standards.

❏ Construction drawings and the written specification (including annotated photographs of details) for tendering and contracting should describe in detail the instructions for job quality that *must* be met by the contractor and those other areas where trade-offs may be possible without sacrificing quality overall or in detail.

❏ Contract documents and instructions to site workers must state general quality standards together with instructions

Photo-drawings are among the most useful formats for describing conservation problems and specifying work, either as advisory materials to help clients and contractors understand what needs doing and how it ought to be done, or as elements of the contract documents themselves. They efficiently describe existing conditions and they help localize areas that are most likely to produce surprises when work begins.

for quality on specific details, emphasizing where standard new-construction approaches are not permissible and making instructions comprehensible to workers, by demonstration if necessary.

❑ Instructions to site supervisors should be the same as those to the contractor and building workers (again, common sense, but not so common practice).

❖ Every recipe or procedure whose results vary with conditions must be tested

on site. Specifications and instructions must express this requirement clearly, allowing sufficient time and assigning responsibility for testing and for assessing results.

❖ Consultants and clients should use pre-tender or pre-construction meetings to verify bidders' or contractors' understanding of specifications, and to inquire how those instructions might be improved (see CONTRACTING AND SUPERVISION and PROFESSIONAL ADVICE FOR HIRE).

East Wall Elevation

General area of plaster repair - Division 9, Sections 9.1 - 9.6 of specifications

Stove is not original to house / stove (1923) acquired by historical society will replace this stove. The replacement stove is a combination electric/wood stove and will be made fully operational

Area of general plaster repair - present condition of plaster is poor, area shows large cracks

Door leads to back staircase to second floor

South Wall Elevation

1. Areas of general plaster repair - plaster show large cracks
2. Location of original and present porcelain sink and taps
3. Door / entrance leads to refrigerator room that is to be reconstructed and will house public washrooms
4. New outlet & light switch, must be secured and plate installed over unit

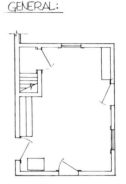

GENERAL:

Area to represent finishes between 195 - 1920

1.) WALLS: Extensive plaster repair needed in areas where indicated, to be done in accordance with Division 9, Sections 9.1 - 9.6 of specifications. Upon completion of plaster repair walls to be primed & painted as specified in the room finish schedule

2.) WOODWORK: Woodwork throughout the kitchen is in relatively good condition, some areas have previously undergone repairs as noted. All woodwork will be painted according the room finish schedule - Division 9, Sections 9.12 - 9.15 of specifications

3.) CEILING: Presently plaster ceiling is in fairly good condition - needs some plaster repair work - surface then to be cleaned & prepared for a fresh layer of paint

4.) FLOORS: Floor surface is presently painted to be treated as specified in Division 9 & re painted as noted in the room finish schedule

5.) SERVICES: Services to be upgraded as stated in Division 16 of specifications approximate locations of electrical outlets & switches are as shown. - Central ceiling fixture must be rewired

North West Corner Elevation

South West Corner Elevation

JOB TIT
MAT
KEEW
DRAWIN
PH

SCALE

References

Though their actual listings are specific to to their locales (Scotland and New York, respectively), see SCOT84, SCOT85 and REST86 for suggestions on what to seek in conservation specialists. Other references about dealing with the professional specialists include COMM83, INSA72, KIRK84, MELV73, MILL86, MITC82, SHOP86 and VILA81. See also "Professional advice for hire" (pages 194-199).

For site supervision, see LEVI78 for an especially good point-by-point guide; see STAH84 for larger buildings and LITC82 for smaller ones. A more general reference on construction supervision, with a section on refurbishment, is FERG86.

Retaining good help

There is as much need for careful hiring and supervision of work as for good planning and design. The quality of conservation work is crucial. Quality can be assured (at least optimized) only if the contractor for every phase of the work is well qualified, and if work is monitored to assure that it meets defined standards and is well and fully co-ordinated with what comes before, during and after.

❖ Ask to see an appropriate demonstration of the skill being hired — ask a researcher for previous reports; an architect or contractor for previous projects; a craftworker for details of previous work. Visits to previous projects are essential; do not rely on descriptions that may be biased (intentionally or not). Unless viewed with a very conscientious eye, photographs of finished work can be particularly misleading; if they're available, look closely at work-in-progress photographs as well. And ask their previous clients about details of projects and their progress, not just the final product.

❖ For a project used as a reference, find out who on the project team did what; in joint ventures or large firms, ascertain individual responsibilities.

❖ If a previous project's quality and success were the result of collaboration, seek to have all of that team, not just its "co-ordinator", retained for your project; often the combination of individuals is greater than their independent contributions. Individuals seldom succeed in conservation work on their own. Conversely, an unsuccessful project does not necessarily mean that all team members performed poorly.

❖ In competitive tendering, which normally seeks the lowest possible price, ensure that a low bid is comprehensive and fully meets the terms of the specifications. The selection process must not abandon the standards of quality and workmanship for what appears to be the lowest price. Though important for new-building work, high standards are even more critical for conservation.

❖ Consultants, contractors and clients should meet very early in the process, even before tendering or starting work. Participants should get to know one another and agree about the work to be done — especially about procedures to follow if things do not go according to plan.

The wide range of skills and practitioners is covered under PROFESSIONAL ADVICE FOR HIRE, which also outlines important cautions to be taken when retaining professionally qualified people for any aspect of conservation.

Balancing cost, time and quality

Supervising any building work involves trade-offs between quality of workmanship and budget and schedule. The final product, including both finished work and balance sheet, must be the criterion of success, whatever may happen during the job.

However, conservation work requires a different sort of balance among these factors than new construction. The overwhelming need to preserve historical and architectural character should give the finished product more weight than short-term economies in balancing schedule, cost and quality. Site and job supervision will require a firmer and more capable hand than usually needed for new work.

Sometimes this means added supervision costs and slower work — to be balanced against the flexibility of working in a building already there, often occupied and paying for itself, as well as long-term savings from better work and less consequent maintenance and repair.

❖ Where possible, have a clerk of works constantly on site to monitor progress and maintain contractually determined quality control, rather than relying solely on periodic visits by architects and other consultants. On-site monitoring may be cost-effective, reducing the number of costly visits by senior consultants, but places a great responsibility on the clerk, who must monitor all aspects of work, even in areas where he or she may not be expert.

❖ Follow a standard text on site supervision for checklists of what to watch for and how to deal with difficulties. Despite the great variety of conditions (and the many different opinions of architects and other building professionals), there is much shared experience in print that is surprisingly poorly used (see margin).

❖ Make notes and instructions on drawings and in specifications complete and unambiguous, so that questions of interpretation are minimized or obviated altogether. Many delays in conservation work are the result not of poor workmanship or "loss" of traditional techniques but of unclear or inconsistent instructions and time wasted waiting for interpretation or clarification.

❖ Keep lines of communication open. Make meetings efficient. Have someone take meeting notes and include these in the project record.

The more complex the work, the greater the need for contractors and workers with demonstrated skills and successful experience in similar work. On small projects, a client may be able to engage directly in certain types of work alongside professionals, or be active in informal supervision of the work. But for larger projects, good management practice often involves delegating responsibilities to an organized team in a consistent, disciplined and professional manner, with much less scope for informality.

Principles

1.1 Planned conservation
2.1 Co-ordinated work
2.2 Co-operation among specialties
2.3 Work in order
2.4 Work at right pace
3.4 Archaeology (site & structure) for reconnaissance
5.1 Priorities of features, priorities of work
5.4 Archaeology (site & structure) for rescue of artifacts

References

Doing things at the right time and in the right order is a central theme of the better references. See, for instance, FEIL82, FERG86, FINE86, INSA72, KIRK84, LEVI78, LYNC82, MELV73, POOR83, SHOP86, TIMM76 and VILA81.

Doing things in order

The most important first step is *not* to demolish or destroy *anything* until its condition, use, potential and value are understood. No approaches of last resort should be taken until all other options have been exhausted. For instance, removing sound interior plaster simply to reach spaces inside walls might make installation of utilities easier, but ignores the aesthetic, thermal and acoustical properties of plaster walls that cannot be replaced by plasterboard. In a conservation project, such gutting is technical incompetence, a sign of an inability to understand a building and to handle conservation work.

The following very basic outline is not necessarily comprehensive for every conservation project; it simply suggests phases and the order of work in general. Much conservation work can run in parallel; for example, interior and exterior work can proceed simultaneously, coming together at such points as window repairs. Parts of a building may be in use while conservation is underway. But do not rush — always leave time for physical and chemical processes to cure properly. Co-ordinate use of exterior scaffolding; its rental, erection and removal are expensive (see STABILIZATION).

Co-ordinating activities such as material deliveries and the use of scaffolding and hoists is absolutely essential to successful conservation work, even more so than for new construction.

Stabilize and secure

❐ Do a full inspection before doing any irreversible work.

❐ Ensure that site services are available throughout the project, including electricity, water, wastewater disposal, and debris disposal.

❐ Provide safe and well-marked temporary access to areas that will remain in normal use during work.

❐ Provide areas in or near building for temporary storage and workspace.

❐ Arrest exterior deterioration, especially roof leaks and areas of moisture damage. *Any temporary repairs at this stage must be reversible.*

❐ Eliminate fire hazards (debris, inoperative doors, etc.).

❐ Eliminate or cordon off hazardous areas.

❐ Secure loose building elements.

❐ Remove standing water.

❐ Inspect for and exterminate insect infestations.

❐ Secure door and window openings against unauthorized entry.

❐ Mask floors, unpainted woodwork and other delicate finishes against damage from clean-up and construction work.

Record and clean up

❐ Clean up loose rubble, taking care to record and store anything of potential value. *Do not pry off loose elements unless they are easily reattachable.*

❐ Photograph, measure and sketch the complete exterior and interior, and add the resulting documents to the project record.

❐ Clean away loose dirt and dust; scrub off peeling paint, but do not (yet) strip it all off (save samples for colour and chemical analysis).

❐ Establish work priorities based on the inspection and on plans and designs for new or continuing use.

❐ Order materials and arrange deliveries and special crafts well before they are needed.

HEAT AND COLD

Particularly sensitive to thermal extremes are painting and masonry cleaning and pointing — none should be done at temperatures below 10°C (50°F). Lime mortars must never be applied in direct, hot sunlight. Certain methods of chemical cleaning must not be carried out in direct sunlight either.

It is sometimes possible to enclose and heat exterior areas temporarily to accelerate work through cold weather, but the shelter must remain heated to keep the workers warm and to let compounds such as mortar cure properly. And curing time may add an extra month or more to the rental and heating charges for the enclosure.

Work in sequence: exterior

❒ Stabilize the structure (temporary and removable reinforcements).

❒ Do site work on adjacent grounds to prevent further deterioration: regrading, drainage, waterproofing.

❒ Repair and reinforce structure for permanent occupancy: foundations, bearing walls, floors (working up from lower floors).

❒ Complete permanent roof repairs, both structural and waterproofing, including flashing and gutters.

❒ Clean exterior surfaces as necessary, including removing paint.

❒ Repair and repoint masonry, replacing deteriorated units as required.

❒ Repair ornamental metal and woodwork.

❒ Repair windows (reglazing where necessary).

❒ Stain and prime exterior surfaces.

❒ Seal and caulk exterior.

❒ Paint exterior.

❒ Clean up around exterior; remove debris.

❒ Complete landscaping.

Work in sequence: interior

❒ Stabilize the structure (temporary and removable reinforcements).

❒ Remove finishes and fixtures where necessary (store for possible salvage).

❒ Repair and reinforce structure for permanent occupancy (working up from lower floors).

❒ Install hidden mechanical services and utilities.

❒ Install insulation, vapour barriers (using great care to prevent moisture problems).

❒ Repair windows (reglazing where necessary).

❒ Clean up debris from plaster, etc.

❒ Make good holes, cracks and other construction damage.

❒ Seal and caulk interior.

❒ Install new finishes.

❒ Complete priming and painting (once dust has died down from previous work).

❒ Repair and reinstall salvaged fixtures.

❒ Install new fixtures.

❒ Repair and refinish masked surfaces.

❒ Clean up.

Seasonal work and contingencies

Construction work is usually seasonal, but an existing building or structure offers considerable flexibility in scheduling. A large portion of conservation takes place inside, and once immediate causes of deterioration are dealt with, interior work can be finished in any season.

On the other hand, roof repair, exterior cleaning, and exterior refinishing must be done in good weather, during the regular spring-to-autumn construction season. Heat, direct sun, cold, and wet conditions can affect curing processes and workers' capabilities and must be controlled as well as possible.

Estimates of time and personnel must also allow for contingencies, delays and surprises. Provide sufficient secure area to stockpile materials and tools, and proper space for an on-site workshop. Even materials ordered well in advance may not arrive on time: keep the schedule as flexible as possible to work around such delays. And keep on hand materials and props for temporary shoring or reinforcement in case of unanticipated structural deterioration or weakness.

Project records and progress diaries

References

Though keeping records during any construction or conservation work should be a matter of common sense, it requires consistency and discipline: see especially FERG86, HECK79, INSA72, KIRK84, LEVI78 and MELV73.

Building from existing records

❖ Incorporate historical documentation into project plans and specifications, in the form of comparable early and modern photographic views or copies of original construction drawings, wherever possible. Such documentation is essential when elements are to be returned to an earlier or original condition or replicated, to prevent "fictionalization" of the historical appearance of a property.

❖ Keep a full copy of research materials on the job (especially drawings and photographs), together with drawings and specifications. Use these materials to give workers and visitors a sense of the direction of the work in progress. Where there is a clerk of works, he or she should have custody of these materials.

❖ Once the contract is awarded, incorporate the contractor's schedules, supporting documents and standard procedures into the project record. Even though these are not contract documents, they may be vital for future maintenance as well as current work. Despite drawings and specifications, site workers often follow their previous training and their foremen's instructions; having a record of these on-the-job changes will help in figuring out later the best means of repair.

Keeping track

❖ Make no irreversible changes without recording, in notes, drawings or photographs, conditions before and after those changes. Such records will be invaluable in case of contingencies and delays due to unforeseen problems and will assist in long-term maintenance.

❖ Record both process and products of any required dismantling in order to assess structure and materials. This may have great value in specifying structural repairs and in understanding how the construction corresponds to conventions of the period or to historical records.

❖ Maintain a running diary of conservation work, by type of work and even by trade or worker. Though the clerk of works must keep a diary as part of the job, encourage everyone on the project to do so. Where a team may be doing several similar projects, sharing experience from one project will aid other work, and even the same job later on.

❖ Keep an account of progress and critical events in comparison to the planned schedule; this will be an invaluable aid in making mid-project adjustments and resolving disputes.

❖ When a contractor or worker suggests procedures different from those in the drawings and specifications for achieving a high-quality result, the suggestion should be taken seriously and adopted if it will achieve an equivalent or better result. *The altered procedure must be recorded in the project records.* This will be great important in resolving any disputes later on. There must be no unauthorized changes in the way work is carried out.

Completed project records

❖ Make *two* copies of a complete dossier of the project, assembled from copies of construction documents (annotated with changes made during work), diaries maintained by the clerk and others, and before-and-after photographs of work in progress. One copy should be filed with the owner of the project, to be part of the maintenance documentation, the second in a suitable local repository for safekeeping and future consultation.

The porch in the historic photograph (top) was reproduced from the evidence of the photograph itself — but on close inspection, the replica (middle) does not quite match. How important such a slight mismatch might be in other cases depends on the specific project — in this case the overall effect is sufficiently close to satisfy most observers.

Keeping notes on the construction documents themselves will be valuable for maintenance and for future repairs.

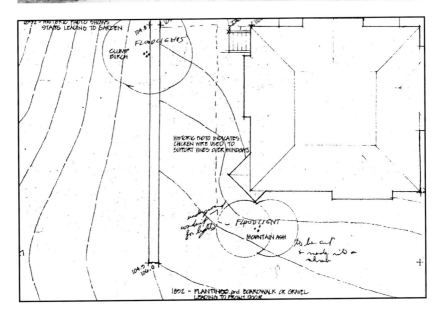

Surprises: on-site reassessments and archaeological finds

References

See KING77, FLAD78 and FEIL82 for different perspectives on chance archaeological finds. For dealing with surprises in and around buildings, see LEVI78, FEIL82, FERG86, INSA72, KIRK84, SHOP86, TRIL72/73 and VILA81.

ARCHAEOLOGICAL FINDS

For advice about chance archaeological finds, contact one of the Ministry of Culture and Communication's archaeological field offices (see the appendix, "Heritage organizations and information resources"). There are offices in London, Ottawa, Sault Ste. Marie, Thunder Bay and Kenora, in addition to the main ministry office in Toronto.

Building archaeology

There is a very thin line between rigorous archaeological exploration anticipated (and authorized) by the Ontario Heritage Act and less formal digging and poking around at a conservation project. Wherever a property has been previously occupied there may be hidden remains in the ground or in concealed spaces of a building. Careful and thorough records must be made of *what* artifacts are found and *where* they are found.

Signs of previous structures may show up as variations in the colour of a lawn or as unevenness of a sodded or paved surface. Within buildings, signs of previous walls or even structural alterations may show up as small changes in painted surfaces, or as small breaks in mouldings or windowframes, or even as a pattern of minute cracks. Whether or not there is a formal archaeological program, this evidence should be recorded as part of the inspection and fault diagnosis and watched for very carefully throughout the project.

❖ In the event of any finds of hidden artifacts, the owner, supervisor or clerk of works should document their type and location, and any associated artifacts. Where archaeological investigation has taken place, its report should be part of the project record, and its author on call to assess chance discoveries.

❖ In the event of *any* doubt — especially about animal or human bones — consult a professional archaeologist (see margin).

Structural hazards

❖ Watch carefully and record processes and products of any required demolition. This will be especially valuable in determining how the structure of an older building actually went together (distinct from how it was meant to go together). *Even the smallest removal must not destabilize all or part of the remaining structure.*

❖ Brace temporarily every doubtful portion of the structure before work begins — indeed, before regular access begins. Make doubly sure that temporary props and supports are on solid footing.

❖ Before new work or new installations, reinforce joists and other members that may have been cut to install services over the years. Structural weakness is seldom inherent in old buildings but is often caused by subsequent "modernizations".

See INSPECTION, RECORDING, and STABILIZATION DURING REPAIRS.

Failures

❖ In the event of any structural shift or failure, even minor, stop work *immediately* and arrange for emergency inspections of both failed areas and adjacent structure.

❖ Stabilize the condition with temporary props and record fully the situation before undertaking *any* remedial work. Often only one element in a complex structure has failed. Wholesale demolition must be resisted until it is clear whether a complete assembly has failed or simply a single element or connection.

See FAULT DIAGNOSIS.

Concealed deterioration

❖ Open up only parts of structure and finished surfaces that must be inspected for hidden deterioration and make these openings in inconspicuous areas. Removing finishes will destroy much of the subtle evidence of hidden conditions. For instance, though foundations may have settled and put a building's features out of plumb, such conditions often have stabilized long ago. Only if there are *recent* patterns of cracks in interior plaster should one consider making more than minimal repairs or reinforcements (apart from any need to upgrade the load-carrying strength of a structure).

❖ Continue to look for hidden deterioration while work is in progress.

❖ Watch closely for signs of weakness or rot around mechanical services, especially plumbing in bathrooms, kitchens and service areas. Allow for delays in the work schedule for replacement of rotten structural members, particularly at joints.

Conservation work may hold surprises, but they should not be unanticipated surprises. The possibilities of archaeological finds, structural weaknesses or hidden material deterioration must always be kept in mind, just in case.

Earth, air and water

Principles

2.2 Co-operation among
   specialties
2.3 Work in order
2.4 Work at right pace
3.3 Informed reconnaissance/
   inspection
3.4 Archaeology (site & structure)
   for reconnaissance
4.5 Respect for setting/context in
   community
4.6 Minimal conjecture/informed
   invention
5.4 Archaeology (site & structure)
   for rescue of artifacts
5.8 Moving as last resort
6.2 Maximum retention
7.7 Gentle cleaning

References

For background on soil and
topographic considerations in
conservation, see CHAP66,
CURT79, FLAD78, THOM81 and
TREA80. For more general issues
of environmental context,
seeKING77, LANG80, TECH86
and WEAV87. For health, safety
and environmental hazards of
conservation activities, see
FEIL82, FERG86, FLAD78,
HIGG85 and MCCA85.

How the ground affects the building

The type of soil, depth of water table, and
slope of ground surrounding a building all
combine to influence the building itself, its
stability and the condition of its materials over
time. Many forms of deterioration can be
traced to poor foundations, and these in turn
to inadequate strength in soils or a high water
table. In rocky areas of the Canadian Shield or
the limestone plains of southeastern Ontario,
even small buildings may rest directly on solid
rock; though the foundations may be solid to
start, high moisture and even running water
beneath the building will hasten deterioration
above.

Where a building (urban or rural) sits on soil,
the level of surrounding ground will often be
different from the original condition, usually
higher, on account of waste disposal and
growth and accumulation of vegetation.
Where this change in grade has altered
drainage or covered previously exposed
features, then corrective measures should be
taken, both to reveal historic details and to
preserve historic materials.

Regrading to historic contours

❖ Remove earth buildup at foundation walls,
   taking the level down to or close to the
   original level, which may be visible as a
   change in materials — for instance, the line
   between masonry walls above original
   grade and stone rubble at and below
   grade.

❖ Where historic contours cannot be
   achieved because of subsequent
   alterations, ensure that soil surrounding
   the foundation is well drained and that
   water drains away from the building.

The perils of backhoe archaeology

❖ Do not dig on a property before
   determining the likelihood of
   archaeological finds. Do a thorough
   archaeological investigation before any
   ground is disturbed and, where there is a
   strong possibility of finding buried
   artifacts, ensure that someone with
   archaeological qualifications is at hand (see
   ARCHAEOLOGICAL INVESTIGATION AND
   REPORTING, and SURPRISES).

❖ Take the same precautions as you would
   for buried utilities. Dig by hand rather
   than machine anywhere there is likelihood
   of disturbing buried objects.

*If water-table conditions change
outside, it may be necessary to
undertake major drainage repairs to
prevent problems inside (below).*

Environmental impacts on buildings

❖ Many causes of building faults are environmental, that is, under very little if any immediate control (see FAULT DIAGNOSIS). Preventative measures may be taken against some of these, however, and periodic inspection and maintenance of heritage properties should take these into account — ensuring that rainwater disposal is functioning well to avoid buildup of acidic precipitation against vulnerable surfaces, and so on.

❖ Human use can wear floor and stairway surfaces beyond safe limits, especially in buildings now in public use that were formerly domestic. Vulnerable wooden surfaces should be covered or foot traffic rerouted away from them, and similar measures taken for any areas subject to heavy use.

❖ The use of salt on exterior walks and drives, and its splashing against exposed walls, comprise a major cause of deterioration. Common salt should not be used as a de-icer anywhere near a building; instead, use calcium chloride (more expensive, but non-corrosive) or clean sand. Sand should be the *only* de-icer used near any important landscape feature with vulnerable vegetation.

Conservation's own environmental impacts

❖ Be more than careful with any conservation treatment that uses toxic chemicals. Check first with environmental officials if there is no information readily available about safe use and disposal. For example, ammonium hydroxide may be useful for cleaning masonry, but cannot be allowed to run off the building face into the ground — a temporary gutter must be placed around the base of the surface being treated (and the cleaning solution recycled and disposed with special care).

❖ Manage the movement of people and materials with care. Precautions that should be part of any construction project — location of waste disposal dumpsters, truck access to the site, workers' safety on scaffolding, and so on — take on added importance in conservation work because of the sometimes restricted site.

Graphic demonstrations of chemical erosion from environmental sources that could have been prevented by closer attention to maintenance — bird droppings (opposite) and de-icing salt (right).

References

Background material on the evolution of some of Ontario's green landscapes can be found in GENT84, HILT86 and LANG78. See MADD85 and NEWC79 for more general information on landscape conservation. The problems of vegetation and buildings are treated in JOHN84, MELV73 and STAH84.

Garden restoration is a specialized field whose technical information resides mostly in specialized journals, though see VONB84 for a good historical survey of what types of landscaping would be appropriate for specific contexts.

Vegetation and buildings

Trees, bushes, vines, hedges and lawns are both assets and liabilities when close to buildings. Most people prefer the contrast between "natural" plant materials and buildings to the absence of greenery. Charm is not a negligible factor in arguing for conservation, and much of the attraction of many old structures consists in their being clad in ivy or creepers, shaded by towering trees, or hemmed in by dense and often colourful foundation planting. Indeed, historic views of homes of the late 19th and early 20th centuries, particularly in the Queen Anne style, often show climbing vines which were as much a part of the overall look and feel of the style as the trellises on which they grew. Shade trees have always been highly regarded companions to buildings, but shrubbery as foundation planting is a more recent taste.

Under many conditions vegetation can draw excess moisture away from a building and shade roof and walls from sun, wind and rain, thereby moderating extremes of weather on those surfaces. But under other conditions it may hold moisture near the building by restricting ventilation. Some planting coexists peacefully with architecture, but some may cause great damage. In all cases, regular attention is needed to detect small problems before they become serious.

Clinging vegetation can be a very attractive part of the character of an older building — but it must be checked constantly, and removed if it is causing damage to the materials or structure of the building.

❖ Use or maintain trees that offer summertime shade to building surfaces and openings, but keep them far enough from the building to avoid root damage to foundations and walls.

❖ Keep eavestroughs and drains free of leaves and roots. Carefully trim vegetation around windows and doorways.

❖ Vines must not be permitted to extend rootlets into the walls, especially into masonry and mortar. Creepers that root in adjacent soil are generally satisfactory, *but avoid or remove any common ivy* (only the variety known as Boston ivy does not extend its hyphae into building cracks). Because the leaves of creepers shade walls, they also keep the walls humid, and this condition must be monitored constantly to prevent deterioration. Clinging vegetation is contentious among conservation professionals (one claim is that climbers help neutralize acidity in rainfall and thereby help protect walls from deterioration).

❖ Watch the building carefully through periodic inspections; if problems of moisture penetration or physical damage can be traced to vegetation, trim or remove it.

❖ Ensure that trellises and other woodwork supporting climbing plants are not overloaded by the weight of greenery. Make sure that birds do not nest in the shelter of climbing plants close to building walls.

Removing destructive vegetation

❖ To remove ivy, sever the vine from its roots and remove all vegetation within reach of the ground. The remainder will dry out and shrink and can then be readily removed. Do not pull living vegetation from a wall, lest bits of the wall come with it.

❖ Roots of not-yet-mature trees near building foundations may invade drains or push foundations so hard that cracks appear in the building. Mature trees are unlikely to alter what is probably a stable situation. Underpinning the structure to remove obvious stress will be expensive.

Removing the trees requires poisoning the roots and waiting until ground conditions become stable, which may take several months.

❖ After removing vegetation with significant root systems, postpone permanent structural alterations until the foundations are stable.

Garden restoration

Restoring gardens is a very specialized area of expertise; even with early written accounts of a property and the research of palaeobotanists, much restoration may be conjectural.

❖ No restored or re-created landscape should be presented as "authentic" without full research and documentation. Historic photographs are especially valuable.

Use period drawings or engravings cautiously, especially those in the many county atlases of the 1860s to 1880s; many views were edited to reveal buildings on their sites or to enhance hoped-for growth of recent plantings.

❖ Gardens and landscapes should be sympathetic to the architecture they surround. For visual clues to help create modern gardens in the proper spirit, historical atlases can indeed be useful.

❖ Dense foundation planting around dwellings was not 19th-century taste; it is thus not an authentic "historic" treatment for early residences (certainly not before the "Craftsman" style of the 20th century) and should not be used or represented as an earlier form of landscaping.

In the rare cases where there is photographic evidence for a historic landscape, it is especially important to note how the garden was integrated with the building — or not.

The small trees planted to match the central columns of the porch have now grown to shade the entire house, a rare effect which adds great visual interest to the house and to the street.

Principles

2.1 Co-ordinated work
2.5 Appropriate skills
3.2 Thorough and documented research
3.3 Informed reconnaissance/ inspection
3.4 Archaeology (site & structure) for reconnaissance
3.5 Specifics of uniqueness (pattern, ensemble, detail)
4.4 Respect for uniqueness (pattern, ensemble, detail)
4.5 Respect for setting/context in community
4.6 Minimal conjecture/informed invention
5.2 Fitting use of existing spaces
5.4 Archaeology (site & structure) for rescue of artifacts
5.8 Moving as last resort
6.2 Maximum retention
8.6 Aided access
9.2 Faithful maintenance
9.4 Conservation commemorated

References

For general background on appropriateness of treatments, see the references to the topics under *Environment* and *Design*. For paving and other horizontal surfaces, see BALL83, CHAM76, DAVE80/86, FEIL82, RESE85 and VONB84. For walls and other masonry structures see BROO77, CONS82, DAVE80/86, GRIM84, OEHR80, POWY29 and WILL83.

Fences, lawns, gates, paving, symmetry, formal axes — all enhance the formal approach to a building, even adding a touch of modest ceremony.

The value of surroundings

The space around a building is both its visual setting and its physical means of access. When a building is completed and first used these twin functions mesh well, but often the demands of one overwhelm the other with time and changes in use. The surroundings of a building lie between the public space of the street and the private spaces inside. In Ontario, if there is any barrier between public and private worlds, it is almost always a fence that may inhibit physical access but invites the eye to look past it to grounds and the building beyond. This intervening space is in private custody but public view — "semi-private". It must be respected, for the way in which we appreciate architecture depends on how we view it, across a greensward or close up against a sidewalk.

The "picture-postcard" view includes the space that sets the building apart from its neighbours and from the viewer. This space, with its topography, greenery, furnishings and lighting, is as important to the heritage value of the architecture as the structural foundations on which the building rests.

The surfaces of this space, particularly its hard surfaces, are also part of the architectural experience of the place as a whole. Traditional paving materials and patterns — of wood, stone, asphalt, brick, concrete, even gravel — have demarcated areas functionally but they also provided visual and tactile delight in their colours and patterns. Though limited in number, they have been used with great inventiveness in many combinations.

Many elements within these spaces and along these paths — walls, terraces, sculptures, monuments — are vital to the heritage value of a property. Their conservation may present the problems of entire buildings on a much smaller but no less serious scale.

Outdoor "rooms", public use and access

❖ Recover and maintain as much as possible the historic approaches to and through a property. Use historic documents and photographs to determine earlier configurations. For instance, do not presume that a classical building necessarily sat in a classically geometrical landscape.

❖ In exploring the archaeology of a property's grounds, look for traces of former pathways, terraces, walls and ornamental structures.

❖ Try to maintain the traditional sense and character of front yards, side yards, and back yards characteristic of Ontario residences and institutions. The public view across a lawn is an essential part of "massing", acting as a visual base of green that sets off the principal façade.

❖ Do not block principal ("postcard") viewing angles with intrusive new elements in the landscape; instead, use any new elements to help define the historic spatial character.

Conserving paved areas

❖ Ensure that paved areas are properly drained; there should be no standing water after rainfalls. Ensure that surfaces have no abrupt breaks, unless intended to be full steps. Repair or replace broken or heaved units and fill potholes promptly. Keep moss and lawns well trimmed, but do not remove greenery where that has become a comfortable part of the pattern of paving units such as flagstones.

❖ Maintain and conserve existing surfaces; repair or replace only deteriorated units (individual bricks or stones).

❖ New paving surfaces should harmonize in colour and visible texture with adjacent buildings. When using paving units, avoid standardized treatments that have no local historical precedents, such as interlocking pastel-coloured concrete tiles in "modern geometric" patterns. Paving units that *do* have extensive Ontario precedents are non-interlocking brick, flagstones, asphalt blocks, wooden blocks on end and granite setts.

❖ Do not destroy steps or parterres to install ramps for aided access; add ramps alongside rather than over top, in order to provide a suitably shallow slope and to avoid making the steps themselves additionally hazardous.

❖ To make aided access discreet, convenient and safe, change the adjacent grade level and slope, where possible, rather than build a ramp structure. Make sure that added slopes and ramps are safe. Use proper lighting. Combine safety and visual continuity by choosing railings compatible in form, material and colour to the delicacy or robustness of the existing building and non-slip surfaces in harmony with other outdoor surfaces (see PROGRAMMING AND USING SPACE).

Walls, fences and monuments

❖ Keep walls, fences and other boundary features in their historic locations and configurations.

❖ Keep retaining walls in good repair, with special care for water drainage around and beneath them. Ensure that the uphill side

does not trap water and ice against the wall (see FOUNDATIONS).

❖ If openings are required in walls or fences, make them in the pattern of materials and techniques typical of historic practices for gates, gateposts, and so on. New openings in walls should not masquerade as "old", but should correspond to earlier practice in proportion and material. For walls, follow good practice guidelines for appropriate materials (see MASONRY and STUCCO, CONCRETE AND COMPOSITES).

❖ Maintain historic lamp standards and lighting fixtures where they survive; consider reproducing missing lamp standards from historic photographs and documents. Though numerous cast-aluminum reproductions of cast-iron originals are available, use only those that match closely the size and proportions of the originals as shown in documentary sources. Use incandescent luminaires to correspond to historic colours of light (see PAINT, COLOUR AND LIGHT).

❖ Some patterns of cedar-rail fencing are meant to be relocated, to periodically redefine pastures or livestock runs. Replace deteriorated posts or rails in kind and do not permanently fasten them with metal connectors that may hasten decay of the wood. Pay close attention to how the pieces go together when taking apart and reassembling these fences — local variations in assembly may be subtle indicators of regional cultural heritage.

❖ Most deterioration of freestanding sculptures and monuments begins with ill-advised repairs to "correct" much less serious decay. Do not use supposed "high-tech" repairs without thorough independent testing and consultation with experts. *Epoxies that inadvertently block or redirect moisture movement within the repaired materials may cause extreme deterioration within months.*

❖ Use chemical "aging" treatments for metals with *extreme* care, and only when existing and repaired material look too different to be perceived as the same material.

See also CEMETERIES AND PRESERVED RUINS.

Traditional hard-paved surfaces include industrial brick and granite setts, which are much more durable and fitting to historic architecture and districts than the standard interlocking concrete pavers often used erroneously as "heritage" paving (right and below). Ramps are often necessary additions to historic buildings, but they cannot be designed and built by formula. They need to be fitted carefully to the individual character of the building and its setting — one solution won't automatically be correct for other cases (bottom right).

References

On cemeteries, see BROO77, CONS82, DAVE80/86, GRIM84, HANK74, NETH81, OEHR80, POWY29 and WILL83.

On the reinforcement and temporary protection of ruined structures, see especially BAXT86, JONE86, KEMP81 and PICH84/84a. On their permanent conservation, see FEIL82, FITC82, FROI86, POWY29 and THOM81.

Monuments on the ground are especially vulnerable to ice damage — water must be made to drain away quickly before it penetrates the surface.

Cemeteries

Grave markers and monuments are exceptionally valuable cultural artifacts, revealing artistic and social concerns of our predecessors in landscapes that are often of exceptional charm. But cemeteries pose very difficult conservation problems, materially and procedurally.

Grave markers sculpted from the relatively soft stone used throughout the 19th century are extremely vulnerable to atmospheric agents of erosion, especially to acidic precipitation — driving rain and snowdrifts push acidic moisture into the pores of limestone and sandstone, where it chemically and physically degrades the stone. Though most good building and sculptural stone develops a hard and durable surface patina with age and weather, microscopic cracks may allow moisture to penetrate; ice and salt crystals then simply pop the skin off the stone. Even granite is vulnerable to this process of decay. Weather erodes most surfaces over long periods, but the more rapid decay of the vulnerable lettering on grave markers lends deteriorated cemeteries particular poignancy. Occasionally very old wooden markers and iron fences survive — even more delicate and difficult to preserve *in situ*.

All conservation work in cemeteries must be preceded by careful inventory and analysis, as is true for any other conservation project. But additional legal concerns must be dealt with under the provincial Cemeteries Act: municipal permissions, notification of descendants, and so on. In the case of burial grounds not currently cared for, it may be difficult to find funds and people to take responsibility for conservation and maintenance. These matters must be addressed during research, inspection and planning, before any major work begins.

❖ Concentrate efforts on maintenance and on stabilization and arrest of further deterioration — don't try to restore an earlier, fresher appearance to monuments and markers. Keep vegetation carefully cropped and settings well maintained.

❖ Ensure that landscaping and drainage problems are corrected before conserving individual monuments. Water must be drained away from the bases of monuments, ideally by subtly adjusting grade and slope rather than by raising monuments on new plinths. Fill in rather than dig. In damp areas, maintain a gravel border surrounding the monument to drain moisture and to keep vegetation (and lawnmowers) from damaging the stone.

❖ Do not use concrete plinths to "protect" monuments; destructive salts may migrate into the stone from the plinth as the cement in the concrete cures. And the many small cracks often found in concrete will draw water up from damp ground and let damaging salts attack the stone.

❖ Retain and conserve monuments and grave markers in their original locations, upright, unless so far deteriorated that they would be quickly obliterated or destroyed by remaining in place (either through continuing degradation by the elements or at the hands of vandals). In cases of severe weakness, consider adding subtle, non-rusting reinforcements of treated timber or metal.

❖ If stones already laid flat for some time are sound and not deteriorating, leave them lying but protect their perimeters from damp and vegetation (see above). Consider removal of markers to protected "commemorative walls" or interior galleries only when there is no other way to protect them from further decay. And *never* embed the markers in concrete.

❖ Use "high-tech" stone consolidants and epoxy repairs with *extreme* caution, and only after thorough independent testing and consultation with experts in stone conservation. Ensure that any compound used in repair has the same or perfectly compatible chemical and physical properties.

See VEGETATION and MASONRY.

The uses of ruins, *in situ*

Ruins have popular romantic appeal, but they are not heritage resources in the same sense as buildings in use — they are preservations of destruction more than reminders of a living community. The original building's use and heritage are only incidental to the fantasy evoked by the "ghost walls" that have survived while the real life has disappeared. Ruins may be much like the myth of "nature", inexplicable and mysterious. They are museum objects — fragments of a once-whole building — taken out of context for display and enjoyment (even though still on their original site). There remains only a portion of heritage value in a preserved ruin.

Ruins have romantic appeal as "memorials" of historic activities, and more pragmatic use as "punctuation" in designs for public parkland.

Deliberate "ruinification" of a building is *not* heritage conservation. But in the wake of inadvertent and tragic destruction, conserving the remains of a heritage resource in ruined form may be appropriate if the material and structure are suitable and if the use and maintenance of the conserved ruin are assured for the long term.

❖ Inspect and diagnose the existing building thoroughly before undertaking any irreversible work. Follow the procedures in INSPECTION, FAULT DIAGNOSIS and PHASING AND SCHEDULING thoroughly and in strict order.

❖ Ensure that every surface that may be subject to weathering is able to survive such weathering; remove or provide suitable protection for former interior finishes.

❖ Make sure that surviving features are structurally stable, by underpinning and consolidating foundations, regrading to shed water away from the ruins, reinforcing unsupported walls either internally or with external bracing, and protecting all wall surfaces from moisture penetration, especially parapets and other horizontal surfaces.

STRAPPING AN
UNSTABLE BUILDING

TEMPORARILY
REINFORCING OPENINGS

Temporary stabilization

❖ If there is any instability in any portion of a partly destroyed building, exercise extreme caution in permitting access or stabilization work; if necessary, do recording work remotely, with binoculars, cameras, photogrammetry and thermography, as required.

❖ Undertake no remedial action without the advice of a qualified engineer *with experience in older structures.*

❖ Properly anchor or found temporary braces and props; place no additional loads on the structure itself, except to relieve existing stresses and restore equilibrium. Pad all props, straps, cables and beams with balks of timber to protect the building's surfaces.

❖ Make sure that props do not puncture or damage the fabric of the building; where possible place braces in window openings to stabilize both sides of a wall in all directions. Temporarily reinforce window openings by filling them in with heavy timber props or concrete blocks.

Permanent preservation and maintenance

Former buildings or structures can be permanently stabilized in such a way as to hide the means of their stabilization or to expose them conspicuously. Either approach is satisfactory on its own, but half-measures are likely to be unsatisfactory both functionally and aesthetically. Original materials and construction may determine which approach is best. Thick walls of brick or stone can be stabilized, reinforced, and made weather-resistant by hidden or subtle means. But it is difficult to preserve structures of timber or combinations of several materials without putting a great deal of the preservation treatment on display as well.

❖ If a ruin is to be treated in a conventionally "romantic" manner (see above) make all traces of structural stabilization and weatherproofing inconspicuous or hidden. Vertical buttresses should be of the same material as surviving walls, but subtly distinguished from them. There should be no obviously new horizontal projections of parapets or sills.

❖ Drainage of water away from the ruin must be inconspicuous; use subtle regrading and gravel bedding around the perimeter rather than constructing a plinth.

❖ If a ruin is to be treated as a sculptural artifact, with little regard for the evocation of "atmosphere", make techniques of stabilization and protection clearly visible, even to the point of erecting a structure or armature to support the ruins, shelter and protect them from weathering, and even allow for viewing at upper levels. In this case, elevation on an artificial platform or plinth would be perfectly in character with the rest of the treatment.

❖ Design all horizontal surfaces to shed water completely and to keep moisture from entering hidden spaces inside a wall. But since no treatment will be perfectly waterproof, provide ventilation to enable moisture to evaporate rather than be trapped in a way that would cause freeze/thaw damage.

❖ Design and construct protective details that are adjustable and repairable. Accommodate expansion/contraction and freeze/thaw cycles — and the consequent structural movements. Unheated structural remains will have to bear daily temperature extremes well beyond those endured by normal buildings.

❖ Inspect vulnerable surfaces frequently — especially horizontal areas — and make repairs as soon as signs of deterioration appear there or in the walls below. Ruins require very special care: they lack the constant maintenance routine that a lived-in building receives, and their surfaces are often vulnerable to weathering from all sides. Keep vegetation under careful control.

It is difficult to adequately protect ruin walls of stone or brick from water penetration. Designs must incorporate parapet or coping details that both shed water and allow trapped moisture to migrate or evaporate without causing damage to the wall, especially in its core. Any conservation treatment must be backed up by regular inspection and maintenance. In this case, the earlier asphalt and concrete caps did not keep water out of the walls, but rather trapped it inside. The newer metal caps intrude somewhat on the "romantic" image of the ruin, but they mean to do a better job of protecting the material and structure.

References

For general references on the maintenance of safe conditions in the course of conservation work, see FEIL82, FERG86, FITC86, FROI86, HODG07, INSA72 and LEVI78. Specific attention to stabilization and reinforcement of weakened or damaged structures during repairs is given in BAXT86, CURT79, JONE86, MACG71 and PICH84/84a.

Scaffolding

Even the smallest building conservation projects require scaffolding as a work platform for everything from initial inspection to final painting and cleaning up. Scaffolding at its most basic is a plank between two stepladders (a single ladder is not a suitable working platform), but work beyond that rather short reach requires steel-tube scaffolds with platforms of wooden planks or steel grating.

Full-scale scaffolding is usually separate from specifications for conservation work and normally the responsibility of the contractor, not the client or consultant. Nevertheless, its uses may go beyond serving as a platform for the contractor. Owners should try to take advantage of these opportunities. Normally, scaffolding has to be erected for exterior work to the full height of the building, sometimes for interior spaces as well. Because of its expense and the time needed to erect and move it, it may loom large in budgets and schedules.

❖ Ensure that scaffolding is provided, erected and maintained by experienced crews under safe conditions.

❖ Provide scaffolding of sufficent strength and stablility to meet the most strenuous demands of the project (usually heavy-material lifts and movements). Scaffolding must satisfy applicable standards and regulations for loading and height. Construction hoists must not exceed the scaffolding's capacities.

❖ Make sure that all scaffolding is well founded and braced, that its weight is not concentrated at points where it will subside or damage building or site, and that building surfaces are protected from stains or impacts by timber balks. Provide safety and weather protection as needed — railings and platform guards for work at any great height; windscreens, tarpaulins and even roofing for bad-weather work.

❖ Make the most of scaffolding when it is available:

❑ Detailed inspections and recording
❑ Preliminary stabilization and temporary repairs; strapping and shoring
❑ Protection of windows and delicate features
❑ Photographic recording, measurement and photogrammetry of details
❑ Removal of features for workshop repairs
❑ Cleaning up vegetation, unblocking drainage
❑ Roof, chimney and drainage repairs
❑ Masonry repair and repointing
❑ Repairs of wall surfaces and woodwork
❑ Installation of new services
❑ Cleaning, painting, refinishing
❑ Reinstallation of repaired components
❑ Final inspections

❖ Where height is not prohibitive, have work and scaffolding move sideways around the building or space rather than dismantling and re-erecting it repeatedly (to save time and assure consistently solid assembly).

❖ Cherry-pickers and mobile construction hoists are ideal for early inspections and recording, but use them only within their specified limits of loading and movement.

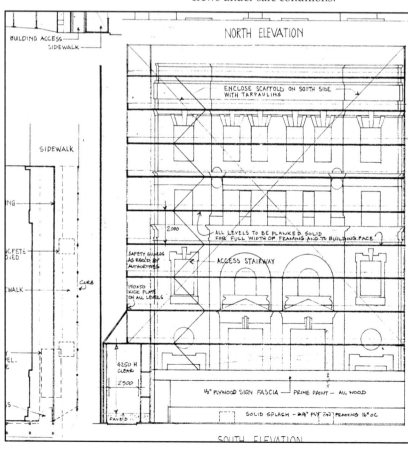

Temporary reinforcement

In cases of advanced deterioration or damage from some recent disaster, it may be necessary to stabilize a structure temporarily with straps, struts, jacks and the like. Only an expert engineer experienced in dealing with old buildings can supervise this work. The structure must be stabilized against the forces of gravity and deterioration, and must bear the strains of conservation work and equipment for months, even years. These loads may be heavier than those of the structure's previous or ultimate uses. As for scaffolding, temporary reinforcements are normally the contractor's responsibility, except on very small projects (without contractors) or very large ones (with special engineering requirements).

It is absolutely essential to take immediate steps to stabilize a structure in the wake of a flood, explosion or other calamity, to keep the building's own weight from causing further deterioration. It is no less important to keep the structure stable during repair and conservation work that may alter the distribution of loads (below). And it is vital that the working conditions are kept safe, by providing temporary handrails, safety barriers, secure outdoor storage, and so on (bottom).

❖ Properly anchor or found temporary braces and props; place no additional loads on the structure itself, except to relieve existing stresses and restore equilibrium. Pad all props, straps, cables and beams with balks of timber to protect the building's surfaces. Treat timbers with preservatives if they are to withstand dampness for any lengthy period, but note that preservatives may stain the building itself.

❖ Make sure that all braces — timber props, steel beams, lally columns, hydraulic jacks, and so on — do not puncture or damage the fabric of the building. Place braces in window openings where possible to stabilize both sides of a wall in all directions (first removing windowframes for workshop repairs). Temporarily reinforce window openings by filling them in with heavy timber props or concrete blocks.

❖ Do not brace the building against itself with props or cables, unless the bracing part of the structure is sound. Be sure not to compromise any *previous* repairs to the structure, especially those involving post-tensioning; these may fail abruptly if not anticipated.

Site workshops and services

❖ Provide sheltered and serviced areas in or adjacent to the project for workshop, office and storage use:

❑ Work areas for repairs to windows, fixtures and so on to be reinstalled in building

❑ Secure storage for plans, specifications, project records

❑ Secure storage for tools, equipment, samples, hardware, etc.

❑ Space for clerk of works or site supervisors to consult plans and specifications, maintain and update project records

❖ Provide sufficient space on site for material storage and waste-disposal dumpsters. Connect and maintain site services — water and electricity especially — properly throughout the work.

❖ Make doubly sure that the site is secured against vandalism and theft from the very beginning of the work. And keep the site as neat as possible — keep vegetation trimmed and the inevitable mess out of public view. The conservation project must try to be as good a neighbour as the building was before and will be afterward.

Foundations

References

For foundation conditions and
problems in residences and other
small buildings, see CUNN84,
DAVE80/86, FITC86, HOLM75,
HUTC80, KIRK84, KITC83,
LYNC82a, MELV73, REMP80 and
SMIT85. For large buildings, see
BAXT86, DIBN85, FEIL82, FITC82,
FROI86, LYNC82a, SMIT85 and
STAH84.

Moisture damage in foundations
is a primary cause of decay in
buildings of every size; in addition
to the references above, see
GRIM84, OXLE83 and TRIL72/73.

Moving buildings creates special
problems for both old building and
new foundation; see CURT79. For
cautions on the problems of
insulation, waterproofing, vapour
barriers, and "aggressive" energy-
conservation retrofits in small
buildings, see HERI87a/87b.

Foundations and building systems

Every building is a system — each part is
connected. Thanks to gravity, the foundation
is at the bottom (literally) of almost every
building problem. Most buildings move, shift
and settle in the few years after construction
as the ground gets used to the new weights
placed on it. Even foundations on bedrock
may move as compressive forces squeeze their
materials against the rock. In general, old-
building foundations are thus far more stable
and secure than those of new buildings. Over
time they have attained equilibrium.

Earth movements and ground water can
unsettle this equilibrium. Several parts of
Ontario, especially in the east, are potential
earthquake zones, but there are no seismic
retrofit requirements for buildings in the
province, as there are, for instance, in
California. Man-made earth movements are
far more serious concerns, especially in the
mining areas of northern Ontario and near
gravel quarries and heavy industries. Adjacent
construction and excavation may also unsettle
once stable foundations. Vibration makes
loose soil act like a liquid, and foundations
have been known to settle unevenly under
such conditions, long after they should have
stabilized.

Variations in ground water are far more
widespread than ground movements; all but
the largest buildings are founded on soil
whose load-carrying capacities change with
moisture content. As urban and agricultural
areas expand, and forests shrink, the water
table tends to drop, soil dries out, and the
ground compresses under the weight of a
building. Installation of storm sewers in small
towns has often led to sudden foundation
settlement in century-old buildings.

With such external influences, it is almost
impossible to take corrective action until the
environment itself stabilizes. In many cases,
settlement will be uniform and will not cause
much harm, apart from small cracks and
misalignment of doors and windows. The
flexibility inherent in small frame structures
allows them to remain sturdy, even though
some of their finishes may suffer.

Changes in the use of a building can also
destabilize both structure and foundation,
especially when loads exceed the capacity of

the original design. There is always a large
"safety" factor in any structure, and old
buildings may have far more generous
margins than closely calculated new
construction, but even these have limits. When
left undisturbed by major renovations or
changes of use, foundations should remain
stable. But they may require reinforcement or
underpinning if loading is to be changed
dramatically.

❖ Ensure that foundations are dry and that
they show no signs of recent movement.
Even timber foundations (common in
bedrock areas) may be perfectly sound and
suitable for continued use *if they remain
dry*. Make sure that new additions or
energy conservation measures do not
cause *new* dampness in foundations.

❖ Where portions of the foundation are to be
more heavily loaded as a consequence of
alteration and adaptation, consider using
structural means within the building to
transfer the loads more evenly across other
parts of the foundation, rather than
reinforcing only parts of the foundation.

❖ If at all possible, finish conservation work
after earlier alterations in the foundations
have stabilized. As much as possible, make
repairs to interior finishes and carpentry in
ways that can accommodate subsequent
movements and adjustments.

Foundations on the outside

❖ Do no excavating until archaeological
concerns have been addressed (see
SURPRISES and EARTH, AIR AND WATER).

❖ Remove (carefully) roots and other
vegetation near or beneath foundations.
Make sure that all downspouts drain well
away from the building.

❖ If there is evidence of dampness (ranging
from loose interior plaster or salt or rust
stains on outside walls near the ground to
running water during storms), drain the
perimeter of the foundation. Inspect and
repair existing drainage. Keep potentially
moist ground at least 20 cm (8") below the
level of the bottom of ground-floor joists
and wall plates of timber-framed
buildings. Inspect regularly to make sure
of this separation.

The stability of foundations depends on the stability of the soil's moisture. The vibration of heavy equipment or a catastrophic explosion may cause damp soil on any slope to shift and let the building collapse (top); it may be necessary to excavate and provide permanent drainage to prevent such a calamity (middle).

❖ Since causes may be difficult to diagnose, have an experienced professional investigate dampness before undertaking repairs, with special care to determine if the dampness is external or internal in origin.

❖ If foundation dampness is the result of a high water table, dig out a trench around the perimeter and fill it with granular material to permit water to drain away from the walls. Waterproofing an existing foundation is difficult and expensive, though where water-table conditions have changed, exterior waterproofing may become necessary. *Beware of sealing the wall in a way that will trap warm humid air from the interior and let it condense inside a cold foundation wall.* Provide weep-holes, drains and ventilation to let water drain out or evaporate. In winter, high interior humidity in a waterproofed foundation may cause damp and condensation from the inside, so that properly installed and maintained vapour barriers and drainage are doubly important.

❖ In extreme cases, dampness may migrate up inside walls to create damp conditions in structure and woodwork above grade. In such cases, if drying and draining the perimeter prove ineffective, consider installing a damp-proof course in the exterior walls to block moisture migration upward. Ensure that such a course is complete and does not concentrate the problem in one place.

❖ Once the causes of damp conditions are dealt with, ensure that stone, brick and mortar in foundation walls are sound. When repointing, use a mortar

formulation similar to what exists, keeping Portland-cement content to a minimum. Ensure that rubble-core foundations (both walls and piers) remain sound, adding grout carefully as necessary to re-establish their original strength.

❖ In the case of differential settlement, it may benecessary to underpin, but only after the cause, internal or external, has been determined. Underpinning by any method is expensive and creates disequilibrium that takes time to stabilize. Repair any drainage problems first. If the soil on which the foundation rests has itself weakened, then the underpinning should spread the load out onto a wider base or transfer the load to a more solid base. If the problem arises from existing or potential overloading in the building, consider redirecting the additional load more broadly within the structural frame.

❖ Avoid covering foundation walls with stucco or insulation; once the basic problems of moisture and movement have been treated, repoint foundation walls to match their historic appearance.

See SUPERSTRUCTURE and MASONRY.

Basements and crawlspaces

❖ When excavating basements and crawlspaces for additional headroom, make sure that foundations retain their load-carrying capacity either by underpinning or maintaining a plinth around all foundation elements.

❖ Inspect, and reinforce where needed, any foundation or basement structural elements weakened by sloppy utility installations or structural changes.

❖ When a previously uninsulated basement is insulated, condensation and dampness from inside may create more havoc in the foundation than water from outside. Make sure that vapour barriers and insulation do not cause condensation within the walls themselves. Though there may be little threat from freeze/thaw cycles below the frost line, there may be uncomfortable dampness and a high likelihood of damage to interior finishes, both old and new.

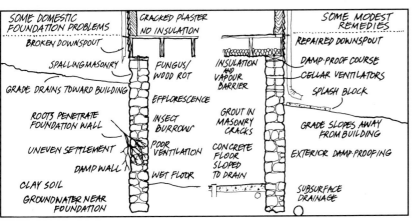

Superstructure: frames, walls and floors

References

Good general reference sources for small-building foundations include BIX85, BOWY80, CUNN84, DAVE80/86, FINE86, FITC86, HOLM75, HUTC80, KITC83, LITC82, MELV73, RADF83, READ82, REMP80, TRIL72/73 and VILA81. For large buildings, see BAXT86, FEIL82, FROI86, STAH84 and TRIL72/73.

Structural problems and repairs in timber are treated in GOOD80, MACG73, MULL81 and WOOD86. Structural problems and repairs in masonry are treated in BEAL87, CONS82, GRIM84, LYNC82a, MACG71, SMIT85, WEIS82 and WILL83.

See the following about specific structural matters: early metal structures, GAYL80 and JAND83; structural elements of commercial façades, MEAD86; fire ratings of outmoded structural types, NIBS80.

Types and materials

The following deals with frames, walls and floors as structural elements. Finishes (and the finishing of exposed structural elements) are dealt with separately as exterior or interior features. Normally, the structure is concealed beneath exterior or interior finishes. Excepting barns, churches, and industrial or engineering structures, exposing the structure is a very recent fashion. In Ontario, even exterior masonry walls are often finishes over a frame rather than part of the main structure.

All walls bear at least their own weight, and often a portion of the loads of the floors and roof above. Nevertheless, most buildings in Ontario from small to large are constructed as a structural frame with a relatively light cladding rather than according to the more traditional European practice of bearing-wall construction. Log construction is essentially a case of bearing walls supporting a small and relatively light roof structure. In many areas, a masonry or clapboard exterior on a house with rather thick walls probably covers an older log structure. Cladding fashionably upgraded of appearance and protected the logs from weathering (as well as stopping drafts).

Most other bearing-wall structures are of stone masonry with timber floors and roofs. Such bearing walls consist of two faces of relatively well-cut stone (sometimes one face is brick) with a core of rubble, sometimes bonded by mortar. Most bearing-wall structures in Ontario are churches; massive walls support elaborate and heavy roof structures.

Brick exteriors are often just cladding; plentiful supplies of timber and sawn lumber for framing made the load-bearing brick walls of European practice obsolete, even in urban areas, where some early building regulations required brick exteriors to prevent the spread of fires. Brick veneer allowed for much larger openings than brick bearing walls and was far more suitable for the complex forms demanded by late-19th-century picturesqueness. Nevertheless, idiosyncratic examples of double- or even triple-thick brick bearing walls seem to occur everywhere. The modern practice of backing a brick face with concrete block did not become common until the 1920s.

Timber frames have come in several varieties. The traditional mortise-and-tenon framing of relatively heavy timber beams and joists arrived from Europe and the United States with each wave of immigration, with subtle variations in practice from group to group. But cheap sawn lumber and machine-made nails made platform- and balloon-framing an instant success by the mid-19th century, pushing traditional heavy-timber construction out of domestic and commercial use. Most such lightweight framing uses "sticks" of small dimensions for wall studs and floor joists, with wooden laths, floorboards and occasional diagonal braces or bridging to make the entire assembly solid. Much more rare was the use of post-and-beam construction, with rigidly braced joints. Where sawn lumber was especially plentiful and cheap, there were occasional structural oddities made of sawn planks stacked up like bricks.

Wrought iron as a structural material, used for engineered structures such as bridges and gas-holders and some framing in large public buildings, was a rarity in 19th-century Ontario. Steel supplanted wrought iron late in the century. Steel's strength permitted much of the eclectic stone and masonry constructions of commerce and public building to be "draped" on a hidden framework that carried most of the load. Steel-reinforced concrete frames appeared soon afterward; some pioneering bridges displayed the new technique and material openly, but in most buildings the concrete frame was concealed behind other materials.

Repairs in general

The basic approaches to conserving heritage structures are to repair in kind wherever possible and to make any repairs easily accessible for inspection and reversible (where necessary). Replacements should be the same material as the original, even the same species of wood where possible, to avoid future deterioration where two incompatible materials abut. Chemical incompatibilities and unanticipated structural movements are likely to continue to trouble the structure if repairs do not fit properly with what exists.

❖ Inspect and record the structural system very carefully and add to that record

While most structures are supported from beneath, there are many instances of structures suspended from above or cantilevered from one side. Every structure must be fully understood, with the help of expert advice as required, before it can be repaired or altered.

throughout conservation work as elements, especially joints, become visible.

❖ Correct any apparent structural problem before continuing other conservation work; correct conditions that may seem only indirectly related to matters at hand as well as more obvious deficiencies. Work up from foundation to roof. Remember, every part of a building is connected.

❖ Do not remove or alter load-bearing structures until the consequences of the change are clearly understood. Do not allow loads to shift so as to overload other parts of the walls or frame. Make no new openings unless the rearrangement of loads is fully resolved.

❖ Use professional architectural and engineering advice in case of any doubts about structural safety or adequacy. Make sure that such consultants are familiar with and sensitive to the problems of conserving existing structures.

❖ Do not add major new loads (heavy dead loads such as mechanical equipment or large numbers of bookshelves or heavy live loads such as public assembly spaces) without ensuring that the capacity of the existing structure is sufficient. Reinforcement should be minimal and unobtrusive — if a new use requires a completely new structure, then it may not be appropriate for that building.

Timber repairs

❖ Use non-destructive testing techniques; use probes gently, especially on smaller timbers. Ensure that all posts and joists are securely seated and that the seats themselves are sound. Note every member that has been cut to permit utility installations in the past and reinforce these. Do not cut any more holes, unless they are fully reinforced.

❖ Correct the causes of timber weakness and decay before undertaking permanent structural repairs. Ensure that any fungus and insect infestations are halted. Remove sections of wood that have lost their strength due to dampness or rot. *Make sure that all remaining wood is sound and dry.* Do not use chemicals or techniques (for

cleaning, caulking, insulation, etc.) that will leave residues harmful to the wood in the long term. Make sure that periodic inspection and maintenance catch deterioration before it becomes severe.

❖ Generally, repair structural weaknesses with splices, braces or flitch plates that can be adjusted or replaced, rather than with epoxies whose bonding properties and chemical characteristics may or may not be satisfactory over the long term. Do not use epoxies for structural wood repairs in any areas where humidity and temperature vary beyond the typically narrow range of normal interiors. Epoxy-laden wood does not absorb moisture and thus does not expand and contract like untreated wood. Whether or not epoxies are satisfactory consolidants for badly deteriorated materials, they are inappropriate for parts of an existing structural system exposed to the elements.

❖ Floors may sag over time under heavy loading. If beams or joists are deformed but do not bounce back after loads are removed, and are otherwise sound and able to support the required loading, do not try to jack them level or bend them straight — use shims or other supplementary means to level flooring. Sometimes beams and joists may be bouncy but structurally sound; these may require stiffening, extra vertical supports, or lighter use altogether.

❖ All timber repairs should allow for movement within a small range to accommodate wood's expansion and contraction with changes in humidity. As much as possible, stabilize humidity and ventilate structural members to allow absorbed moisture to escape — especially vital for sealed and vapour-protected areas. Allow for variation of moisture content *within* heavier members that lie between spaces with different humidities.

❖ Where reinforcing cannot achieve long-term stability, replace timbers with wood of similar dimensions, species and moisture content. New timber is seldom properly seasoned or kiln-dried, and may shrink or twist — connectors and joints should be adjustable to accommodate such movements. Ideally, store replacement

timbers where they will be used long
enough to bring their moisture content to
the same level as the existing structure.

❖ Use fastening devices appropriate to the
existing structure; if increased loads
require more strength, use external
connectors that spread the load uniformly.
Ensure that any chemical preservative in
new wood cannot migrate and cause
staining or chemical deterioration of other
building components.

❖ If replacing deteriorated timbers with
other structural materials, ensure that
every connection is able to resolve
differential movement without disturbing
other parts of the structure.

*Most small brick buildings, whether
domestic or not, have wooden frames
supporting their brick skins (above).
Their frames are often weakened over
the years, sometimes severely, by
numerous cuts and holes for utilities,
and may require repair and
reinforcement (right). Heavy timber
structures require massive
reinforcement at joints to resist loads
and vibrations, and in traditional
practice these are simply but
elegantly detailed in iron or wood
(below right).*

Masonry repairs

❖ Record and monitor all cracks and
discontinuities in masonry walls, both
between units and in the surfaces of
individual units. Look especially for
missing mortar and other evidence of
weakness in the core of a load-bearing
masonry wall. If water has for a long time
been able to penetrate the core, do not be
surprised to find that the core may have
been washed out altogether, creating
severe stresses in the surface masonry.

❖ Do all foundation repairs before
permanent work on walls — most cracks
in masonry walls are based on foundation
problems. And repair framing that bears
on masonry before making final repairs to
the walls themselves. Where weakness or
decay in floor systems has altered the
loading on supporting walls, redistribute
the loading properly before fixing the
walls.

*Solid masonry structures may shift
in time and reveal cracks that must
be watched carefully for recent
movements. In this case, the shifting
was traced to weakened exterior
walls, whose buttresses required
rebuilding to regain their ability to
hold up the roof (opposite).*

❖ Use mortars softer and weaker than the
masonry units they hold. Stresses and
small movements in walls must be
resolved in the assembly as a whole and
must not be transferred to individual units
through hard mortars (see MASONRY).

❖ Grouting of masonry walls requires skilled
and experienced workers and careful
supervision. Make sure that any pressure-
grouting of rubble cores is not so powerful
as to dislodge the masonry units
themselves. Grouts should be as carefully

mixed as mortars, with very little Portland cement.

❖ For masonry veneers connected to the structure with metal ties, make the ties secure — they often rust through in places, leaving the brick only barely attached to the structure. Allow for thermal expansion or contraction in any reinforcements and connections. Locate new ties at masonry joints, *not* at holes drilled through the masonry itself.

❖ Replace rusted metal ties. Use only rust-free metal reinforcements or connectors. Stainless steel, though expensive, is far preferable to galvanized metal. Hot-dipped galvanized nails and ties may be adequate where risk of moisture entrapment is very low. Vapour and liquid moisture may penetrate walls, no matter how well sealed. When iron connectors rust they expand, shifting and cracking masonry before letting go altogether.

❖ Replacement units should be as strong and durable as what they replace. Replace in kind — do not substitute sandstones and limestones for one another. Ensure that stone is worked and laid with its bedding planes horizontal, to minimize moisture penetration and consequent spalling. Mortar should be mixed to match existing work both physically and chemically, and its pointing should follow the existing pattern. Replacement bricks should be of equivalent hardness, smoothness and porosity, to provide similar structural strength and durability. Ideally, they should come from the same yard as those they replace.

Traditionally exposed structures

Because they will be on view, repairs to exposed structures must respect much more rigorously the heritage character of the building. Churches are most sensitive because their structures are adorned and decorated. Barns, mills and factories are expected to be more robust and can accept far more robust repair work.

The size and complexity of these structures will usually require the aid of architectural and engineering consultants familiar with historic construction practices.

❖ Heavy timber structures (barns, mills and the like) require careful inspection to ensure that vibrations and movements have not displaced any members or joints. If they remain in heavy use, inspect them frequently; use simple strain gauges to measure movement.

❖ These structures may also require reinforcement where cuts in the structure permitted insertion of services or shafts. The seating of beams on stone walls is especially vulnerable to loosening from vibration. Many heavy timber structures have already been reinforced with iron or steel tie rods, and more such reinforcement may be needed to keep outer walls from spreading under load and vibration.

❖ The open trusses of many church interiors are among the most impressive of architectural feats, even at the modest scale of most Ontario churches. Take very special care to maintain their dignity while repairing any decay. Once all causes of deterioration have been treated (often foundation and buttress failures due to the weight of the roof), make repairs such as the insertion of flitch plates as much as possible on the hidden upper side of timbers. If the church is kept heated throughout the winter, the interior environment may prove sufficiently stable to consider epoxy repairs. Tie rods have often proved necessary to keep side walls and buttresses from spreading under the roof's weight, and these may be preferable to the more drastic reinforcement and enlargement of the buttresses themselves or the addition of new truss elements.

See WOOD AND PLASTER.

Concrete, iron and steel

Though concrete, iron and steel are thought of as especially modern building materials, older structures made of them require major conservation work if they are to survive. Most conspicuous are engineering structures such as bridges, vulnerable to weathering and to chemical corrosion from road salt. But the engineering achievements seen in the impressive trusses of arenas and armouries deserve conservation no less than the stylish architectural clothing of the exteriors. The size

Because exposed structures have such distinctive visual impact, whether sacred or secular, they require and deserve special care in repair and reinforcement (opposite). Wrought iron and other metal frameworks can be reinforced to a certain point without much effect on their appearance, but their use (in this case the maximum loading of the bridge) may have to be regulated to avoid the problems of more radical reinforcement (above, top). Reinforced concrete has become an extremely common structural type, but it is seldom exposed, apart from engineering structures, because of the difficulty of making minor repairs without marring its appearance (above).

and complexity of *these* structures require structural experts familiar with the historic background of modern construction practices.

❖ Steel structures must be protected from weathering, by paint or by enclosure. Regular maintenance is essential; corrosion and rust must be arrested immediately on discovery.

❖ Reinforcement for increased loading on existing steel structures should be as discreet as possible. Use materials and techniques similar to those of the existing structure — use several small members rather than fewer larger members. Where possible, resolve the distribution of forces by reinforcement in tension, by cables or rods rather than beams or girders. Use the lightest-weight technique. If replacement is necessary, replace in kind.

❖ Major concrete repairs are quite difficult to carry out in a manner that restores both structural integrity and original appearance. Exposed reinforced concrete degrades under attack from salts, allowing moisture to get at the reinforcing bars, which corrode, rust and expand, popping off more concrete, exposing more steel, and so on. Proprietary compounds to fill cracks must be used in a program of regular maintenance. If deterioration goes too far, the only reasonable conservation treatment may be replication in new concrete.

❖ "Plastic" repairs of concrete forms should match the existing contours, aggregate, colour and strength of material as closely as possible (concrete is one material that is hard to match *too* closely). Patches must be keyed into the remaining concrete to provide a contiguous surface against water and water-borne salts. Paints or silicone-based coatings do not prevent water penetration for long and must be constantly renewed. It is better to design elements that let water drain quickly away without being trapped.

See METALWORK and STUCCO, CONCRETE AND COMPOSITES.

Principles

References

For general information on repairs to all types of roofing on small buildings, especially houses, see BOWY80, CUNN84, DAVE80/86, FINE86, HANS83, HUTC80, KAPL78/86, KIRK84, KITC83, LABI80, LITC82, LOND84, LYNC82, MELV73, POOR83, READ73, READ82 and STLOnda. For larger and more complex buildings see FEIL82 and STAH84.

For examples of appropriate materials and styles for early residences, see MACR63, MACR75 and MCAL84. See MACE98, RADF83 and POWY29 for early specifications and drawings of roof construction. The special problems of metal roofing are covered in GAYL80, INSA72, PETE76 and TIMM76. Of the small-building sources noted above, LABI80 and POOR83 have useful advice on repairs to slate roofing, while DAVE80/86 and LITC82 cover chimney repairs for old houses (see also WILL83).

Types and materials

The roof is the most exposed part of a building; it often dominates a building's visual character, but is also the single element most vulnerable to weathering and thus to periodic change. Even when well maintained (and inaccessibility makes maintenance difficult) roofing materials do not last as long as other parts of the exterior. Much deterioration throughout a building is caused by too much moisture in the wrong place over a period of time — and much of this moisture gets in through gaps or weaknesses in the roofing, especially at junctions or edges. At some points in a building's life an owner will face a crucial decision whether to continue repairs or to replace the roofing entirely. In these cases, where conservation may mean renewal rather than repair, the craft, durability and visual impact of the old must be recalled very carefully by the new.

Roofing materials in 19th-century Ontario included shingles in wood, slate, and metal, as well as continuous seamed sheets of metal. Metals for roofing included copper, tin-plated iron, terne-plated iron (terne is a lead/tin alloy), and (very rarely) lead. The early 20th century added asphalt shingles and clay and concrete tiles to the repertoire. With few exceptions, the general lightness of structures (compared to European precedents) was echoed in lightweight roofing materials — copper rather than lead, thin slates rather than heavy stone flags. Even lowly asphalt has had a long career on roofs, tested by the Royal Engineers as waterproof roofing in Kingston as early as 1840.

Roofing techniques distinguish between flat or very shallow roofs where water-*proofing* is needed to resist moisture penetration from standing or slowly evaporating water and snow, and more or less steep roofs which emphasize rapid water-*shedding*.

In Ontario, flat and shallow roofs are usually covered with continuous sealed membranes of tar or bitumen (usually laid with gravel to protect the membrane) on a built-up base of paper and felt over a wooden substructure of joists and roof boards. Much rarer for low-pitch roofs is sheet metal (copper or terne-plate) with interlocking flat seams — extremes of temperature make metal roofs especially vulnerable to creeping, curling and punctures.

A flat roof must retain its integrity despite accumulations of rain and snow as well as tremendous variations in temperature from day to day — even hour to hour. Many tar-and-gravel roofs on quite old buildings sit on top of worn-out metal. Few built-up roofs last long without leaking, though the effective life of a well-maintained flat roof range from 10 years to perhaps 30.

On sloping roofs, metal roll or sheet roofing provides a smooth, relatively impervious surface, but can fail at seams and joints as well as at punctures. Thermal expansion and contraction tax every part of a metal roof — most deterioration comes at folds or standing seams that cannot move enough to relieve strains. The use of standing seams or even wooden battens at seams gives metal roofs a characteristic vertical emphasis and also offers the metal considerable room to expand and contract.

Repairing metal roofing is expensive and requires experienced experts; poor short-term repairs will accelerate deterioration. Shingle roofing in any material is more vulnerable to leaks between units and at flashings, but it is more amenable to bit-by-bit repairs; a roof's overall life can be extended by those repairs, but only to a point. The flashing and drainage of all sloped roofs are critical, for any water build-up can back up underneath shingles or sheets by capillary action, as if the roof were sucking on a straw. Locating sources of leaks may not be so easy as looking for obvious dampness; much moisture may be coming via capillary action from the side or even from below.

❖ Carefully assess the remaining life expectancy of a roof before deciding to repair or replace part or all of its surface — especially slate roofs, where many slates may or may not be reusable (see "Replacement", below).

❖ Look and feel very carefully in attic spaces for subtle signs of damp or rot that may not be apparent from above. Inspect the roof in wet weather to see it at its worst.

❖ Ensure that the space beneath the roof is properly ventilated, so that any moisture can readily evaporate without damage to structure or materials and to dissipate summertime heat build-up.

In extreme cases such as steeples, roofing repairs require special scaffolding and extra safety precautions.

❖ Make certain the roofing is properly anchored and that the anchors are not corroded or broken.

❖ Make vents, skylights and other new elements fit as discreetly as possible, both visually and materially. Flash and seal any openings fully and inspect them regularly. There are many traditional ways to conceal or incorporate such elements, as part of the roofing itself or in conjunction with gables, dormers or chimneys (see VISUAL HARMONY AND GOOD FIT).

❖ Make sure there is proper protection against damage by lightning, especially for high buildings in rural areas. Lightning rods on barns and churches may or may not be properly grounded; if not, they will be worse than nothing in the event of storms.

Repairs

❖ Arrest deterioration and repair problems in the roof *structure* before final repairs on the roof *surface*. Remove wood damaged by infestation or rot and replace with sound material. If replacing roof boards with plywood sheathing, provide sufficient ventilation between roofing and sheathing. Make sure that the roof has temporary covering while it is open for repairs.

❖ Be especially careful about safety on sloped roofs. Work in cool weather. Take special precautions when working on brittle slate roofs (soft-soled shoes, wooden planks or ladders to obviate walking on slates, and so on) — sloppy repair work may break more slates than it fixes.

❖ *Never* use bituminous (tar) patches on metal or shingle roofs. Such patches do not cure a leak; they only postpone its damage for a short while. They are almost completely irreversible and often cannot be fixed without complete replacement of the underlying material.

❖ Match the colour, dimensions, texture and material of surrounding roofing when replacing individual units or sheets. In the case of slates, maintain any polychrome patterns that may exist. Ensure that substitute units are fastened in a way and with materials that will not hasten

deterioration around them. Do not artificially age the appearance of new sections of copper — in time, they will fit into the general appearance of the roof without assistance.

❖ Ensure chemical and physical compatibility between roofing, fastenings and flashings. Do not use copper with cedar shingles. Do not use different metals together — fasten copper with copper, terne-plate with lead-coated nails, and so on. Decorative iron cresting designed for slate roofing will not go with a copper replacement roof. Watch for signs of corrosion of metal flashings and drains from stone particles eroded from slate roofs and replace deteriorated troughs and downspouts.

Replacement

❖ Wherever possible, replace worn-out roofing with the same materials. Where there is sufficient documentary or archaeological information, consider replacing modern short-life roofing with the more durable covering of the building's earlier years. Do not presume that the original material was necessarily wood shingles or copper sheeting. Consider a conjectural "period" substitution only when it proves impossible to determine the authentic materials and techniques used for the roofing (or when the historic technology is no longer available), and then only treatments commonly used in the region during the period of construction.

❖ Do not lay new roofing over top of existing roofing. Ensure that roofing can expand and contract without losing its integrity.

❖ Consider the choice between repair or replacement of slate roofing with the following in mind:

❑ Soundness of the slates in general

❑ Integrity and durability of existing flashing

❑ Capacity of existing roof structure

❑ Percentage of slates that can be re-used — thickness, brittleness, sound nail-holes, cracking

❑ Estimated life of sound slates

☐ Sources for replacements; new or used; colour-matching

☐ Time and labour costs

☐ Estimated life of the renewed roof as a whole

❖ Interim short-lived roof coverings should be similar in colour and texture to what is replaced or to the early covering ("interim" may be a long period of time).

❖ Be especially cautious when replacing slates with lightweight simulations; in assessing relative costs, consider these as short-lived alternatives until their durability has been proved. Match as well as possible the texture, colour, and details of the specific building rather than accepting the standard offered by the supplier.

Gables, eaves and dormers

❖ Inspect all roof valleys very carefully at regular intervals, especially the tops of short valleys at dormers, and repair any problems immediately.

❖ Make flashings secure at every junction or penetration of the roof. Do not rely on mastics or adhesives alone to prevent capillary action and moisture penetration. There are many traditionally proven details for such junctions; do not invent a new one where an old one will do quite well. Wherever water may run down a surface (such as fascia mouldings, soffits, sills or brackets), provide a drip edge (a groove or slot in the horizontal surface beneath) to keep a film of water from creeping into the joints below.

❖ Provide proper eavestroughs and downspouts to channel water away from the walls below. These should be discreet — retain and repair built-in gutters rather than attach new troughs. New troughs and downspouts should be visually "thin" and follow corners or angles in walls where possible. Add new downspouts especially where flat roofs do not drain away storm water fast enough.

❖ Keep rooftop decorations in good repair and flash very carefully where they are fastened through the roof. Ground all projections against lightning.

❖ Replace missing features only on the basis of conclusive documentation and use original materials and colours where possible.

See EXTERIOR WOODWORK and METALWORK.

Renewing a wooden roof requires removal of accumulated surfaces, repair of any deterioration in the underlying substructure, and provision for sufficient ventilation beneath the roofing to prevent future problems. Here, following traditional designs, the rain gutter is being reincorporated into the edge of the roof rather than as a separate trough.

Chimneys

❖ Inspect chimneys and flues regularly (at least annually) for structural soundness and proper operation. Ensure that chimney caps and linings are sound and that firestops and flues are in working order if the chimney is to be in use. Flashing is especially important; much roof deterioration is found around chimneys.

❖ Make sure the chimney is vertical and structurally stable. Ensure that flue gases over the years have not damaged mortar — if they have, it will probably be necessary to take the chimney down and rebuild it. If a furnace has been converted to natural gas, look carefully for chimney problems caused by excessive condensation. In repointing, follow the general guidelines for mortar mixing and application. Make sure all flashing is secure and effective.

❖ Replace masonry with units of the same type, colour, dimension and durability; do not replace proper brick or stone chimneys with metal pipes.

❖ Protect and retain ornamented chimneys and chimney pots, which are important parts of the building profile. Repair or replace cracked or otherwise damaged chimney pots; replacements should be new pots of similar size and shape.

See MASONRY.

All projections and structures on the roof, from finials to chimneys, cupolas, hatches and attic dormers, require careful flashing and regular inspection to keep water and dampness from causing damage beneath the weather-resisting covering.

Masonry: brick, stone, block, terra cotta

References

There is a great deal of general coverage of masonry repairs in the bibliography. For new masonry, the best source is BEAL87. For conservation treatments, the most comprehensive are general DAVE80/86, FEIL82, JOHN84, MEAD86 and STAH84. See also BOWY80, FACA87/87a, FROI86, GRIM84, HUTC80, INSA72, LOND84b, LYNC82a, MELV73, OEHR80, RAMS88, REMP80, SMIT85, TECH82, TIMM76 and TRIL72/73.

For stone in particular, see CONS82, PRIN81, SCHO85 and WEIS82; for brick, NASH86. Older technical treatises include HODG07, MACE98, RADF83 and WARL53.

For cleaning and pointing, see ASHU77, ASHU83, HIGG85, MONC83 and WILL83.

Types and materials

Masonry construction consists of heavy individual load-bearing units — bricks, blocks of stone, concrete block, clay tile, pre-cast units in terra cotta (clay) or cast stone (cement), and even blocks of glass — bedded and consolidated by mortar. Masonry is almost ideal for resisting compressive forces, but terrible for tensile forces. Its principal use has been in exterior walls of buildings. Though some important older engineering works have been made in stone or brick, the European traditions of massive arched or vaulted masonry structures gave way to lightweight framing techniques in the 19th century, and few such structures survive in Ontario. Masonry construction will last centuries if its units are properly manufactured and erected.

Mortars for masonry combine sand, lime and cement in varying proportions to permit the entire wall to act as a unit in resisting compressive stresses (even where that wall is only a skin over the principal structure behind). Mortar itself is not a very strong structural material. Modern construction uses mortar with a great deal of cement to bind hard bricks into very rigid walls with frequent control joints to allow for thermal expansion and contraction. Historic construction (almost every pre-1920 building) used softer mortar with very little cement, binding together bricks or building stone of varying hardness to produce walls that could absorb stresses and thermal movements with few if any control joints.

The greatest danger to historic masonry construction is usually from relatively recent repairs using hard mortar of high cement content. The "philosophy" of mortar has been reversed in this century. In historic practice, a small portion of cement was added to the lime to help stiffen the mix and keep the mortar in place while it cured; in modern practice a small portion of lime is added to the cement to keep the mortar workable long enough to be laid smoothly. Hard mortar transmits stresses to the brick or stone; soft mortar absorbs stresses *from* the masonry. Hard-mortar repairs simply crack and crush the relatively soft stone or old brick, often in very short time.

Many conservation projects must pay more attention to repair of damage caused by *previous* "modern" repairs than to simple deterioration of aging originals.

Brick

Bricks are manufactured from clay and tend to take their colour and chemical properties from that clay. Their porosity and hardness depend on their firing, often on their location in the kiln. Most historic brick masonry was produced in small batches and fired as a batch in a small kiln; modern bricks are produced and fired in a continuous process with far greater uniformity. In old buildings, face brick is usually far more durable than interior brick, or sometimes even the side or rear walls. Not all brick was unpainted — in some neighbourhoods, soft brick was used instead of face brick for all exterior walls, and paint provided the weatherproof skin.

Bricks are vulnerable to mechanical damage from overstressing, freezing, and crystallization of salts in migrating moisture. Their long-term preservation requires that moisture be kept out of the walls or can escape in a non-damaging way if it *does* get inside. Soft flexible mortar is the traditional safety valve for older brick. Periodic repointing may be needed to repair deterioration and is far preferable to replacing the bricks themselves.

❖ Finish structural repairs, especially around door and window openings vulnerable to movement, before working on visible masonry repairs.

❖ Repair vertical fractures, both structurally and cosmetically, from bottom to top; if reinforcement of the brickwork is necessary, use only non-rusting (non-ferrous or stainless steel) ties.

❖ Do not seal brick surfaces with silicones or consolidants, which trap water vapour behind the surface of the brick; when that vapour condenses, it may freeze or leach salts that will eventually destroy the brick face. Similarly, do not slap stucco on a deteriorated brick surface to hide the problem; it will simply mask further deterioration that will eventually crumble both brick and stucco. Far more acceptable is repointing with porous mortar that lets the wall "breathe" to the outside, allowing moisture to migrate and evaporate through the mortar, not the brick.

See BEAL77 for the most
thorough treatment of all masonry
types and techniques, though its
emphasis is on modern practice.
Early texts on masonry offer
excellent information on how
things used to be done, and thus
on how to make compatible
repairs: for instance, see
MACE98 or HODG07 (out of print,
but accessible through libraries),
or WARL53 (available as a
reprint). See also the advice in
HIGG85 and STAH84.

Varieties of masonry materials and techniques.

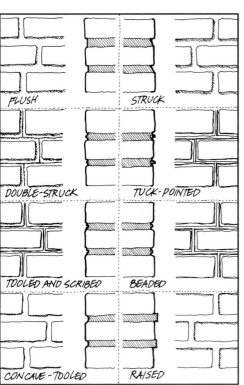

FLUSH   STRUCK

DOUBLE-STRUCK   TUCK-POINTED

TOOLED AND SCRIBED   BEADED

CONCAVE-TOOLED   RAISED

REGIONAL VARIETY

There has been a tremendous variety of masonry construction in Ontario; the historic use of specific types and colours of brick or stone has given many areas a distinct character. Many areas were built almost entirely in brick, because of fashion and to prevent the spread of fire in towns. The Victorian taste for polychrome brickwork, often accented in stone, combined with the timing of development to dominate the look of many southern Ontario towns and villages. This regional identity broke down with subsequent centralization of larger brickyards and abandonment of quarries as stone construction gave way to concrete.

Making rough bricks into fine ones — a traditional but rarely surviving pointing method that is difficult to recover once painted over.

❖ Once the source of brickwork decay has been repaired, repoint only in areas where mortar is loosened or crumbling. As much as possible, do not remove sound mortar. But poke and probe to make sure that what is left really is sound.

❖ Before repointing, cut out crumbled material until you reach sound mortar to which the new mortar can adhere. Use hand tools to reduce the risk of damage to the brick. Only skilled and experienced operators should use power-chisels, and then only lightweight models. Do not use a power-saw. No matter how carefully used, power tools will damage bricks if you cannot see what you are working on. Look at the piles of brick dust around sites where power tools have been used to cut out mortar. Most of that dust is from the no-longer weather-resistant brick faces and edges.

❖ Repoint masonry walls using as close an approximation as possible of the historic formulation, profile, width and colour of mortar. Use sand for colouring rather than less permanent pigment (unless the original really did use pigment). Match the colour of a freshly exposed section of original mortar rather than a weathered area — eventually, the "new" mortar will age and weather to match the existing surface. Do not "butter" or "scrub" the joints; besides looking very sloppy, the thin feathered edges of such joints crack and break easily, funneling water into the joint and creating even worse damage.

❖ Before repointing, thoroughly wet the adjacent bricks to keep the mortar from drying too quickly before it cures properly.

❖ Use a mortar mix no stronger or stiffer than the historic mortar. *Do not use modern formulations with high proportions of Portland cement.* If possible, take a sample of *sound* original mortar (whose lime content has not been leached away or altered in subsequent repointings), have it analyzed by a laboratory, and use that specific formula for repointing. Laboratory analysis should take into account the variabilities of the original application and the effects of impurities in the original mixture.

❖ Never apply lime mortars in temperatures near or below freezing or in hot, direct sunlight. In either case, the mortar will never attain its structural strength and other properties.

❖ Never use caulking as a replacement or covering for mortar.

❖ Where the faces of bricks have spalled and crumbled, replace them in kind, matching the bonding pattern and the units' dimensions, colour, and texture. For matching purposes use actual samples, not just pictures of samples. Use only first-quality face brick for exterior replacements. Use old bricks from a salvage yard or, if necessary, bricks scavenged from an inconspicuous part of the same building to match on a conspicuous face. Do not use salvaged bricks that have been sitting directly on the ground for any length of time — they may have absorbed ground salts that will cause efflorescence later on.

❖ In replacing special shapes of brick, do not expose cut or rubbed edges to weathering if posssible. Custom-shaped replacement bricks are almost impossible to find and may have to be made by cutting down a standard brick. (This may be the one condition where coating a brick with a water-repellent treatment may be satisfactory, *but only on new brick*; regular inspections and recoating may be necessary).

❖ Where isolated brick surfaces in a generally uniform wall require replacement, consider refacing the brick with a synthetic surface made up of brick dust and an appropriate resin bonded to the sound remnants of the original. This will require great skill in matching colour, porosity and surface texture and should be considered a last resort, but it may prove satisfactory. This is similar to the more typical "plastic" repairs of stone (see below). Very skilled hands may be able to replicate unobtainable custom-shaped units.

MIXING MORTAR

In general, the cement content of mortars for historic masonry must be no greater than one-twelfth of their dry volume, and this must be *white* Portland cement rather than gray.

For very weak or soft bricks, use an ASTM (American Society for Testing and Materials) type K mortar: 1 part white Portland cement, 3 parts hydrated lime, 12 parts sand. For more typical machine-made face bricks in more exposed conditions, use an ASTM type O mortar: 1 part white Portland cement, 2 parts hydrated lime, 9 parts sand. Do not use additives such as plasticizers in any of these mixes. And, above all, do not use caulking as a mortar substitute.

Stone requires similar caution, especially for sandstones and the weaker limestones. As for brickwork, use a "weak" mortar mix compatible with the existing formulation and with the stone. Whenever possible work from a laboratory analysis of the existing mortar, but for most sandstones, the ASTM type O mortar should be satisfactory. Limestone in good condition and granite can both stand a more cementitious mix if necessary (ASTM type N: 1 part white Portland cement, 1 part hydrated lime, 6 parts sand) but do not let the cement content exceed the lime. As above, avoid plasticizers and caulking.

Cautions: repoint in temperate, shaded conditions and keep pointing wet long enough for it to cure properly. See ASHU83 and BEAL87 for more technical information on mortars.

Stone

Though the appearance of most Ontario towns, at least in the south, is dominated by brick construction, building stone appears in an extraordinary variety of types and forms throughout the province. Though churches and public buildings offer the most conspicuous examples of stone masonry, there are concentrations of limestone commercial buildings in towns as far apart as Perth and St. Marys, farmhouses in granite "fieldstone" all along the glacial ridges north of Lake Ontario, and even cobblestone façades in Paris and in Sidney Township. The Rideau Canal and its adjacent houses and towns comprise a special concentration of stone architecture, and even a few stone-arch bridges survive, from Pakenham to St. Marys.

For most coursed and dressed masonry, limestone has proved generally more available, workable and durable than sandstone, but many large mansions and public buildings used the reddish Credit Valley sandstone to good effect in contrast with smooth brick of similar colour. As the railway network widened at the end of the 19th century, construction stone moved far beyond the immediate locale of specific quarries. Many of the province's larger stone-faced structures of the 20th century were clad in limestone imported from Indiana or Manitoba. Marble (metamorphosed from, but softer than, limestone) has been imported for decorative exterior work, but since it weathers poorly in extreme climates, few Ontario examples survive.

Building stone's physical and chemical properties vary tremendously, and even the most solid-looking of stone can be eroded rapidly by weathering. Though weathering does give most building stone a protective hardened crust or patina, stone is more or less porous to moisture and is no less vulnerable than brick to deterioration caused by hard-mortar repairs. Apart from granite, building stone is normally sedimentary in formation, built up in layers or bedding planes. Limestones and sandstones are best quarried and laid with those planes horizontal, but there are examples of stones laid with their planes vertical, and these exposed faces may simply spall off in thin flakes or sheets as trapped water freezes or its dissolved salts crystallize. Though early stone structures were of bearing-wall construction, most late-19th- and 20th-century stone walls were often simply cladding on a steel or concrete frame beneath.

Good building stone can be worked or sculpted into astonishing varieties of forms, though the requisite skills have become exceedingly rare. The exposed face of coursed stonework may be either rusticated or dressed smooth (ashlar); there are also many examples of decorative surface treatments such as vermiculation. High Victorian Gothic and Romanesque Revival tastes often combined different surfaces on the same wall, including sculpted heads and simulated vegetation. Many buildings exhibit puzzling projecting blocks of unfinished stone, testimony to the construction budget having given out before the stonecarver could finish his work.

Few Ontario quarries still provide building stone apart from gravel. Accordingly, finding precisely matching replacements from the original quarry is almost impossible. Because of Europe's much longer tradition of stone construction, there have been many attempts there to develop chemical consolidants to prevent further deterioration of already decaying stone surfaces. These imported compounds must be considered experimental, even though some have been tested for a decade or more. They should be applied only by experts under very careful controls, and only on surfaces beyond other repair techniques.

❖ Finish structural repairs, especially around door and window openings vulnerable to movement, before doing visible masonry repairs. Repair vertical fractures, both structurally and cosmetically, from bottom to top. In the case of bearing-wall construction, consolidate the insides of the walls with cementitious grout if there are voids or weaknesses; use only non-rusting reinforcing bars of stainless steel or non-ferrous metal (see FOUNDATIONS and SUPERSTRUCTURE).

❖ Repoint only in areas where mortar is loosened or crumbling. Do not remove sound mortar. Cut out deteriorated mortar by hand and repoint using the historic formulation, profile, width and colour of mortar (see above). The above-mentioned caution about "buttered" joints applies doubly for stone, especially rubblestone; no matter how irregular the joints, resist the temptation to even up the wall surface by plastering it with mortar; the inevitable water penetration may eventually weaken the wall.

❖ When applying lime-based mortars, respect the same cautions as those for brick — never apply mortar in extreme temperatures and thoroughly wet the surrounding stone to keep the moisture from leaving the mortar before it cures properly (see above).

❖ Whenever possible, replace irreparably deteriorated stone in kind. Ideally, replacement stone should come from a similar bed in the same quarry, quarried and bedded similarly (unless the decayed stone was improperly quarried in the first place). Where closely matching stone is unavailable from any source, consider swapping stone from inconspicuous parts of the building to more conspicuous areas, using less critical substitutes for the first area.

❖ Ensure that replacements for ashlar and other coursed work are horizontally (naturally) bedded and that in arched, vaulted, or decorative repairs the bedding is oriented to use its strength in the best direction.

❖ Where substitutes are hard to find, and the material is a fairly strong limestone or granite, consider carefully "quarrying" the units already on the building. With suitable reinforcement, a damaged stone may be moved forward in its place and its surface re-dressed. Alternatively, a skilled mason can split a thick unit in two, dress the new surface to match the old, and reintegrate it into the structure with non-ferrous bolts or dowels. Only a specialized and experienced contractor should attempt this rather destructive form of rescue, and only after testing first in an inconspicuous area.

❖ An alternative substitute may be a cast-stone replica of the damaged masonry, using cement, appropriate epoxies, stone dust and aggregate to match the colour, texture and structural capacity of the

original. With skill, cast stone technology can produce units as durable as natural stone, but it is critical to match colour and texture to avoid an unacceptably pasty, concrete-like surface. This may be the only satisfactory means to replace or replicate missing or badly damaged decorative masonry (see "Replacements and substitutions", below) but should be considered a last resort.

❖ If replacing stone from a different source, take special care to use the same type of stone; substitute sandstone for sandstone, limestone for limestone, and so on. Limestone and sandstone are particularly incompatible in one respect — acid precipitation washing the surface of limestone creates a mildly carbonated water that leaches the calcium carbonate out of any sandstone beneath it, and calcium carbonate may be the only thing keeping the sandstone from becoming structurally useless sand.

❖ Because they are irreversible, use chemical consolidants only with *extreme* caution and expert advice. For instance, alkoxysilanes have been used successfully to consolidate siliceous sandstones — but if your sandstone isn't siliceous, or if your silane isn't applied properly, you will end up with even worse deterioration. The only traditional consolidant generally recommended is a lime wash on limestone — essentially application of a protective coating of the stone itself in liquid form. Do not apply a lime wash to sandstone.

❖ Repair impact damage or broken stone with a "dutchman", an insert of matching natural stone or compatible cast stone facsimile cut to size by a skilled stonemason and put in place with a stable epoxy filler and non-rusting anchor or dowel.

❖ "Composite patching", using mixtures of stone dust, lime, cement and possibly epoxy, may be an acceptable interim treatment for decayed stone where it is necessary to protect the remaining sound stone from further weathering and decay. Such patches must be removable when a more durable repair can be made. It is extremely difficult to avoid a very pasty, concrete-like surface texture in the poorly

Though some of this pointing may be rough and in need of repair, its sloped profile has kept water from running into the wall.

See MEAD86 for more technical information and further references on terra cotta. Also useful are early editions of "Architectural Graphic Standards" (see RAMS88).

controlled conditions of the construction site (and too much epoxy may interfere with moisture movement in surrounding stone). Match the chemistry and physical properties of the surrounding stone and use non-rusting ties and reinforcements to bind the patch securely to the stone. This technique requires a rare combination of skills and generally should be confined to inconspicuous areas.

Terra cotta and clay tile

Terra cotta and its more mundane cousin, structural clay tile, are fired clay products still in production, but much less popular than they were from the 1880s to the 1930s. Terra cotta is hollow and much lighter than stone.

In its heyday, terra cotta was moulded to imitate carved stone or almost any other shape and simply bolted onto a substructure. Its composition and manufacture limited the size of individual pieces, but these could be readily combined as masonry units to emulate larger features in the same way small wooden mouldings could be assembled to make large cornices. The characteristic ceramic glaze on most terra cotta was applied in a separate operation from the shaping of the basic unit.

Most terra cotta in Ontario was imported from huge factories in the northeastern United States. None of these plants survives. Though small workshops can produce custom units and a few small factories in the United States still make production runs, decorative terra cotta on existing buildings is essentially irreplaceable.

Terra cotta is a brittle material that deteriorates quickly when stressed beyond its limited capacity. It is quite difficult to repair. Most problems are caused by failure of fastenings. Bolts and brackets rust and fail, often weakened by thermal expansion and contraction in the terra cotta itself or by structural movements behind the units. Individual units jostle one another, creating added stress and finally cracking or breaking completely. The ceramic glaze is vulnerable to extremes of temperature, but the frequent light crazing of the glaze does not mean that the unit has lost its strength or integrity.

❖ Even if the glazing has hairline cracks from ceramic crazing, do not paint or cover terra

cotta with waterproof coatings. Just as with brick, water vapour will inevitably penetrate the unit from behind and needs to be able to evaporate to the outside. If sealed beneath the surface, water will condense and in cold weather frost will destroy the glaze.

❖ Ensure that the mortar between the units is soft and flexible, to absorb stresses and movements. If necessary, add control or relieving joints to long runs of units to remove external stresses. Remove and replace any rusting bolts or anchors with new non-rusting connectors.

❖ Never use heavy-duty acidic compounds to clean terra cotta; hydrofluoric acid, even well diluted, causes great damage to the ceramic glaze.

❖ Secure cracked but otherwise sound pieces with reinforced resins of tested formulation. Large sections or those with more severely deteriorated anchorages can be refixed with non-ferrous anchors grouted in epoxy.

❖ If it is necessary to replace a unit, try to find craftworkers or small shops familiar with casting and firing ceramics for outdoor conditions. If using an existing unit as a pattern, enlarge the mould for the replacement slightly to allow for shrinking during firing. Take the opportunity to make and store spare units. Ensure that new units are fastened with rustproof connectors and bedded in soft mortar.

❖ Consider substitute materials for replacements only in extreme cases. It is very hard to match the glazed finish of terra cotta (though acrylic/epoxy finishes come close). Cast stone may be a satisfactory substitute for unglazed terra cotta, but it is heavy and special care is needed to prevent damage to adjacent units. Glass-reinforced plastic or cement has been used as a substitute for cornices and panels. Consult recent technical literature for advice, and follow expert advice (see "Replacements and substitutions", below).

Elegant glazed terra cotta surrounded many windows in early 20th century commercial architecture (regrettably, the window itself has not been so well treated as the frame).

Cast stone and block

With the right touch and mixes, cast or "artificial" stone can be moulded into different shapes as easily as clay. Very similar in composition to concrete, cast stone involves preparing a dry mix of cement and sand or other aggregate and adding a specific amount of water to form a paste that can be cast or moulded into any required shape. It came into common use for steps, lintels, garden ornaments and other small elements in the late 19th century, but its more sophisticated use as a coping and facing material for buildings emerged about 1900 as concrete technology matured. The most conspicuous use of cast stone was to clad steel- or concrete-frame structures with panels that emulated carved stone ornament and dressed stone walls (for a good deal less money than either). Cast stone came reinforced or unreinforced, in a variety of colours, textures and trade names, such as Roman stone or angel stone.

There were and are many different formulations for cast stone (some proprietary), and not all have proved durable over time. The material may break down through faulty mixtures, poor casting, corroded reinforcement or fastenings, and all the other agents of chemical decay that afflict natural stone. Nevertheless, cast stone is very durable, in some respects even sturdier than some of the natural stone it can emulate. Its technology survives primarily in the making of garden ornaments. Epoxies and resins now offer additional strength to the cement and

aggregate mixtures. Cast stone remains useful as a substitute for stone masonry, to repair both deteriorated natural stone and "historic" cast stone.

Concrete "breeze" block first appeared early this century, as another aspect of concrete's leap to prominence in construction, but was rarely used as a visible material. In the suburbs and small towns built in the 1910s and 1920s, examples survive of houses and even the odd church in moulded blocks of standard size made to look something like rusticated limestone.

❖ Before any attempt at repair of cast stone features, undertake a laboratory analysis of a sample. There was and is a tremendous variety of mixes and aggregates, some incompatible with one another. Matching the material accurately requires detailed investigation of additives used to produce colouring and texture.

❖ Arrest any moisture problems, repair underlying structural deterioration, and ensure the soundness of all anchors and joints before starting cosmetic work. Make sure that reinforcing within the feature has not weakened or rusted — remove any rusted metal before patching. If deterioration is severe it may be best to recast the unit altogether.

❖ Patch cracks or pits in cast stone with a plastic repair made from a mix of cement and aggregate similar to that used originally. Make sure the patch is well keyed to sound original material. Dutchmen repairs may also be satisfactory. Any coatings or paints must "breathe", letting interior moisture escape and evaporate.

❖ For replacements, make moulds from a sound original, recast the elements using the same formula, colour and texture, and reinstall with non-rusting anchors. Moulds can be made to the same size as the copy; cast stone does not shrink significantly in preparation.

❖ Consider using cast stone for its historic use, as a material to replicate expensive or missing stonework; investigate the current technical literature for its use as a substitute (see "Replacements and substitutions", below).

Concrete block has never become an elegant construction material, but it has appeared and reappeared in many patterns for modest residential and commercial buildings — even the occasional church — since the early 1900s.

Romanesque and Classical styles of carved stone ornamentation — the rusticated styles gained particular popularity in the late 19th century for the pragmatic reason that they weathered and aged more graciously than the precise and polished styles.

The problems of bad masonry cleaning have been so widespread in Ontario that the Ministry of Culture and Communications asked a consultant to prepare sample specifications for both cleaning and repointing — see HIGG85. See MEAD86 about replacements and substitute materials.

Cornices, corbels, and carvings

There is a great wealth of decorative detail in brick and stone ornaments and projections, especially in the Gothic and Romanesque revivals of the late 19th century. These especially fine details are unfortunately very vulnerable to erosion, and there are few stonecarvers able to carve replacements or new decoration in the style of the historic details.

❖ Inspect all projecting masonry features regularly. Ensure that anchorages are solid and rust-free, and flashings intact and sufficiently sloped to let water drain away quickly. Take immediate action to correct problems and prevent further decay.

❖ Use chemical consolidants only with great caution, and only on the basis of expert advice (see above).

❖ Follow the advice under "Stone", above, regarding the uses of dutchmen and plastic repairs.

❖ Only when important ornamentation has severely and irreversibly deteriorated due to atmospheric pollution or other long-term influences — and preventive maintenance has failed to stop this decay — should removal and storage of original work and replacement with replicas be considered. Substitutes must maintain the visible character of the original features without creating conditions for further deterioration.

Cleaning

Masonry does not need to be cleaned nearly as often as it is, or as deeply. Careless cleaning can seriously damage masonry. Many buildings sandblasted barely a decade ago have lost much of their exterior because of weathering of the raw surfaces exposed as the protective skin of the brick or stone was literally blown away. Water jets at high pressure may do even worse damage, both eroding the surface and driving water deep into the wall. Poor chemical cleaning deposits salts inside the masonry that come out as stains and crystals, crumbling the surface microscopically just as surely as a blast of sand.

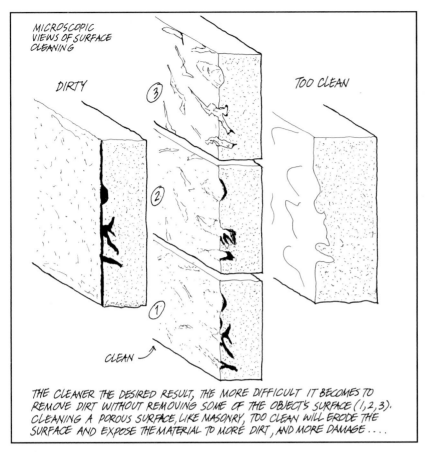

MICROSCOPIC VIEWS OF SURFACE CLEANING

DIRTY

TOO CLEAN

③ ② ①

CLEAN →

THE CLEANER THE DESIRED RESULT, THE MORE DIFFICULT IT BECOMES TO REMOVE DIRT WITHOUT REMOVING SOME OF THE OBJECT'S SURFACE (1,2,3). CLEANING A POROUS SURFACE, LIKE MASONRY, TOO CLEAN WILL ERODE THE SURFACE AND EXPOSE THE MATERIAL TO MORE DIRT, AND MORE DAMAGE....

A low-pressure water-soaking for limestone — slow but effective, so long as the water can evaporate without harming the interior of the walls (above). Sandblasting on the other hand produces harrowing results — and here it did not even remove all of the paint (right).

It is vital to establish the *level of clean* required for the specific job and not to clean any more deeply than absolutely necessary.

❖ Clean masonry only to uncover deterioration, to halt further deterioration, or to remove organic deposits. Do not remove patina that protects the interior of the unit, but do ensure that the patina is not itself a source of chemical decay.

❖ Where masonry has been painted during most or all of its existence, do not strip the paint to the unprotected masonry, except to repaint. Use vapour-permeable paints to prevent moisture build-up from inside.

❖ Do not erode the building surface. Do not clean so deeply into the surface that the surface itself is removed along with the dirt. Use the gentlest cleaning method possible and use more time rather than caustic chemicals and high pressure to complete the job. Do not sandblast or use abrasive high-pressure water or compressed air blasts on any historic masonry.

❖ Clean exterior masonry only in suitable weather, preferably in moderate conditions in spring or early fall. Do not use cleaning chemicals in hot, direct sunlight. Do no exterior cleaning in winter.

❖ Mask delicate surfaces carefully. Use no chemicals that will form salts in reaction to the masonry. Do not let cleaning residues get absorbed into the masonry. Test-clean inconspicuous sample areas first and follow proper conservation specifications fully. Test patches of cleaning methods in inconspicuous places. Make these patches big enough to be reliable samples — at least 1.5 metres square. The architect, client and contractor must all agree on the test results and on the method to be used overall.

See PAINT, COLOUR AND LIGHT for other cautions about exterior cleaning.

Plastic repairs require frequent inspection and maintenance if underlying deterioration has not been corrected, and in any case require the skill of a sculptor to match the texture of the adjacent masonry. Repairs that look more like stucco than the stone or brick they intend to emulate cannot be considered satisfactory.

Replacements and substitutions

Modern construction products — fibreglass (glass-fibre-reinforced plastic), glass-fibre-reinforced cement, and polymer concrete — may or may not be useful substitutes for decayed masonry. Each of these, as well as the "historic" substitute, cast stone (see above), has advantages and disadvantages as a masonry substitute. Because conservation work emphasizes durability far more than new-building technology, even such well-known substitutes as fibreglass must still be considered experimental for conservation. The lifespan of historic masonry is properly measured in centuries, but modern substitutes may last only decades. Substitutes should thus be considered more as items of long-term maintenance rather than as permanent replacements. The best and most durable replacements are the original materials themselves.

❖ Attach replacement elements securely to the structure, with non-rusting bolts and anchors. Do not permit replacement features of substitute materials to carry loads other than their own. And do not let the weight of replacements bear on other non-structural elements.

❖ As much as possible, use modern substitutes that are long-lived and durable for the particular situation, especially with regard to their finishes and colours, both wet and dry. Because these factors change with new developments, check the most recent technical literature for data on longevity. For example, though glass-reinforced plastics are generally long-lived, they deteriorate under the ultraviolet component of daylight, meaning that they must be painted or coated and maintained no less rigorously than, say, painted ferrous metal (for which they may be a substitute, as well as for masonry).

❖ Always allow for shrinkage in moulding new materials from existing features — each material has different thermal characteristics.

❖ Ensure that drainage details do not channel water into existing elements. Do not rely for moisture protection solely on mastics or caulking, which must be regularly maintained and renewed.

Woodwork repairs — for both cladding and ornament — have long been the subject of do-it-yourself and home-repair magazines and books. For the most part, their advice is accurate and sensible, but special care must be taken to keep as much of the existing sound woodwork as posssible and to make repairs that won't hasten further decay. Good conservation-minded guides include BOWY80, CUNN84, HANS83, HOLM75, KAPL78/86, KIRK84, LOND86, MELV73, MILN79, POOR83, REMP80 and TECH82. Other more popular treatments have good advice , but use with care; see FINE86, JOHN83, LITC82, READ73, READ82 and WOOD83.

More technical background is available in FEIL82, FROI86, INSA72, LOCK86, LOCK86a, MULL81, MUNN83, PRIN81, RAMS88, STAH84, TIMM76, WOOD86 and WRIG86. Old building catalogues and manuals can also be helpful; see MACE98 and RADF83.

For examples of woodwork style and ornament, see BLAK69, BROL82, LANG78, MACR63, MACR75, MCAL84 and VICT84.

Properties, manufacture, deterioration

Wood is the most common of building materials. It is strong yet light and easily worked; variously coloured and grained yet a good base for paints and coatings; structurally durable yet ideal for ornamental carving and furnishings. It has always been relatively cheap and readily available throughout Ontario from the beginning of settlement. The temperate forests of the south offered a vast profusion of species, from the white pine for ships' timbers to the cherry, oak and elm sought by cabinetmakers. The coniferous forests of the Shield produced excellent softwoods for structure and ornament.

Most historic structural and exterior woodwork was of softwood, most interior finishes and furnishings hardwood. Only the ubiquitous pine seemed equally at home inside and out. Almost every stick of wood in historic Ontario buildings and furnishings came from domestic forests, often a mere stone's-throw away, but the province's modern timber production is concentrated instead on pulp, paper and plywood.

For all its advantages, wood is also afflicted with numerous weaknesses. It is flammable. It is vulnerable to biological decay from moisture, insects and fungus, especially under certain combinations of darkness, humidity and temperature. Dampness is wood's enemy, just as it is masonry's. Rapid cycles of alternating wet and dry conditions in unfinished or poorly protected wood cause cracking and checking that will admit water and lead to further decay. Most species used for exterior woodwork thus require at least one water-repellent coating. Wood's most common "overcoat" is paint, which itself weathers and requires regular renewal.

General repair and preservation

❖ Keep all exterior woodwork well maintained and painted. Inspect regularly and frequently for any signs of deterioration. Decay is often first evident in blistering or peeling paint, generally symptomatic of moisture problems.

❖ Correct any source of degradation, whether infestation or moisture penetration, and ensure structural stability before making cosmetic repairs.

❖ Use only gentle means to clean or strip wood of finishes before repairing and refinishing. Do not remove sound, well-bonded paint. Do not sandblast or water-blast wood under any circumstances. Beware of scorching wood with hot-air guns or electric heat plates. Use chemicals only as part of a cleaning process (to soften paint for scraping, not to dissolve it altogether) — do not risk permanently impregnating wood with them.

❖ Make sure all exterior wood is properly finished to prevent its deterioration; only rot-resistant woods such as red cedar can be left unfinished with relative impunity. Paint is the most frequent historic form of protection to prevent constant wetting/drying cycles from attacking the wood. Follow traditional practices for scraping, sanding, cleaning, filling, splicing, treating, priming and painting wooden surfaces.

❖ Consider replacing decayed exterior woodwork with a sound substitute only when the wood has lost its material integrity and its ability to hold its surface coating. Substitute in kind, with wood of the same species, and with the same moisture content. Store replacement timbers at the worksite long enough to permit their moisture content to match the existing woodwork.

❖ Use preservative-treated or water-repellent-treated wood for all exterior work, *but ensure that preservatives do not interfere with paint adhesion.*

❖ Do not cover wood with ostensibly "impervious" coverings (vinyl or aluminum cladding, for instance) that trap moisture against wooden surfaces in darkness. Such conditions are ideal for insect infestation and fungus growth.

❖ Use traditional subtle details such as drip edges to prevent water films running into wood junctions and joints. Do not rely exclusively on caulking for such purposes. Take special care to protect exposed end grains against water penetration.

See also SUPERSTRUCTURE; PAINT, COLOUR AND LIGHT; and WOOD AND PLASTER.

Cladding

Wood has provided opportunities for amazingly rich wall textures, even on modest buildings — vinyl or aluminum cannot replicate such richness, and as replacement siding will cause damage both aesthetic and material.

Wooden cladding is a frequent feature of residential and agricultural buildings, especially in areas once well-served by local sawmills. There are two primary types: boards and shingles. Traditional board siding is usually horizontal, but it is not only "clapboard"; it may also be drop, bevel or shiplap. Vertical board-and-batten siding is found most often on 19th-century rural cottages or farm buildings. Though much more common on seacoasts than in Ontario, shingle siding appeared on many buildings in mid-19th-century settlements on the Canadian Shield and reappeared as a decorative feature of eclectic revivals in the 1880s and 1890s.

Cladding deteriorates primarily because of trapped moisture and consequent rot as well as insect infestation. Despite nail holes and other damage, sound cladding may survive beneath stucco, aluminum or vinyl coverings. If maintained and protected by periodic painting or staining, wood cladding will last as long as the structure, but at certain points, especially corners and near the eaves or the ground, it can be vulnerable to attacks by dampness, fungus or insects. Moisture is almost always the primary culprit, and good ventilation almost always the saviour.

❖ Make spot repairs to wooden siding in kind. Keep its surface well maintained and regularly painted (if painted originally).

❖ Before undertaking cladding repairs in response to visible deterioration, first cure any moisture penetration from eaves or other sources, and make all needed structural repairs.

❖ Follow the instructions in a good home repair manual in making any spot repairs. Use the same species of wood and install it with the grain running the same way. Use only exterior-grade galvanized nails. Use only one nail per stud to permit thermal movements.

❖ Entire walls requiring replacement on account of advanced decay should be replaced in wood, with the same dimensions and profiles as original.

❖ Do not replace or cover generally sound wooden cladding with allegedly maintenance-free materials. Aluminum and vinyl emulations of wood are not maintenance-free; they are far more vulnerable to impact than wood and difficult to repair. They also cover over decay that will inevitably worsen.

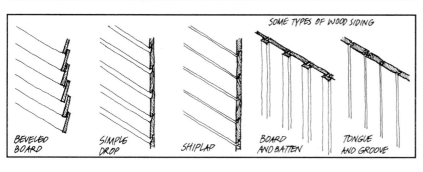

SOME TYPES OF WOOD SIDING

BEVELED BOARD   SIMPLE DROP   SHIPLAP   BOARD AND BATTEN   TONGUE AND GROOVE

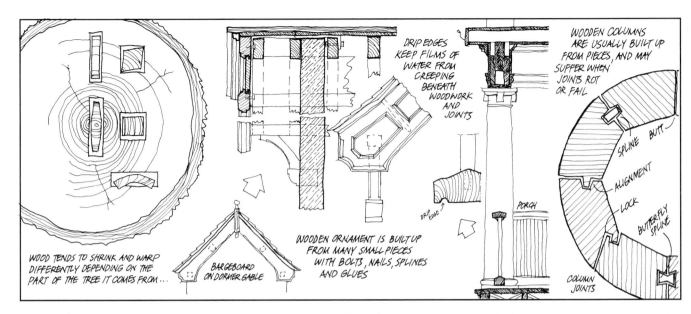

DRIP EDGES KEEP FILMS OF WATER FROM CREEPING BENEATH WOODWORK AND JOINTS

WOODEN COLUMNS ARE USUALLY BUILT UP FROM PIECES, AND MAY SUFFER WHEN JOINTS ROT OR FAIL

SPLINE BUTT

ALIGNMENT

LOCK

BUTTERFLY SPLINE

DRIP EDGE

PORCH

COLUMN JOINTS

WOOD TENDS TO SHRINK AND WARP DIFFERENTLY DEPENDING ON THE PART OF THE TREE IT COMES FROM ...

BARGEBOARD ON DORMER GABLE

WOODEN ORNAMENT IS BUILT UP FROM MANY SMALL PIECES WITH BOLTS, NAILS, SPLINES AND GLUES

(opposite)
Ensembles of wood cladding and ornament require regular maintenance and painting (upper left), vulnerable as they are to weathering from above (middle left) and damp and chemicals from the ground beneath. But paint can't be permitted to accumulate indefinitely — from time to time, with great care, it must be removed (middle right) and rotted elements repaired or replaced (bottom right).

Occasionally, advanced deterioration forces replacement of large areas of cladding — careful attention needs to be paid to the minor irregularities of the original as well as to the integration of gutters and downspouts (below).

Detail and ornament

Even modest historic buildings may display a wealth of mouldings, window and door surrounds, gingerbread, scrollwork, turned work, shutters and louvres. The 19th and early 20th centuries maintained a considerable craft tradition in woodworking, even in the midst of the mass-produced millwork of industrialized construction. Cabinetmaker and carpenter were not divorced from one another as radically as now. Countless small mills and shops dotted the province, yet there was a recognizable consistency to much decorative work, representing not only a formal tradition (shared through millwork catalogues and pattern books) but also the limitations of habit, similar tools, and factory production. Great effort went into making the mass-produced appear ornate and hand-tooled, but wood's workability and availability kept the small woodworker in business too.

Carved, sawn and turned detail is very vulnerable to decay and requires constant attention. Its relative vulnerability is matched, however, by its relative ease of reproduction by skilled hands.

❖ Ensure that fastenings of wooden ornament are secure, and that they are free from rust. Correct causes of deterioration before any repairs and look especially at *earlier* repairs for signs of decay.

❖ Patch cracks and holes with chemically compatible wood fillers or with wood splices of same species and cut. Use epoxies carefully, ensuring that their thermal and moisture properties match those of the surrounding wood.

❖ Replace only wood that has irreparably deteriorated, leaving all sound wood intact. Use stable, non-shrinking glues (for instance, calcium caseinate is a strong bonding agent, with centuries of use to prove its reliability). Treat stripped and exposed wood with a water-repellent mixture before refinishing (see above).

❖ Wherever wood is structurally sound and its surface reasonably undamaged, repair rather than replace it. Make any replacements precisely according to the existing feature, an obvious mate, or pictorial evidence of the original. Use the same species or another with similar cut,

moisture content and material performance. Use stock items for replacements only when they match originals accurately.

❖ Make new details carefully to prevent water absorption and consequent rot. Changes from traditional practice (for instance, use of built-up sections to replicate solid timbers) may lead to problems unless the new elements are properly protected. Do not rely on caulking to keep water out. Make sure that horizontal surfaces have sufficient slope to shed standing water, and provide drip edges along sills, cornices and similar features.

❖ In areas of highly modelled woodwork, wood repair must be the first choice, but fibreglass replacements can be satisfactory if accurately moulded to match details and if painted to match the historic appearance. Fibreglass will not be as durable as properly maintained wood. Make sure that junctions between fibreglass and wood do not inadvertently force water into end grain or concealed pockets in the existing woodwork.

❖ Take complex pieces such as ornate scrollwork or columns and their capitals and bases off the building to repair and refinish them in controlled workshop conditions. Repair their anchorages and reattach them with non-rusting connectors, allowing for the wood to expand and contract with changes in moisture and temperature. Do not fasten or re-fasten wood so tightly that stress cracks appear later.

❖ Maintain or restore the operation and hardware of shutters, paying special attention to removal of paint build-ups that have restricted or blocked movement. Restore missing operable shutters (as operable) only where historical and material evidence indicates their earlier existence.

❖ Inspect ventilation louvres regularly to ensure that they function as designed; install rustproof interior screens, inspect constantly for bird and animal infestations, and make sure that any signs of rot are arrested quickly.

References

See GAYL80 for technical
information on most exterior
metals and repair techniques.
MEAD86 deals comprehensively
with repairs and substitutions for
metalwork on façades, and
includes more recent technical
references.

Other technical references include
FEIL82, FROI86, INSA72,
JAND83, KEMP81, STAH84 and
TIMM76. More modest
maintenance and repair methods
may be found in CHAM76,
DAVE80/86, JOHN84, LOND84
and SHOP86.

*Stamped sheet iron used to imitate
carved woodwork (which in its turn
mimicked stone).*

Architectural metals: materials and types

Though lead and copper had been used as
building materials for millennia, the 19th and
early 20th centuries added a tremendous
variety of metals for uses in structure,
cladding, hardware, and even humble utilities.
For architectural conservationists, their variety
is both exhilarating and daunting:

❑ Cast iron for structure: columns, plumbing

❑ Cast iron for ornament: fences, shop
    windows, shopfronts, lamp standards,
    street and park furniture, hardware, small
    sculpture

❑ Wrought iron for structure: beams, joists,
    fasteners, and engineering structures,
    especially bridges (superseded by steel)

❑ Wrought iron for ornament: hardware,
    fences, gates, grilles, window frames

❑ Cast brass/bronze, monel metal
    (nickel/copper): hardware, sculpture,
    doors and doorways

❑ Steel for structure: beams, columns,
    reinforcing bars

❑ Steel for ornament: windowframes,
    stainless or enameled panels

❑ Copper: sheet roofing, flashing, shingle
    roofing, sculpture, doors and doorways,
    plumbing

❑ Sheet iron (zinc-galvanized, tin-plated,
    terne-plated, or painted; usually both
    coated *and* painted): ceilings and panelling
    (interior and exterior), ornamentation,
    cornices, window surrounds, sheet
    roofing, shingle roofing, flashing

❑ Lead: sheet roofing, flashing, small
    sculpture, plumbing

❑ Aluminum (extruded, sheet and cast):
    windows, doors and doorways, hardware,
    sculpture

Metals are exceptionally durable yet
surprisingly vulnerable to deterioration.
Though hard and able to sustain loads that
either compress or stretch their molecular
structure, they tend to react with water-borne
chemical agents that radically reduce their
strength. Metals conduct heat very easily and
expand and contract with even small changes
in temperature. All installations and
fastenings of structural or decorative metal
must accommodate thermal expansion and
contraction. Traditional sheet-metal
fabrication and details took this into account
by having lots of angles that could flex in
response to movements (ornate decorations in
metal were as much functionally apt as
aesthetically fashionable), but age makes
metal brittle and the flexing begins to cause
cracking.

Most metal failures are due to the rusting of
ferrous (iron) elements, especially connectors
between elements. Except for stainless steel —
iron alloyed with chromium — all ferrous
metals (cast, wrought and sheet iron) require
coating or painting to prevent rust. All
architectural metals are vulnerable to acid
precipitation, though even clean water can
lead to problems when it enables electrolytic
currents to pass between adjacent dissimilar
metals. This "galvanic action" ionizes metal
surfaces and causes a chemical reaction that
eats into the metal. Copper and iron or steel
are the most unfriendly of metals in this
respect, and iron corrosion is often traceable
directly to adjacent copper. Even stainless steel
is corroded by galvanic action when in contact
with aluminum.

❖ Before any conservation work identify the
   metal accurately. Clean thoroughly before
   diagnosis, treatment and repainting or
   recoating. Cover metals meant to be
   covered (ferrous); uncover metals meant to
   be uncovered (copper, bronze, stainless
   steel).

❖ Replace badly deteriorated metal in kind;
   do not under any circumstances replace
   one metal with any other metal that may
   lead to corrosion. If using non-metallic
   materials as substitutes (see below), ensure
   that new metallic connectors do not
   establish galvanic action.

Decorative cast iron

Prefabricated building components of cast iron were used extensively world-wide in the mid-19th century for both structural and decorative purposes. Because of the ready availability of timber in Ontario, decorative cast iron did not make much of a mark on the province's architecture, and cast-iron catalogue-type commercial façades were rare (though iron fences, gates, ornaments and lamp standards were widespread). Cast iron has good compressive strength and, though less susceptible to oxidation than sheet iron, rust is a constant problem. Cast iron is very brittle and resists tension poorly.

Cast iron deteriorates if poorly installed or not maintained; it may also suffer structural fatigue and failure if poor casting techniques build stresses into the metal. The chief agent of deterioration is water, especially getting into joints and connectors, where it leads to corrosion unseen and unchecked.

❖ Arrest all sources of water penetration and corrosion first — repair structural connections and drainage and ensure maximum protection from moisture penetration, either liquid or vapour. Remove every sign of rust or corrosion. Cast iron is very brittle — do not bang or try to bend it.

❖ Ensure that no copper flashing or decoration directly touches iron and that water does not run down from any copper or copper-alloy element onto iron.

❖ Tighten bolts and connectors to draw loosened sections together but make sure thermal expansion and contraction are still permitted. To seal gaps, use only the highest-performance elastomers (these synthetic compunds are hard to paint over but can be pigmented in mixing). Alternatively, use panels or fillers of galvanized sheet metal, carefully prepared, to bridge large gaps. Use auto-body putty for small holes and cracks — its expansion factor is similar to iron's.

❖ Clean cast iron mechanically, with wire brush, scraper, or very low-pressure dry-grit blasting (maximum 100 psi). Use chemical rust removers with great care and protect adjacent surfaces (for these to be most effective, consider removing the element and reinstalling it after cleaning and priming under workshop conditions). *Use neither water nor water-based chemicals, nor high-pressure grit.* Remove any previous cement or other incompatible patches that may attract moisture to the iron.

❖ Prime cast iron *immediately* after cleaning, within no more than a few hours. Use an appropriate rust-inhibiting primer: red lead in an oil vehicle is best for long-term protection, but it covers poorly and is especially poisonous. Alternatives are zinc phosphate and zinc chromate. For both priming and painting, alkyd or oil vehicles provide a better paint bond than latex, because they dry more slowly.

❖ If cast iron is too weakened or corroded to repair (and where the original pattern exists), recast and replace decayed components. New cast-iron replacements are both difficult and expensive if the original pattern no longer exists. A sound existing component may be used as a pattern, but the mould must be about 1.5 per cent larger than the final dimensions, to allow for shrinkage in cooling. Use substitute materials such as cast aluminum only with the greatest care — see "Replacements and substitutions", below.

Decorative sheet metal

Decorative sheet metal — usually galvanized and painted iron in 19th-century practice, and as often unpainted copper or other non-ferrous alloy in the present century — often imitated other forms of wood or stone. The complexities of these forms and their attachments, and general lack of maintenance of features out of reach of the ground, have enabled corrosion of such elements to proceed unchecked, making many repairs very difficult.

❖ Repair or replace wooden or metal supports and backing as necessary before working on metal surfaces. In most small buildings, the backing is wood, often decayed from rot or infestation (good historic precedent for not slapping modern metal siding on top of sound wood). Make sure that any concealed metal anchors or brackets are themselves sound; remove all signs of rust.

❖ Ensure that there are suffcient expansion joints and that they function without overstressing sheet metal or connectors; carefully add expansion or relief joints where needed.

❖ All connectors must match the metals they connect. Remove all connectors that show signs of corrosion from galvanic action and replace with ones that do not. Be especially careful to keep copper and iron well apart.

❖ Clean sheet metal extremely carefully. Be even more cautious than for cast iron so as not to erode the plating — no grit-blasting, not even at low pressure — and leave sound paint layers intact. Use no water-based cleaning treatments. Repair any broken soldered joints with equivalent solder and flux.

❖ For sheet metal, particularly galvanized iron, use auto-body putty to patch and fill small holes and dents.

❖ For large patches with new metal, use a similar metal/plating combination as that of the base to accommodate thermal expansion and to prevent galvanic action in the old material. Solder or rivet the new patches, sealing with an elastomeric compound to keep out water.

❖ Large patches with glass-reinforced plastic may be a satisfactory alternative only if they accommodate the thermal expansion of the metal; the plastic must be fully primed and painted to protect it from ultraviolet light.

❖ To paint sheet metal follow the same procedures as for cast iron — prepare a clean surface (do not clean to the bare metal if older paint is sound), use the proper primer (compatible with existing paint chemistry), and build up several coats of primer and finish enamel.

❖ Consider artificially "aging" copper with weak acid only with very great caution, and only to reduce the contrast with existing patina, not to attain it instantly; beware of acid runoff causing problems below.

For flashing, see also ROOFING.

Some of the range of historic architectural metals, from cast and wrought iron fencing, to pressed metal replicas of stone, to copper, brass and lead in commercial windows (opposite), and to structural steel (above, top). For repairs beyond basic maintenance, it may be necessary to detach metal elements and work on them indoors (above).

Brass, bronze and other non-ferrous sculptural metals

❖ Do not assume that a discoloured surface on a non-ferrous metal is a beneficial patina. Consult with a specialist to determine if the patina is protecting the metal; if there is pitting or obvious loss of metal, then the patina is probably corrosive and should be removed.

❖ Use domestic brass- and bronze-cleaning compounds or impregnated polishing cloths for non-ferrous features. A weak oxalic acid solution with fine pumice powder seems especially effective for most exterior dirt. A controversial treatment that some experts advocate and others oppose is mechanical cleaning of exposed sculptural surfaces with *very* low pressure glass-bead peening (80 to 100 psi), after masking surroundings carefully or removing the feature altogether for treatment in controlled workshop conditions and subsequent reattachment. This technique will alter the surface of the metal and may or may not be acceptable — accordingly, get more than one expert opinion about its suitability for particular conditions.

❖ Where surfaces such as doors, railings and hardware are subjected to constant public use, apply protective lacquer to the metal surface and maintain it regularly.

❖ Consider replacing individual elements only where deterioration is far advanced, that is, when metal is weakened or missing. Replace elements in the same metal wherever possible — use fine-art conservation skills for repairs.

❖ Maintain all metal hardware in working order. Keeping fasteners and hinges properly tightened and lubricated will reduce wear and tear. Do not paint unpainted surfaces.

❖ Pay constant attention to maintenance; never use corrosive de-icing salts near non-ferrous metals.

Replacements and substitutions

Because modern materials and fashions have completely overwhelmed many earlier "high-tech" materials and suppliers, it may not be possible to find identical replacements for metal features. Reproduction of badly deteriorated features in the appropriate metal from moulds taken off sound existing material is possible, though it will require the expertise and workshop of a specialist, such as a specialty hardware supplier or even a fine-art craftworker. Satisfactory substitute materials may include cast aluminum, glass-fibre-reinforced cement, and fibreglass (glass-fibre-reinforced plastic). But the use of substitutes must be a last resort, used only where necessary to re-establish overall visual integrity of the whole.

❖ Do not use substitute sculptural materials to carry heavy loads; for instance, cast aluminum is much weaker in compression than a cast-iron original it may replace, requiring structural reinforcement.

❖ Establish long-term durability of substitutes, especially their finishes and colours (both wet and dry), before considering their use. Check recent technical literature for data.

❖ Allow for shrinkage in moulding new materials from existing features. Each material has different thermal characteristics; for instance, cast aluminum shrinks twice as much as cast iron in cooling.

❖ Make sure that structural connections are secure and non-rusting. Do not transfer loads to any existing non-structural features.

❖ Design and fabricate drainage details that channel water away from existing material; do not rely for water protection exclusively on mastics or caulking, which must be regularly maintained and periodically renewed.

References

For basic repairs to stucco, see KAPL78/86 and POOR83. Other books dealing with small-scale stucco and cement work include FINE86, HANS83, KITC83, LEGN79, LITC82, OLDH85 and READ82. For more technical help, including old building texts, see HUGH86, MACE98, MEAD86, RADF83, RAMS88 and STAG76.

The most concise yet useful book dealing with the range of historic and modern formulations for stucco, mortar and plaster is ASHU83.

Concrete and terrazzo repairs are far more demanding technically, and require special expertise, borrowing chemistry and technique from both limestone and plaster conservation; see MEAD86 and TIMM76.

Stucco

Stucco, sometimes known as rendering, is simply a lime (or lime-and-cement) mortar plastered onto a lath hung on the exterior walls of a building. It is a very old technique. Properly formulated and applied, stucco can be as durable as the mortar between bricks. Indeed, stucco's composition is very much like masonry mortar (though stiffer), with different proportions of cement, lime, and sand or other aggregate.

Early stucco was much like interior plaster, primarily a lime-and-sand mixture with animal hair, straw or other binders to improve material integrity. Its surface was built up in two or three coats for maximum strength and durability — the rough first ("scratch" or "brown") coat tied the mix to the lath, and the final finish coat provided texture and colour. In some cases, its surface was scored to imitate ashlar or moulded with a pattern of "bricks", the grooves painted to simulate mortar lines. In the late 19th- and early 20th-century revival styles, various textures were added to the finish coat with plasterer's tools to imitate traditional European textures.

As Portland cement became commonly available, late 19th- and early 20th-century stucco used a mix that added increasing portions of cement to the lime until the mix was about half and half, with a further four or five parts of sand or fine gravel for surface texture. Metal lath also came into common use before 1900.

Traditionally, stucco was seldom painted (once painted it requires regular *re*painting). Rather, it usually took its colour from the aggregate and any permanent pigment mixed in to the finish coat.

Like exposed mortar, stucco is quite stiff and vulnerable to cracking and crumbling. Water may penetrate behind the surface and lead to rot in the wooden lath, or foundations and structures may settle and shift, or the stucco may lose its bond with the supporting lath because of poor formulation or application. Sometimes later repair patches with high cement content will worsen conditions in the older and softer lime stucco.

❖ Ensure that any textured or decorated stucco is accurately recorded before repairs

begin. Note carefully the thickness of stucco relative to wood trim and maintain that dimension in any repair. Take careful and accurate colour samples of existing stucco, using both weathered and freshly broken samples, and store these for colour-matching purposes. Measure accurately the locations and dimensions of simulated ashlar or other motifs and replicate these in the course of any major repairs.

❖ Remove cracked, crumbling or damaged stucco to a sound base (in most cases the wooden or metal lath). Repair the lath as required. Duplicate the original stucco formulation in strength, composition and texture as well as possible, adding if necessary stabilizing material to keep the mix from shrinking as it dries.

❖ Match the historic finish colour and texture carefully in any repairs, using a sample of freshly broken material, and take into account the different colour of wet and dry materials and the effects of time (weather-borne dirt may darken the surface over time, but fading pigments may lighten it). Size and colour of aggregates in the mix are essential characteristics — all sorts of ingredients have been added to stucco, such as pulverized cinders, to accent its finished surface. Try to reproduce the conditions of the original application and the effects of impurities in the original mixture (in difficult cases, laboratory analysis may be necessary).

❖ Reproduce any special markings, such as "ashlar" scoring, based on the recorded features.

❖ In the case of a primary elevation, consider repairing the entire wall plane where it is critical to have a consistent colour, but generally do not remove sound stucco. Do not paint stucco if it is not already painted.

❖ Moisture content is critical to successful stucco patches — don't make patches too wet (they will crack as they dry) but do keep them damp for a couple of days once applied. Dampen the stucco surrounding the repair as well. As in traditional practice, build up repairs in at least two or three coats to ensure sound bonding and curing.

STUCCO — ON ROUGH BRICK, OR WOODEN OR
METAL LATH CAN BE VERY
DURABLE, BUT REPAIRS MUST
FOLLOW THE ORIGINAL METHOD,
WITH SEVERAL COATS.
1 - BASE (OR SCRATCH)
2 - SCRATCH
3 - FINISH

ASHLAR-
SCORED,
ON
BRICK

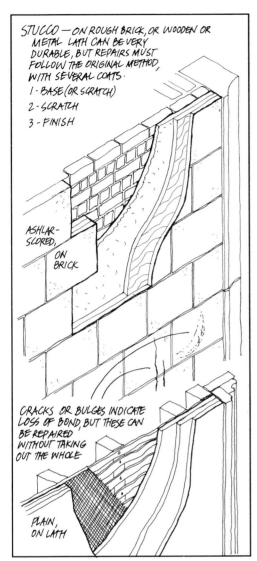

CRACKS OR BULGES INDICATE
LOSS OF BOND, BUT THESE CAN
BE REPAIRED
WITHOUT TAKING
OUT THE WHOLE

PLAIN,
ON LATH

*Stucco has been a much-used
exterior surface in every era of
Ontario architecture, from the ashlar
imitations of Upper Canadian
Georgian fashion (above right), to the
classical revivals of the early 20th
century (right), where the traditional
lime-and-sand stucco has been
"modernized" into cast-in-place and
factory-made cement ornament.*

Cast-in-place concrete and terrazzo

Reinforced concrete was invented in the mid-19th century, but its use as a deliberately exposed surface began only early in the present century on bridges and other engineering structures. Concrete is made of cement, sand and gravel in varying proportions, cast into a temporary container around an armature of steel reinforcing bars or mesh. The combination of steel and concrete bonded together is far stronger than concrete alone, enabling the entire assembly to carry forces of both tension and compression. Concrete can be moulded with surfaces other than flat and even textures, but exterior curing conditions vary so much that cast-in-place

ornament has not proved very durable. Terrazzo is a special application of concrete with marble chips in the aggregate, with the final surface of the mass ground down and polished.

Concrete is in effect artificial limestone. It deteriorates in the presence of moisture and dissolved salts, which break down the bonding within the hardened mix and attack the steel reinforcing bars, which then rust. The rust in turn removes the essential bond between the steel and the concrete and drastically reduces the assembly's overall integrity and strength. The very nature of the material means that all repairs must be done on site.

❖ Before any concrete repair, undertake a full laboratory analysis of a sample taken from an inconspicuous, sound area. There has been a tremendous historical variety of mixes and aggregates, and some combinations of cement and aggregate will be incompatible with one another and with the original work.

❖ Complete the necessary structural repairs before working on finished surfaces, especially around openings. Repair vertical fractures from bottom to top.

❖ Make sure that any reinforcing exposed in the course of repair is fully de-rusted before applying patches; if necessary, add reinforcing bars or mesh to tie in the repair and strengthen the assembly where the structure is weak.

❖ Most concrete surfaces can be patched with identical material as a plastic repair; make sure that patches are pre-tested to be chemically compatible and are well keyed to the original work. Epoxy resins can be used to help bind the new patch into the original material. It is impossible to patch exposed concrete without leaving visible signs of the work, so concentrate instead on matching the surface texture.

❖ Clean concrete as if it were limestone masonry — *use no acids.*

See also MASONRY.

Concrete can be a durable surface as well as a structural material (below), but its early 20th-century use as a cast-in-place artificial stone has turned out to have been very vulnerable to high humidity and corrosion beneath its surface. It is almost impossible to patch discreetly (bottom).

Composite, eclectic, and other modern materials

Just as with architectural metals, a great wealth of new decorative treatments arrived early in the 20th century to cover exterior walls and floors, especially in commercial buildings. These "modern" materials included ceramic tiles, asphalt blocks, plastics, "structural" glass facing and glass masonry. Not all have proved durable. Many are no longer in current use, replaced by newer fashions and materials. Most of these "composite" surfaces are very brittle and vulnerable to impact. Some can be repaired or replicated with current materials, though conspicuous factory-made materials such as solid-coloured structural glass (known by brand names such as vitrolite or Carrara glass) are very difficult to replicate unit-by-unit while maintaining the smoothness or consistency characteristic of their "look". There are few standard procedures for conserving these materials.

Mid-20th-century storefronts often combine several "modern" (or modernized) materials — terrazzo floors, structural glass panels, frameless glazing and aluminum trim (above). Glass block is another modernistic material that has cycled in and out of fashion for commercial buildings (right).

❖ In dealing with irreplaceable "modern" materials, follow the general principles of regular inspection and maintenance, correcting basic causes of deterioration first, replacing in kind, and not transferring deterioration to adjacent features with poor repairs.

❖ Consult specialists and follow their advice, especially artists and craftworkers using similar technology and materials.

❖ Most storefront glass or tile facings were installed as veneers over an earlier surface or structure — seated on shelf angles, fastened with asphalt-type mastic, and flashed with aluminum moulding. In attempting repairs, carefully remove mouldings, then panels or tiles. Remove dirt and repair any hidden deterioration, reapply panels with high-grade mastic, reinstall metal trim, and caulk carefully. Inspect the finished work regularly.

❖ It is no longer possible to find perfect replacements for damaged "structural" glass in most colours, except from wreckers' yards — most colours of structural glass are no longer produced (check with manufacturers for colours still available). Coloured acrylic or polycarbonate sheets, rear-painted clear glass sandwiches, or enamelled substitutes may suffice, depending on colour and location. Consider moving sound panels from inconspicuous areas (as in last-resort masonry repairs) to maximize consistency in highly visible areas.

❖ Glass blocks are fairly durable but may crack because of undue stress or washing out of mortar. Repair causes of stress as for masonry and arrest any water penetration. Replace damaged units in kind as far as possible, bedded in soft mortar that matches the original. Do not substitute caulking for mortar. Consult manufacturers for availability of new units to match old; sometimes a skilled craftworker can fine-tune finishes of interior faces of glass blocks to match the originals.

References

Advisory texts on window repair
seldom emphasize preserving
existing forms or materials.
Among the best conservation-
minded sources are DAVE80/86,
HAYN87, KAPL78/86,
LOND84a/85 and POOR83.
Others include BOWY80,
CUNN84, DUTO85, FINE86,
HANS83, JOHN83, JOHN84,
KIRK84, KITC83, LITC82,
LYNC82, MELV73, MULL81,
OLDH85, PYKE80, READ82,
SHOP86, SMIT84, STLOnd,
TECH82 and VILA81.

Some sources describe
dimensions, materials and
operation of historic windows;
these will be useful in replacing
vanished originals with
appropriate substitutes. See
BRAY80, CHIT80, EHRE84,
JAND83, MACE98, MCAL84,
NATI80, POWY29, PRIZ75,
RADF83, REMP80, TUNI86 and
VICT84.

Modern replacements, even in
the same material, seldom
replicate precisely the dimensions
and profiles of historic muntins
and mullions. For cases where
this difficulty has been overcome,
see HAYN87. See SEDW83 and
HERI87a/87b for sensitive energy
retrofits of existing windows.

The special importance of windows

Windows are not simply glass. They are
assembled from several materials and
components and present almost all of the
conservation problems of a building in
miniature. They are also among the most
conspicuous of any building's features. Their
arrangement and design define much of the
style and even the "personality" of a building.
Windows help define building character
because they catch the eye from the outside,
directing the viewer's attention from one part
of the elevation to another, punctuating the
façade. Windows are the most-used part of a
building (visually, physically, decoratively),
where human contact between inside and
outside is maintained. They permit and define
views both in and out, provide light and
ventilation for human occupants, and enable a
whole range of environmental adjustments —
the building's own "breathing". The original
windows give us something of the experience
of the original view, the opportunity to see out
of the building in the way its early occupants
did, even if the view itself has changed.

Because they are used a great deal, windows
are very vulnerable to wear and tear, weather
and weathering, and the requirements of
changing interior uses. They require
considerable maintenance but don't often get
enough. They thus require repairs in the
course of almost every conservation project.
As with more basic materials, the essential
conservation principles are to repair rather
than replace and replace in kind when too far
decayed for repairs.

When evaluating the importance of windows
in any project, from a district study to actual
repairs, consider the following characteristics:

❑ Date/era of installation (original, early
alteration, late alteration)

❑ Location, stylistic association with building
as a whole, with other windows in
building

❑ Size, shape, glazing divisions (typical and
atypical)

❑ Manner of operation (see types, below)

❑ Materials, profiles and dimensions (frame,
sash, muntins, mullions, surrounds, etc.)

❑ Glazing type (crown, cylinder, plate,
stained, etc.)

❑ Craftsmanship of components and
assembly (quality of materials; handwork
v. millwork)

❑ Rarity of type (technologically or
stylistically)

❑ Hardware and accessories (awnings,
shutters)

Frame, sash and glass

The frames and sash of almost all 19th-century
windows in Ontario were assembled from
wooden millwork, usually softwood (though
softwood and hardwood were used for larger
windows). Only timber provided the strength
and flexibility to hold the delicate (and
expensive) glass panes, to open and close for
ventilation, and to tolerate the extremes of the
local climate. Even within the cast-iron
commercial fronts, the windows themselves
were invariably framed in wood.

Until the turn of the 20th century, almost all
windows except fixed-pane shopfronts and
leaded stained-glass church windows were
operable (ventilation for these was provided
through small transom openings). Only with
the eclectic Queen Anne styles were some of
the larger parts of residential windows
permanently fixed, and from that time even
the top panes of "double-hung" windows
have often been fixed. The most common
frame type, the double-hung wooden sliding
sash window, is usually labelled by the
subdivisions of its major halves — six (panes)
over six, one over one, and so on. The wooden
window remains the most common in use for
small buildings even today, though often
transformed by vinyl coatings, aluminum
storms and even vacuum-sealed double
glazing.

Metal windowframes appeared late in the 19th
century, but their common use takes off with
mass-produced steel sash after 1910, for
commercial, industrial and even residential
windows. Leaded glass appears in historic
Ontario church and residence windows as a
reminder of historic fashion rather than
through any need to use small panes.

Within the sash itself, the glass is normally
held in place by metal glazier's points and
flexible putty within an angle of wooden
moulding known as a muntin (or astragal). In

larger windows a secondary wooden glazing strip may reinforce the muntin. The profile of the muntin — often unique to an individual worker or mill, though within the limits of a given style — is an extremely valuable artifact of the locale and era of the building. A knowledgeable eye can date a window, and often the building itself, by the profile and dimension of its smallest member.

Most 19th-century windowpanes were made as crown glass (blowing and twirling the molten glass into a large disk) or as cylinder glass (blowing the glass as a large "bottle", slicing off the ends, and laying the cylinder out as a small flat sheet). Available by the 1840s, the much larger and stronger panes permitted by the plate-glass method enabled a major change in the look and function of windows as the need for muntins disappeared (to reappear later as a conspicuous element of the many revival styles). Factory-made glass flooring, glass block and wired glass (or "fire-glass") emerged as important new materials around 1900, especially in response to insurance demands and fire codes.

Repair and rehabilitation

❖ Carefully inspect and record each window, comparing its present state closely with historic photographs whenever possible. Test the window's operation and look for deterioration of frame and/or sash, failure of putty, caulking or glazing, obvious air or moisture infiltration or condensation, and paint failure, especially on bottom rails and at the sill. Most deterioration occurs in the bottom third or so of a unit — but check the soundness of the upper part as well. Ensure that metal-covered window elements (especially shopfronts with sheet brass or copper over a wooden frame) do not hide rot in the wood beneath.

❖ Make sure that all wood is free from rot, damp and infestation, that all metal is free from rust, and that glazing putty is sound and remains flexible without cracking.

❖ Repair windows rather than replace them if they contribute greatly to architectural character and are largely sound and intact. When a window can be repaired with readily available techniques and materials, can have its broken panes replaced without damage to sash, and can fit together and operate properly, repair it.

❖ Replace badly deteriorated components in kind when the rest of the window is sound or can be repaired. In making replacements, maintain the integrity and appearance of the entire window and maintain or restore its operability, wherever possible, in its original mode. Reproduce wooden mouldings precisely according to those in existing windows of the same vintage; avoid modern stock mouldings unless their match is perfect.

❖ Retain the existing glazing as much as possible, especially where it has irreplaceable aesthetic qualities of form, light and colour; make special efforts to protect and retain curved glazing. Ensure that replacement panes have sufficient thermal expansion room within the sash and that the putty is sufficiently flexible to allow movement without damaging either muntins or glass.

❖ For wooden windows, use linseed-oil-based putty and assure its proper bonding with cleaned and prepared wood. Prepare the wood with a linseed-oil treatment and very carefully paint over the putty (but not the glass) to maintain its softness and flexibility. Do not "butter" putty on sloppily — besides looking bad, the thin feathery edges will allow water to creep in to the wood.

❖ Retain and repair historic window hardware; replace missing hardware in kind. Do not cover over old windowframes with metal or plastic. Restore the operation of the upper sash of a double-hung window wherever possible: apart from "authenticity", an open upper sash offers much-improved warm-weather ventilation.

❖ Remove excessive paint build-up but leave sound paint that adheres well and does not interfere with the window's operation. Determine previous paint types and colours through paint analysis in course of repair and add that information to the project records for use in both current and future work.

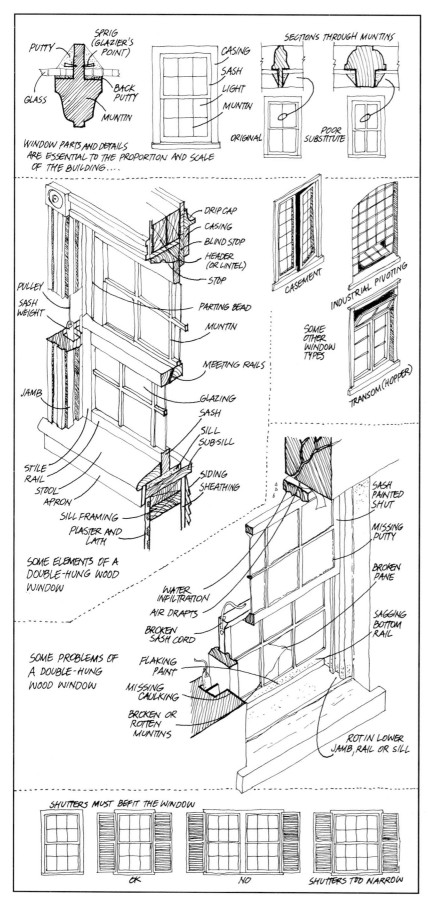

WINDOW PARTS AND DETAILS ARE ESSENTIAL TO THE PROPORTION AND SCALE OF THE BUILDING....

SOME ELEMENTS OF A DOUBLE-HUNG WOOD WINDOW

SOME PROBLEMS OF A DOUBLE-HUNG WOOD WINDOW

SHUTTERS MUST BEFIT THE WINDOW

❖ Remove all rust from metal frames and sash; prime metal surfaces immediately after cleaning (see METALWORK).

❖ Repaint in suitable colours — either in those of the original or in colours more generally authentic to the neighbourhood in an earlier period (see PAINT, COLOUR AND LIGHT).

❖ Replace or add proper weatherstripping at all openings, as either compression seals or sliding seals. Metal, vinyl, rubber, polypropylene, and felt strips each have their best locations and are far more durable than adhesive-backed foam, which does not allow sliding. Do not let weatherstripping bind or restrict window operation. Caulk carefully, and discreetly, to provide an air seal between mouldings and walls.

❖ Take special care, if inserting second panes of glass into wooden sash, to maintain original muntin dimensions and profiles. If accuracy is not possible without severely weakening the window or damaging existing glazing — or if the existing glazing is original or of special importance and survives generally intact — use an alternative form of double glazing (see below).

See also EXTERIOR WOODWORK and METALWORK.

Replacements and restorations

❖ Replace a window unit only when the majority of the window is missing or severely damaged or where it no longer fits properly and cannot be adjusted to fit and maintain its function. Even where there is historical evidence of an earlier window, do not pull out a reasonably well-fitting, compatible, and functioning window from a later period unless necessary. Do not replace an existing and fitting one-over-one double-hung window with an "earlier" six-over-six or other restoration of a presumed earlier window. The existing window may have its own value and authenticity which a restoration would lack, and that value should be taken into account in making decisions.

❖ Replace inappropriate "modernizations", such as horizontal metal sliders and fixed

modern frames, where these compromise or distort the overall architectural character of the building, as evident in neighbouring buildings or historic photographs and drawings. Choose conscientiously (that is, on the basis of research) whether to restore to an authentic original or simply to a compatible model.

❖ Do not replace inconsequential or neutral windows that may have replaced earlier windows but nevertheless fit reasonably and do not detract from the overall character of the building or from other windows.

❖ Maintain or if necessary recover the historic size and shape of all window openings. Neither expand the openings, nor fill them in, except to make good previous damaging modifications. If interior ceilings are to be lowered or furred down, ensure that the ceiling drop is set back sufficiently from the window to enable its visual and functional continuity.

❖ If windows must be blocked in because of major functional change, look hard at the program to determine if the function cannot be satisfied with windows retained in their historic forms and locations. If, as a very last resort, windows must be covered over from the interior, maintain their *exterior* appearance as windows.

❖ In replacing windows, match (from documentary sources or surviving mates) historic profiles, shapes, dimensions and divisions of frame, sash, muntins and surrounds. Add hardware and window accessories such as awnings and shutters only on the basis of evidence from thorough research.

❖ Take special care, if using double-glazed replacements, to maintain accurately the muntin dimensions and profiles of the originals — use alternative double glazing otherwise (see below).

What not to do to historic windows.

Operable exterior storm windows are traditional energy-conserving features of historic buildings, especially residences and small commercial buildings (top). It is possible to add a layer of glazing within the sash itself, taking care to maintain the operation and appearance of the window (above). And though it is also possible to double-glaze individual panes or lights, taking care to preserve the distinctive profiles of the historic sash and muntins, this particular example (right) loses that historic appearance.

Storm windows, double glazing

There exist several options for upgrading the insulation and acoustical performance of windows, including removable exterior storms, fixed operable exterior storms, interior operable storms, interior fixed glazing on sash or on removable magnetic frames, and sealed-unit replacement. Selecting the most appropriate depends on how important is the character of the existing window, relative cost of the work, and potential savings over time in reduced energy expenditures. Historic windows should be upgraded only when the work can be done without permanently damaging or compromising their visual and material character. Simple air-sealing measures — weatherstripping and caulking — will improve a window's thermal and acoustic performance considerably. Keep energy-saving ambitions realistic: windows account for no more than 15 to 20 per cent of the heat moving into or out of a building.

❖ Consider using either independent storm windows or double glass for sliding sash. For other types, double glazing will often be more satisfactory than storms because of conflicting movements and unduly restricted ventilation.

❖ Where they exist, retain and use wooden storm windows. Usually custom-made, they may be as old as the original windows.

❖ Where there are no existing exterior storm windows and where interior storms are impracticable, install new exterior storms as discreet (and discrete) complements to historically valuable windows. Make glazing divisions coincide, using the same or larger (not smaller) divisions. Wooden storms are preferable to aluminum, as better visual matches and insulators, but thin aluminum or steel sections, anodized or painted to blend in with the frame and sash, may be satisfactory.

❖ Be *very* cautious about using fixed exterior glazing (whether glass or polycarbonate) over leaded or stained glass — the greenhouse effect will heat the air space between the panes and weaken leading. Make sure that the air space is as deep as possible, and ventilate it fully to the exterior. This is not an energy-saving

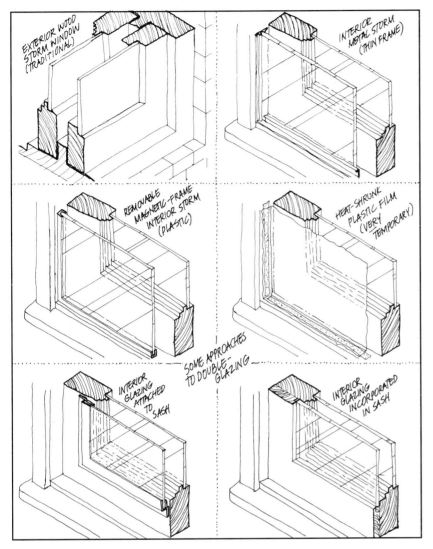

A difficult case — though energy conservation, security and preservation of hardware are achieved, is its appearance satisfactory (and is it properly ventilated)?

measure, but rather a form of security against windstorms and vandalism. Never use curved or bubble-formed plastics over historic glazing.

❖ Interior storm windows (operable or fixed) are preferable to new exterior storms in terms of maintenance and preservation of exterior appearance, though they do leave the existing window exposed to the elements. To reduce or eliminate condensation between fixed interior glazing and exterior glass, assure proper ventilation of the air space — small openings at top and bottom of the exterior sash will permit condensation to evaporate quickly. Do not rely on dessicant materials, which must be constantly renewed. The fixed pane should be removable for cleaning.

❖ To double-glaze non-sliding types of sash, it is possible to use a pane of lightweight glass or plastic fastened to the interior of both fixed and moving parts of the sash, with neoprene gaskets to prevent air leakage and condensation between panes. A lightweight addition rather than standard glass will obviate the need to replace hinges and hardware with heavier-duty substitutes. Additional panes must clear the moving parts of the window.

❖ Do not install double vacuum-sealed units in delicate muntins in good condition — this does away with sound existing glazing, and the wooden section is seldom deep enough to rabbet out without weakening the sash or to conceal the spacer in the insulated unit. And the weight of glass will more than double.

See BALANCING HERITAGE, COMFORT AND ENERGY EFFICIENCY.

Details

❖ Make supreme efforts to maintain and preserve special forms of glazing — early irregular ("antique") glass, curved glass, leaded glass, stained glass, art glass, etched glass, moulded glass — their variety, especially around the turn of the century, was extraordinary. These are very rarely replaceable and give distinction to many buildings. Particularly vulnerable are manufactured types no longer in

Operating fabric awnings were almost universal window accoutrements early this century, and can still be useful — but care must be taken to follow traditional forms and materials, as here (top). Very eclectic façades (above) may require different conservation treatments for each window.

production and extremely difficult to repair or replicate, even in custom workshops.

❖ Be especially careful in repairing frames and sash with curved glass. If broken, replace with curved glass of same dimensions whenever possible. Consider only pre-formed polycarbonate sheet as a substitute — bent acrylic sheets are not durable, and segments of flat glass are completely unacceptable visually and functionally.

❖ Make sure that the lead cames of stained or leaded glass are sound and that any glazing putty is still flexible; remove excess, "plastered" putty. Restore missing glass only where there is good photographic evidence of its original appearance. Remove the window for any major repairs. Refer conservation of any irreplaceable historic stained or leaded glass to a specialist.

❖ Maintain and restore the use of original window hardware — sash locks, latches, sash balances, hinges, cranks and pivots. Where such hardware has gone missing, consider rearranging what survives among similar windows within the building — rehabilitate and recycle original hardware in more conspicuous locations and use new or reproduction hardware elsewhere.

❖ Replace decayed awning fabric and rehabilitate operable awnings. Never use metal or plasticized awnings as substitutes.

❖ Maintain operable exterior shutters in working order. Under no circumstances replace them with non-operable plastic or metal simulations. Restore missing shutters only on the basis of research, and then only as operable elements. If there is any doubt about the historical existence of shutters, do not put new ones on.

❖ Where they survive, retain and repair built-in interior shutters. Maintain and continue to use interior shades, blinds, draperies, as part of window operation (see FIXTURES).

For glass block and panels, see STUCCO, CONCRETE AND COMPOSITES.

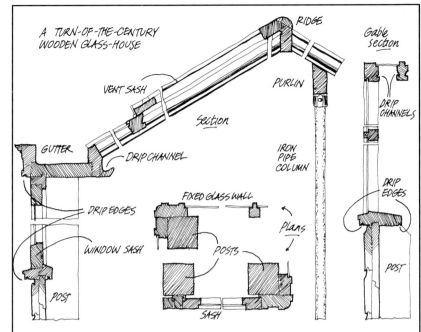

A TURN-OF-THE-CENTURY WOODEN GLASS-HOUSE

RIDGE

Gable section

VENT SASH

PURLIN

DRIP CHANNELS

Section

GUTTER

DRIP CHANNEL

IRON PIPE COLUMN

DRIP EDGES

DRIP EDGES

FIXED GLASS WALL

Plans

WINDOW SASH

POSTS

POST

POST

SASH

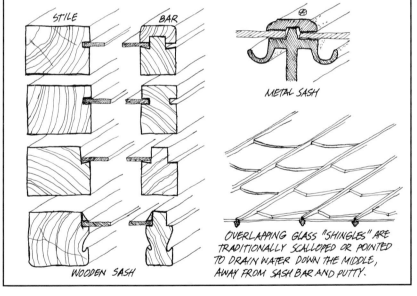

VARIETIES OF GREENHOUSE AND CONSERVATORY GLAZING BARS — OFTEN, THE GLASS SIMPLY RESTS IN THE GROOVES, FREE TO ACCOMMODATE STRUCTURAL MOVEMENT. MORE ADVANCED STRUCTURES INCORPORATE CONDENSATION CHANNELS THROUGHOUT.

STILE

BAR

METAL SASH

WOODEN SASH

OVERLAPPING GLASS "SHINGLES" ARE TRADITIONALLY SCALLOPED OR POINTED TO DRAIN WATER DOWN THE MIDDLE, AWAY FROM SASH BAR AND PUTTY.

Skylights and conservatories

High year-round humidity and thermal extremes between inside and outside can cause great stresses and deterioration in cast-iron glasshouses, and dampness and putty deterioration can afflict wood-frame structures with rot. Well-detailed glasshouses have features to drain away the inevitable condensation without damaging the structural frame, as well as ventilating louvres to prevent both heat and humidity from building up to excessive levels.

❖ Inspect glass structures regularly for signs of putty failure and paint deterioration and ensure that condensation does not accumulate as standing water anywhere in the structure. Keep the ventilation system in good repair and ensure its regular use.

❖ Assess the existing structure and glazing very carefully and repair any flaws in structure and drainage before working on glazing repairs. Where glass is laid as overlapping "shingles", its lower edges are sometimes scalloped. Maintain these, even in replacements — this elemental detail keeps water away from putty and frame.

❖ Where iron elements or structures are so badly rusted as to be irreparable, use replacement sections cast or built up in metal that match the original profiles and dimensions (concealing any structural reinforcements within hollow sections as much as possible). Provide for both ventilation and drainage following historic practice — do not rely on modern mechanical equipment.

See METALWORK and EXTERIOR WOODWORK.

Principles

1.3 Balance of use and preservation (cautious conversion)

2.5 Appropriate skills

3.5 Specifics of uniqueness (pattern, ensemble, detail)

4.2 Respect for period/historic continuity, sequence

4.4 Respect for uniqueness (pattern, ensemble, detail)

4.6 Minimal conjecture/informed invention

5.1 Priorities of features, priorities of work

5.3 Minimal alteration, minimal intrusiveness

5.6 Minimal removals

5.7 Reconstruction for wholeness

6.2 Maximum retention

6.4 Respect for craft

6.5 Safe working conditions

7.1 Traditional repair (proven technology)

7.2 Replacement in kind/ recycled materials

7.4 Cautious high-tech repair

7.6 Maintainable repairs

8.3 Complementary additions

8.4 Independent additions

8.5 Energy conservation

8.6 Aided access

9.2 Faithful maintenance

References

Most entrance and porch problems and repairs for residences involve wood; see the references in "Exterior woodwork", particularly BOWY80, CUNN84, DAVE80/86, HANS83, HOLM75, KAPL78/86, KIRK84, LOND86, MELV73, MILN79, POOR83, REMP80, STLOnd and TECH82. For examples of appropriate historic styles and patterns, see BLAK69, GREE74, MACR63, MACR75, MCAL84, TUNI86 and VICT84.

More technical background may be found in FEIL82, FROI86, INSA72, LOCK86, LOCK86a, MULL81, MUNN83, PRIN81, STAH84, TIMM76 and WOOD86. On handicapped access, see BALL83; on energy-conserving retrofits, see SEDW83.

The importance of entrances

The entrance of a building complements its windows — the "invitation" and attractiveness of the façade can be confirmed or destroyed by the way the entrance itself appears and works. Doorways set the visual, tactile and spatial "tone" for the functional relation between inside and outside. *Using* a building means going in and out of its doors constantly. Entrances establish the human scale of a building (or its lack of scale). They also establish a protocol for its use — there is always a *primary* entrance, in addition to one or many subsidiary ways in, even if the visual distinction is only ceremonial. The most elaborate historic entrances were "aedicules" — little buildings in themselves.

Porches expanded these little buildings into useful exterior spaces. Ontario's climatic extremes prompted builders to provide a shelter that not only protected an important entrance in winter but also offered a shaded platform for the enjoyment of its often sub-tropical summers. The generous porch or verandah was among the most conspicuous features of North American residential architecture in the late 19th and early 20th centuries, spanning stylistic boundaries with a profusion of forms. The grandest porches belonged to the inns of coaching and early railway travel, covering principal façades with two or even three levels of porch, accessible from every room.

Because they are close to hand and eye, finishes and details of doorways and porches are much like those of furniture — and closely related to what most people consider, whether justifiably or not, the "style" of the building. They are details more of cabinetmaker than carpenter.

Because they are so heavily used and have so many parts, entrances (like windows) require considerable maintenance to repair the damages of weathering and human wear and tear. Lack of maintenance at the entrance leads to the most obvious (though not necessarily the worst) deterioration in the building.

For the relation of entrances to the property beyond the building's walls, see SPATIAL DEFINITION AND HARD LANDSCAPING; for main-street commerce, see STOREFRONTS.

Doors and doorways

❖ As far as possible, maintain the primary entrance in its historic location in both plan (functionally) and elevation (visually) — retain the historic patterns of access and building entrances in any new use. Do not insert a *new* entrance in a front or other principal elevation. Whenever possible, satisfy code requirements for increased exit dimensions without modifying architecturally valuable doorways — use other existing access points or add new ones discreetly.

❖ Inspect and record existing entrances very carefully. Before any work — even temporary repairs — look carefully for and record archaeological traces of earlier features (colour changes, stains, nail holes, left-over paint ridges indicating historic trim, and so on).

❖ If the original or an early door survives, make very special efforts to retain and repair it. Use surviving original or early doors as models for accurate reproductions in other locations on the same building. Unfortunately, doors are often treated like furniture and are often removed. If you are fortunate enough to have an original door, or one that appears to have been in place for a long time, hang onto it.

❖ *Do not fake historic doors and details.* Do not install "period" doors emulating originals that cannot be documented from historic photographs, and most certainly none that antedates the building itself. To be considered compatible, modern complements should be similar in material, size, depth, proportion and styling and should not dominate the overall impression of the doorway or building.

❖ Retain, repair and maintain historic hardware where it survives. If hardware is missing, use complementary modern fittings or reproduction hardware that coincides with the original era of building or some later period — never an earlier period.

❖ Maintain the features comprising the door surrounds (entablatures, sidelights, fanlights, pilasters and the like). Restore missing features only with firm evidence

ENTRANCE ELEMENTS

Doorways

❒ Principal doors (single, double, solid, paneled, composite, glazed)

❒ Pilasters and engaged columns

❒ Sidelights

❒ Fanlights and transoms

❒ Pediments and entablatures

❒ Hardware (hinges, handles, locks, etc.)

❒ Storm and screen doors

Porches and verandahs

❒ Vestibules

❒ Columns and piers

❒ Railings and balustrades

❒ Floors

❒ Lighting fixtures

❒ Planters and benches

❒ Steps and ramps

(documentary, photographic and archaeological). Repair deteriorated glazing in kind. Use clear glazing and simple patterns unless there is sufficient general documentation to permit a sympathetic and artistic modern substitute that evokes the colour and pattern of the appropriate period.

❖ Do not embellish secondary entrances as if they were formerly more important by adding (fake) reproduction sidelights, fanlights, and so on.

❖ Maintain the physical integrity of historic doors. Do not bolt panic hardware, automatic closers, locks, and other such additions *through* the door — indeed, try to avoid such hardware by, for instance, using non-historic entrances and modern doors to satisfy code-related exit requirements.

❖ Storm and screen doors should be simple and compatible in colour and proportion to the main door. Follow an approach

similar to the guidelines for exterior storm windows: make a storm door a discreet complement to the existing door; make glazing and screening divisions coincide, using the same or larger rather than smaller divisions; use wooden members rather than metal where possible (though a thin-section aluminum or steel door, anodized or painted to blend in, may be a satisfactory alternative). Remove incompatible storm doors and replace them with more fitting designs. Where feasible, use an interior door to make a heat-conserving vestibule in lieu of a storm door.

❖ Maintain all doors and doorways faithfully and frequently, repairing any damage at the earliest opportunity.

See EXTERIOR WOODWORK and WINDOWS.

Porches and verandahs

❖ Inspect carefully for water-related damage, especially around posts and balustrades. Repair all structural flaws before working on details, ensuring that foundations are sound and well drained.

❖ Ensure that stone or cast-stone balustrades are well anchored. Remove all superficial

Original or early doors (far right) — even vintage screen doors (right hand door, above) — are vital to the unique character of entrances. Treating them as portable artifacts (right) simply steals from the original location to dress up another place with false antiquity.

rust and protect iron connectors and elements with suitable primer and paint. Replace any seriously corroded cast-stone connectors with non-ferrous or stainless bolts. Repair damaged units with "plastic" or dutchman inserts. Replace units only as a last resort, and then only in the original material (moulded from adjacent sound elements; see MASONRY).

❖ Renew the anchorages of cast- or wrought-iron railings in stone following historic practice (usually molten sulphur or lead in a reverse-cut cavity). As an alternative, use modern epoxy fastenings very carefully, ensuring that any expansion of the epoxy will not destroy surrounding stone.

❖ Treat wooden porch floors and other exposed woodwork with water-repellent preservatives before refinishing. Replace only irreparably rotten members — clean, sand and fill the others as necessary (see EXTERIOR WOODWORK).

❖ When considering the permanent enclosure of open porches, follow the model of the historic practice used for summer screening. Keep glazing and screening behind the perimeter columns and balustrades, use the thinnest possible framing members, and maintain the integrity of all perimeter features as both visually and structurally separate. Retain the historic "transparency" of the porch as much as possible — do not use smoked or reflective glass to enclose it.

❖ Retain and conserve upper-storey porches and balconies, even where not original, where these have become important to the historic character of the building. Ensure that they are well founded and properly fastened and flashed at walls and roofs. Make sure that the porch does not compromise the foundation and exterior of the building — provide for independent structural movements. Restore missing features only on the basis of historical photographs and archaeology.

Porches to suit their houses — from small Regency porticos, to double height porches of former inns (though the new door unfortunately violates an original window), to ornate Victorian verandahs.

Steps and ramps

❖ Make sure that the foundations of exterior steps are secure. Since they usually lack a basement beneath, steps are often vulnerable to the heaving of freezing and thawing ground. Ensure that surroundings are well drained. Exterior steps should be level, with only just enough slope to drain water away quickly. The steps should be sound, with no deep cracks or missing chips.

The design and materials of steps should complement the architecture of the building — for instance, though wood is often the traditional material for front steps of 19th-century houses, concrete is often the proper material for steps to early 20th century dwellings.

❖ In repairing stone steps, ensure that patching matches colour, texture, profile and hardness of existing steps. For small patches, use stone dust mixed into a lime-and-cement mortar and make sample mixes to test colour, curing, and ultimate strength and hardness. Let these tests stand at least several weeks and compare their hardness with that of the existing stone; the mortar must be neither harder nor softer. Use only stainless-steel reinforcing to help bond larger mortar patches. Allow sufficient curing time in moist conditions and match the final profile and surface carefully to the original (a very dilute muriatic acid solution may help harmonize the grain and surface of such repairs).

❖ For more severe damage, consider dutchman repairs or replacement of steps with stone of matching qualities (see MASONRY).

❖ Keep wooden steps well maintained. Replace rotten or heavily worn steps in kind. Renew the paint on wooden steps more frequently than on decorative ornament or walls but do not let layers of paint build up so much on top that deterioration from below is masked or even aided (see EXTERIOR WOODWORK).

❖ Where there is or will be elevator access within a building, plan handicapped-access ramping to descend into the building rather than rise to it, adding a second principal entrance while preserving the original entrance (see PROGRAMMING AND USING SPACE).

❖ Where new raised ramps prove necessary, use forms and materials similar to or sympathetic with those of the building. New work should defer visually to what exists. Ramps should seem "light" in mass, proportion and detail — they should not (and need not) obscure significant views and elevations. In planning spaces and access, consider the ramp entrance as a second principal, not second-*class*, entrance but do not compromise the integrity of the historic entrance (see SPATIAL DEFINITION AND HARD LANDSCAPING).

❖ Do not use corrosive de-icing agents on any exterior steps or ramps — especially not sodium chloride (see TAKING CARE).

References

Storefront conservation requires first of all an appreciation of context and planning; see BROW80, CAPP86, CUMI85, DUTO85, EDWA46, FACA87/87a, FLEM82, HOLD85, JOHN84, NATI80, REAL81, RESE85, THUR83, WARN78, WILL78 and WORS69.

For materials and details, see references in other *Exterior features*, but especially GAYL80, MEAD86, NIBS80, SHOP86 and TECH82. Helpful older texts include MACE98 and RADF83.

See also GREE74, LONG87 and STEN81 for background on storefront forms.

Display and the street

Storefronts are rather peculiar architectural assemblages, standing (physically, and in time) between the rapidly changing commercial displays inside and the usually very stable historic main-street façades above. Conservation of historic storefronts must be considered within constantly altering contexts: the store and its stock change, neighbouring stores change, the community changes. Co-ordination of old and new is thus a constant preoccupation. It is often difficult to balance the rapidly changing cycles of retail style and the architectural heritage of the building. The challenge is to maintain the continuity of main-street change over time, to recognize and respect changes and contrasts between façade and storefront.

Having begun as the front parlours of merchants' houses, storefronts took their modern form as soon as their proprietors were able to afford large glass display windows. The multi-paned cylinder-glass windows of Georgian storefronts gave way to large Victorian plate-glass fronts in the 1840s and 1850s. The display window dominated the ground floor. The shop entrance lay in a deep, narrow passage in the centre or to the side, and the doorway to the upper storeys was also pushed to one side. The window became a deep space within the shop, almost a separate room. This basic organization has persisted, with some changes in location and depth of doorways and in the frames for glass and surrounding panels.

Storefront architecture must make a strong impression for its retail space, with little regard for, often in spite of, the rest of the building. For historic storefronts, visual contrast has been the rule much of the time. To attract the eye, the large glass display windows and their slender pillars contrasted with the masonry and ornament of the façade above. The floor of the entrance contrasted in colour and material with the sidewalk. The large and vivid signs contrasted in scale and colour with their sedate architectural frames. But as hard as it tried, the storefront was always subordinate to the larger frame of the entire façade. The plane of the façade defined quite clearly the line between public and commercial territory. Even the most garish signage sat in frames within the façade or

hung discreetly at its edges. And even the generous canvas awnings withdrew into a pocket within the front of the building itself.

Just like the entrances of other buildings, storefronts require considerable maintenance because of constant heavy use. They are vulnerable to human wear and tear, to the weather, and of course to constant and often arbitrary changes in retail functions and fashions. The details of storefronts are furniture-like, but not domestic — they are closely related to what most people consider to be the "style" of the shop and of shopping, not of the larger building.

It is vital to distinguish, both historically and currently, between the more or less permanent architecture of the storefront as part of the overall façade and the changeable displays *within* the storefront. It is absolutely essential to maintain these in balance so that changing retail fashion does not destroy the heritage value of the architecture above and adjacent.

❖ Where an existing storefront is physically sound and compatible with overall building façade through its design, details and proportions — even though of a different "period", subsequent to the original building — maintain and repair it rather than replace it. Maintain the generally characteristic containment of the storefront by the façade by removing additions attached in front of or outside this "frame" (including fluorescent sign boxes along the fascia), unless these are actual originals or restorations based on early historic photographs.

❖ Where an existing storefront does not fit with the historic character of the building, consider replacing it by revealing the earlier front beneath (if recoverable), by installing a more fitting modern design, or by restoring (with proper research and documentation) an authentic earlier appearance. Consider any storefront replaceable that covers over historic material with bland or poorly fitting materials and features of no intrinsic merit, or that encroaches into the street beyond the historic edges of the building, or that is profoundly dissonant when seen in context with its neighbours, so long as the overall façade is not damaged or devalued.

See CAPP86, HOLD85 and FLEM82 for more discussion about the matter of respect for historic façades in commercial areas in the course of changing retail fashions. See LONG87 for a unique guide to the historic variety of main-street building forms that frame storefronts.

So long as the many changes in store fashion are contained within the storefront, the upper storeys of a commercial block can be maintained and conserved (though this one, below, has lost a cornice). Covering historic façades merely to contain store signs mocks the neighbouring buildings and makes the street as a whole much less attractive (bottom).

❖ Where the physical condition of a storefront (either existing or concealed) is too poor to repair without massive replacement and where it is considered appropriate to recover a genuine earlier appearance, restore that appearance using existing materials, building archaeology and archival photographs, with as little conjecture as possible. Use firm evidence to reproduce an earlier front rather than conjectural evidence about the actual original. Use surviving materials as models for colour and detail, reproducing in kind as much as possible.

❖ Keep the established store *front* distinguishable from the changing store *display.*

❖ *Do not falsify history.* Do not give a storefront a "period" look antedating the era, status and locale of the original building — no American Colonial coach lamps, for instance. Do not put a Georgian front on a Victorian building, nor a Victorian front on an Art Deco building. But maintain fitting historic "modernizations" where they enhance the building and street (see above). Use historic photographs and building archaeology as guidance for any modification or reproduction to an earlier appearance.

See VISUAL APPROACHES AND RESULTS.

Façade/storefront/sign

❖ Inspect very carefully for finishes and materials hidden behind existing storefronts. Assess likely damage to concealed surfaces: holes for nails and bolts, missing projecting elements such as cornices and pilasters, and so on. Assess as well the historic, aesthetic and functional merits of the existing front before considering re-exposing concealed fronts (there may be more than one).

❖ Use historic photographs to establish the styles and types of sign appropriate to a building within its district during the era of its construction and early life and use these as models for contemporary signs. New signs may be far more adventurous and bold than modern false-historic modesty may consider appropriate yet remain architecturally compatible if they are based on evident local historic practices and fitting modern designs.

❖ Do not automatically remove all projecting signs, as often mandated in commercial area improvements. Determine if they are themselves important historic and character-defining features of intrinsic value and rarity that should be repaired and maintained. Evaluate such signs with the same criteria as those for non-original storefronts that may deserve retention and repair (see above). Pay particular attention to retaining early non-standardized, non-illuminated or neon-tube signs unique to that building or street.

❖ Ensure that fixtures and fastenings of projecting signs are well anchored and are not causing deterioration of the masonry or woodwork of the façade.

❖ Do not use back-lit fluorescent sign boxes against the fascia and remove them during major repairs. Apart from their poor fit with the façade — they project beyond the historic "frame" — they are seldom if ever properly flashed to prevent water penetration and lead to material deterioration behind. Consider their continued use only if boxes and fittings can be recessed into the fascia without damage to the historic structure.

❖ Retain, repair and maintain operable canvas awnings where they survive and

consider restoring missing operable awnings in appropriate locations where there is evidence for their earlier existence. Awnings reduce summer heat gain tremendously and provide shelter from rain. Keep awnings and mechanisms in good repair, replace fabric when it begins to deteriorate. Do not use fixed canvas, plastic or metal canopies as substitutes.

❖ Follow historic practices in lighting storefronts and upper façades. Illuminate buildings in colours and patterns that bring out the essential forms and profiles visible in daylight. Use incandescent or similar light sources to render accurately building and material colours. Use front-illuminated signs.

See PAINT, COLOUR AND LIGHT.

Windows, doors and details

Despite the many changes in storefront fashion, there has been remarkable continuity in storefront features. The major element has always been glass — though each era may have framed the glass differently, the recessed entrance allowing the display apparently to "project" has remained the basic configuration for a century and a half.

❖ Maintain the distinctive setbacks, recesses, framing structure, materials and details of storefront glazing in repairs or replacements.

❖ Maintain the proportions of glass to solid characteristic of the historic storefront. Do not brick in or block up portions of windows or replace large panes of glass with false "period" subdivisions. Maintain glazed transoms above the entrance doors. Conceal air conditioners in sleeve units in panelled areas rather than obstruct glazing (better still, move the unit to the rear of the store).

❖ Clean, restore and maintain any painted-over non-ferrous metal surfaces. Pay particular attention to conservation of copper and bronze frames — clean carefully, making sure to correct any structural problems. Make any necessary reinforcements as discreet as possible.

❖ Conserve energy in existing storefronts by glazing the rear of the display area defined

(opposite)
Traditional main-street details still attractive and useful for shoppers and residents: the retractable awning (top); the double-glazed display window that helps insulate the interior of the store (middle); the front-lit sign over a double-height deep-bay window to display goods and let both daylight and artificial light reach the interior (bottom left); and doorways to upper-storey residences or offices that maintain the style and detail of the whole (bottom right).

(right)
A false "period" look is out of place when it confuses what is genuinely historic about the building (top). Some renewed storefronts co-exist peacefully with the older façade above by respecting general symmetry and proportion (upper middle), but others collide badly (lower middle). Sometimes the traces of earlier historic elements show through, awaiting recovery (bottom).

by the window and entrance recess or by using blinds or curtains to separate the display area as an intermediate thermal buffer. Just as for any other type of window, effect the greatest savings by simple caulking and weatherstripping.

❖ Avoid stock modern replacement doors and hardware; recycle or reproduce existing features when upgrading doors to modern requirements.

See EXTERIOR WOODWORK, METALWORK, WINDOWS, and ENTRANCES.

Panels and paving

❖ When attempting to recover earlier hidden finishes, remove existing materials very carefully to avoid worsening the damage to hidden surfaces.

❖ In making repairs, use substitute materials discreetly; consider rearranging panels of irreproducible materials such as "structural" glass to maintain its continuity in conspicuous locations, especially near and below eye level.

❖ Protect and maintain ornamental paving: terrazzo, brass inlays, contrasting tile, concrete, asphalt or brick patterns. These sometimes contain names or symbols of earlier shops. Maintain glass-block paving where it survives, within the storefront or beneath the sidewalk in front.

❖ Maintain sidewalk hoists in good repair. If a hoist is not used often, test its operation regularly.

❖ If it is necessary to install a unit air conditioner in a panelled area, conserve and store the removed panels for future re-use. Make vents and drainage for the unit discreet. Do not let condensate from the unit drain across paving.

See SPATIAL DEFINITION AND HARD LANDSCAPING, and STUCCO, CONCRETE AND COMPOSITES.

References

Since paint must be renewed periodically, there are many references on cleaning, preparation and applying new paint; see READ82, SHAK85, CUNN84, FERG86, KAPL78/86, KIRK84, LANG78, LYNC82, OLDH85, POOR83, SHOP86, TECH82 and VILA81.

Good conservation practice requires careful analysis of what exists — its chemistry, physics and colour — and involves more specialized technical aid. Such specialized problems are covered in JAND83, CHAM76, DAVE80/86, FEIL82, HUGH86, JOHN84, SCHO85, STAH84, TIMM76 and WRIG86.

On historic and contemporary approaches to colour, see LENC82, PRIZ75, MOSS87, POMA87, MILL71, ONEI71, PARR85 and PORT82. For guidance on paint sampling, and on matching colour and chemistry, see KITC83, MILL77 and FEIL82. For help on preparation and repainting for conservation projects, see OLDH85, POOR83 and DAVE80/86.

There are few published sources for exterior lighting; see FLEM82 and JAND83.

The mechanics of exterior paint

Until the late 19th century, the most common exterior paint was whitewash, a mixture of lime and water with some linseed oil mixed in for good measure. Though many different vehicles and binders were used for indoor painting (casein, tempera, and so on), few of these were durable or inexpensive enough for exterior use. Coloured pigments in linseed oil were expensive and used only on the buildings of the wealthy. Stucco was coloured with pigment laid into the finish coat; woodwork was most commonly stained and varnished, or whitewashed. Mixing paints was itself a skilled trade. Pre-mixed oil-based exterior paints as we know them today did not become widely available until the 1870s.

Exterior paint must be renewed regularly. Even in the 19th century, the recognized life of an exterior linseed-oil-based paint was 5 to 15 years. Whitewashing was an *annual* job. Accordingly, many historic surfaces, where not stripped to their base material, may retain traces of a dozen or more applications of paint, two or three coats for each application. Some exterior surfaces were painted with sand mixed in for a roughened, stone-like texture. The profusion of exterior colours we now associate with the 19th century did not appear until the broad distribution of paint manufacturers' catalogues late in the century.

A well-formulated exterior paint (historic or modern) deteriorates very slowly from the effects of weathering, but much more rapidly from moisture penetrating and compromising its bond with previous layers or with its base material. Paint is flexible and forgiving, to a point. It may blister, check, craze, crack, peel, alligator or simply fall off a deteriorated surface. Indeed, paint deterioration is a very useful symptom of worse problems beneath.

Modern pigments tend to be more stable than historic colours. Modern alkyd (resin) and latex vehicles tend to show brush marks less than do oil-based paints. On the other hand, latex emulsions bond poorly to historic paints unless very well primed and they still do not cover as well as alkyds or oils. Generally, alkyd or old-fashioned linseed-oil paints provide more covering power and a more durable finish for old-building work than do latex paints. Some people believe that oil paint has a depth of colour subtly different from

latex that is more appropriate to historic settings.

Regular repainting should destroy as little as possible of what lies beneath; ideally, it should physically erode or be sanded down at each renewal only as much as needed to prevent excessive build-up.

❖ Do no cleaning or repainting until samples of paint are taken from all exterior surfaces. Save, catalogue and analyze samples for colour and, if necessary, paint chemistry. Catalogue samples fully and accurately, keying locations to photographs and drawings. Store paint samples along with project records for future reference.

❖ Take paint samples from many places, even on what appears to be the same surface, and especially on any raised or embossed surfaces — these are likely to have had accents of several colours at one time or another.

❖ Take paint samples both as chips of peeled or broken paint and as feathered or sanded patches that indicate the layering of colours over time.

❖ Paint all surfaces that were historically painted. Do not strip previously painted wood to its base and varnish or seal it to appear unpainted — this is historically inauthentic, and exterior varnish will break down under ultraviolet light and expose the wood to atmospheric damage unless regularly renewed (and it must be renewed more frequently than paint).

Though this paint has clearly "failed", its underlying woodwork shows no decay.

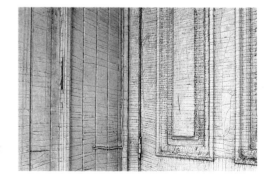

Detailed ornament cannot accept many coats of paint before it loses its focus and texture. Preparing it for fresh paint must be a very careful job (top and above). Sometimes (in this case because of an unfortunate demolition), long-obscured painted signs are revealed, and these deserve protection as virtual archaeological resources (above right).

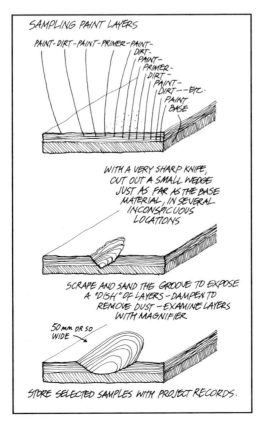

SAMPLING PAINT LAYERS

PAINT-DIRT-PAINT-PRIMER-PAINT-
DIRT-
PAINT-
PRIMER-
DIRT-
PAINT-
DIRT---ETC.
PAINT
BASE

WITH A VERY SHARP KNIFE, CUT OUT A SMALL WEDGE JUST AS FAR AS THE BASE MATERIAL, IN SEVERAL INCONSPICUOUS LOCATIONS

SCRAPE AND SAND THE GROOVE TO EXPOSE A "DISH" OF LAYERS - DAMPEN TO REMOVE DUST - EXAMINE LAYERS WITH MAGNIFIER

50 mm OR SO WIDE

STORE SELECTED SAMPLES WITH PROJECT RECORDS.

Cleaning and preparation

There are many guides to proper exterior painting practice; the notes below refer specifically to repainting conserved elements.

❖ Complete all basic repairs and replacements and remove surface dust and grime, before preparing, priming and painting. Be sure that surfaces to be painted are *dry*. The best times for exterior painting are spring and fall.

❖ Scrape and sand painted surfaces only as deep as necessary to reach a sound base, whether previous paint or base material. Do not strip *all* previous paint except to repair base-material decay, to restore operation of a movable feature (for instance, window sash), or to reveal the profile and modelling of details obscured by paint build-up. Once they are exposed, prime all unfinished wood surfaces, taking special care to mask knots.

❖ Take appropriate safety precautions when removing lead-based paint: wear a face mask and coveralls and dispose of the very poisonous residues carefully.

❖ Use an air gun or electric heat plate to help remove paint rather than a blowtorch, which may ignite trapped dust or the wood beneath the paint or release toxic fumes from lead-based paint.

❖ Clean and sand all surfaces and completely remove residues of any sanding, brick or mortar dust, and cleaning chemicals. Sanding alone will not remove mildew or mould — use a proper fungicide.

❖ Choose the appropriate primer to bind finish coats of paint to base material; there are different primers for metal, wood and masonry. Consult paint manufacturers' technical specifications to be sure of the right choice.

❖ As much as possible use, oil or alkyd exterior primers and paints over existing paints, which are likely to be oil-based themselves (unless quite recent). If using latex, cover the previous oil paint with an oil-based primer; even a latex primer will not bond well to oil enamel. Always sand between coats of primer and finish paint.

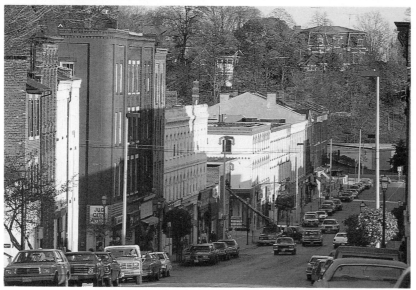

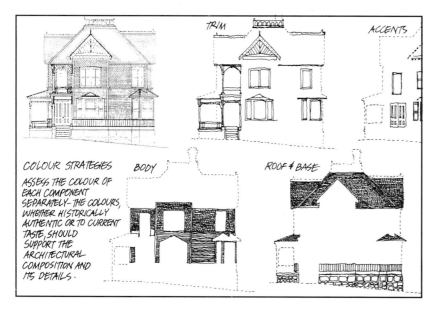

COLOUR STRATEGIES

ASSESS THE COLOUR OF
EACH COMPONENT
SEPARATELY- THE COLOURS,
WHETHER HISTORICALLY
AUTHENTIC OR TO CURRENT
TASTE, SHOULD
SUPPORT THE
ARCHITECTURAL
COMPOSITION AND
ITS DETAILS.

TRIM   ACCENTS

BODY   ROOF & BASE

The right colours

❖ In matching historic colours, consider above all the very changeable quality of daylight; its colour temperature (visual coolness or warmth) varies during the day and during the year. As much as possible, assess and compare colours under a variety of lighting conditions, especially those that affect the building itself.

❖ When judging historic colours from paint samples, do not confuse primer and finish colours. A high-powered magnifier or low-powered microscope should reveal traces of dust on the exterior surface of the actual finish colour.

❖ Since many pigments oxidize and fade with time and with varying exposure to light, start to determine historic colours from samples taken where sunlight does not reach or from the underside of a colour layer (viewed under the microscope). The oil vehicle holding the pigment will yellow in darkened areas, including those covered by subsequent layers of paint. Historic colours may not be as yellow as they would first appear from such samples. A paint sample with a pale blue surface and a deep green interior may well have been deep blue originally. And in historic practice, pigments were not ground as finely as they are today, so that old painted surfaces may seem to have a somewhat different visual depth than those painted recently. When in doubt, consult a conservation expert familiar with the chemical and physical aging of paint.

❖ When matching historic and contemporary colours, use dry samples with similar finish; the colour of paint in the tin will be quite different from its finished appearance (matte, gloss, or in between). Even if periodically cleaned, and apart from their photochemical fading, all colours will soften with dust.

❖ Do not be slavish about matching the original colour, but do pick a colour appropriate to the era and style(s) of the building. Paint is as much a maintenance item as a permanent feature; every cleaning operation will reveal many layers of paint, often of different colours to suit the changing moods of the owner.

The wall mural is becoming popular as a focus of community activity and pride (and occasionally reviving as an advertising medium). It can coexist with historic architecture if care is taken not to conflict with the form and details of the building. Side walls are thus far more suitable for artwork than principal façades.

Few original exterior lighting standards or fixtures survive — in recreating their presence, it is important to base replicas on those used formerly in the given community, not on generic models (right). Rather than using the now virtually universal backlit fluorescent boxes, historic building fronts and signs should be illuminated from in front and above, following historic precedents (bottom).

(opposite)
Colours vary in appearance by time of day and time of year — selecting or matching old and new must involve careful understanding of the colour and quality of light, both natural and artificial.

❖ Select colours from a spectrum appropriate to the neighbourhood and period; if the original woodwork was painted a horribly murky maroon that you desperately don't want, choose another dark colour of that period, perhaps one that a neighbour might have used — but refer to local historical and archaeological evidence for the choice.

❖ For most mid- to late-19th-century buildings, follow the general Victorian colour strategy of reinforcing the effects of projecting and receding planes; use darker colours for doors and window sash than for their surrounding frames, to emphasize openings receding into the façade.

❖ Use a matte or dull finish on painted metal surfaces to make them appear solid; the play of light on inevitably irregular gloss finish weakens their visual presence.

Exterior lighting

❖ Maintain historic lamp standards and lighting fixtures where they survive; consider reproducing missing lamp standards from historical photographs and documents. Though there are numerous cast-aluminum reproductions of cast-iron originals available, use only those that match closely the size and proportions of surviving originals or as shown in documentary sources. Paint lamp standards to match original colours, based on paint samples from the existing or a nearby standard.

❖ Use incandescent luminaires to correspond to historic colours of light.

❖ When floodlighting or illuminating buildings, ensure that wiring and lighting are fastened to the building in a manner that will not cause deterioration of masonry or woodwork and will not create combustible conditions.

❖ Illuminate buildings in colours and patterns that bring out the essential forms and profiles visible in daylight. Use incandescent or similar light sources to render accurately building and material colours. Use front-illuminated signs.

Principles

References

For general matters of planning interior spaces in existing buildings, see AUST88, NATI80, STAH84, WARN78 and WILL78. For background on appreciating existing spatial character and detail, see ICOM86, KIRK84, LAND82, MILL87, OLDH85, POOR83, RADF83, SEAL79, THOR84 and VICT84.

Technical aspects of repairs and replacements are covered in references to other topics in *Interior features*, but in general see CHAM76, DAVE80/86, FEIL82, FINE86, HANS83, OLDH85, POOR83, SAND84, STAH84, TECH82 and VILA81. Matters of handicapped accessibility are dealt with in BALL83, and fire safety in NIBS80 and PARNnd.

For descriptions and availability of legal regulations, see Appendix 5, "Codes and regulations for conservation work in Ontario".

The life of interiors

Interior spaces must change to meet new problems and requirements much more frequently than exteriors. Interiors are subjected rarely to the corrosive weathering endured by exterior surfaces but often to the perhaps more severe effects of human use and abuse. Interior features may have survived virtually unchanged for a century or more — or radically altered every decade.

The general public rarely sees private interiors, so that the public interest in conserving interior architecture is less compelling than for exteriors. But many important public or publicly accessible spaces demand attention and conservation. Just as there is a growing taste for the "antique" in furniture and domestic artifacts, so there is growing interest in conserving interiors of genuine heritage value, beyond the more typical restorations of dubious authenticity.

Interiors vary even more than exteriors, though most spaces are domestic in character and small in scale. Large factory spaces are wide open and undefined; highly specialized interiors such as theatres are very clearly laid out and walled in. Each type requires a different approach to understanding and preserving its character, and each demands a different approach to new insertions.

Consequently, there is a much wider range of possibilities for architectural conservation of interior spaces than for building exteriors. This range covers radical alteration and reverential restoration, and all points in between, none of which can be automatically ruled out in planning the conservation of specific spaces. Much depends on what may have survived from the original or early period of the building. Rooms and spaces may be unaltered in both layout and surface treatment. Or the layout may survive with mildly or greatly altered finishes. Or all permanent traces of earlier occupants may have disappeared, except for some ghostly outlines of vanished partitions or plasterwork.

The conservation principles are clear in calling for maximal retention of the valuable material that still exists from the past, but new requirements for habitability and function may require some difficult choices and compromises. Good conservation practice must tilt the balance in favour of preservation by insisting on and capitalizing on the flexibility and adaptability of users and functions rather than by making the building "flex" to suit an arbitrary standard.

New-building codes and old-building heritage

Literal interpretation of codes for new construction can have devastating effects on existing buildings — nowhere more drastically than in planning and finishing of their interiors. Building officials have some discretion in interpreting code requirements, and many are prepared to consider means of satisfying safety requirements other than the standard approaches required by the Ontario Building Code or the Ontario Fire Code retrofit regulations. The scope for that discretion is partly built into those documents. The Building Code permits many compliance alternatives for residential occupancies in existing buildings, as well as a process for approving other alternative measures case by case. Compliance alternatives for other occupancies have been under study since 1985, and special cases have been allowed. The Fire Code permits alternatives to the standard requirements on the basis of a qualified life safety study and the discretion of the local fire official.

Specialized professionals in fire safety and code interpretation can help develop strategies to accommodate the safe performance required by the codes in ways that will minimize disruption of the historic and architectural value of a building's spaces and circulation routes. The advice that follows is meant to provide the foundation for such strategies so as to maximize conservation of what deserves to be retained. Achievement of those strategies will necessarily be the subject of negotiations and of experts — and certainly the subject of another book altogether.

(opposite)
The qualities of light, view and detail in interiors are well worth preserving in order to enhance existing or new uses (top, middle). Even some of the properties of plain surfaces such as plaster, here unfortunately removed (bottom), cannot be reproduced.

Conserving interior character

❖ Assess and record existing floor plan(s) before making any decisions about arrangement or rearrangement of uses in rooms. Do not alter or demolish defining walls and partitions of any notable spaces.

❖ Assign priorities of value to individual spaces — those to be preserved as is or faithfully restored, those that can be altered with respect, those that can be altered radically, and those that can be treated as completely new work. Follow these priorities rigorously, especially in using existing spaces for new uses.

❖ Pay careful attention to *all* the characteristics of interior spaces and their points of access — structure, dimensions, surface materials and textures, lighting, acoustics, ventilation, and relation to adjacent spaces (see INSPECTION). Use these attributes as guides for improving the qualities of existing and new uses.

❖ Do not puncture or alter floors, ceilings or walls that define important and highly visible rooms and spaces, unless every alternative has been thoroughly evaluated.

❖ Maintain ceiling heights and surfaces as much as possible. Do not lower ceilings in any important space or room: as much as possible try to avoid doing so even in less important spaces. Preserve ornamented ceilings in the course of conservation. Remove discordant fixtures that impinge on or cut through historic surfaces and make good the damage.

❖ Retain or re-establish the historic conditions of daylighting in any conserved interior space. Wherever possible, unblock obscured windows, clerestories or skylights; use traditional means such as operable blinds, shutters and curtains to control the light.

❖ Whenever possible, do not remove interior finishes and features; cover them over if need be (with readily removable materials) but add or leave alone rather than subtract any sound and stable material.

❖ If finishes and features must be removed, record fully all removals, especially hidden finishes when they are exposed. Treat such removals with the same respect accorded

When conservation work involves major disruptions of interior spaces — in this case the excavation of a new basement — it is vital to protect finishes from damage with interior "hoarding" (above and right).

archaeological sites — note the layering of wallpapers and paints and signs of previously covered-over ornamentation (see INTERIOR FINISHES).

❖ Keep the building secure from unauthorized visitors before and during all interior work. The popularity and recyclability of interior trim and fixtures make them vulnerable to vandalism and theft. If temporarily removing any features for safe storage, record their location first, keep a complete inventory of features in storage, and assign custodial responsibility for their safety and return.

❖ Where distinctive interior spaces have been subdivided previously in a nondescript or even damaging manner but retain comprehensible traces of their former ornament and scale, remove the subdivisions and re-establish the whole. Remove partitions, dropped ceilings and intrusive fixtures that distort the space or butt into earlier decorative details.

❖ Do not obscure historic interior elements and finishes with heavy furniture or new partitions — indeed, wherever possible arrange furnishings in ways that respect historic traffic patterns and formal symmetries or asymmetries of the space.

Stairways and their vertical spaces are often the most exciting interior spaces, whether in a power plant or a house, though new-building codes sometimes make them difficult to retain.

Circulation and access

❖ Maintain historic sequences and patterns of access and circulation. Restore the use of any blocked passageways where these can serve the rehabilitated or new use of the building. Do not relocate important historic entrances and hallways.

❖ Do not remove or relocate interior doors and doorways, even if they are no longer to be used. Lock them and leave them undisturbed.

❖ Do not cut new doorways into existing walls when an existing doorway can be adapted for the purpose. Make new doorways simple and unobtrusive: locate them in logical relationship to existing openings and symmetries, and detail them using the proportions and spirit of historic openings, without attempting slavishly precise replication.

❖ Make any necessary code-mandated safety additions discrete and removable; do not damage historic materials. Added fire doors in corridors should be glazed as much as possible or installed as normally opened with alarm-actuated automatic closers. Emergency-exit signs should be as small as possible and mounted so as to cause as little damage to historic surfaces as possible.

See PROGRAMMING AND USING SPACE.

Lightwells are not common features in historic residences, and are thus especially valuable (below); here, fire codes required that a glazed barrier be installed. It is even more rare that vintage elevator cabs survive (indeed, this one exists only because it was out of use for 50 years). Documentary or physical evidence may provide enough information to enable restoration of their finishes and materials while accommodating modern operating standards.

Stairs

❖ Retain stairways in their historic locations and maintain their use in the building's circulation system. Enclose open stairways only where there is no alternative means of complying with current building regulations; make such enclosures as visually open as possible to retain at least an impression of their historic context.

❖ Assure the structural integrity of all staircases before undertaking finishing work. Reinforce the capacity of the stair if required by changes in use but in such a way that they do not damage historic materials and finishes; they should be adjustable and reversible.

❖ Tighten any rods and bolts that hold the staircase structure and balustrade together. Make no repairs that will block future accessibility to such adjustments.

❖ Reverse and reinstall wooden or marble treads only when they are *excessively* worn; leave such signs of age and use so long as they pose no hazard.

❖ Maintain the proportions, dimensions, and direction(s) — straight, angled, curved, switchback — of stairways requiring reconstruction or major repairs.

Elevators

Early elevator cabs in many office blocks and public buildings were splendid wood and metal extravagances in classical or modernistic styles. Renovations to accommodate increasingly strict operational standards have left very few cabs with their historic materials, finishes and colours intact. Where early designs and finishes remain, take every possible action to retain and restore their historic character. Where historic photographs and drawings survive, consider restoring elevator interiors to their original appearance in any upgrading of their function.

Woodwork and plaster

References

The most careful and exhaustive of the careful texts for interior woodwork repair is DAVE80/86. Good backups are KAPL86 and POOR83. LITC82 and LITC83 are useful for technique, but suggest some things that are not good conservation in general — use with caution. For plaster, STAG76 is by far the most encyclopaedic guide, for both traditional and modern plasterwork and framing. ASHU83 covers earlier traditional practice and formulas briefly but comprehensively. FEIL82 covers the tricky removal repair and re-erection of decorative plaster. KAPL78/86 and POOR83 deal well with do-it-yourself domestic work. See CHAM76 and SAND84 regarding maintenance.

Older texts are quite useful for fastening details of both wood and plaster; see MACE98, RADF83 and VICT84.

See also FINE86, JOHN83, KIRK84, LAND82, OLDH85, PRIN81, REMP80, SEAL79, SHOP86, STAH84, THOR84, TIMM76 and VILA81.

Craft and style

The character of interior spaces lies in the colour, texture and modulation of their fixed surfaces of wood and plaster no less than their changing furnishings and artifacts. Both wood and plaster are readily workable materials and display the skill of the hands (and sometimes machines) that made them and the stylistic preferences of their periods. These factors, along with their proximity to hand and eye, make them vulnerable to use and abuse as well as periodic modernization. Because they can be reproduced with considerable fidelity to historic originals, new reproductions must be faithful to true originals distinctive to the building, locale and period.

Historic interior trim has both functional and aesthetic attributes. Mouldings and applied ornaments physically conceal imperfections and gaps in surfaces and joints, sometimes even hiding the edges of "secret" operable panels or doors. They also distract the eye from imperfections that cannot be concealed, an important role both functionally and aesthetically. Chair rails and wainscots protect brittle plaster from impacts; picture rails permit hanging of decorations without constant damage from nails and picture hooks. Cornices and friezes alter the impression of height or lack of height in rooms of awkward proportions; they may even conceal or enhance artificial lighting.

Window and door frames cover the awkward construction — and the occasional adjustment or reconstruction — of the actual opening. They also add visual interest and style to the ceremony of entering and leaving. Most historic interior trim has been painted, sometimes with grained or marbled surfaces to conceal its more humble insides — both wood and plaster can be made to produce similar three-dimensional effects and are often used together beneath the paint.

Wooden and plaster trim of particular size and profile makes an aesthetic "bridge" to details of furnishings — light, classically proportioned Georgian furniture fits more assuredly with the interior spaces of its own time than with the heavier shapes and styles of High Victorian eclecticism. Furniture of some periods can fit into rooms of other periods, but some matches of furniture and architecture are more successful than others.

Interior woodwork is vulnerable to fungus, insects and damp, especially where it is adjacent to hidden moist conditions. In extreme cases of wood rot or decay, the accumulation of painted surface may be the only thing holding the element together. Plasterwork is also a victim of moist conditions — it may break down directly or lose its grip on its backing lath, and the wooden lath itself may fall victim to structural movements or its own decay.

Woodwork repair and replacement

Much of the advice about exterior woodwork applies equally to interiors. The agents of wood decay are not so aggressive inside, though interior woodwork may be attacked by dampness, insects and rot through the structure behind and may suffer impact damage and general wear and tear from the exposed (human) side as well.

❖ Inspect carefully for any signs of wood deterioration from insect or fungus infestation before beginning interior woodwork repairs. Check for hidden damage by knocking on apparently sound wooden surfaces to determine their solidity. Cure the source of any infestation and replace any infested wood.

❖ Make all required structural repairs and correct damp conditions before beginning work on interior wood trim. Reinforce any sagging wooden flooring by strengthening joists and inserting shims where floorboards no longer bear on a joist.

❖ Store all new wood for interior work inside the building in conditions of similar moisture and temperature (out of harm's way) long enough to stabilize its dimensions. Don't fix *any* new wood into permanent position until it has "seasoned", for several weeks at least.

❖ Remove damaged trim for repairs (or to permit structural or plaster work) only when necessary. Pry moulding or casing very gently from its backing, doing as little damage as possible to adjacent plaster or woodwork. Use cardboard or wooden wedges and blocks as cushions and pry the trim off a bit at a time rather than all at once.

Well crafted woodwork and plaster complement each other, with motifs that even follow through to the tile floor.

❖ Use dovetails, tenons, dowels, splines and other wood-to-wood joints in keying new wood to old, rather than (or in addition to) metal fasteners. Do not glue woodwork to other finishes. Keep any epoxy or filler repairs from adhering to other surfaces.

❖ Replace severely damaged trim with wood of the same species, cut and section. Replace simple mouldings in one piece; build up complicated sections from two or more simpler sections. Do not use plastic or metal replicas of wooden moulding.

❖ Do not replace missing trim with mouldings out of character or style with the style(s) of the building. Use fine-quality millwork to fill in for missing trim of that character, rougher sections to suit a less refined context, and so on.

See SUPERSTRUCTURE and EXTERIOR WOODWORK.

Plaster and lath

Plaster at its most basic is simply powdered lime or gypsum, mixed in water and normally applied to a supporting lath — traditionally a series of wooden strips fastened to wall studs or ceiling joists; more recently a heavy-duty metal mesh. Its base coat, traditionally reinforced with binders such as animal hair and inert aggregates such as sand, pushes through and "keys" to the lath. A second coat of similar constitution, keyed in turn to the roughened or scratched surface of the base, straightens out any obvious irregularities. The third coat, its surface whitened and smoothed (in traditional practice with added lime), provides a relatively soft but sound base for paint or wallcoverings. Historic lime-based plaster tends to be softer and more porous than modern gypsum-based plaster, Though the two can and do bond to each other reasonably well under dry and stable conditions, dampness will bring out their different rates of absorption and expansion or shrinkage, creating stresses and cracks, even disintegration.

Drywall (plasterboard, sheetrock, gypsum board, Gyproc, etc.), a hard plaster board with a paper surface, has now supplanted most wet-plaster work, either as a surface for direct finish or as a substitute for the base coats and lath beneath a more traditional finish coat. Traditional plaster on lath is usually thicker

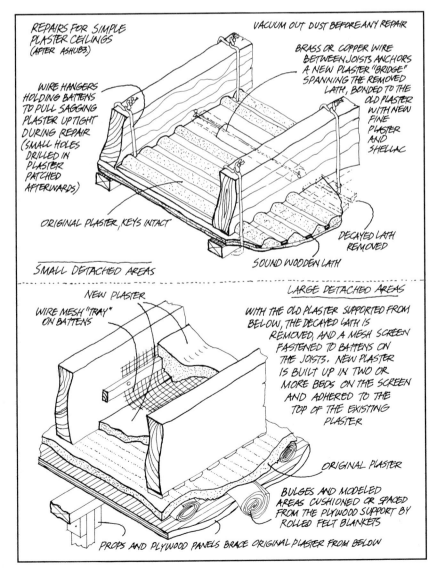

REPAIRS FOR SIMPLE PLASTER CEILINGS (AFTER ASHURB.)

VACUUM OUT DUST BEFORE ANY REPAIR

BRASS OR COPPER WIRE BETWEEN JOISTS ANCHORS A NEW PLASTER "BRIDGE" SPANNING THE REMOVED LATH, BONDED TO THE OLD PLASTER WITH NEW FINE PLASTER AND SHELLAC

WIRE HANGERS HOLDING BATTENS TO PULL SAGGING PLASTER UPTIGHT DURING REPAIR (SMALL HOLES DRILLED IN PLASTER PATCHED AFTERWARDS)

ORIGINAL PLASTER, KEYS INTACT

DECAYED LATH REMOVED

SOUND WOODEN LATH

SMALL DETACHED AREAS

LARGE DETACHED AREAS

NEW PLASTER

WIRE MESH "TRAY" ON BATTENS

WITH THE OLD PLASTER SUPPORTED FROM BELOW, THE DECAYED LATH IS REMOVED, AND A MESH SCREEN FASTENED TO BATTENS ON THE JOISTS. NEW PLASTER IS BUILT UP IN TWO OR MORE BEDS ON THE SCREEN AND ADHERED TO THE TOP OF THE EXISTING PLASTER

ORIGINAL PLASTER

BULGES AND MODELED AREAS CUSHIONED OR SPACED FROM THE PLYWOOD SUPPORT BY ROLLED FELT BLANKETS

PROPS AND PLYWOOD PANELS BRACE ORIGINAL PLASTER FROM BELOW

than drywall and much slower to apply (it needs to dry and cure properly between coats). It demands more skill in application, but because it is softer and thicker, it is a far better absorber and insulator of sound than drywall. It absorbs noise rather than transmitting it and deadens the harshness of reflected sounds.

❖ Make sure that existing plaster is sound, solid, and well-keyed to its lath. Where the surface has bulged, crumbled or detached,

An ornamental plaster ceiling worth preserving (above): though the sprinkler system's pipes interfere with it visually, they have not actually caused much physical damage; perhaps they may be concealed in the course of future work. And a woodwork detail worth preserving (right): sliding wood doors with overlapping covers that conceal the slots when the doors are fully retracted.

concealed moisture is most often the culprit. Ensure that no exterior surface leaks are letting water in behind the plaster; keep humidity differences between rooms to a minimum. Repair all subsurface problems before finish plaster work.

❖ In patching small cracks or areas of damage, make sure that the edges of the existing plaster have been cleaned up and undercut to hold the patching material. Use a non-shrinking compound to fill in damaged areas and use at least two coats for any repair (even three if keying the repair directly to the lath), making the final finish coat no thicker than 3 mm (about an eighth of an inch).

❖ In major repairs, where large sections of plaster require replacement, maintain the thickness of the original plaster in whatever combination of wood, metal, or gypsum lath and new plaster is used. Remove carefully any wooden trim before working on the repair and refasten it afterwards in the same location.

❖ Wet the wooden lath before applying any plaster repair that must key to the lath, to keep it from drawing water out of the drying plaster too quickly. In addition, when using a bonding agent to help tie the repair to the existing plaster, use a compound formulated specifically for plaster, not a more general-purpose agent.

❖ In repairing or replacing concealed utilities or correcting structural deficiencies, remove as little sound plaster as possible. Do not gut old plaster walls and ceilings wholesale. Do not remove sound historic plaster merely to substitute plasterboard. Historic plaster has a number of hard-to-reproduce thermal and acoustical characteristics; it is not merely a neutral flat surface.

❖ Retain and repair existing bowed or sagging ceilings rather than replace them, if at all possible (for both acoustical and decorative considerations; see below). The lath itself may have separated from the joists, or the plaster may have lost many of its keys into the lath (because of other structural problems, moisture, deterioration of the nails holding the lath, even animal infestations). Reattach loose lath and detached but sound plaster from above (by temporarily lifting floorboards if necessary), vacuuming out all accumulated debris and broken plaster, repairing any broken lath, and screwing detached lath back into the joists. Make sure to undercut the edges of any plaster removed for these repairs, to permit a good bond with subsequent patches. Large areas of sagging may be pushed back into place from below and reinforced from above by bonding new plaster to the old to re-key it to the lath, reinforced with wire mesh and battens tied to the joists as required.

❖ In reattaching wall lath that has pulled away from partition studs or the structure itself, remove only enough plaster to reconnect the lath securely (with screws and with perforated or wire-mesh washers to help key the repair) and cover the repair with plaster of similar composition to the rest of the wall. More severe problems can be handled with techniques similar to those for ceilings.

❖ Give all plaster repairs sufficient time to dry and cure properly. Allow extra time for the finish coat to cure before applying paint or other coating.

❖ Before refinishing repairs, apply a coat of white shellac over new plaster to seal its surface and keep it from absorbing moisture from paint or other covering.

A mildly eclectic Victorian public interior (below), with an ornate plaster ceiling rose yet modest Classical woodwork. A more unusual example (bottom) of Georgian plasterwork: the decorative baseboards, cornices and door surrounds are different in each room.

Decorative plaster

Decorative plaster ranges from relatively simple cornices that keep irregularities of domestic walls from clashing too horribly with irregularities in their ceilings to the ornate coffered ceilings of monumental public interiors. In between are mouldings, brackets, columns, pilasters, baseboards, ceiling medallions, even architectural sculpture. Plasterwork was recognized as a sculptural skill, and its practitioners were regarded as expert craftsmen. As building became industrialized in the 19th century, many of these ornate features were mass-produced as prefabricated plaster-and-wood concoctions, attached by less skilled labourers and plastered into place.

❖ Consult an expert before undertaking major repairs of any decorative plaster. Anything beyond the most simple repair of cracks or pits in plaster ornament is the province of skilled craftworkers. In many cases ceiling rosettes and cornices may be consolidated and repaired along the lines of the basic repairs above. But in extreme cases the decoration will have to be carefully removed and reattached, often piece by piece.

❖ If decorative plaster has disappeared or deteriorated so badly that its substructure and internal composition cannot be rehabilitated, replace or restore the feature according to project records and historical documentation. Some ornamental plaster firms stock cast-plaster cornices, columns and other interior features that may match exactly a deteriorated feature. They may also make a mould in latex or plaster of a sound existing feature for replication in plaster-of-paris or a stronger compound. These can be attached to the wall or ceiling structure with screws or bolts, and any small gaps plastered over discreetly.

❖ Do not, however, install a stock decoration as "historic" without evidence for such a feature's historic existence. In the absence of interior photographs, inspection of the ceiling plasterwork from above should indicate locations where ornaments and fixtures were formerly fastened, and inspection from below may reveal a faint outline of a former ornament.

Interior finishes

References

There are many quite helpful references for repairing and reproducing interior finishes, but the most important book to mention here is SAND84 — though it is specifically about cleaning and housekeeping, it is those that are in fact the most careful conservation treatments.

For guidance on paint sampling, and on matching colour and chemistry, see KITC83, MILL77 and FEIL82. For help on preparation and repainting for conservation projects, see DAVE80/86, OLDH85, POOR83 and WRIG86. On special painted finishes, see ONEI71 and PARR85, for wood, see JOHN83.

Other useful sources are FINE86, KAPL78/86, KIRK84, LAND82, MCCA85, MILL87, PAIN78, SEAL79, SHOP86, STAG76, STAH84, THOR84, TIMM76 and VILA81.

Respecting interior finishes

It is extremely rare for interior finishes to survive use, age and changing fashion for more than a few years without being altered or covered over. Traces of early finishes may appear inside subsequent walls, or beneath mouldings or repairs, and may be corroborated by historic photographs, even family snapshots. Because historic "authenticity" must vie with current taste in renewing the finish of many interiors, the modern-day use of the space must direct conservation and maintenance decisions — a private residence endures wear and tear quite different from that of a museum-house.

❖ Protect all delicate surfaces and finishes from inadvertent damage during conservation. Do the work in order, so that any repairs to such surfaces are carried out at the end, after heavy-duty tasks are completed and cleaned up.

❖ Repair any underlying deterioration behind the surfaces of walls, floors and ceilings before conserving their finishes or refinishing. Correct any moisture damage, consolidate weakened base material, and stabilize any structural problems. Cure any damp conditions. Interior finishing should be the last major task. Clean up major messes before delicate finishing work.

❖ Use only the gentlest means possible in cleaning surfaces and finishes. Safeguard texture and sheen where these are essential qualities of the interior. Clean all delicate finishes by hand.

❖ Unless there is evidence of significant material deterioration, do not add protective finish to historically unfinished materials.

❖ Do not alter the character of historical finishes — do not substitute a stripped-and-sealed wood finish for a previously painted or grained finish.

❖ Do not expose an unfinished structural or historically hidden surface by removing historic finishes.

Paint

❖ Take paint samples from all surfaces requiring renewal of paint and analyze and catalogue them with the project records. Determine the type of woodwork beneath the layers of paint; if hardwood, look very closely for signs that it may have originally had a clear finish (softwoods, even when used as finished flooring, tend to have been painted from the beginning, often grained to resemble hardwood).

❖ Be especially watchful for indications of stencil work, marbling, graining, and even figurative art painted directly onto the walls. Wherever possible, maintain or restore early decorative finishes, but at the very least cover them with easily removable protection (strippable wallpaper or removable varnish) before refinishing. Consult an expert on paint or fine art conservation before either revealing or covering any historic decorative finishes.

❖ If the actual historic colours are not suitable for current taste, at least maintain the general qualities of lightness or darkness appropriate to the original period and to other adjacent finishes. In regard to "authenticity" of colour, see PAINT, COLOUR AND LIGHT.

Taking special care to record colour schemes, as well as the progress of careful cleaning.

The process of restoring the original marbled finish to the plaster walls, pilasters and details, based on colours and patterns identified by documentary research and professional paint analysis (below).

❖ Maintain historically painted surfaces as painted surfaces. Repair damage to base materials and to painted finishes as required and record both the pre-existing state and the finished one for inclusion in the property's maintenance files.

❖ Use the gentlest means possible to remove deteriorated paint and remove only down to the next sound layer unless paint build-up obscures or conceals profiles of decorative trim. Keep a record of the colours of all paint layers removed.

❖ In removing lead-based paints, take all appropriate safety measures — wear a safety-approved face-mask, wash up thoroughly after each session, and dispose of all residues carefully in sealed containers. Do not sand lead-painted surfaces. Do not use a blowtorch to soften interior paint; hot-air guns or heat plates are sufficient aids and offer the least risk of releasing toxic lead as vapour or dust.

❖ Preserve and protect decorative paint finishes such as marbling and graining. Clean them with the most gentle methods possible (by hand, with art gum or bread dough). Where they are too extensively damaged to repair, reproduce them according to traditional techniques.

❖ Use vapour-*permeable* paint on interior walls where it is necessary that repairs and undercoats "breathe" and maintain equilibrium with the interior environment.

❖ Use vapour-*impermeable* paints on interior surfaces of exterior walls to help any vapour barrier keep humid interior air from condensing or freezing in the exterior parts of the wall section.

❖ When painting embossed features such as radiators, match their colour combinations to historic precedents and to the paint colours of the room as a whole. Paint the background colour last, wiping the embossed surfaces to reveal the highlight colour.

Other historic painting techniques that involve special care in conservation and restoration include stencilling and painting embossed surfaces (below).

Wallpapers and fabrics

❖ In taking paint samples or in removing existing wall finishes, identify and record any traces of wallpaper or wall fabric in the layers beneath the existing surface. If possible, uncover as much of a single pattern-repeat as possible; if it is particularly old and rare (consult appropriate reference works or someone with knowledge of historic interiors), record it at life-size for the historical records of the building and the project.

❖ In some instances it may be possible to restore portions of old wallpaper, but consult an expert. Consider reproducing the original paper or replicating a similar pattern as a new finish if appropriate to the new use of the space. Be very careful not to damage the paper if removing it as a sample for reproduction.

❖ Conserve existing wallpaper if it is reasonably sound and historically valuable. Clean it with the gentlest means possible. Consult a conservator well versed in historic interiors when considering restoration — even cleaning — of any rare and valuable covering.

floors had linoleum or even wall-to-wall carpeting installed directly on the subfloor. Traditional subfloors were invariably softwood good enough for a floor structure but not to be exposed.

❖ Provide protective coverings over delicate finishes in areas of heavy use. Put padded carpeting, or even a separate protective wooden floor, over historic wooden or tile floors in areas of heavy foot traffic.

❖ Be wary of using "low-maintenance" finishes, especially polyurethane, on woodwork. They will not adhere well to the wood if earlier finishes were oil-based or if there have been putty repairs to splits or nailholes. Polyurethane is hard and rigid and will not forgive movements in wood, especially softwood. It is prone to impact damage and burns and is hard to spot-repair. Oils, waxes, varnishes and shellacs are far preferable for wooden surfaces.

❖ Retain sound historic linoleum floors where possible. If they are damaged, replace them in kind or with a substitute material of colour and texture that match the historic finish as closely as possible.

Floors

❖ Do not expose and treat wooden subfloors as finish flooring. Perhaps there never was a wooden floor on the subfloor; many late-19th- and early-20th-century residential

Behind a hinged wallpapered panel survives an important preserved archaeological fragment — a sample of the finishes before restoration (below).

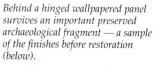

Other finishes

(opposite and below)
This house is a treasure-chest of late 19th-century interior finishes — paint, tile, plaster, woodwork — all carefully treated in different ways. Some, such as the fresco-like wall and ceiling paintings and the tiled vestibule, have been protected and maintained rather than restored, while other walls and floors have been re-stencilled according to historic practice and surviving bits of old paint.

❖ Retain and protect any ornate manufactured finishes such as pressed-metal ceilings or wall-panelling, embossed wallpapers or Lincrusta-Walton dados or friezes. Replace these in kind if badly deteriorated. If at all possible use an authentic pattern from the building for matching and reproduction rather than a non-matching stock pattern. To make small pressed-metal repairs, use a patch of auto-body putty compound moulded from a wax impression of a sound portion or sculpted to match the embossing; make sure that the patch is keyed neatly into the original.

❖ Remove paint and any other coatings built up over historically unpainted metal finishes. Use an appropriately gentle cleaning technique and restore as well as possible the characteristic sheen of the surface — do not presume that the finish of brass, for instance, was necessarily mirror-bright. Use paste wax or clear lacquer of similar sheen to protect brass and bronze from heavy use. Do not use heavy or abrasive polishes.

❖ Retain and repair early ceramic-tile wall and floor surfaces rather than replace them. Ceramics are especially durable interior finishes, though damaged by impact. Ensure that damp conditions and moisture damage are attended to before any repairs — where necessary, replace damaged or rotted subsurface woodwork with treated or marine-grade wood and make sure that the area behind the repairs is ventilated to reduce future dampness. If a perfect match cannot be made, reattach broken tiles rather than replace them with new — rearrange them if need be to place sound tiles in conspicuous areas.

References

Most advice about maintenance or replacement of fixtures is part and parcel of other conservation work; for general advice, see FEIL82, FINE86, GAYL80, HANS83, KAPL78/86, KIRK84, LYNC82, MILL77, MILL87, SHOP86, STAH84, STEP72, TECH82, THOR84 and VILA81.

Keeping, reusing, recycling

Fixed features of interior architecture shade gradually into movable furnishings. Features such as fireplaces, lighting fixtures, doors, built-in cabinetry, sinks and bathtubs, ventilation grilles and radiators sit astride the visible and tactile boundary between real and movable property. They often also comprise the "interface" between the normally hidden utilities and the appearance and uses of the interior.

Where interior fixtures survive that are distinctly part of the original or early years of a building, they afford a great opportunity to "key" rehabilitated or new uses and furnishings into existing spaces, just as plaster keys to its lath. Unfortunately, like doors, fixed (but detachable) fixtures tend to travel about like furniture in the antique market — and even into museums. This is both a problem and an opportunity: if fixtures have survived the antique hunters it is possible to recycle them within a building where they can no longer be useful in their original context or when they can complete a more prominent interior.

Some interior fixtures may be historically important for their use or technology as well as (or perhaps despite) their appearance. Industrial and commercial spaces may have many strictly utilitarian features — fire-hose cabinets, glazed partitions, machinery and so on — that may or may not still function but evoke historical activities. There is a trade in these utilitarian objects as well, so that many end up in shops or museums. When such items remain in a historic building, they offer an opportunity to give the building a new role in re-presenting and celebrating its own history, as a sort of museum without museum walls that keeps more of its history and interest alive as part of its everyday use.

❖ Retain and restore the operation of historic interior hardware — doorknobs and locks, kick panels, window latches, and so on. Do not substitute "period" hardware out of character and style with the building, and certainly none that antedates the building.

❖ Retain — where necessary restore — the quality and quantity of the original artificial lighting. Do not add "period" fixtures that were never there to increase overall lighting. Most historic interiors were not lit at the high-energy levels typical today. Provide discrete task lighting to satisfy any increased functional requirements and use concealed indirect lighting to supplement overall levels only if necessary.

❖ Retain and repair surviving fireplaces and mantels (even where they will no longer be used as fireplaces). Mantelpieces have been made out of almost every imaginable material and combination of materials, including hardwood, slate, ceramic tile, cast iron and marble. Refinish their surfaces according to the material. If a disused fireplace is to be used once more, ensure that the flue is clear and operable, that the chimney lining has been cleaned of hazardous creosote and other residues, and that the chimney itself is structurally sound from bottom to top.

❖ Retain and repair kitchen and bathroom fixtures, repairing their plumbing and refinishing them as required. Cure any moisture damage in the woodwork beneath, seal all junctions and gaps against water penetration, and keep those seals maintained. When seeking reproduction or replacement faucets and other fittings, try to find accurate matches to the originals where there is some evidence of their appearance. Retain and repair any historic marble or glazed washroom partitions and surfaces.

❖ Repair and restore the operation of interior window shutters. Remove excess paint build-up and ensure that shutters fold and fit properly into their pockets.

❖ Continue to use interior shades, blinds and draperies, as part of window operation.

❖ Do not automatically dispose of hardware or fixtures no longer integral to the building's basic uses. Retain and recycle fixtures to other purposes where possible, when they possess intrinsic visual or historical importance and can be used and interpreted to add interest to interior spaces of size and function suitable for their display.

New fixtures to match or fit

❖ Replace missing features in kind where possible — if necessary, where some elements (radiators, for example) are missing, consider swapping surviving features from less important locations and consolidate historic features in prominent areas. Base any substitutions on historic photographs and on archaeological traces of earlier fixtures.

❖ For modern services, use simple and inconspicuous fixtures that correspond in colour, dimension and proportion to their surroundings. Do not use inauthentic "period" fixtures — Georgian-style ornamental electrical switchplates and other obviously "olde-style" modern features.

❖ Incorporate the air handling and ventilating louvres of concealed systems discreetly, as slots or grilles aligned with and disguised by mouldings, cornices, baseboards and other linear features. Conceal them as well as possible, painting them to match adjacent interior colours where it is not possible to mask them otherwise.

❖ New radiators and other service elements should stand clear of historic surfaces and be relocatable or replaceable without damaging those surfaces.

❖ Where interiors retain their historic formality of space and finish, install smoke detectors, alarms and sprinkler heads using concealed hardware. Use recessed ceiling detectors and pop-down sprinkler heads. Alarm panels should be clearly visible and located near principal access points but should not impinge upon or damage historical elements and finishes.

When the occasional stroke of good fortune leaves mantels, fireplaces, ceramic fixtures and the like intact and in place, utmost effort should go into retaining them (top, middle).

Distinctive modern lighting in a formal classical interior lights the space well, follows the shape of the room, and does not confuse old and new — but this solution may be too bold for other situations (bottom).

References

The best checklist for
maintenance of mechanical and
electrical systems is CHAM76.
For guidance on general domestic
repair and maintenance, see
BLAC81, BLAC86, CENT86 and
MCCA85.

Few sources look directly at both
mechanical systems and heritage
conservation to reconcile their
potential conflicts; see HERI86a
and HERI87a/87b. Domestic
retrofits and upgrading are
covered in COE84, FINE86,
HUNT85, KAPL78/86, KNIG87,
MELV73, NATC83, OLDH85,
POOR83, SEDW83, VILA81 and
WING83. Larger-scale examples
are included in ELEY84, REID84,
SHOP86 and STAH84.

Maintaining and upgrading "hidden" systems

Few historic buildings survive with their
original wiring, plumbing or ductwork intact.
Those services did not exist when most
"historic" buildings were erected, and
mechanical and electrical services have tended
to wear out long before structures and
finishes. Even in new construction, services
have a much shorter life expectancy than the
structure; in calculating the costs of a new
building over its predicted lifetime, most
estimators include major mechanical repairs
as frequently as every eight years.

Apart from the specialized mechanical and
electrical services required for industries and
office towers, many different things and
connections snake through even a small
building's hidden spaces:

❑ Heating and ventilating — ducts, furnaces,
  pipes, controls, grilles, vents, boilers,
  compressors, heat pumps, central vacuum
  systems, air conditioners

❑ Plumbing — pipes, radiators, vents,
  valves, boilers

❑ Electricity — conduits, wires, junction and
  switch boxes, light switches, fixtures,
  outlets, alarms, sensors, transformers,
  generators, telephone cables, computer
  cables, switches, terminals, controls

Most of these change far more rapidly than
the architecture and structure of any building,
sometimes more rapidly than interior layouts.
Their importance for architectural
conservation is indirect but profound. Leaks
and condensation from heating and plumbing
systems can create damp conditions that may
damage structure and finishes; faulty wiring
can cause the fire that burns the building
down.

Repairs and replacements

❖ Whenever possible, retain and upgrade
  existing mechanical systems rather than
  replace them — not so much because of
  any intrinsic heritage value as because of
  potential damage to interior spaces and
  finishes in the course of replacements.

Nevertheless, if the life of a mechanical system
cannot be usefully extended because of its age
and poor condition, replace its hidden
components with the most durable possible
substitutes and maintain the appearance and
finish of the system's visible features.

❖ Ensure sufficient structural capacity to
  hold new mechanical equipment. Though
  an ideal location for some equipment may
  be in the attic or roof space, do not install
  any large heavy equipment that would
  disfigure the building's profile, transmit
  excessive vibration to the structure, or
  greatly increase the chance of leakage or
  condensation within the structure. As
  much as possible, locate new equipment in
  basement areas, existing service wings or
  areas or in new additions designed to
  support and conceal them properly. Ensure
  sufficient ventilation and access space in
  all equipment rooms and shafts.

❖ Do not replace a hot-water or steam
  heating system with a new forced-air
  system unless air ducts can be
  incorporated without impinging on or
  cutting through important historic spaces
  and finishes. Piping is much easier to
  conceal than ductwork. It may be possible
  to incorporate ducts in risers in a new
  addition, but ensure that horizontal
  ductwork can be accommodated without
  undue damage to the existing building.

❖ Do not cut through structural supports to
  install services. Repair or reinforce
  previously damaged supports. Wherever
  possible use existing gaps, shafts, chases
  and service spaces for new or replacement
  pipes and conduits.

❖ Insert louvres, grilles and vents as
  discreetly as possible.

❖ Ensure that all new pipes and conduits can
  be reached for repairs without damage to
  historic finishes and materials. Use
  existing openings as access hatches where
  possible or locate service shafts in modern
  additions.

See FIXTURES, INTERIOR FINISHES.

Internal environment

The new or rehabilitated internal environment must not hasten deterioration of the building that contains it. Upgrading of some systems and aggressive energy conservation measures can cause condensation that may lead quickly to far worse deterioration from trapped moisture in the structure and finishes. Fumes or decay products from new materials can attack the existing fabric or even create problems for occupants (urea formaldehyde insulation being the best known example).

❖ Maintain a stable equilibrium of temperature and humidity. Humidify the interior in winter only when there are requisite air and vapour seals properly installed and do not make it so humid as to trap condensation within exterior walls or spaces, where moisture may freeze and cause structural or material deterioration.

❖ Use vapour barriers wherever necessary to keep warm humid interior air from condensing against cold exterior surfaces, but also ensure that areas where moisture may be trapped are ventilated to permit evaporation. In general, because they have usually established an equilibrium already, let old buildings "breathe" to the outside.

❖ Only where sufficient precautions against condensation have been taken in the fabric of a historic building should its environment be joined with that of an air-conditioned addition. Do not permit air and vapour pressure from a new addition to drive moist air *into* the fabric of the old building. As much as possible keep their environments separate, especially their humidities.

See BALANCING HERITAGE, COMFORT AND ENERGY EFFICIENCY.

In some buildings the mechanical equipment is the major inhabitant, deserving of special attention in its own right for how it looks as well as what it does (top).

In residences, regular attention must be given to heating and plumbing (middle), and to the damage that humidity and condensation can cause in inadequately ventilated areas (bottom).

Balancing heritage, comfort, and energy efficiency

Principles

1.3 Balance of use and preservation (cautious conversion)

2.6 Second opinions when in doubt

5.3 Minimal alteration, minimal intrusiveness

7.3 Reversible repair

7.4 Cautious high-tech repair

7.5 Recipes tested before application

7.6 Maintainable repairs

8.5 Energy conservation

References

For more technical detail on the problems of overly enthusiastic energy conservation retrofits, and on some satisfactory alternatives to the conventional approaches, see HERI86, HERI86a, and HERI87a/87b. Good additional background information is available in POOR83 and SEDW83. Mechanical retrofits are covered in COE84, KNIG87 and WING83.

Other useful sources include CENT86, ENER84, HUGH86, KAPL78/86, NATC83, SHOP86, STAH84, TECH82, THUR83 and VILA81.

Environmental equilibrium in old buildings

Though energy conservation has become a watchword of the past decade, the struggle to keep warm in Ontario winters (and cool during parts of its summers) is not a new phenomenon. Every building has been constructed both to keep out the elements as much as possible and to offer a comfortable interior environment. But whereas traditional approaches to wintertime comfort involved fireplaces, stoves, doors, windows, heavy sweaters and heavy curtains, modern standards demand that the entire building be comfortably warm, despite fuel costs. Modern energy-conserving strategies are correspondingly more technical and comprehensive, and that means trying to adjust the building itself to retain its heat in winter far more than its builders could have anticipated.

Much of the adjustment is still in the hands of occupants, whether or not the building is inherently energy-efficient. Consider windows. Curtains, windowshades, shutters and operable windows help keep warm air from leaking through cold windows in winter and yet cool and ventilate the same area in the heat of summer. Winter performance will improve with better weatherstripping and perhaps double-glazing; summer performance with better shading and the free air flow of natural ventilation (or with double glass and air conditioner — cooler but less efficient).

But radical differences in temperature create the risk of condensation in the height of both seasons. Condensation — with consequent frost damage and salt crystallization in masonry walls, rot and disintegration in mouldy woodwork, peeling and disintegration in plaster and paint — is the major evil lurking inside too-heavily sealed and insulated historic buildings. The visual damage wrought by slapping new-building parts onto structures of architectural and historical distinction may not bring imminent collapse, but wood rot and spalling brick will.

❖ Maintain, and use, the inherently energy-conserving and comfort-enhancing architectural features of historic buildings:

❑ Vestibules as winter air locks, porches to cut winter winds and protect entrances

❑ Porches for summer shade

❑ Gable vents to help keep attics dry

❑ Thermal mass of masonry walls to even out daily temperature extremes

❑ Operable windows for flow-through summer ventilation

❑ Operable interior shutters for winter window insulation and draft-proofing

❑ Drapes, curtains and blinds for winter window insulation and draft-proofing

❑ Operable exterior shutters for wind-proofing and summer shading

❑ Exterior awnings, interior windowshades for summer shading

❖ Keep interior humidity within a range that will not lead to damage by condensation. Ventilate all areas tending to dampness — kitchens, baths, basements, laundry areas, potentially leaky attics. Do not dry laundry inside without direct exterior ventilation (this is often the major source of household humidity).

❖ Turn the thermostat down (manually or automatically) at night during winter. Close doors to seldom-used rooms to reduce the area needing full heating.

❖ Keep heating and ventilating mechanisms — furnace, vents, water heater, plumbing, ductwork, etc. — well maintained.

The hazards of enthusiastic energy conservation

Most manuals on energy-conserving retrofits ignore the architectural character of the existing building. Much of their advice is worthwhile as far as it goes — it simply goes too far. Keep in mind the following hazards and constraints.

❖ Inspect thoroughly for energy-conserving potential in a historic building and incorporate appropriate measures as part of the larger conservation project. But beware — energy savings alone will not pay back much more than the costs of modest caulking and weatherstripping and updating the efficiency of mechanical equipment.

❖ Air-sealing — tightening up the flow of air through exterior walls by weather-

Traditional and effective energy-conserving measures: winter vestibule, often removable in summer (below); double-glazing — a standard window inside, a complementing storm window outside, and an insulating air-space between — together with heavy drapery that makes another air-space inside (right).

The deep, wide porch is a traditional architectural feature that provides shade in summertime heat and shelter against winter winds (above).

Energy conservation taken far too far, hiding almost all traces of the building in a cocoon of insulation and vinyl siding that is likely to cause decay far more expensive to repair than any possible savings in heating bills (right).

stripping, caulking and repairing cracks — is the most generally useful and least problematic energy-conserving strategy for historic buildings. But ensure that there will be sufficient air changes to ventilate living spaces and prevent build-up of harmful exhausts (most notably carbon monoxide and other furnace-combustion by-products) — don't "tighten" a building without providing enough ventilation for the health of the occupants.

❖ Generally, do not insulate without using vapour barriers and air barriers *on the warm side of the insulation*, but select and install these barriers very carefully. The wrong material — or even inadvertent gaps or tears in the right material — may well concentrate accumulations of moisture and drastically increase the risk of condensation and its attendant damage.

❖ Ensure as much as possible that moisture does not condense where it will lead to damage in the form of wood rot, corrosion or freezing. Be especially careful about relative locations of insulation and air and vapour barriers. Be especially watchful for signs of paint deterioration that may betray moisture build-up or rot. Vent high-moisture areas (baths, laundries, etc.) directly to the outside.

❖ Make sure that reused fireplaces and chimneys have been brought up to modern safety standards and that there are no exposed wood members in chimneys. Be wary of automatic flue dampers and similar modern combustion devices in a partly recycled system; they may not function properly.

❖ Provide sufficient air space around insulated features — especially electrical devices — to prevent overheating that may lead to fire.

❖ When installing new insulation, do not inadvertently leave water pipes in uninsulated conditions.

See FOUNDATIONS, ROOFING and WINDOWS.

References

For aspects of the visual relations of old and new, see BENT85, CHIT85, EDWA46, GOON80, HIST78, ICOM86, LANG78, LYNC72, MADS76, NATI80, PYE78 and RENY86. For guides to historic styles and features see, for instance, BLUM77, CHIT85, LONG87 and POPP83, as well as other sources noted in "Elements and styles" (page 20).

Functional aspects of planning and structure are discussed in BALL83, BAXT86, BUIL86, FEIL82, FERG86, NIBS80 and REID84.

Both visual and functional aspects of building additions are treated in ALEX77, BAKE83, BINN82, DIBN85, HOW86, PYKE80, SHOP86, STEP72 and TECH82.

See also the references in "Visual approaches and results" (page 84).

Though controversy may result from attempts to treat historic façades with less than complete reverence, there may be good reasons for it. Here, the historic façade had been covered by a 1950s metal screen whose fasteners had damaged much of the original masonry beneath. Architect, client and municipality agreed to respect what was salvageable rather than restore or recreate the original throughout. The new openings echo the proportions and rhythm of the historic windows, and the overall effect distinguishes old and new very clearly.

Old and new/context and contrast

Though it may not be recognizable in many modern projects, a central tenet of architectural design has always been respect for context, for the visual fit of the new work to its existing surroundings. Traditionally — at least until some Victorian styles — this respect for context has meant "fitting in" rather than "standing out", being a good neighbour to existing buildings and spaces, at least in towns and cities. The isolated building in suburb or countryside also "fitted in", but according to a different set of rules involving landscape and historical references to isolated "model" buildings of the past.

Victorian eclecticism added *contrast* to the architect's repertoire of respecting context. Though new buildings could be as wild as they liked, their extravagances were still within a definite context. Though battles to catch the Victorian eye were fierce, the more pragmatic considerations of property ownership and building cost, material and height still gave most streets overall consistency of form and character.

The modern "non-historical" styles of the 20th century furthered these contrasts to the extreme. So long as they were isolated examples in a larger backdrop of 19th-century buildings, they merely added variety and interest to the generally consistent mix.

Indeed, the modern styles seemed to *require* this backdrop of "the old", to stand out in that much sharper relief by contrast.

The modern styles themselves succeeded too well; they have not served to establish their *own* kind of context. Few modern buildings are good neighbours. Technology has permitted new buildings vastly out of scale and form with its surroundings. Historic architecture (whatever the merits of individual buildings) establishes a comfortable sense of continuity, but cannot tolerate unlimited contrast. Where the limit lies is difficult to say. How many per cent new to how many per cent old — or how many per cent *fitting* to how many per cent *rude*?

Not just for the sake of the building next door must new designs be fitting rather than rude. There is no longer enough historic context to tolerate the back-handed slap anywhere. New buildings must regain the amenity value offered by historic patterns of space, dimension and detail. Where they adjoin historic architecture, new buildings must strive to be good neighbours by helping to extend the context established by the old. An addition or neighbour to a historic building should stand on its own as a historic building of its own time — it must add to history, not take history away.

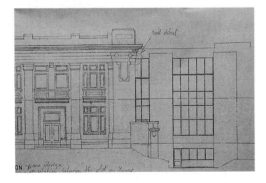

The opposites of good fit: new work that devalues the old, from the use of the front door as a fireplace and chimney (top); to the burial of half of the original brick façade, still visible on the left, inside a casing of stucco (above); to the mismatching of windows and walls in a new addition to an old building (right).

Four strategies of recognition and accommodation of new to old were elaborated in VISUAL APPROACHES AND RESULTS:

> Reconstitution/period reproduction
> Approximation/complement
> Cautious contrast/self-effacement
> Radical contrast

The application of one of these strategies (or those that may lie in between) will vary with each case. But there are general correspondences between new and old that should apply to all new work in historic buildings, whether as exterior additions, interior additions, or the spaces between the two. VISUAL APPROACHES AND RESULTS dealt with the ensemble of old *and* new; the following remarks emphasize the new.

Making new harmonize with old

❖ New elements should relate clearly to one or more of the distinguishing characteristics of historic buildings. The profile and exterior materials of historic architecture are its most readily perceived character-defining aspects — ensure that the profile and exterior materials of the new harmonize with the old. Harmony is a complex relationship in music, and in architecture. A close match may not be harmonious at all if it attracts attention to clashing details. Use the criteria and features set out in "Identifying architectural character" (see INSPECTION).

❖ New work should stand on its own merits visually. Additions to the plan of a historic building should be demarcated in elevations by a clearly recognizable junction between old and new. Such a vertical line or feature need not be conspicuous but it should reveal the change from one period of building to another, regardless of the styles of each.

❖ Use new construction to provide services, accessibility and other modern requirements that cannot fit comfortably in the historic building.

❖ Design elevations for new additions based on features, materials, proportions, scales or symmetries of the adjacent existing elevations. Fronts should correspond and harmonize with fronts, rears with rears. Again, use the criteria and features set out in "Identifying architectural character" (see INSPECTION).

❖ As far as possible, do not add to the height or roof of a historic building. Even the smallest change to a roofline alters the overall character of a building tremendously, and the larger the addition, the greater the damage, until at some point (depending on the scale and style of the original) the whole will appear to be a large new building with a small old façade tacked onto the front. At that point, the heritage value of the original may be reduced to that of a moved or disembodied façade.

❖ As far as possible, keep the height and bulk of new additions smaller than the existing building. When downtown conditions demand a much larger building than the historic building, the "addition" should be made to appear independent and *be* independent, excepting any smaller additions for services (see above).

❖ Make any bridges or independent connections appear to be light in visual terms and harmonious in material and detail to the historic building. Such connectors should join the existing building as far as possible at existing openings, preferably doorways or windows sufficiently large to enable their surrounds to be retained.

❖ Make vents, skylights and other new elements on the roof fit as discreetly as possible, both visually and materially. There are many traditional ways to conceal or incorporate such elements, as part of the roofing itself, or in conjunction with gables, dormers or chimneys.

❖ Keep satellite dishes, aerials, air conditioners and other "servant" features to the side or rear, the traditional places for such add-ons.

See INSPECTION and VISUAL APPROACHES AND RESULTS.

The tradition of new residential additions is an old one — here (below) it may not be immediately obvious whether the larger elements were added to the smaller ones, or vice versa (though closer inspection will tell), but the whole is a harmonious blend of profile and detail that can serve as a model for even the most contemporary treatment. For industrial buildings, robustness and size of an original may permit a robust modern addition, here set back on the roof (bottom left).

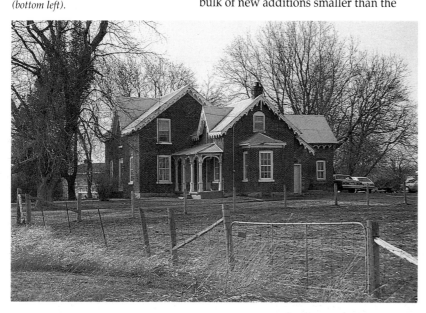

In making an exterior wall into part of an interior space, it is important to make the connection without demeaning the old. Here, on one hand, the actual physical connection has not been done well, butting the concrete to the stone with caulking, obscuring the texture of the older material and erasing some of the historic traces in the arched openings for the sake of neatness — but the overall character of the new space permits appreciation of the former exterior as an important historic element, daylit from above as it was before (opposite, bottom right, and below).

Connections — access and use

❖ Use new construction to provide services, improved access and other modern requirements that cannot fit comfortably in the historic building.

❖ Design new spaces and entrances to correspond with the historic spaces and entrances, using new access to satisfy building and other code requirements instead of altering historic spaces and finishes.

❖ Make floor levels of new construction correspond to existing floor levels of the historic building as far as possible. But try to incorporate necessary level changes and ramps within new construction in providing for handicapped access.

❖ Where a required elevator cannot be installed in the historic building, use a new addition to provide both elevator and links to floor levels of the existing building. Where floor levels cannot be made to correspond between old and new, use a double-sided elevator to permit connections between them.

❖ Keep new additions well fire-separated so as not to force the existing building to meet potentially damaging new-building requirements.

See PROGRAMMING AND USING SPACE and INTERIOR SPACES AND CIRCULATION.

Good neighbours: fitting new work to the old

❖ Use mouldings, flashings and expansion covers for their traditional purposes — to conceal junctions or gaps yet allow access to them if necessary — rather than make butt joints with sealants that will deteriorate in a few years. Covers and mouldings should appear to go from the new to the old, to make clear that the new is making gestures (snuggling up?) to the old, not vice versa.

❖ Always drain water from new additions *away* from the existing building.

❖ Keep the structures of new and old independent from one another, unless the new is designed deliberately to reinforce or stabilize the old (for instance, a new stair or service shaft to provide lateral stability to the older structure).

❖ Keep the foundations of the new independent from those of the old unless part of a purposeful underpinning of the old; do not compromise the existing foundation in new excavations.

❖ Ensure that adjacent materials do not have adverse chemical or physical reactions to one another. For example, be particularly careful about galvanic action where the same metal flashings cover both old and new.

Taking care: building operation and preventive maintenance

References

For periodic maintenance procedures and checklists, and for cleaning materials and techniques, see CHAM76, MCCA85, MILL80, MONC83, POOR83, STAH84 and SAND84.

Exterior maintenance is also treated in ASHU77, BLAC81, DAVE80/86, HOLL86, HOLM75, JOHN84, MEAD86 and SIMP78. For interior features, see also BLAC81, DAVE80/86 and STAG76.

Periodic inspections

Daily, weekly and seasonal cycles of weathering and human use will take their toll on any building. The common assumption is that new or renovated buildings become "immune" to deterioration by virtue of the effort and expenditure involved in durable finishes, careful weatherproofing and new structure or utilities. This is very far from the truth. Even the newest building — *especially* the newest building — requires vigilance to spot errors in construction or sloppy installations where one of the many causes of deterioration might gain a foothold. No conservation project is truly finished. Each job must be inspected and maintained in the succeeding months and years to sustain the value and integrity of the conservation work and to slow deterioration as much as possible.

❖ Develop a schedule for periodic inspection suitable for the size and complexity of the building or site. Follow the general sequence of features laid out in INSPECTION. Pay special attention to the items listed under FAULT DIAGNOSIS.

❖ Give every building a thorough visual once-over, both inside and out, after major storms to check for leaks, water stains, blistered paint or other signs of water penetration that does not immediately dry out. Be sure to include quick looks into attics, basements and crawl spaces.

❖ Undertake a regular inspection, both inside and outside, at half-year intervals to deal specifically with moisture penetration and related problems. Ideally, such inspections take place in spring and fall. In the spring, pay special attention to problems hidden by winter snows, as well as more insidious decay from condensation. In the fall, pay attention to maintenance items, especially to cleaning out blocked drainage.

❖ Perform a more thorough inspection every year to check for faults in weather-seals; plant, insect or animal infestations; paint deterioration; cracks in plaster or woodwork; and human wear and tear on interior and exterior finishes. This sort of inspection is best done in late spring or late summer to leave time for any corrective work to be done in reasonable weather.

❖ Undertake a full and comprehensive inspection of the entire building and site at least every five years, with complete records kept for comparison to records of previous inspections as well as the original work. This inspection should be at least as attentive as the full-scale investigation needed for the original conservation work (though it will obviously take much less time). Pay special attention to any possible structural movements and to the operation and durability of utilities, particularly where these have been maintained through earlier modifications.

❖ Compile complete and clear records of all periodic inspections and attach these to the archive of information gathered for the project in the first place. This will be especially important in determining if errors in the project may be to blame for any general or localized deterioration.

Maintenance manuals and procedures

It is absolutely essential to have procedures and cautions for ongoing maintenance and repairs spelled out for every conservation project, though many procedures are commonsense and uniform from building to building. Most procedures will be tied to periodic inspections; for instance, blocked gutters and drains identified in an autumn inspection should be cleaned out then and there. This may mean, for this particular example, that in climbing the ladder to inspect the eavestrough, you should have a bag ready to carry the things pulled out of the trough or downspout.

❖ Prepare a comprehensive maintenance manual, to include: a basic checklist of work items and their priorities; how often they should be carried out; the time, people and tools required for the work; names and telephone numbers of consultants, suppliers and emergency contacts; and copies of the relevant drawings and specifications from the conservation work. Keep one copy of the manual readily available at the building itself; file a second copy securely in another place. In the case of a public building, or one of particular importance that may have received financial assistance

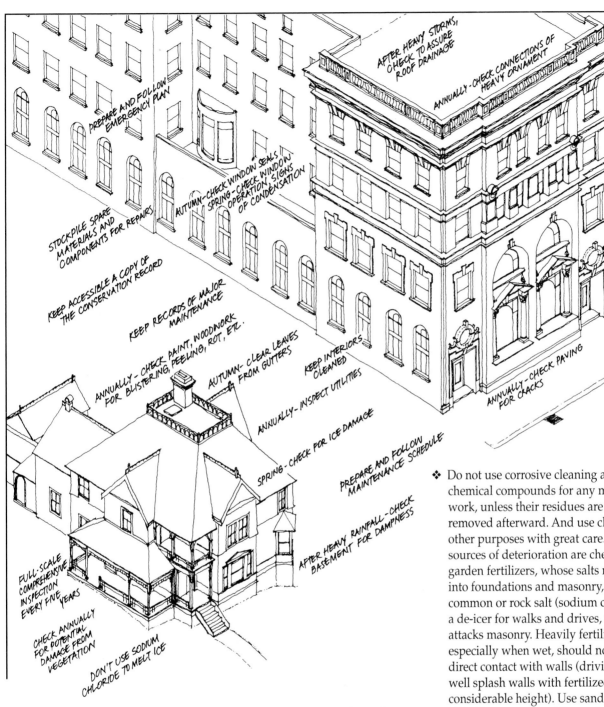

Labels on the illustration:

AFTER HEAVY STORMS, CHECK TO ASSURE ROOF DRAINAGE

ANNUALLY - CHECK CONNECTIONS OF HEAVY ORNAMENT

PREPARE AND FOLLOW EMERGENCY PLAN

AUTUMN - CHECK WINDOW SEALS
SPRING - CHECK WINDOW OPERATION SIGNS OF CONDENSATION

STOCKPILE SPARE MATERIALS AND COMPONENTS FOR REPAIRS

KEEP ACCESSIBLE A COPY OF THE CONSERVATION RECORD

KEEP RECORDS OF MAJOR MAINTENANCE

ANNUALLY - CHECK PAINT, WOODWORK FOR BLISTERING, PEELING, ROT, ETC.

AUTUMN - CLEAR LEAVES FROM GUTTERS

KEEP INTERIORS CLEANED

ANNUALLY - INSPECT UTILITIES

SPRING - CHECK FOR ICE DAMAGE

PREPARE AND FOLLOW MAINTENANCE SCHEDULE

AFTER HEAVY RAINFALL - CHECK BASEMENT FOR DAMPNESS

ANNUALLY - CHECK PAVING FOR CRACKS

FULL-SCALE COMPREHENSIVE INSPECTION EVERY FIVE YEARS

CHECK ANNUALLY FOR POTENTIAL DAMAGE FROM VEGETATION

DON'T USE SODIUM CHLORIDE TO MELT ICE

for its conservation, file an additional copy with the municipality or LACAC, or with the granting agency, to facilitate its availability in emergencies.

❖ Keep on hand a stock of spare materials for use in repairs — items like bricks, tiles, castings, fixtures and pre-cut lumber. Keep records and colour samples of all paints and finishes that will have to be renewed periodically.

❖ Do not use corrosive cleaning agents or chemical compounds for any maintenance work, unless their residues are completely removed afterward. And use chemicals for other purposes with great care. Two sources of deterioration are chemical garden fertilizers, whose salts may migrate into foundations and masonry, and common or rock salt (sodium chloride) as a de-icer for walks and drives, which also attacks masonry. Heavily fertilized soil, especially when wet, should not come in direct contact with walls (driving rain may well splash walls with fertilized soil to a considerable height). Use sand or calcium chloride on snow and ice as alternatives to common salt.

❖ Maintain environmental controls and procedures within specified limits to obviate condensation or material deterioration. Keep records of any changes made to those procedures, and their effects. Take special care to ensure that all ventilation elements are operating and maintained throughout the year.

WAYS AND MEANS

The basic purpose of preservation is not to arrest time but to mediate sensitively with the forces of change. It is to understand the present as a product of the past and a modifier of the future.

John W. Lawrence,
Tulane University, 1970

Professional advice for hire

Professional services or do-it-yourself?

The growing importance of heritage conservation has prompted a corresponding development of professional expertise. In addition to the existing range of planning and building professionals, advisers with specialized talents and experience are available for every conservation activity, from research to restoration. Many of these specialists have established professional associations to share information and maintain principles and standards for the quality of their work.

There may be little room in the budget to afford conservation expertise. But every part of every project must be appraised to see where such help might offer short- or long-term savings that would more than pay for the consultation. A professional's experience on many individual projects adds up to a wealth of knowledge that can minimize or prevent problems, and it is often worth a modest fee to borrow that experience for the job at hand.

For any construction project, old or new, the crucial starting point is the matter of project planning and co-ordination. Owners must decide whether to do their own co-ordinating, and undertake to bring in appropriate specialists,or to hand overall supervision to someone else — perhaps to an architect, engineer or general contractor. Doing-it-oneself can be very time-consuming, cutting into time, convenience and even income. But the advantages of close personal attention and responsibility may include some cost savings, as well as an unparalleled learning opportunity and the ultimate personal pride in the results of the work. There may be, however, legal limitations on how much building work can be done by a non-professional. At some point, even the most avid do-it-yourselfer may have to bring in an expert for a special item of work or to help oversee the project.

It is very rare that an owner can hand over complete responsibility to a co-ordinator for an old-building project, because there will be adjustments during the work that will require "policy" decisions. Though they should be avoided by careful planning, complete reversals may occur in the course of even the best-planned work. No old-building project ever goes completely by the book (not even

this book). Owner-clients should consider a project co-ordinator insurance against the worst — to help minimize avoidable risks and reduce the damage from unavoidable events — and paragon — someone whose talent will add value to the final product.

But co-ordinators cannot do everything. Most old-building projects cover a variety of work that exceeds the range of services normally offered by the architects and engineers who have traditionally co-ordinated construction work or even those offered by independent project managers. On the smallest projects a co-ordinator will be *do*er as well as manager; on larger jobs, some firms may try to cover all the work, but they will probably retain and supervise specialized sub-contractors. This can put a strain on the client, who may have to deal with disagreements among co-ordinator and specialists. Even as co-ordinator, an adviser is simply one who advises, and the client must take ultimate responsibility for every important decision. A good co-ordinator will help make those decisions more informed and palatable but cannot and must not make them without the client's understanding and support.

A project co-ordinator — or an owner acting in that capacity — will have to identify which specialties must be brought in for the project and when, and which functions can be carried out by less expert workers (or even by the owner). In the earliest phases, there will need to be planning and research to evaluate the resource, to identify its most important qualities and to determine appropriate treatments. This can involve several specialties, from historian and archaeologist to photographer and conservator. Design and specification of the necessary and optional work may require similar specialties if the problems identified earlier prove untypical. Assessment of structural and other deficiencies requires a rare and deft combination of construction knowledge and understanding of historic materials and techniques available from few architects or engineers unaided by specialists.

Standard construction documents are seldom applicable to old-building work; specifications must be developed by someone with special experience and must be based on thorough reporting of existing conditions, something

---

Definition of a consultant — someone called in to share the blame.

Dr John Parker

Most private practitioners belong to one or more organizations representing their profession as a whole or their specific expertise in heritage work. Besides associations representing architects, engineers and planners, there are groups such as ICOMOS Canada, the Association for Preservation Technology, and the Association of Heritage Consultants, whose members are drawn from many of the "trades" comprising the heritage field. Consulting assistance should be sought through the membership of such groups, who are pledged to uphold the highest possible standards of quality and workmanship. Names and addresses for these organizations may be found in Appendix 6, "Heritage organizations and information resources".

unnecessary for conventional new work. Sometimes there are economies to be made by replacing some usual construction drawings with suitably clear annotated photographs, but the written specifications need to be correspondingly precise and knowledgeable.

And then there is supervision.

Exhaustive research, sensitive design, careful specification — all will come to grief if the work is done poorly. Bad work can rarely be undone. Sometimes it will be hidden from view and rear its dangerous head only in the event of a failure or even collapse. Without the most diligent care and attention to everything from research to final clean-up (and maintenance after . . .), there will be plenty of chances for misunderstanding, slap-dash work, even damage to features meant to be preserved by the project.

Site supervision for old-building work is unlike that for new construction. For larger projects, it may even mean having a resident site supervisor all the time: a clerk of works. Close supervision does not mean hovering over foremen and workers as if they were galley slaves; the idea is to help improve the quality on site by bringing in previous experience with conservation problems to solve new ones as they crop up. In practice, this means establishing standards for quality on the job at the beginning of the project, using samples and demonstrations to make clear the sort of work that will merit approval at the *end* of the project. The contractor may be well versed in conservation problems and able to make up for deficiencies in the contract documents, but a client or architect should never count on such magic.

Personnel engaged for any stage of a conservation project should be able to demonstrate their adherence to the highest possible standards of knowledge and craft. They should belong to professional organizations and should work in some manner for the advancement of their specialty as a whole. In the end, the ultimate test for all of the preparatory work on a building conservation project is a durable, honest, well-preserved final product on paper and on the ground — something that will endure to the credit of all its contributors.

Generalists

Planners work under a variety of labels nowadays, from management consultants to environmentalists and surveyors, but their training and experience may equip them to co-ordinate many of the conservation activities that surround but do not include the construction process itself. They may be listed in directories according to various specialties. Some have specialized as **heritage planners** through on-the-job experience, since there is no specific training for them in Canada and few programs elsewhere. Heritage planning is both specialized and generalized. Though focused on but one "kind" of resource — old places and things — the very variety and complexity of these resources require heritage planners to have an exceptionally broad base of skills. In practice, heritage planners, environmental planners, resource managers and urban planners should be able to co-ordinate — and do — most conservation research, analysis and planning. But the more effective practitioners will have a solid understanding of heritage resources and the built environment through thorough grounding in history, human geography, architectural history or material culture studies.

Architects seem the "generalists" best placed and trained to be comprehensive co-ordinators of building conservation work, from even the earliest stages of research and planning. But in North America few architects receive any training in the special concerns and problems of conservation. Few architects treat existing features with very much respect, and many historic buildings have been stripped of valuable and useful heritage features at an architect's orders as a matter of course before replacement work is even designed. Selecting an architect for conservation work requires careful attention to the needs of the project at hand, together with an assessment of the architect's understanding and sensitivity in previous projects, both as designed and as completed. Demonstrated skill in site supervision is essential, even though it seldom involves more than a quarter of the fee. The experience and satisfaction of previous clients may play a large role in the selection of an architect. Frequently, an architectural firm's success depends on specific personnel, and a client can and should insist on having a previously successful team retained together. On larger projects someone with conservation experience may work as a specialist with another co-ordinating architect. While there are competent and experienced specialists without special training, many have received qualifications from advanced university programs outside Canada. Some practitioners have begun to call themselves "conservation architects", though the title is not used consistently.

Engineers and **project managers** are competing with and taking over many of the construction-related responsibilities of architects, even though they may not be trained in all of the areas required for architectural qualification or for building work in general. In Canada education of engineers is if anything more deficient than that of architects for conservation purposes, but there are specialists with conservation skills who have learned from experience (and their numbers are growing as old-building work increases). Project management is a relatively recent specialization, elevating the role of construction co-ordinator to that of construction director responsible for all work, including even retention of architects as one of several types of "specialist" (see "Clients, consultants and contracts", below). Again, there are few project managers with the special understanding required for most conservation work — conventional project management accelerates construction schedules by deliberately dispensing with the preparatory work essential to conservation. Here, as for architects, previous results are the only reliable test of an engineer's or project manager's capabilities for conservation projects, whether independently or as part of a team.

Building contractors can act as both co-ordinators and doers of the work. Some contractors are very skilled at conservation work, often because their work-force contains specialists trained in traditional methods in Europe. A good contractor may be able to make up for some lapses on the architect's part, but just as often a contractor or builder will not take the required care or precautions demanded by the conservation specifications. On many construction jobs, the owner will have to deal with both an architect and a general contractor, each with separate contract and separate legal status, and this can get very confusing. Architect and contractor must work well with one another to make a success of conservation work. Because of the cyclical nature of construction, the best workers may not be available for conservation work — contractors and their regular trades often get too busy during economic booms and may leave the field altogether when things are too slow. A good, sensitive contractor working unhurriedly with careful, well-conceived plans is the closest an owner will get to a guarantee of success on a conservation project. Regrettably, such people are rare.

Specialists

Architectural researchers and **architectural historians**, trained academically or through many years of reading, writing and seasoned observation, can quickly unearth much of the background needed to determine the associational value of a building or site and relate a given place to others of its type and era. They can cut through the mountains of marginal documentation to find the useful information. They can and do teach others about the importance of historic buildings, districts and towns. The publication of "academic" books about Ontario architecture in the last two decades by architectural historians has done a great deal to establish a far more positive climate for conservation, and the book-writers and their students are now adding to that knowledge town by town and building by building. Researchers who deals with the nuances of the new uses and functions of a building, often called **architectural programmers**, can help co-ordinate new uses and old spaces to advantage.

Archaeologists, trained in anthropology or classical studies but seasoned in trenches, pits and basements, certainly dig up information much more directly than their documentary colleagues. A skilled historical archaeologist can make reliable inferences from fragmentary evidence that combines with the historical evidence to locate missing features, illumine the lives of early inhabitants, or disprove the invented tales of a romanticized past. But historical archaeology requires sensibilities and interests that not every archaeologist possesses. The key to successful archaeological exploration of building and site is the archaeologist's ability to mesh tangible evidence and findings with those of other building specialists to solve practical problems quickly.

Building investigators are specialists in the inspection, recording and diagnosis of building faults. The "building surveyor" is a legally recognized and regulated professional in Britain, but has not yet attained such status in North America. Often trained in architecture or building technology, inspectors with a special eye for historical detail and technique may prove invaluable in diagnosing the causes of deterioration and in tracking down solutions to puzzling difficulties. Where original drawings do not exist, building investigators may record dimensions and materials and produce measured drawings upon which conservation specifications may be based. Many investigators combine these talents with more general research skills to offer comprehensive building reports for conservation projects.

Architectural photographers and **photogrammetrists** can make precise and unambiguous records of buildings and sites before, during and after conservation work. Their photographs can be used by architects and specifiers instead of or in addition to drawings, saving time and sometimes expense. Not just anyone with a camera qualifies as an architectural photographer, however. Expensive equipment, large-format negatives, and an unusually keen sense for composition and lighting are beyond the average shutterbug. Terrestrial photogrammetry can provide, at additional expense, images good enough to stand in for measured drawings when plotted on a computer-aided system. As yet, there are few building photogrammetrists in Canada, but they may multiply as newer and less expensive equipment improves in quality.

Landscape architects and **land surveyors**, though seldom trained in any explicit aspect of heritage conservation, may offer site assessment services that mesh well with archaeological and building survey work and can be retained in conjunction with those specialists when larger sites and districts are under consideration.

Conservators and **materials scientists** are laboratory-based problem-solvers, familiar with the physics and chemistry of building materials and able to prescribe recipes such as mortar mixes and cleaning formulas. Fine-art conservators can offer particularly useful help with materials such as paint, woodwork and metal, though there is often a special challenge to translate their laboratory prescriptions to workable treatments on a building site.

Interior designers may sometimes go beyond conventional popular tastes for European "antiques" to an understanding for the historic forms and styles of Ontario communities, whether high-style or commonplace, and a corresponding skill in the conservation of furnishings and finishes. An old-building interior of good quality that has survived modification is a rare phenomenon, and should be entrusted only to a knowledgeable designer who can treat it with almost museological care.

Museologists receive training in several areas surrounding the core concern for the portable artifact and its conservation. Consequently, they may be able to assist the resolution of specialized problems identified through archaeology or historical research, by suggesting ways to integrate others' work in a way that respects the integrity of the whole.

Building craft workers and special tradespeople with traditional training and many years' experience may have learned as a matter of course many of the special conservation repair techniques studied so assiduously by professionals at graduate schools. Only the contractors for whom they work may know of (and perhaps jealously guard) their special skills. Though there are growing numbers of such specialists, they may be hard to find. And in some of the older trades, such as stonecarving, practitioners have almost completely disappeared.

Custom fabricators may be able to repair or replicate building elements in their workshops in cases where on-site repairs have become too difficult. Perhaps the most called-for components are window sash and other types of custom millwork. There are still many rural and small-town mills and shops that will do such work well, but, like good building workers, their existence is advertised only by word of mouth.

Clerks of works keep track of the conservation work on the jobsite. Though sometimes juniors in an architect's office, they often have solid construction experience and may consider themselves to be budding conservation architects. They must possess considerable patience and attentiveness, and must know building and repair techniques very well. Site supervision is a delicate and crucial task, and its practitioners must be thorough, disciplined and diplomatic.

Construction managers may be retained directly by clients to manage the construction phases of a project, as co-ordinator of a team comprising architect, contractor and other specialists as required. Construction management, traditionally part of the general contractor's role, adds to the responsibilities of a clerk of works the independence and authority to deal directly with everyone involved in the project. The flexibility of the role can be of great advantage to conservation, if the manager has the requisite understanding of old buildings and traditional practices to go with more general co-ordinating skills.

Managing projects

All types of construction have become more complex in recent years on account of increasing specialization of buildings, builders, consultants, and regulations. For conservation, which comprises much more than standard building work, the potential variety of ways of running the work, from research and planning to maintenance and repair, is even more complex. The roles of the many professionals described above depend on the type and scale of project and on client preferences.

Owners should be aware of the variety of ways that conservation projects can be managed. In traditional building practice, clients contract separately with an architect to prepare plans and drawings and a general contractor to carry them out, sometimes with the architect's supervision. But as building practice has broken up into more specialties, clients have more options for how the specialties relate to each other.
In project management, an individual or firm becomes virtual dictator of the work, and all the client's decisions and approvals are

funneled through the project manager's office. In construction management, an individual or firm becomes co-ordinator of a team, more referee and counsellor than dictator. In some cases, these functions are still carried out within an architect's responsibilities, but in complex projects the architect may lose that "oversight" function. Complexity is not simply a matter of size or expense — in conservation, even relatively small projects may require several specialties and close attention to their co-operation.

In contrast with this specialization of function, what are known as design-build firms may offer all these services under one roof. This comprehensive approach, where teamwork is made consistent over many projects, is primarily a new-construction technique best suited to projects with little variation. Unless a conventional design-build firm has individuals already skilled in conservation, it is unlikely that its approach can meet the varying demands of conservation.

Of these approaches and their variants, construction management seems to offer the most adaptability to the often changing conditions within conservation projects. But, no less than any other form of management, it requires talented and co-operative individuals to make it work.

This range of options for building conservation has parallels in the wider spheres of land-use and environmental planning, where independent specialists co-ordinated by heritage planners and management consultants are in competition with planning or engineering firms that offer a multitude of services. Either approach may offer the right services and personnel for a given job, from environmental assessment to landscape restoration. Again, the best results will come from co-ordinated teams of skilled individuals working together.

Clients, consultants and contracts

In retaining professional help, it is essential to look most closely at a consultant's or contractor's previous work and to take more than one look and hear more than one opinion about that work. Conservation requires both very specific skills and a very broad vision. It requires both assured experience and willingness to keep learning. There exist guidebooks for the selection of professional services in general as well as manuals for the professionals themselves on the development and selling of their services. The best general guide is the published advice available to the "other side" — consultants should learn about procurement, clients about marketing. Beyond that, keep asking questions of the prospective consultant (and of the client, too), to become aware of both talents and limitations in a "partnership" for a specific project. This will be true for any aspect of conservation from studies to maintenance, but especially so in selecting someone to co-ordinate the work of others.

To maximize the value of professional advice, clients, consultants and contractors should all take advantage of free (and almost free) help as well.

No matter how simple the work, it is vital to use proper legal contracts to regulate and assure quality of work. For building conservation, the construction documents themselves are legal agreements, not merely instructions, and their breach can cause legal problems as well as building decay. Architects and engineers use standard forms of contract documents, and it may be useful to examine these before getting into any legal agreements with consultants or contractors. These standard forms are generally useful (in some cases even mandatory), but they seldom fit many conditions encountered in conservation work. An owner may require several contracts for a single project, and their interrelations will be as important to the success of the work as their individual contents.

Even where a client fulfills many or all of these functions on a do-it-yourself basis, it is vital to keep them well organized. Though it may lead to an almost schizoid separation of personalities, an owner must be clear, when making crucial decisions every step of the way, whether he or she is acting as client, co-ordinator, or specialist.

Professional advice for free (and almost free)

There are many almost-free information resources in the form of books about conservation practice generally, or about specific aspects or components of conservation work. The references throughout the "Good practice" guidelines include both specialized texts and general works. Listed below are the more general and comprehensive of these publications.

Planning/principles: CUMI85, FRAM84, GUID82, HIST80, HUME83, MCPH84, NEWC79, REST86, TECH86, TIMM76

Integrated/technical: BOWY80, FEIL82, FROI86, HOLL86, INTE82, LANG78, LITC82, MACE98, MADD85, POWY29, RAMS88, SHOP86, SMIT78, STAH84, TECH82, TIMM76

Small buildings: HOLM75, KITC83, LYNC82

Residential: ARTL85, CUNN84, DAVE80/86, HANS83, HOW86, HUTC80, KAPL78/86, KIRK84, LAND79, LAND82, LAVA82, LEGN79, LEST77, MELV73, MILN79, POOR83, PUIB85, READ82, RENO85, SAUN87, STEP72

Commercial/main street: DUTO85, JOHN84, MEAD86

Maintenance: CHAM76, SAND84

French-language (general): FROI86, LAVA82, PUIB85, GUID82, RENO85

Finding and using advisory services

Recent expansion of conservation activity has built on a much older foundation of public movements to conserve history and its artifacts. In Ontario, such movements preceded Confederation — the Historical Society of Upper Canada was founded in 1861. Local historical and genealogical societies began to promote record-keeping and commemoration of local history more than a century ago. The Ontario Historical Society, to which thousands of individuals and more than two hundred organizations belong, dates from 1888. The more specific interest in architectural conservation is also quite venerable. The York Pioneer and Historical Society began to restore the Sharon Temple as a local museum in 1917; the Architectural Conservancy of Ontario was founded in 1932.

Because of this tradition of community interest and activity, many organizations and individuals can offer information and advice about a wide range of conservation problems. Information resources are lodged in libraries, archives, museums and publications and in the shared knowledge of many people involved in voluntary organizations. These resources are of inestimable value to those researching and evaluating communities and individual properties and may even be able to help in solving conservation problems. What help may be available will vary from place to place, however. And though there are provincial and federal resources for advice and assistance, these cannot replace local initiatives and local resources.

Local architectural committees

The Ontario Heritage Act has enabled municipalities to establish local architectural conservation advisory committees (LACACs). These citizens' committees advise municipal councils on any matter relating to the legal designation and conservation of buildings of historic or architectural value, as individual properties or as heritage conservation districts. In practice, a committee's activities often go far beyond simply recommending that specific places be designated, one by one. In order to prepare for the future, many committees make plans and inventories to identify and recognize important properties, rather than simply react to requests or threats.

They actively promote their heritage, staging public events, producing and distributing walking tour guides and other educational materials, and supporting local research and publication. Some LACACs offer practical advice (in larger communities, through a professional staff) on appropriate preservation, restoration and maintenance techniques. Many LACACs are, however, learners themselves, and their principal advisory role may be as co-ordinators of information and resources.

Members of a LACAC or its advisory staff are best contacted through the municipal clerk's office (though in some municipalities an inquiry may have to be a bit persistent, since such functions may be carried on by a historical board or other civic agency not known expressly as a LACAC). By April 1988, there were 175 LACACs in the province, and the number continues to grow.

Local heritage organizations and allied groups

Even in places where there is no LACAC, there are always individuals and groups with interests in and knowledge about local and regional architecture and history. Most communities have local museums or public libraries; curators and librarians are invariably knowledgeable about heritage groups and activities in their locale. They can offer information about buildings and sites in their collections and archives and can direct inquiries to larger centres or to local individuals with special knowledge. Libraries can find any conservation literature in print through interlibrary loan.

Many municipalities, counties and regions compile and maintain archives of documents. These can include tax and assessment records, personal and municipal papers, photographs, drawings and local newspapers, as well as collections of local historical publications. They may also have microfilm copies of important documents from other collections. All these may be useful for individual building research as well as for broader investigations. Local churches may also have such collections.

There are hundreds of historical and genealogical societies in Ontario, many with

Current addresses for the organizations mentioned in the text, with telephone numbers where available, can be found in Appendix 6, "Heritage organizations and information resources". See Appendix 7 for a current list of LACACs. Provincial government services and responsibilities for legislation are indexed and described generally in the annual "KWIC Index to Services" available from the Ontario Government Bookstore (see Appendix 6).

information about buildings and sites of heritage importance. In certain cases there may be a regional foundation dedicated to heritage conservation, with resources to undertake conservation work directly. For instance, both Frontenac County and Waterloo Region have active heritage foundations. These and other groups and their members often have collections of papers and photographs that can offer the patient researcher much essential information for conservation work. Many groups are themselves members of the Ontario Historical Society. Even local service clubs and ethnic organizations may have valuable information and documentation about the cultural history of their communities that can prove useful to conservation projects. Though some groups may have technical expertise in conservation, this is not often the case; their value is in the shared interest and knowledge they can offer about history and places.

Province-wide organizations

In addition to professional associations, province-wide interest groups may well have information and advice for specific cases. The Ontario Historical Society, as the principal umbrella organization of historical societies and the like, may be able to direct inquiries about regions or subjects to appropriate groups or individuals. Recently, the OHS offered a program of technical consulting services that enabled municipalities without local expertise to avail themselves of qualified consultants on a need-to-know basis.

The Architectural Conservancy of Ontario and its several regional chapters comprise a host of knowledgeable and dedicated enthusiasts who can advise on many aspects of architectural heritage. Similarly, members of the Ontario Society for Industrial Archaeology can assist those with interests in the industrial past of the province. There are many other such groups with special interests; they may be tracked down through local contacts, the Ontario Historical Society, or regional offices of the Ontario Ministry of Culture and Communications. Becoming a member of such groups offers opportunities to gather information, share knowledge and assist others in conservation, and permits access to allied national or international organizations.

Publicly endowed organizations

Though the Ontario Heritage Foundation may be better known for its financial assistance to conservation, it also provides information and technical advice to those who seek it or channels such requests to the professional staff in the Ministry of Culture and Communications who assist the Foundation. The Foundation sponsors conferences and seminars on conservation and produces advisory publications on specific topics. The Foundation's experience in conserving its own properties has generated considerable documentation; though little has been published, its files may have much useful information about individual problems.

Heritage Canada is a federally chartered but independent non-profit organization that promotes conservation of cultural heritage at the national level. Based in Ottawa, Heritage Canada publishes bi-monthly magazines with articles and technical advice on many areas of conservation activity and practice (*Canadian Heritage* and *Continuité*). It also has a reference centre in its Ottawa office, sometimes available by appointment for research visits. With local co-operation, Heritage Canada operates a "Main Street" program in several communities in Canada and has produced comprehensive information packages and seminars of technical advice for downtown revitalization and storefront rehabilitation.

Heritage in government

Few municipal governments have sufficient resources to retain heritage expertise on permanent staff, though this is changing as planning and building departments begin to recognize the need for such in-house expertise. Some larger towns, cities and regional municipalities have staff whose work includes heritage conservation. But for Ontario the major concentrations of professional expertise in government are the Heritage Branch of the Ontario Ministry of Culture and Communications in Toronto, and the National Historic Parks and Sites Directorate of Environment Canada in Ottawa. Both offices have professionals skilled in all aspects of conservation, from research to repair, and collections of reference materials for consultation. Both maintain contacts with allied professionals in other parts of their respective governments. Both have undertaken many specialized research projects; though few have been published, there is considerable documentation available for serious research on many topics and areas.

The federal government maintains the Canadian Inventory of Historic Building, a database of many buildings constructed up to the 1880s in Ontario and other eastern provinces (to the 1910s in the west). Though a descriptive dossier may be available for buildings in even the smallest community, the CIHB's data are by no means comprehensive. Its strength lies in its topical or thematic studies of building and structure types, and there are now published references for canals, courthouses, schools, town halls and lighthouses, among others, as well as surveys of selected Canadian architectural styles and techniques.

Both the Archives of Ontario (Toronto) and the National Archives of Canada (Ottawa) preserve extensive holdings of government records, as well as large collections of historic photographs, maps and architectural drawings. Particularly useful for architectural research are their holdings of old fire insurance atlases of many towns and cities.

Other government agencies

Governmental interest in heritage conservation is not restricted to heritage agencies. Provincial and federal departments concerned with housing, industry, public works, agriculture, environment and energy have all established some interest in one or another sphere of heritage conservation, from planning highways to insulating houses. Some agencies have published advisory materials that can apply to conserving architecture and other heritage resources. But these publications must be used with care and discretion, for much of their advice is directed toward new construction rather than the much more complicated matters of preservation and maintenance of existing places. Energy conservation and retrofit are particularly sensitive issues, and much conventional retrofit advice cannot be applied without

damaging the fabric and appearance of historic buildings.

Both federal and provincial governments publish general guides to all their programs; information about their potential for heritage conservation may be sought through heritage agencies.

Educational and cultural institutions

There are no full-fledged architectural conservation programs established in Canadian universities or technical colleges, though there are prospects that some will exist in the very near future. Nevertheless, there are individuals in departments of architecture, geography or history with their own interests in heritage, and such departments may well have academic studies and surveys of regional architecture invaluable as background for conservation work. As early as the 1930s some universities supported work on surveys or drawings of historic architecture in Ontario, as well as on regional studies with architectural aspects. Universities, especially the older institutions, have extensive archival holdings of historic documents, drawings and photographs rivalling those of government (and not necessarily restricted to immediate local interest). One special collection of note is at the Canadian Centre for Architecture in Montréal, whose rapidly growing archives and library should in the long run offer considerable documentation for many areas in Ontario as well as the rest of North America.

Periodicals

Conservation has begun to attract a good deal of attention as a commercial activity, and a series of special-interest magazines has grown up in addition to publications directed to professional audiences. These magazines offer useful information, though much must be used with caution unless reliably tested. Perhaps their most valuable contribution is their advertising for suppliers and fabricators, since a great deal of heritage work requires skills and materials not readily available in the corner hardware store.

A good statement of what LACACs have done, and can do. Since May 1986, the BRIC program mentioned in the letter has been replaced by new programs that offer similar grants in aid of conservation work in Ontario.

Dear Resident;

This L.A.C.A.C. committee was formed in Oct. 1984 in response to the threat to the Lyndhurst Bridge. We have become known for the part we took in the controversy over that issue, and we are proud of the contribution we made toward the final decision to restore the old bridge. We would now like to clarify our purpose and our aims for the future.

We are essentially a group of community-minded citizens who have decided to take an active role in preserving the things that make our township unique. Those among us who are natives of the township decided many years ago to stay here and help make this a better place to live, rather than go where the pastures looked greener. Those of us who have come here recently were attracted by the same features we are trying to save. We believe that a sense of pride in our past is essential to a strong and stable future, and we applaud the Government of Ontario for addressing that issue through the Ontario Heritage Act. We hope to make that Act work to the advantage of this township, and in that endeavour we request the cooperation of all residents.

We hope to foster an attitude of sympathy toward the old architecture in the township. Whereas, for many years, our old-fashioned houses, stores, and industries were seen as a liability that drove our young people away; those same old buildings have now become assets. They give our residents a sense of being part of a long tradition, and they attract newcomers who feel a lack of tradition in their lives. It is now a privilege to own some of our oldest houses and stores, and, as with most privileges, there is a responsibility to the community of which that architecture is a part, to defend it against such hazards as aluminum siding, "picture windows", aluminum storefronts, unsympathetic renovations, and needless destruction.

We would like to suggest alternatives to these detrimental renovations and help people find sources of restoration materials and services. Buildings that qualify according to our formula can be designated by our Township Council to bring them under the protection of the Ontario Heritage Act. Once designated, those buildings are eligible for grants under the Building Rehabilitation and Improvement Campaign (BRIC), which pay half the cost of exterior restoration, up to a maximum of $2000 per year. The BRIC program, however, is due to expire at the end of 1986, and we are expecting the announcement of a new program to replace it. In the meantime, we are researching and preparing to designate buildings chosen on the basis of merit and need for protection.

This committee has taken the additional incentive to establish an archives for the Township, where all descriptions of historical material may be deposited. At present it consists of a single filing cabinet, but we hope to expand into a large unit that will stand in the Council Chamber and hold file cabinets, flat plan files, book cases, microfilms, and a card index to the collection. It will be open for users and donors at any time the Municipal Building is open. We need any sort of written or printed material that sheds light on what conditions were like in this township, province, or country, prior to W.W. II. This includes, but is not limited to, diaries, letters, business records or agreements, trade directories, histories, family trees, photographs, maps, land grants, memoirs, etc. These things are often of no monetary value, and were usually sent to the dump in the past. We especially want identified photos of people and places in this township. Old photos of buildings can be the evidence that makes a restoration qualify for a BRIC grant.

The archives also needs donations of money or materials that are not included in our budget, such as a filing cabinet (two drawer, legal size), a plan file, encapsulating materials, book cases, and eventually, a microfilm reader.

Let's finally get started on building a mutual pride in our community by appreciating what our ancestors did and built here. In that field we are already 70 years behind our neighbours south of the border.

Thank you.

Local Architectural Conservation Advisory Committee, Township of Rear of Leeds and Lansdowne, May 1986

Conservation at law

The Ontario Heritage Act

This legislation is central to the protection and conservation of man-made heritage resources in the province, though it is by no means the only law that affects heritage. The Act authorizes the Ontario Heritage Foundation to promote heritage conservation by giving advice to the Minister of Culture and Communications, by owning and conserving property, by aiding conservation activities of others, and by maintaining a register of municipally designated properties. The Act enables municipal governments to designate and protect properties deemed to be of architectural or historic interest, whether singly or in districts, and further permits establishment of local architectural conservation advisory committees (LACACs) to advise municipal councils. It permits the Minister of Culture and Communications to designate archaeological sites and regulate archaeological exploration anywhere in Ontario. The Act also enables the Foundation and municipalities to acquire conservation easements on properties, in order to assure their conservation while leaving their use and enjoyment in private hands. The Act provides as well for the usual procedures and penalties normal to provincial legislation.

Part IV designation applies to properties of architectural or historical interest, as defined by a municipal council in consultation with its LACAC; the Act itself does not provide explicit criteria for designation. After a specified set of steps — that provide for public notice, consultations with property owners, public submissions, and administrative appeals — a property may be designated by municipal by-law. This by-law, with its accompanying reasons for designation, is registered on the title of the property and authorizes the municipality to delay the issuing of demolition permits or to require approval in advance for any alterations that might affect the reasons for designation. Designation makes the owner eligible to apply for any heritage grant-aid that may be available from municipal or provincial programs tied to the Act.

Part V designation applies to heritage conservation districts: municipally defined areas of distinctive architecture and/or landscape that may include several properties.

The procedures and effects of district designation are similar to Part IV designation with respect to individual properties, but Part V designation can also affect new construction on all properties within the district, enabling a municipality to ensure that new development will fit well with the character of its surroundings in scale, material and character. A district may also affect streets and other public lands within its bounds, allowing for comprehensive designs for rehabilitating both public and private property. District designation is reviewed and granted through the local-area planning process, culminating in a hearing of the Ontario Municipal Board.

Part VI designation enables the Minister of Culture and Communications to protect archaeological sites, including ruins; it is not a municipal responsibility. The Minister has the power to stop work on a site where archaeological remains may be threatened and to declare any site permanently out of bounds for excavation or other destruction. All archaeological work is regulated through the issuing of licenses by the Minister on the advice of the Ontario Heritage Foundation. Archaeological artifacts belong to the people of Ontario, and any unauthorized archaeological work is considered a serious offence.

Conservation easements may be acquired and held by the Ontario Heritage Foundation, by municipal governments or by heritage agencies so delegated by the Foundation. They permit the acquisition of one right from the bigger bundle of rights that make up ownership of real property. A conservation easement is a commitment by the owner of the property's title to conserve and maintain the features described in the easement; these may include interior or exterior features, landscape elements, even specified views. Once attached to the property, the easement is an inalienable part of the title, binding future owners to the same conditions. Easements have important advantages for both sides of the deal; the easement holder gets a guarantee that the property's heritage value will be conserved by the owner, and the owner is often able to obtain in return financial aid for the property's conservation.

It is enough . . . that the privately created ingredient of property receive a reasonable return. . . . All else is society's contribution by the sweat of its brow and the expenditure of its funds. To that extent society is also entitled to its due.

New York State Court of Appeals, 1978

The statutes noted here are cited more fully in Appendix 1 and Appendix 5. The most readily available guides to the Ontario Heritage Act are FRAM84 for individual buildings, and CUMI85 for districts. The Ministry of Culture and Communications also publishes advisory pamphlets on archaeological conservation and on heritage conservation easements, both available through ministry offices. Provincial government services and responsibilities for legislation are indexed and described generally in the annual "KWIC Index to Services".

The Planning Act and the Environmental Assessment Act

The Planning Act empowers Ontario municipalities to regulate the use of public and private lands within their boundaries, including preparation of general and local-area plans and their implementation in municipal legislation, especially zoning by-laws. The Act enables municipalities to negotiate agreements with landowners about conditions for developing properties in addition to zoning requirements and further enables them to undertake special studies and plans for redevelopment areas. Most of the Act's powers are subject to approval by senior levels of government, including regional authorization of site-plan and subdivision-plan approvals, ministerial approval of official plan documents, and administrative reviews, approvals and appeals before the Ontario Municipal Board.

The Planning Act has an effect on heritage resources in municipalities at least as great as the Ontario Heritage Act, since it governs the uses to which buildings may be put and the context in which they will continue to exist in the future. Plans after all will affect *all* buildings and properties, whether designated or not (and the vast majority of properties that may merit designation have not been designated). A town cannot enact a heritage conservation district without having amended its official plan to allow for heritage districts in general. Any alteration of permitted uses to enable an existing building to be adapted to new uses is a planning matter.

Because planning and heritage are so intertwined, dealing with heritage matters is most often part of the responsibilities of a planning department or consultant, and most heritage inquiries end up with planning officials (see "Municipal policies", below).

Ontario's Environmental Assessment Act requires that all major developments be assessed for their impact on the environment as a whole and that measures be taken in planning and construction to ameliorate these effects as much as possible. In practice, the bulk of these projects are public developments; most private undertakings take place within municipalities where development is already regulated by planning and zoning (though there are occasional overlaps). The Act's definition of environment is quite broad and includes man-made features of architectural, historical, archaeological and scenic value.

In general, major environmental disturbances such as highways, electrical transmission lines, minesites and even tourist facilities can be immensely damaging to heritage features, and the most effective impact-reducing strategy is usually avoidance. But where avoidance is impossible, then as much as possible heritage resources are inventoried, recorded, protected during construction, and re-used or modified to cope with their new context. Demolition should be only a *very* last resort.

Because of the Environmental Assessment Act's insistence on thorough study of the environment before any change is contemplated, environmental studies have gathered much information on the heritage features of large areas of the province beyond municipal boundaries. Accordingly, many collections of data in environmental reports may prove useful to researchers on history, architecture and archaeology. The Act's provisions for protecting environmental resources apply to buildings no less than wetlands, and these procedures are far more comprehensive than those of the Ontario Heritage Act.

Maintenance and occupancy by-laws

In Ontario, the Planning Act and the Municipal Act authorize and in certain cases compel municipalities to enact property standards in the form of "maintenance and occupancy" by-laws which establish standards for the security and upkeep of properties. Abandonment and neglect of property are a blight on surrounding properties, and municipalities have powers to enter and clean up dereliction and charge the expense to the property owner's taxes. Such powers have kept most of the province's municipalities relatively free of abandoned and derelict buildings, but sometimes at the cost of rushing the demolition (or completely insensitive modernization) of properties whose conservation could not be instantly assured. The effect of these by-laws on heritage structures varies from place to place, but they do offer a minimum standard of serviceability that even the most modest conservation project must surpass.

Ontario Building Code

The Ontario Building Code is a uniform standard for construction practice across the province, though its enforcement is a municipal responsibility. The Code was devised to regulate new construction and in consequence can conflict seriously with existing buildings, many built under earlier regulations or no regulation at all. Recognizing this, the provincial government has begun to modify the Code to recognize the value of older construction techniques and to enable older buildings to meet performance standards rather than the absolute minima that comprise the regulations for totally new construction. Part XI enables owners and builders to seek "compliance alternatives" (suggested in the Code itself) or "alternative measures" (proposed by owner or consultant) for residential occupancies in buildings being rehabilitated or converted from other uses. This involves some flexibility on the part of local building officials, but it has proved an effective approach in terms of economics, aesthetics and safety. Work is in progress to extend such provisions to other uses but has been complicated by the many permutations of conversion from one use to another.

This flexible approach to regulation can permit retention of much more of a building's character in the throes of its conservation for renewed use than would be possible with strict adherence to new-construction techniques. Its price is the need to know more about the techniques of the building's original construction, an area not yet well enough known by very many owners, architects and builders.

Other conservation-related regulations

Other aspects of provincial law bear directly on conservation work. The Occupational Health and Safety Act and its regulations provide for worker safety on construction sites (among other places) and spell out procedures for avoiding unsafe practices. The Environmental Protection Act regulates the use of chemicals and hazardous substances on and around worksites; many conservation techniques, especially cleaning, can be very hazardous to workers and surrounding properties if not carried out strictly according to regulations and specifications. The Ontario Fire Code governs fire safety measures for all buildings, old and new, and contains "retrofit" provisions that empower fire officials to order modifications to buildings for fire-safety reasons, regardless of whether or not any work is being done to a building. These retrofit powers are meant to mesh with the requirements of the Ontario Building Code, and this may mean life-safety studies and negotiations about performance standards similar to those for residential renovation.

Municipal policies

Some towns and cities have taken more initiative than others with these legal tools. For instance, the city of Toronto has included provisions in its official plan to offer a density "bonus" (added floor area for new development) to projects in the central area of the city that incorporate and rehabilitate historic buildings. Toronto also allows the use of "surplus" density rights to be transferred from sites with historic buildings to adjacent or nearby properties. The sale of such density rights may generate funds to help conserve the historic buildings themselves. Toronto has also received authority beyond the powers available in the Ontario Heritage Act to restrain demolition of designated properties.

These and other strategies for combining the goals of city planning and heritage conservation have been tentatively explored by other municipalities. The Planning Act's authorization of special development agreements enables municipalities to negotiate such deals on a project-by-project basis, so that there is as yet little consistency from place to place or from time to time within the province.

Financing conservation

Investing in heritage

It should be obvious (even from the basic principles of conservation) that for any property of heritage importance to survive, it must have an economically viable use and user. In turn, such use depends on the more general economic conditions of a community and its region. A decision to invest in a property of historic or architectural interest can be justified on historic or aesthetic grounds only so far, and then economic utility must carry the day. This is true for both public and private ownership — even the historic-house museum must help support itself financially.

The key to evaluating the financial aspects of heritage is to consider most carefully what professionals call "life-cycle costs" — the complete costs of capital improvements and operating expenses amortized over the expected life of the building (not merely the life of its mortgage). At its most comprehensive, a life-cycle cost analysis may take into account even the energy consumption (and costs) built into the manufacturing of building materials. For projects supported by public agencies, the analysis may also include indirect benefits to adjacent economic activities (for instance, expenditures in nearby businesses by visitors to a cultural facility). By understanding all aspects of building construction and operation costs beyond the simple short-term analysis, an owner can assess how much an existing building can contribute to long-term costs and savings by balancing the financial and other credits represented by its existing state against the costs of conservation and rehabilitation for renewed use into the future.

In most cases, a cold-blooded analysis of this sort will not demonstrate huge savings for conservation over new construction — nor, for that matter, will new construction have much of an edge either. But when the non-financial contributions of heritage buildings are added to the balance (summed up in such elusive characteristics as pride of place and community stability), conservation invariably ends up being far more sensible and *economical*, in the broad sense of the word, than demolition and new construction as a way to renew properties and communities.

Conventional lending

Most construction is financed through loans from credit institutions: banks, trust companies, credit unions, insurance companies. These are generally conservative institutions. In Canada, that means (somewhat perversely) that they lend less money and attach more stringent conditions to conservation projects than to new construction. The reasons for this boil down to the tremendous incentives given new construction by the current system of taxation and government expenditure. This fiscal context has existed for many decades, in order to promote general economic development, and is unlikely to be much modified in the foreseeable future, even under the federal tax-reform proposals of 1987.

For instance, a bank may offer 75 per cent financing of a new-building project with a five-year term, but only 60 per cent on a three-year term for a rehabilitation project (and at a higher interest rate). The differential reflects the bank's lower opinion of the future worth of the rehabilitation project, and forces the owner to be far more aggressive about other sources of financing or far less generous in spending money on conservation work. This is so despite the undeniable financial advantages of most rehabilitation projects — occupants may be able to move in sooner to generate cash flow, some repairs can proceed while users are occupying other parts of the building, and government approvals can often take place more quickly than for new buildings, especially in built-up neighbourhoods.

The biggest problem with this attitude of conventional lenders is the dangerous cost-cutting that such discounted lending encourages. Rehabilitation projects are doubly constrained, first by a taxation system that bonuses new construction by permitting accelerated depreciation of new work, and then by the unwillingness of lenders to extend credit on the same terms as new work. Only where an institution is satisfied that the local property market will grow faster than the norm and make the rehabilitation project *immediately* worth more than the purchase price plus improvements will there be any prospect of financing to new-building norms. And in those cases, property speculation will

---

A good architect can make an old house look a lot better by just discussing the cost of a new one.

Anonymous

For comments and advice on private-sector financing, see REAL81, BENN79, REIN79, WARN78 and NATI76. For public-sector projects, see REAL81 and KALM80b. Grant and loan programs change frequently; for current programs, check with the Heritage Branch of the Ministry of Culture and Communications.

probably have pushed the purchase price up even before work begins. The financial success of privately funded conservation is thus as much a matter of luck and good timing as it is of cool calculation.

For income-generating projects, lenders will expect to see a fully worked-out balance sheet of revenues, capital expenditures and operating expenditures. In many cases, they will also want evidence that tenants or users have already committed themselves to the project and may even wish to see the designs and specifications for the building work itself. On the positive side, the availability of grants or loans from public agencies for heritage work may loosen up the purse-strings and prompt a higher contribution from a lender. For owner-occupied residences in larger centres, it is now much less difficult than it once was to get mortgage-based financing for "home improvements", but in other areas it may prove difficult to get such financing without some government guarantee.

Grant and loan programs

Provincial and federal governments have been unwilling to make fundamental changes in the fiscal context affecting building and conservation. Instead, they have established programs of direct grant or loan support for building conservation and rehabilitation. These programs come in several guises. Almost all direct assistance for conservation comes from provincial and provincially aided municipal programs; it may take the form of specific "heritage" aid, more general community renewal assistance, or help from funds aimed even more broadly at economic development at a regional or sectoral scale.

Heritage-directed aid in Ontario comes primarily from the Ministry of Culture and Communications and the Ontario Heritage Foundation; in some cases these provincial funds supplement municipal financial assistance. In all cases, the owner is expected to raise the lion's share of the funding required for any project. There have been and continue to be programs directed at different conditions. There may be municipally administered grants made available on a broad basis to owners of any designated property for work needed to conserve the features for which the property was

designated. More substantial funding for similar work may be made available directly from the ministry or the Foundation for commercial rehabilitation projects, for heritage district improvements, and for conservation work on cultural, institutional and community facilities. The ministry or the Foundation may also provide aid to non-capital heritage projects, such as studies, inventories, publications and events that themselves expand public awareness and activity in heritage conservation.

In recent years the ministry has encouraged and aided the formation of community heritage funds to extend such support to an even wider range of situations. Nevertheless, there are no permanent programs for such assistance. Their availability in the long term will depend on how well the present generation of programs fare.

Some municipalities, aided or not by matching dollars from the province, have small-scale heritage foundations for special projects, and help from these funds should be sought for projects of local importance.

Community development and renewal programs are funded by several provincial agencies, most notably the ministries of Housing and Municipal Affairs. These programs provide support for everything from planning studies to capital expenditures for upgrading utilities and community buildings. They are not directed specifically to heritage conservation, but are clearly of great influence on local opportunities for conservation work. There are also more focused programs that promote upgrading of housing and conversion of non-residential buildings into housing units. Special programs assist revitalization of main-street commercial areas and commercial façades.

These programs are normally available only through municipalities; they are tied to municipal planning policies and initiatives and, in the case of commercial areas, they are often linked with formally established business improvement areas. There have been many cases of close co-operation between community development and renewal projects and explicit heritage projects, to the point where two agencies may both contribute to different aspects of one project or area.

Economic development incentives

sometimes offer assistance toward heritage projects that happen to meet wider regional development goals. Such incentives are usually restricted to areas whose economies are not prospering, though small business development aid is normally available throughout the province. The most conspicuous programs, through the Ministry of Tourism and Recreation, comprise assistance to "tourism infrastructure", to facilities (and to supporting studies and plans) that offer accommodation and support to

tourists and visitors, rather than to the building of actual attractions. Such capital assistance can be invaluable in conserving places away from urban centres. Programs to assist the establishment of small businesses may also be useful in capital work on existing buildings, and thus to heritage conservation.

From time to time, special funding agreements between federal and provincial agencies permit capital assistance to cultural facilities, industries and other groups whose programs may include the revitalization of buildings or sites of heritage importance. Such programs, though infrequent, may offer assistance far beyond the levels available through heritage-specific funds.

Taxation

There exists in the United States a program of income tax credits for "certified" rehabilitation work, that is, building conservation work that meets the standards of the Secretary of the Interior for quality and integrity. This program, though altered somewhat in recent years, has prompted private investments of billions of dollars in high-qualityarchitectural conservation. No such program exists at either federal or provincial levels in Canada. Nor are there breaks in property taxation for heritage conservation. Unlike the United Kingdom, Canada offers no exemption from sales tax for materials and fees for building conservation. Accordingly, much of the grant aid available from sources outlined above will go toward paying taxes on all aspects of the work. These taxes also apply to new construction — but new construction is allowed a more rapid rate of capital depreciation, and thus a better tax advantage. Despite lobbying by preservation groups, there has been little action to change this situation in recent federal or provincial tax-reform proposals.

APPENDICES

About the Ontario Heritage Foundation

The Foundation's legal mandate and authority are spelled out in the Ontario Heritage Act, R.S.O. 1980, c. 337, Part II.

Conserving the provincial inheritance

Established in 1968, the Ontario Heritage Foundation works to promote and protect the tangible resources of artifacts, properties, buildings, structures and landscapes that make up the province's rich and irreplaceable heritage. The Foundation's mandate also provides that it encourage everyone in the province to conserve these resources.

The Foundation is an agency of the government of Ontario, guided by a board of private citizens representing all parts of Ontario, each with a strong interest or talent in one of the many aspects of heritage conservation.

The Foundation gives financial aid and practical help to private individuals and public bodies actively conserving the archaeological, architectural, historical and natural resources that comprise the province's cultural heritage. It also acts as steward of many valuable properties, both movable and immovable, that have come as gifts from generous benefactors to the people of the province.

The Foundation owns many types of property outright, from collections of fine art and archaeological artifacts to buildings and tracts of land. It also holds many conservation easements, legal rights pertaining to specific lands or buildings that effectively make the Foundation a partner in the care of a property in order to protect those characteristics important to the provincial heritage while enabling its owner to use and enjoy the property. Many of these easements have been acquired in exchange for grant assistance to the conservation of buildings.

The real properties owned by the Foundation are used and managed so as to conserve all of their heritage values — architectural, archaeological, historical and natural — in harmony and balance. The Foundation tries to be a model trustee and custodian of its properties, making them available for sympathetic use by tenants or by the general public when appropriate. Similarly, where it holds an easement, the Foundation encourages the owner to maintain the property's heritage character to the highest possible standards while keeping the property in productive use.

In general, given the costs of maintaining properties and the personal care required to maintain them well, the Foundation works as much as possible with other private and public owners to conserve their properties in active use in their communities. In promoting conservation by others, the Foundation provides grant aid, organizational assistance and technical advice and information.

Nature

There are many properties in Ontario with important biological and scenic characteristics that have been spared development and destruction. Distinctive landforms, endangered wetlands, forest remnants and other wildlands and landscapes are all important and irreplaceable vestiges of the province's environmental history. Though some of these are protected in parks and reserves, there remain tracts of land in private or government ownership whose conservation for the future is by no means assured.

Working with an alliance of organizations dedicated to nature conservation, the Foundation encourages protection of this natural heritage by accepting deeds of gift of such lands, by negotiating and holding conservation easements to ensure their legal protection, and by acquiring important properties with special funds granted by the provincial government. By demonstrating principles and practices of wise land-use management, the Foundation aims to protect the most precious of these lands and encourage other custodians of natural heritage to follow its example.

The Foundation has a special role in protecting natural heritage along the length of the Niagara Escarpment and, with the co-operation of the Niagara Escarpment, Commission is acquiring many important properties from Queenston to Tobermory.

Archaeology

Archaeological exploration seeks an understanding of the past, from the earliest settlements and passages of prehistory to the minutiae of life in the modern world, in its material traces. By examining these traces in the configuration of cultivated landscapes, material remains found underground or underwater, artistic expressions of cultures otherwise forgotten, or even rubbish found around and inside a building under repair, amateur and professional archaeologists can recover important and useful knowledge of the past and of the present.

The Foundation advises the Minister of Culture and Communications on the issuing of licences required for archaeological projects in Ontario and on the designation of sites under the Ontario Heritage Act.

The Foundation gives grants in aid of archaeological research, fieldwork and analysis, as well as more broadly conceived educational and promotional initiatives. It also offers professional advice to groups and individuals engaged in scholarly and popular projects with archaeological applications. From time to time the Foundation may even act as a trustee to protect an important archaeological property from damage.

History

Ontario's history can be likened to a vast fabric, whose many threads represent the stories of individuals and communities, places and events, themes and variations. Each of these threads is special; the fabric they form is unique. Understanding and maintenance of this precious cloth of cultural history demand care and attention to the memories represented by those countless threads. If the threads are not maintained, communities lose their continuity and vitality, sometimes with unfortunate practical consequences. Recognizing this, many communities commemorate and celebrate their pasts in a wide variety of ways, from parties to publications.

The Foundation supports the conservation of history by giving financial aid to groups and individuals for historical research, publications, conferences, travelling displays, museum installations, and a variety of special projects initiated by communities. The Foundation takes an active role in organizing regional heritage festivals and conclaves to promote community pride in cultural heritage and to offer practical advice for its continuing protection.

The Foundation also erects markers commemorating important places, events and personages in provincial history; there are more than a thousand blue-and-gold plaques throughout Ontario.

Architecture

Structures of architectural or historical importance are valuable reminders of our past as well as significant places for present and future use and enjoyment. Each community in the province has been endowed with buildings, monuments, structures, and entire neighbourhoods or districts that give it distinction and vitality. Even apparently modest structures of no great antiquity can be valuable assets to a community's appearance and its economic vitality. But old buildings have distinct problems, too, and it may be difficult to keep their historic character intact while fitting them out for modern uses and requirements.

The Foundation offers grant aid or loans to encourage conservation of important structures in the province. It also channels practical advice on conservation to individuals and groups, including many local architectural conservation advisory groups that protect and conserve buildings and districts in communities throughout Ontario.

The Foundation takes a very broad view of what is architecture. It has aided repair, rehabilitation and restoration of houses, mills, churches, courthouses, schools, even bridges. It has also assisted publication of many books and guides promoting appreciation of architecture in communities, both as individual landmarks and as distinctive districts of many complementary buildings. It has begun to publish practical information — such as this book — on how best to conserve the province's architectural heritage while keeping it useful for current and future needs.

The Venice Charter

International Charter for the Conservation and Restoration of Monuments and Sites

Venice: International Council on Monuments and Sites, 1966.

The Venice Charter is the foundation for several subsequent adaptations and refinements. There are comprehensive national documents based on its precepts, as well as international charters for specialized aspects. Of particular interest are the following:

The Florence Charter on Historic Gardens, 1982 (ICOMOS)

Recommendation concerning the preservation of cultural property endangered by public or private works, 1968 (UNESCO General Conference, Paris)

Recommendation concerning the safeguarding and contemporary role of historic areas, 1976 (UNESCO General Conference, Nairobi)*

The Burra Charter for the Conservation of Places of Cultural Significance, 1981 (ICOMOS Australia)

Archeology and Historic Preservation: Secretary of the Interior's Standards and Guidelines, 1983 (U.S. National Park Service)*

The Secretary of the Interior's Standards for Rehabilitation and Guidelines for Rehabilitating Historic Buildings, 1983 [revised] (U.S. National Park Service)*

The Appleton Charter for the Protection and Enhancement of the Built Environment, 1983 (ICOMOS Canada)

Code of Ethics and Guidance for Practice, 1985 (International Institute of Conservators — Canadian Group)

Copies of these texts are available through ICOMOS Canada; those with an asterisk (*) may be found in KEUN84.

Imbued with a message from the past, the historic monuments of generations of people remain to the present day as living witnesses of their age-old traditions. People are becoming more and more conscious of the unity of human values and regard ancient monuments as a common heritage. The common responsibility to safeguard them for future generations is recognized. It is our duty to hand them on in the full richness of their authenticity.

It is essential that the principles guiding the preservation and restoration of ancient buildings should be agreed and be laid down on an international basis, with each country being responsible for applying the plan within the framework of its own culture and traditions.

By defining these basic principles for the first time, the Athens Charter of 1931 contributed towards the development of an extensive international movement which has assumed concrete form in national developments, in the work of ICOM and UNESCO and in the establishment by the latter of the International Centre for the Study of the Preservation and the Restoration of Cultural Property. Increasing awareness and critical study have been brought to bear on problems which have continually become more complex and varied; now the time has come to examine the Charter afresh in order to make a thorough study of the principles involved and to enlarge its scope in a new document.

Accordingly, the IInd International Congress of Architects and Technicians of Historic Monuments, which met in Venice from May 25th to 31st 1964, approved the following text:

DEFINITIONS

Article 1.   The concept of an historic monument embraces not only the single architectural work but also the evidence of a particular civilisation, a significant development or an historic event. This applies not only to great works of art but also to more modest works of the past which have acquired cultural significance with the passing of time.

Article 2.   The conservation and restoration of monuments must have recourse to all the sciences and techniques which can contribute to the study and safeguarding of the architectural heritage.

AIM

Article 4.   The intention in conserving and restoring monuments is to safeguard them no less as works of art than as historical evidence.

CONSERVATION

Article 4.   It is essential to the conservation of monuments that they be maintained on a permanent basis.

Article 5.   The conservation of monuments is always facilitated by making use of them for some socially useful purpose. Such use is therefore desirable but it must not change the lay-out or decoration of the building. It is within these limits only that modifications demanded by a change of function should be envisaged and may be permitted.

Article 6.   The conservation of a monument implies preserving a setting which is not out of scale. Wherever the traditional setting exists, it must be kept. No new construction, demolition or modification which would alter the relations of mass and colour must be allowed.

Article 7.   A monument is inseparable from the history to which it bears witness and from the setting in which it occurs. The moving of all or part of a monument cannot be allowed except where the safeguarding of that monument demands it or where it is justified by national or international interests of paramount importance.

Article 8.   Items of sculpture, painting or decoration which form an integral part of a monument may only be removed from it if this is the sole means of ensuring their preservation.

RESTORATION

Article 9.   The process of restoration is a highly specialised operation. Its aim is to preserve and reveal the aesthetic and historic value of the monument and is based on respect for original material and authentic documents. It must stop at the point where conjecture begins, and in this case moreover any extra work which is indispensable must be distinct from the architectural composition and must bear a contemporary stamp. The restoration in any case must be preceded and followed by an archaeological and historical study of the monument.

Article 10.   Where traditional techniques prove inadequate, the consolidation of a monument can be achieved by the use of any modern technique for conservation and construction, the efficacy of which has been shown by scientific data and proved by experience.

Article 11.   The valid contribution of all periods to the building of a monument must be respected, since unity of style is not the aim of a restoration. When a building includes the superimposed work of different periods, the revealing of the underlying state can only be justified in exceptional circumstances and when what is removed is of little interest and the material which is brought to light is of great historical, archaeological or aesthetic value, and its state of preservation good enough to justify the action. Evaluation of the importance of the elements involved and the decision as to what may be destroyed cannot rest solely on the individual in charge of the work.

Article 12.   Replacements of missing parts must integrate harmoniously with the whole, but at the same time must be distinguishable from the original so that restoration does not falsify the artistic or historic evidence.

Article 13.   Additions cannot be allowed except in so far as they do not detract from the interesting parts of the building, its traditional setting, the balance of its composition and its relation with its surroundings.

HISTORIC SITES

Article 14.   The sites of monuments must be the object of special care in order to safeguard their integrity and ensure that they are cleared and presented in a seemly manner. The work of conservation and restoration carried out in such places should be inspired by the principles set forth in the foregoing articles.

EXCAVATIONS

Article 15.   Excavations should be carried out in accordance with scientific standards and the recommendation defining international principles to be applied in the case of archaeological excavation adopted by UNESCO in 1956.

Ruins must be maintained and measures necessary for the permanent conservation and protection of architectural features and of objects discovered must be taken. Furthermore, every means must be taken to facilitate the understanding of the monument and to reveal it without ever distorting its meaning.

All reconstruction work should however be ruled out *a priori*. Only anastylosis, that is to say, the reassembling of existing but dismembered parts can be permitted. The material used for integration should always be recognisable and its use should be the least that will ensure the conservation of a monument and the reinstatement of its form.

PUBLICATION

Article 16.   In all works of preservation, restoration or excavation, there should always be precise documentation in the form of analytical and critical reports, illustrated with drawings and photographs.

Every stage of the work of clearing, consolidation, rearrangement and integration, as well as technical and formal features identified during the course of the work, should be included. This record should be placed in the archives of a public institution and made available to research workers. It is recommended that the report should be published.

The Appleton Charter

The Appleton Charter for the Protection and Enhancement of the Built Environment.

Ottawa: ICOMOS Canada (English-Speaking Committee), Fall 1983.

A. Preamble

This charter acknowledges *The International Charter for the Conservation of Monuments and Sites* (Venice, 1964), the Australia ICOMOS *Charter for the Conservation of Places of Cultural Significance* (the Burra Charter of February 23, 1981), and the *Charter for the Preservation of Québec's Heritage* (Declaration of Deschambaults), without which it could not exist.

It further recognizes that the sound management of the built environment is an important cultural activity; and that conservation is an essential component of the management process.

B. Framework

Intervention within the built environment may occur at many *levels* (from preservation to redevelopment), at many *scales* (from individual building elements to entire sites), and will be characterized by one or more *activities*, ranging from maintenance to addition.

Though any given project may combine intervention scales. levels and activities, projects should be characterized by a clearly stated goal against which small-scale decisions may be measured.

The appropriate level of intervention can only be chosen after careful consideration of the merits of the following:

- cultural significance
- condition and integrity of the fabric
- contextual value
- appropriate use of available physical, social and economic resources

Decisions concerning the relative importance of these factors must represent as broadly based a consensus as possible.

Legitimate consensus will involve public participation and must precede initiation of work.

The relationship between scales of intervention, levels of intervention, and intervention activities is summarized below.

	Activity			
Levels of Intervention	Maintenance	Stabilization	Removal	Addition
Preservation	●	●		
Period Restoration	●	●	●	●
Rehabilitation	●	●	●	●
Period Reconstruction				●
Redevelopment				●

Levels of Intervention

Preservation — retention of the existing form, material and integrity of site.

Period Restoration — recovery of an earlier form, material and integrity of a site.

Rehabilitation — modification of a resource to contemporary functional standards, which may involve adaptation for new use.

Period Reconstruction — recreation of vanished or irreversibly deteriorated resources.

Redevelopment — insertion of contemporary structures or additions sympathetic to the setting.

Activities

Maintenance — continual activity to ensure the longevity of the resource without irreversible or damaging intervention.

Stabilization — a periodic activity to halt deterioration and to put the existing form and materials of a site into a state of equilibrium, with minimal change.

Removal — a periodic activity: modification which involves the subtraction of surfaces, layers, volumes and/or elements.

Addition — aperiodic activity: modification which involves the introduction of new material.

C. Principles

Respect for the existing fabric is fundamental to the activities of protection and enhancement.

The process of protection and enhancement must recognize all interests, and have recourse to all fields of expertise which can contribute to the study and safeguarding of a resource.

In intervening at the scales, levels, and activities described, measures in support of the protection and enhancement of the built environment will involve adherence to the following principles:

Protection: Protection may involve stabilization; it must involve a continuing program of maintenance.

Artefactual value — Sites of the highest cultural significance are to be considered primarily as artefacts, demanding protection as fragile and complex historical monuments.

Setting — Any element of the built environment is inseparable from the history to which it bears witness, and from the setting in which it occurs. Consequently, all interventions must deal with the whole as well as with the parts.

Relocation — Relocation and dismantling of an existing resource should be employed only as a last resort, if protection cannot be achieved by other means.

Enhancement: The activities of removal or addition are characteristic of measures in support of enhancement of the heritage resource.

Use — A property should be used for its originally intended purpose. If this is not feasible, every reasonable effort shall be made to provide a compatible use which requires minimal alteration. Consideration of new use should begin with respect for existing and original traditional patterns of movement and layout.

Additions — New volumes, materials and finishes may be required to satisfy new uses or requirements. They should echo contemporary ideas but respect and enhance the spirit of the original.

Environmental Control — Systems of insulation, environmental control, and other servicing should be upgraded in ways which respect the existing and traditional equilibria and do not set in motion processes of deterioration.

D. Practice

Documentation — The better a resource is understood and interpreted, the better it will be protected and enhanced.

In order to properly understand and interpret a site, there must be a comprehensive investigation of all those qualities which invest a structure with significance.

This activity must precede activity at the site.

Work on site must itself be documented and recorded.

Conjecture — Activities which involve the recovery or recreation of earlier forms must be limited to those forms which can be achieved without conjecture.

Distinguishability — New work should be identifiable on close inspection or to the trained eye, but should not impair the aestetic integrity or coherence of the whole.

Materials and Techniques — Materials and techniques should respect traditional practice unless modern substitutes for which a firm scientific basis exists, which have been supported by a body of experience and which provide significant advantage can be identified.

Patina — Patina forms part of the historic integrity of a resource, and its destruction should be allowed only when essential to the protection of the fabric. Falsification of patina should be avoided.

Reversibilty — The use of reversible processes is always to be preferrred to allow the widest options for future development or the correction of unforeseen problems, or where the integrity of the resource could be affected.

Integrity — Structural and technological integrity must be respected and will require attention to performance as well as to appearance.

Standards for building conservation projects grant-aided by the Ontario Heritage Foundation

Adopted as policy by the Ontario Heritage Foundation, September 1985

1. Building conservation projects shall be undertaken only on the basis of a responsible and sufficient investigation of the historical and architectural aspects of the existing building and site.

2. The existing state of the building and site shall be recorded before a project is undertaken, and changes made in the course of a project shall be properly documented in relation to that record.

3. Repair and reconstruction activities shall be phased and managed to protect and respect the historic fabric of the building.

4. Every reasonable effort shall be made to provide a compatible use for a property which requires minimal alteration of the building or site in its environment, or to use a property for its originally intended purpose.

5. The distinguishing original qualities or character of a building or site in its environment shall not be destroyed. The removal or alteration of any historic material or distinctive architectural features should be avoided whenever possible.

6. All buildings and sites shall be recognized as products of their own time. Alterations having no historical basis that seek to blur the distinction between the historic and new portions of the project shall be discouraged.

7. Changes that may have taken place in the course of time are evidence of the history and development of a building or site and its environment. Whenever these changes have acquired significance in their own right, they shall be recognized and respected.

8. Distinctive stylistic features or examples of skilled craftsmanship which characterize a building or site shall be retained and respected. Additional work shall complement and sympathetically enhance the distinctive historic features of the building.

9. Deteriorated architectural features shall be repaired rather than replaced wherever possible. In the event replacement is necessary, the selection of new materials should be treated with sensitivity.

10. The surface cleaning of buildings shall be undertaken only with the gentlest means possible. Sandblasting and other cleaning methods that needlessly erode or damage the historic fabric of the building shall not be undertaken.

11. Every reasonable effort shall be made to protect and preserve archaeological resources affected by or adjacent to the project.

12. Contemporary design for alterations or additions to existing properties shall not be discouraged when such alterations and additions do not destroy significant historical, architectural, or cultural material, and when such design is compatible with the size, scale, colour, material, and character of the property, neighbourhood or environment.

13. Whenever possible, new additions or alterations to buildings shall be done in such a manner that if such additions or alterations were to be removed in the future, the essential form and integrity of the building would be unimpaired.

Codes and regulations for conservation work in Ontario

Copies of provincial acts and regulations are available in person at the Ontario Government Bookstore, 880 Bay Street, Toronto; by mail from MGS Publication Services, 5th floor, 880 Bay Street, Toronto M7A 1N8; or by telephone — in Toronto: 965-6015; from outside Toronto, toll-free: 1-800-268-7540; from area code 807: ask the operator for Zenith 67200.

Construction and building rehabilitation

The *Ontario Building Code* governs almost all construction activities, and contains special provisions for renovation and for handicapped access that may affect old-building work. The Code is administered by local officials — to start with, talk to the local building inspector or building department. For further information contact the Ontario Buildings Branch, Ministry of Housing, 777 Bay Street, 3rd floor, Toronto M5G 2E5, telephone (416) 585-6666. Local officials and the Buildings Branch are similarly responsible for the *Plumbing Code*. Electrical work is regulated by the *Electrical Safety Code*, administered by Ontario Hydro (700 University Avenue, Toronto M5G 1X6, telephone (416) 592-3721).

Fire safety

Ontario Fire Code Regulation 730/81 enables officials to inspect and in some cases to require the upgrading (retrofit) of fire safety features in existing buildings. Such upgrading may often overlap with work under the Building Code. Matters of fire safety in existing buildings are dealt with by local fire departments and by the Office of the Fire Marshal (Technical, Research and Consulting Services, 7 Overlea Boulevard, 3rd floor, Toronto M4H 1A8, telephone (416) 965-4851 or 965-4855).

Occupational health and safety

Construction work, even on small projects, can be hazardous, and site safety is accordingly regulated by the government under the *Occupational Health and Safety Act*. The Ministry of Labour maintains a network of site offices for inspection, investigation and technical advice. Information is available through the Construction Health and Safety Branch, 400 University Avenue, 8th floor, Toronto M7A 1T7, telephone (416) 965-7161 or 1-800-268-8013.

Environmental protection

For the most part, conservation work does not create hazardous waste or effluent but in some cases, such as the rehabilitation of old industrial or mining sites, projects may expose long-hidden toxic materials. The *Environmental Protection Act* requires great care to be taken on such sites. For information (including the location of regional offices) contact the Investigations and Enforcement Branch, Ministry of the Environment, 1 St. Clair Avenue West, Toronto M4V 1K6, telephone (416) 323-4831. Where masonry cleaning involves the use and disposal of toxic chemicals, special approvals for the work may be required by the local municipality or by the Ministry of the Environment.

Archaeological licensing

Archaeological exploration in Ontario must be authorized by a licence issued by the Minister of Culture and Communications under the *Ontario Heritage Act, Part VI* (see *Conservation at law* and *Archaeological investigation and recording*). For information, contact one of the Ministry's archaeological field offices, listed in the following section.

Cemetery conservation

Human remains uncovered in the course of conservation or archaeological exploration must be dealt with under the *Cemeteries Act*, and may well require police investigation before anything else may be done on the site. For information, contact the Cemeteries Branch, Ministry of Consumer and Commercial Relations, 101 Bloor Street West, 6th floor, Toronto M5S 2Z5, telephone (416) 963-0511.

Heritage organizations and information resources

The names, addresses and telephone numbers of these organizations are current as of January 1988.

Provincial government publications are available in person at the Ontario Government Bookstore, 880 Bay Street, Toronto; by mail from MGS Publication Services, 5th floor, 880 Bay Street, Toronto M7A 1N8; or by telephone — in Toronto: 965-6015; from outside Toronto, toll-free: 1-800-268-7540; from area code 807: ask the operator for Zenith 67200.

Federal government publications are available through authorized bookstore agents and other bookstores, or by mail from the Canadian Government Publishing Centre, Supply and Services Canada, Hull, Québec K1A 0S9. A list of Parks research publications is available from Research Publications, Environment Canada–Parks, 1600 Liverpool Court, Ottawa, Ontario K1A 1G2.

An especially thorough guide to periodicals on the built environment, including many with either complete emphasis or occasional articles on conservation, is GRET86.

Archaeological Field Offices, Ontario Ministry of Culture and Communications
207 First Street South, P.O. Box 2880, Kenora, Ontario P9N 3X8 (807) 468-8928
55 Centre Street, London, Ontario N6J 1T4 (519) 433-8401
1 Nicholas Street, Suite 1105, Ottawa, Ontario K1N 7B7 (613) 566-3731
390 Bay Street, 3rd floor, Sault Ste. Marie, Ontario P6A 2A7 (705) 253-2625
1825 East Arthur Street, Thunder Bay "F", Ontario P7E 5N7 (807) 475-1683

Archindont (Architectural Index of Ontario)
Fine Arts Department, 2nd floor, Metropolitan Toronto Central Reference Library,
789 Yonge Street, Toronto, Ontario M4W 2G8 (416) 393-7077

Architectural Conservancy of Ontario
Ontario Heritage Centre, 10 Adelaide Street East, Toronto, Ontario M5C 1J3 (416) 367-8075

Archives of Ontario
77 Grenville Street, Toronto, Ontario M7A 2R9 (416) 965-4030

Association of Heritage Consultants
P.O. Box 1023, Station F, Toronto, Ontario M4Y 2T7

Association for Preservation Technology (APT)
Box 2487, Station D, Ottawa, Ontario K1P 5W6 (613) 238-1972

Association of Professional Engineers of Ontario
1155 Yonge Street, Suite 101, Toronto, Ontario M4T 2Y5 (416) 961-1100

Canadian Centre for Architecture/Centre canadien d'architecture (CCA)
1440 ouest, rue Sainte-Catherine, 2ème étage, Montréal, Québec H3G 1R8 (514) 871-1418

Canadian Conservation Institute
1030 Innes Road, Ottawa, Ontario K1A 0M8 (613) 998-3721

Canadian Institute of Planners
30-46 Elgin Street, Ottawa, Ontario K1P 5K6 (613) 233-2105

Canadian Inventory of Historic Building
Architectural History Branch, National Historic Parks and Sites Directorate, Environment Canada–Parks, Terrasses de la Chaudière, Hull, Québec
(mailing address: Ottawa, Ontario K1A 1G2) (819) 994-2866

Canadian Oral History Association
P.O. Box 2064, Station D, Ottawa, Ontario K1P 5W3

Conservation Review Board
2nd floor, 77 Bloor Street West, Toronto, Ontario M7A 2R9 (416) 965-1432

Eastern Ontario Archivists Association
c/o National Archives of Canada (see below)

Federal Heritage Buildings Review Office (FHBRO)
Realty Services, Public Works Canada, Sir Charles Tupper Building, Confederation Heights, Riverside Drive, Ottawa, Ontario K1A 0M2 (613) 998-8582

Heritage Branch, Ontario Ministry of Culture and Communications
2nd floor, 77 Bloor Street West, Toronto, Ontario M7A 2R9 (416) 965-7635
Architecture and Heritage Planning — (416) 965-4961
Archaeology and Natural Heritage — (416) 965-4490 / 965-8199
Historical Resources and Museums — (416) 965-3937 / 965-4021
Heritage Properties — (416) 965-5727 / 963-2874

Heritage Canada Foundation
P.O. Box 1358, Station B, Ottawa, Ontario K1P 5R4   (613) 237-1066

ICOMOS Canada
P.O. Box 737, Station B, Ottawa, Ontario K1P 5R4

Multicultural History Society of Ontario
43 Queen's Park Crescent East, Toronto, Ontario M5S 2C3   (416) 979-2973

National Archives of Canada
395 Wellington Street, Ottawa, Ontario K1A 0N3   (613) 995-5138

National Research Council
Institute for Research in Construction, Building M-20, Montreal Road,
Ottawa, Ontario K1A 0R6   (613) 993-2607

Ontario Association of Architects
50 Park Road, Toronto, Ontario M4W 2N5   (416) 968-0188

Ontario Heritage Foundation
2nd floor, 77 Bloor Street West, Toronto, Ontario M7A 2R9   (416) 965-9504

Ontario Historical Society
5151 Yonge Street, Willowdale, Ontario M2N 5P2   (416) 226-9011

Ontario Museum Association
465 King Street East, Unit 13, Toronto, Ontario M5A 1L6   (416) 367-3677

Ontario Professional Planners Institute (an affiliate of C.I.P.)
3206 Yonge Street, Toronto, Ontario M4N 2L3   (416) 483-1873

Ontario Society for Industrial Archaeology
c/o Institute for the History and Philosophy of Science and Technology (IHPST), Victoria
College, University of Toronto, Toronto, Ontario M5S 1A1

Restoration Services Division, Engineering and Architecture Branch
Environment Canada–Parks/Public Works Canada, Terrasses de la Chaudière, Hull, Québec
(mailing address: Ottawa, Ontario K1A 1G2)   (819) 997-0335

Society for Industrial Archeology
National Museum of American History, Room 5020, Washington D.C. 20560, USA

Society for the Study of Architecture in Canada
Box 2302, Station D, Ottawa, Ontario K1P 5W5

Southwestern Ontario Archivists Association
c/o Municipal Archives, Windsor Public Library, 850 Ouellette Avenue,
Windsor, Ontario N9A 4M9   (519) 255-6782

Toronto Area Archivists Group
Box 97, Station F, Toronto, Ontario M4Y 2L4

Local architectural conservation advisory committees (LACACS)

LACAC members are appointed by municipal councils. To contact LACACs, telephone or write the clerk of the municipality, listed in the blue pages of telephone directories. This list is current as of April 1988; for more up-to-date information contact Architecture and Heritage Planning, Heritage Branch, Ontario Ministry of Culture and Communications, 2nd floor, 77 Bloor Street West, Toronto, Ontario M7A 2R9; telephone (416) 965-4961

Ajax
Alexandria
Almonte (with Ramsay twp.)
Amherstburg
Ancaster
Anson, Hinden and Minden (twp.)
Aurora
Aylmer
Barrie
Bastard and South Burgess (twp.)
Bath
Bayfield
Belleville
Bexley (twp.)
Bothwell
Brampton
Brantford
Brockville
Brussels
Burlington
Caledon
Cambridge
Campbellford (with Seymour twp.)
Carleton Place
Cavan (twp.)
Chatham
Chesterville
Clinton
Cobourg
Colchester South
Coldwater
Collingwood
Cornwall
Cumberland (twp.)
Deep River
Delhi (twp.)
Dresden
Dundas
Dungannon (twp.)
East Gwillimbury
East York
Eganville
Elora
Eramosa (twp.)
Etobicoke
Fenelon Falls
Fergus
Flamborough (twp.)
Forest
Fort Frances
Gananoque
Georgina (twp.)
Glanbrook (twp.)
Gloucester
Goderich
Goulbourn (twp.)
Grand Valley
Grattan (twp.)

Gravenhurst
Grimsby
Guelph
Haldimand (town)
Haldimand (twp.)
Halton Hills
Hamilton (city)
Hamilton (twp.)
Hanover
Hawkesbury
Hearst
Highgate
Huntsville
Kincardine
King (twp.)
Kingston
Kingsville
Kirkland Lake
Kitchener
Lakefield
Lanark
Leamington
Lindsay
London (city)
London (twp.)
Madoc (twp.)
Markham
McNab (twp.)
Merrickville
Millbrook
Milton
Mississauga
Muskoka Lakes (twp.)
Nanticoke
Napanee
Nepean
Newcastle
New Liskeard
Newmarket
Niagara Falls
Niagara-on-the-Lake
North Dumfries (twp.)
North York
Norwich (twp.)
Oakville
Orangeville
Orillia
Ottawa
Owen Sound
Paris
Parkhill
Parry Sound
Pelham
Pembroke
Penetanguishene
Percy (twp.)
Perth
Peterborough
Petrolia

Pickering (town)
Pittsburgh (twp.)
Port Burwell
Port Colborne
Port Hope
Port Stanley
Prescott
Prince (twp.)
Prince Edward (county)
Puslinch (twp.)
Ramsay (twp.; with Almonte)
Rear of Leeds and Lansdowne (twp.)
Renfrew
Richmond Hill
Rideau (twp.)
Ridgetown
Rockcliffe Park
St. Catharines
St. Joseph (twp.)
St. Marys
St. Thomas
Sarnia
Sault Ste. Marie
Scarborough
Seaforth
Seymour (twp.; with Campbellford)
Simcoe
Smiths Falls
South Crosby (twp.)
South Dumfries (twp.)
Southampton
Stratford
Sudbury
Tecumseth (twp.)
Thamesville
Thorold
Thunder Bay
Tillsonburg
Toronto
Trenton
Tuckersmith (twp.)
Uxbridge (twp.)
Vankleek Hill
Vaughan
Victoria Harbour
Wainfleet (twp.)
Walkerton
Waterloo
Welland
Wellesley (twp.)
Whitby
Wilmot (twp.)
Windsor
Wingham
Woodstock
Woolwich (twp.)
Yarmouth (twp.)
York (city)

A note on glossaries of technical and specialized terms

Conservation terminology can become quite overwhelming, but there are many good sources for basic as well as detailed definitions; the more comprehensive standard dictionaries will also contain many terms. All the references cited here have useful glossaries; they are listed fully in the bibliography.

Planning and general conservation terms

Scattered throughout MADD85 are wide-ranging and thoughtful definitions for many terms of planning, financing and law, understanding of which may be essential to the success of heritage conservation efforts (see especially pages 12, 57, 202, 275, 311, 332, 343, 352 and 393)

Descriptive terms for historical styles and simple building elements

Easily available paperbacks with general usefulness as "field guides" to styles include POPP83 (with a good but elementary glossary), BLUM77 (a thorough visual dictionary of terms in context with styles), and FLEM80 (the most comprehensive, but with a heavy bias to Britain and Europe). The CIHB guide for field recorders (BRAY80) has an excellent systematic lexicon of descriptive terms. For Classical styles and elements, CHIT85 and STRA86 permit deeper understanding of orders and proportions.

Glossaries appear in several architectural guides specific to Ontario. Each of MACR63, MACR75 and MACR83 contains a cogent glossary tailored to the building type covered by the book. Though focused on buildings in Prince Edward County, the visual catalogue in CRUI84 is useful for most rural southern Ontario architecture. And MCHU85, though about Toronto, has a basic list of terms applicable to urban Ontario.

Many recent books about historic houses in North America define terms specific to residential elements — the best of these is MCAL84 (the whole book is really a visual glossary, the most comprehensive of all); WALK81 is more basic but still useful. A recent guide that defines terms for main-street architecture is LONG87.

Technical terms (especially historic practices, special elements and conservation techniques)

The most thorough and readily available dictionary for architectural and building terminology is HARR75. Comprehensive technical manuals for conservation that contain extensive glossaries are STAH84 and FEIL82. A guide of more modest scope to technical terms is in LEGN79, developed for residential architecture in Chicago but applicable to small urban buildings in Ontario.

Good glossaries for special areas within conservation may be found in CHAM80 (archaeology), BEAL87 (masonry), STAG76 (plastering) and PARR85 (painting and interior finishes).

French-language sources

The technical glossary in FEIL82 is multilingual, including English and French, but the French-language equivalents are based on usage in France rather than Canada; the French-English lexicon in BUTT81 is similarly European. To correct this, the province of Quebec has produced an exhaustive French-English dictionary for construction, CONS82a. A more basic French-only lexicon from Québec for small-building conservation appears in ENTR85.

ALEX77 Alexander, Christopher, Sara Ishikawa, et al. *A Pattern Language: Towns, Buildings, Construction*. New York: Oxford University Press, 1977.

AMEN83 *L'amenagement, l'urbanisme et le patrimoine*. Québec: Ministère des Affaires culturelles, 1983.

ARCR85 *L'architecture en representation*. Paris: Ministère de la Culture, 1985.

ARTH72 Arthur, Eric and Dudley Witney. *The Barn: A Vanishing Landmark in North America*. Toronto: McClelland and Stewart, 1972.

ARTL85 Artley, Alexandra, and John Martin Robinson. *The New Georgian Handbook*. London: Ebury Press, 1985.

ASHU77 Ashurst, John. *Cleaning Stone and Brick* (Technical pamphlet 4). London: Society for the Preservation of Ancient Buildings, 1977.

ASHU83 Ashurst, John. *Mortars, Plasters and Renders in Conservation*. London: Ecclesiastical Architects and Surveyors Assoc., 1983.

ASHU84 Ashurst, John, and Francis G. Dimes. *Stone in Building: Its Use and Potential Today*. London: Stone Federation, 1984.

AUST88 Austin, Richard L., ed. *Adaptive Reuse: Issues and Case Studies in Building Preservation*. New York: Van Nostrand Reinhold, 1988.

BAIL75 Bailly, G. H. *The Architectural Heritage*. London: Stanley Thornes, 1975.

BAKE83 Baker, David. *Living with the Past*. Bedford, UK: David Baker, 1983.

BALL83 Ballantyne, Duncan S. *Accommodation of Disabled Visitors at Historic Sites in the National Park System*. Washington, DC: US Department of the Interior (NPS), 1983.

BAXT86 Baxter, Alan, and Associates. *Structural Renovation of Traditional Buildings*. London: CIRIA, 1986.

BEAL87 Beall, Christine. *Masonry Design and Detailing for Architects, Engineers, and Builders*. New York: McGraw-Hill, 1987.

BECK80 Becker, Norman. *The Complete Book of Home Inspection*. New York: McGraw-Hill, 1980.

BELL85 Bell, Charlotte, R. *Federal Historic Preservation Case Law*. Washington, DC: Advisory Council on Historic Preservation, 1985.

BENN79 Benn, Bruce, Deepak Karma, and Marc Denhez. *How to Plan for Renovations*. Ottawa: Heritage Canada, 1979.

BENT85 Bentley, Ian, Alan Alcock, Paul Murrain, et al. *Responsive Environments: A Manual for Designers*. London: Architectural Press, 1985.

BINN82 Binney, Marcus, and Kit Martin. *The Country House: To Be or Not To Be*. London: SAVE Britain's Heritage, 1982.

BIX85 Bix, Cynthia, ed. *Sunset Home Repair Handbook*. Menlo Park, CA: Lane Publishing, 1985.

BLAC81 Blackburn, Graham. *An Illustrated Calendar of Home Repair*. New York: Richard Marek, 1981.

BLAC86 Blackburn, Graham. *Quick and Easy Home Repair*. New York: Ballantine, 1986.

BLAK69 Blake, Verschoyle Benson, and Ralph Greenhill. *Rural Ontario*. Toronto: University of Toronto Press, 1969.

BLUM77 Blumenson, John J.-G. *Identifying American Architecture*. Nashville: AASLH, 1977.

BORC78 Borchers, Perry E. *Photogrammetric Recording of Cultural Resources*. Washington, DC: US Department of the Interior (NPS), 1978.

BOWY79 Bowyer, Jack. *Guide to Domestic Building Surveys* (third edition). London: Architectural Press, 1979.

BOWY80 Bowyer, Jack. *Vernacular Building Conservation*. London: Architectural Press, 1980.

BRAY80 Bray, R., S. Dale, W. Grainger, R. Harrold. *Exterior Recording Training Manual* (revised edition). Ottawa: Parks Canada (CIHB), 1980.

BROL82 Brolin, Brent, and Jean Richards. *Sourcebook of Architectural Ornament*. New York: Van Nostrand Reinhold, 1982.

BROO77 Brooks, Alan. *Dry Stone Walling: A Practical Conservation Handbook*. London: British Trust for Conservation Volunteers, 1977.

BROW80 Browne, Carolyn. *The Mechanics of Sign Control*. Chicago: American Planning Association, 1983.

BUCH83 Buchanan, Terry. *Photographing Historic Buildings*. London: HMSO, 1983.

BUCO76 Bucovetsky, Joseph, and Michelle Greenwald. *Townsend Traces: Heritage Conservation in Townsend New Town*. Toronto: Ministry of Culture and Recreation, 1976.

BUIL77 *Built Environment . . . How to Conduct Environmental Education Workshops*. Washington, DC: American Institutes of Architects, 1977.

BUIL85 Building Research Board. *Building Diagnostics: A Conceptual Framework*. Washington, DC: National Academy Press, 1985.

BUIL86 Building Research Board. *Programming Practices in the Building Process: Opportunities for Improvement*. Washington, DC: National Academy Press, 1986.

BUSC87 Busch, Akiko. *The Photography of Architecture*. New York: Van Nostrand Reinhold, 1987.

BUTT81 Butterworth, Basil, and Janine Flitz. *Dictionary of Building Terms: English-French, French-English*. London: Construction Press, 1981.

CAPP86 Cappe, Lorne. *Window on Toronto*. Toronto: City of Toronto Planning and Development Department, 1986.

CARS82 Carson, Alan, and Robert Dunlop. *Inspecting a House: A Guide for Buyers, Owners and Renovators*. Toronto: General Publishing, 1982.

CART83 Carter, Margaret. *Researching Heritage Buildings*. Ottawa: Parks Canada, 1983.

CART83a Carter, Margaret. *Faire des recherches sur les bâtiments anciens*. Ottawa: Parks Canada, 1983.

CART83b Carter, Margaret, ed. *Early Canadian Court Houses*. Ottawa: Environment Canada–Parks, 1983.

CENT86 Centaur Associates. *Tips for an Energy Efficient Apartment*. Washington, DC: US Department of Energy, 1986.

CHAM73 Chambers, J. Henry. *Rectified Photography and Photo Drawings for Historic Preservation* (draft). Washington, DC: US Department of the Interior (NPS), 1973.

CHAM76 Chambers, J. Henry. *Cyclical Maintenance for Historic Buildings*. Washington, DC: US Department of the Interior (NPS), 1976.

CHAM80 Champion, Sara. *Dictionary of Terms and Techniques in Archaeology*. New York: Everest House, 1980.

CHAMnd Chambers, J. Henry. *Using Photogrammetry to Monitor Materials Deterioration and Structural Problems*. Washington, DC: US Department of the Interior (NPS), nd.

CHAP66 Chapman, L. J., and D. F. Putnam. *The Physiography of Southern Ontario* (second edition). Toronto: University of Toronto Press, 1966.

CHAR84 Charles, F.W.B., and Mary Charles. *Conservation of Timber Buildings*. London: Hutchinson, 1984.

CHIT80 Chitham, Robert. *Measured Drawings for Architects*. London: Architectural Press, 1980.

CHIT85 Chitham, Robert. *The Classical Orders of Architecture*. New York: Rizzoli, 1985.

COE84 Coe, Gigi, Michael R. Eaton, Michael M. Garland. *The Home Energy Decision Book*. San Francisco: Sierra Club, 1984.

COMM83 Committee on Historic Resources. *Preservation Practice* (AIA Handbook, C-1). Washington, DC: American Institute of Architects, 1983.

COMPnd *Complete Handbook* [for properties in designated historic districts]. Mobile: Architectural Review Board, nd.

CONS82 *Conservation of Historic Stone Buildings and Monuments*. Washington, DC: National Academy Press, 1982.

CONS82a *Construction*. Québec: Office de la langue française (Banque de terminologie du Québec), 1982.

CONV83 *Conventions and Recommendations of Unesco Concerning the Protection of the Cultural Heritage*. Paris: United Nations Educational, Scientific and Cultural Organization, 1983

CRIT84 *Critères de rénovation et restauration: documentation*. Montréal: Héritage Montréal, 1984.

CROS70 Crosby, Theo. *The Necessary Monument*. Greenwich, CT: New York Graphic Society, 1970.

CRUI84 Cruickshank, Tom, and Peter John Stokes. *The Settler's Dream: A Pictorial History of the Older Buildings of Prince Edward County*. Picton: County of Prince Edward, 1984.

CUMI84 Cuming, David J. *Discovering Heritage Bridges on Ontario's Roads*. Erin, Ontario: Boston Mills Press, 1984.

CUMI85 Cuming, David J., and Mark Fram. *Ontario's Heritage Conservation District Guidelines*. Toronto: Ministry of Citizenship and Culture, 1985.

CUNN84 Cunnington, Pamela. *Care for Old Houses*. Sherborne, Dorset: Prism Alpha, 1984.

CURR63 Currie, A.W. *Canadian Economic Development* (fourth edition). Toronto: Nelson, 1963.

CURT79 Curtis, John Obed. *Moving Historic Buildings*. Washington, DC: US Department of the Interior (HCRS), 1979.

DAVE80 Davey, Andy, Bob Heath, Desmond Hodges, et al. *The Care and Conservation of Georgian Houses* (second edition). London: Architectural Press, 1980.

DAVE86 Davey, Andy, Bob Heath, Desmond Hodges, et al. *The Care and Conservation of Georgian Houses* (third edition). London: Architectural Press, 1986.

DEAN69 Dean, William G., ed. *Economic Atlas of Ontario*. Toronto: University of Toronto Press, 1969.

DECA87 de Caraffe, Marc, C.A. Hale, Dana Johnson, G.E. Mills, and Margaret Carter. *Town Halls of Canada*. Ottawa: Environment Canada–Parks, 1987

DENH78 Denhez, Marc. *Heritage Fights Back*. Toronto: Fitzhenry and Whiteside, 1978.

DIBN85 Dibner, David R., and Amy Dibner-Dunlap. *Building Additions Design*. New York: McGraw-Hill, 1985.

DUTO85 DuToit, Roger, Architects. *Planning and Design for Commercial Façade Improvements*. Toronto: Ministry of Municipal Affairs, 1985.

EAST67 Easterbrook, W.T., and M.H. Watkins. *Approaches to Canadian Economic History*. Toronto: McClelland and Stewart, 1967.

EDWA46 Edwards, A. Trystan. *Good and Bad Manners in Architecture* (second edition). London: John Tiranti, 1946.

EHRE84 Ehrenkrantz Group. *Window Rehabilitation: A Manual for Historic Buildings* (draft). New York: New York Landmarks Conservancy, 1984.

ELEY84 Eley, Peter, and John Worthington. *Industrial Rehabilitation: The Use of Redundant Buildings for Small Enterprises*. London: Architectural Press, 1984.

ENER84 *Energy Saving in Religious Buildings: Putting Practical Ideas to Work*. Toronto: Ministry of Energy, 1984.

ENTR85 *Entretien et restauration, de la fondation à la toiture*. Québec: Conseil des monuments et sites, 1985.

EVER86 Evers, Christopher. *The Old-House Doctor*. Woodstock, NY: Overlook Press, 1986.

FACA87 *Facades: Improving Commercial Building Fronts*. Toronto: Ministry of Municipal Affairs, 1987

FACA87a *Façades: Rénovation des façades d'immeubles commerciaux*. Toronto: Ministère des Affaires municipales, 1987

FALC81 Falconer, Keith, and Geoffrey Hay. *The Recording of Industrial Sites: A Review*. London: Council for British Archaeology, 1981

FALK77 Falkner, Ann. *Without Our Past*. Toronto: University of Toronto Press, 1977

FAWC76 Fawcett, Jane, ed. *The Future of the Past*. New York: Whitney Library of Design, 1976.

FEIL82 Feilden, Bernard M. *Conservation of Historic Buildings*. London: Butterworths, 1982.

FERG86 Ferguson, Ian, and Eric Mitchell. *Quality on Site*. London: Batsford, 1986.

FERR77 Ferro, Maximilian L. *How to Love and Care for Your Old Building in New Bedford*. New Bedford, MA: City of New Bedford, 1977.

FINE86 *Fine Homebuilding Remodeling Ideas*. Newtown, CT: Taunton Press, 1986.

FITC82 Fitch, James Marston. *Historic Preservation: Curatorial Management of the Built World*. New York: McGraw-Hill, 1982.

FITC86 Fitchen, John. *Building Construction Before Mechanization*. Cambridge, MA: MIT Press, 1986.

FLAD78 Fladmark, Knut R. *A Guide to Basic Archaeological Fieldwork Procedures*. Burnaby, BC: Simon Fraser University, 1978.

FLEM80 Fleming, John, Hugh Honour, and Nikolaus Pevsner. *The Penguin Dictionary of Architecture* (third edition). Harmondsworth: Penguin, 1980.

FLEM82 Fleming, Ronald Lee. *Facade Stories: Changing Faces of Main Street Storefronts and How to Care for Them*. New York: Hastings House, 1982.

FRAM84 Fram, Mark. *A Heritage Conservation Primer*. Toronto: Ministry of Citizenship and Culture, 1984.

FRAM84a Fram, Mark, and John Weiler, eds. *Continuity with Change* (second edition). Toronto: Dundurn Press, 1984.

FROI86 Froidevaux, Yves-Marie. *Techniques de l'architecture ancienne: Construction et restauration*. Liege: Pierre Mardaga, 1986.

GAYL80 Gayle, Margot, David W. Look, and John G. Waite. *Metals in America's Historic Buildings: Uses and Preservation Treatments*. Washington, DC: US Department of the Interior (NPS), 1980.

GEBH77 Gebhard, David, and Tom Martinson. *A Guide to the Architecture of Minnesota*. Minneapolis: University of Minnesota Press, 1977.

GENT84 Gentilcore, R. Louis, and C. Grant Head. *Ontario's History in Maps*. Toronto: University of Toronto Press, 1984.

GLAS83 Glassford, Peggy. *Appearance Codes for Small Communities*. Chicago: American Planning Association, 1983.

GOOD80 Goodall, Harrison, and Renée Friedman. *Log Structures: Preservation and Problem-Solving*. Nashville: AASLH, 1980.

GOOD85 *Good Buildings Good Times: A Manual of Program Ideas for Promoting Local Architecture*. Albany, NY: Preservation League of New York State, 1985.

GOON80 *Good Neighbors: Building Next to History*. Denver: Colorado Historical Society, 1980.

GREE74 Greenhill, Ralph, Douglas Richardson, Ken Macpherson. *Ontario Towns*. Ottawa: Oberon, 1974.

GRET86 Gretes, Frances C. *Directory of International Periodicals and Newsletters on the Built Environment*. New York: Van Nostrand Reinhold, 1986.

GRIM84 Grimmer, Anne E. *A Glossary of Historic Masonry Deterioration Problems and Preservation Treatments*. Washington, DC: US Department of the Interior (NPS), 1984.

GUID82 *Guide pour la conservation et la mise en valeur de l'architecture du Vieux-Québec*. Québec: Service de l'urbanisme, division du Vieux-Québec et du patrimoine, 1982.

HANK74 Hanks, Carole. *Early Ontario Gravestones*. Toronto: McGraw-Hill Ryerson, 1974

HANS83 Hanson, Shirley, and Nancy Hubby. *Preserving and Maintaining the Older Home*. New York: McGraw-Hill, 1983.

HARR75 Harris, Cyril M., ed. *Dictionary of Architecture and Construction*. New York: McGraw-Hill, 1975.

HARR87 Harris, R. Cole, ed. *Historical Atlas of Canada: Volume 1: From the Beginning to 1800*. Toronto: University of Toronto Press, 1987.

HAYN87 Haynes, Wesley. "Windows: Techniques for Restoration and Replacement." *Architectural Record* 175, no. 7 (June 1987): 150–165.

HECK79 Hecker, John C., and Sylvanus W. Doughty. *Planning for Exterior Work on the First Parish Church, Portland Maine: Using Photographs as Project Documentation*. Washington, DC: US Department of the Interior (HCRS), 1979.

HELD83 Heldmann, Carl. *Managing Your Own Restoration Project*. New York: Putnam, 1983.

HERI80 *Heritage Studies on the Rideau-Quinte-Trent-Severn Waterways*. Toronto: Ministry of Culture and Recreation, 1980.

HERI86 *Heritage-Energy: An Annotated Bibliography*. Toronto: Ministry of Citizenship and Culture, 1986.

HERI86a *Heritage-Energy: A Compendium of Relevant Literature*. Toronto: Ministry of Citizenship and Culture, 1986.

HERI87 *Heritage Buildings and Energy Conservation*. Toronto: Ministry of Energy, 1987.

HERI87a *HeritagEnergy Conservation Guidelines*. Toronto: Ministry of Citizenship and Culture/Ministry of Energy, 1987.

HERI87b *Patrimoine-énergie: Directives pour une double conservation*. Toronto: Ministry of Citizenship and Culture/Ministry of Energy, 1987.

HIGG85 Higgins, Spencer R. *Annotated Master Specifications for the Cleaning and Repointing of Historic Masonry*. Toronto: Ministry of Citizenship and Culture, 1985.

HILL82 Hill, Nicholas. *Conservation of Historic Streetscapes*. Goderich: Nicholas Hill, 1982.

HILT86 Hilts, Stewart G., et al., eds. *Islands of Green: Natural Heritage Protection in Ontario*. Toronto: Ontario Heritage Foundation, 1986.

HIST74 *Historic Preservation Handbook: A Guide for Volunteers*. Atlanta: Department of Natural Resources, 1974.

HIST78 *Historic Preservation Plan for the Central Area General Neighborhood Renewal Area, Savannah, Georgia*. Washington, DC: US Dept. of Housing and Urban Development, 1978.

HIST80 Historic Preservation Program. *The Burlington Book: Architecture, History, Future*. Burlington, VT: University of Vermont, 1980.

HODG07 Hodgson, Fred T., ed. *Cyclopedia of the Building Trades* (volume 1 - masonry, etc.). Chicago: American Building Trades School, 1907.

HOLD85 Holdsworth, Deryck, ed. *Reviving Main Street*. Toronto: University of Toronto Press, 1985.

HOLL86 Hollis, Malcolm. *Surveying Buildings* (second edition). London: Surveyors Publications, 1986.

HOLM75 Holmström, Ingmar, and Christina Sanström. *Maintenance of Old Buildings*. Stockholm: National Swedish Institute for Building Research, 1975.

HOTT79 Hotton, Peter. *So You Want to Fix Up an Old House*. Boston: Little, Brown, 1979.

HOW86 *How to Plan and Design Additions*. San Francisco: Ortho Books, 1986.

HUGH86 Hughes, Philip. *The Need for Old Buildings to "Breathe"* (SPAB Information Sheet no. 4). London: Society for the Preservation of Ancient Buildings, 1986.

HUME83 Hume, Gary L., Kay D. Weeks, et al. *The Secretary of the Interior's Standards for Rehabilitation and Guidelines for Rehabilitating Historic Buildings* (revised 1983). Washington, DC: US Department of the Interior (NPS), 1983.

HUMP80 Humphreys, Barbara A., and Meredith Sykes. *The Buildings of Canada*. Ottawa: Parks Canada, 1980.

HUNT85 Hunt, Alistair. *Electrical Installations in Old Buildings* (Technical pamphlet 9). London: Society for the Preservation of Ancient Buildings, 1985.

HUTC80 Hutchins, Nigel. *Restoring Old Houses*. Toronto: Van Nostrand Reinhold, 1980.

HUTC82 Hutchins, Nigel. *Restoring Houses of Brick and Stone*. Toronto: Van Nostrand Reinhold, 1982.

ICOM86 ICOMOS-France. *Créer dans le créé*. Paris: Electa Moniteur, 1986.

INSA72 Insall, Donald W. *The Care of Old Buildings Today: A Practical Guide*. London: Architectural Press, 1972.

INTE82 *Interpreting the Secretary of the Interior's Standards for Rehabilitation* (volume 1). Washington, DC: US Department of the Interior (NPS), 1982.

INTE86 *Intellectual Property Rights in an Age of Electronics and Information*. Washington, DC: Office of Technology Assessment, 1986.

JAND83 Jandl, H. Ward, ed. *The Technology of Historic American Buildings*. Washington, DC: Foundation for Preservation Technology, 1983.

JOHN83 Johnson, Edwin. *Old House Woodwork Restoration*. Englewood Cliffs, NJ: Prentice-Hall, 1983.

JOHN84 Johnson, LeRoy, Jr., ed. *Handbook of Maintenance Techniques [Galveston, Texas]*. Austin: Texas Historical Commission, 1984.

JONE86 Jones, Barclay G., ed. *Protecting Historic Architecture and Museum Collections from Natural Disasters*. Boston: Butterworths, 1986.

KAHN78 Kahn, Lloyd, ed. *Shelter II*. Bolinas, CA: Shelter Publications, 1978.

KALM77 Kalman, Harold. *The Conservation of Ontario Churches*. Toronto: Ministry of Culture and Recreation, 1977.

KALM80 Kalman, Harold. *The Evaluation of Historic Buildings*. Ottawa: Parks Canada, 1980.

KALM80a Kalman, Harold. *Évaluation des bâtiments historiques*. Ottawa: Parks Canada, 1980.

KALM80b Kalman, Harold D., Keith Wagland, and Robert Bailey. *Encore: Recycling Public Buildings for the Arts*. Don Mills: Corpus, 1980.

KAPL78 Kaplan, Helaine S., and Blair Prentice. *Rehab Right*. Oakland, CA: City of Oakland Planning Department, 1978.

KAPL86 Kaplan Prentice, Helaine S., and Blair Prentice. *Rehab Right* (revised edition). Berkeley, CA: Ten Speed Press, 1986.

KEMP81 Kemp, Emory L., and Theodore Anton Sande, eds. *Historic Preservation of Engineering Works*. New York: American Society of Civil Engineers, 1981.

KEUN84 Keune, Russell V., ed. *The Historic Preservation Yearbook* (first edition, 1984/85). Bethesda, MD: Adler & Adler, 1984.

KING77 King, Thomas F., Patricia Parker Hickman, and Gary Berg. *Anthropology in Historic Preservation*. New York: Academic Press, 1977.

KIRK84 Kirk, John T. *The Impecunious House Restorer*. New York: Alfred A. Knopf, 1984.

KITC83 Kitchen, Judith L. *Old-Building Owner's Manual*. Columbus, OH: Ohio Historical Society, 1983.

KNEV86 Knevitt, Charles. *Perspectives: An Anthology of 1001 Architectural Quotations*. London: Lund Humphries, 1986.

KNIG87 Knight, Paul A. *Mechanical Systems Retrofit Manual: A Guide for Residential Design*. New York: Van Nostrand Reinhold, 1987.

LABI80 Labine, Clem, and Carolyn Flaherty, eds. *The Old-House Journal Compendium*. Woodstock, NY: Overlook Press, 1980.

LAND79 Lander, Hugh. *House & Cottage Conversion: The Do's and Don'ts*. Redruth, Cornwall: Acanthus Books, 1979.

LAND82 Lander, Hugh. *House & Cottage Interiors: Do's and Don'ts*. Redruth, Cornwall: Acanthus Books, 1982.

LANG78 Lang, J. Christopher. *Building with Nantucket in Mind*. Nantucket, MA: Nantucket Historic District Commission, 1978.

LANG80 Lang, Reg, and Audrey Armour. *Environmental Planning Resourcebook*. Montreal: Environment Canada, Lands Directorate, 1980.

LAVA82 Lavallée, Johanne, Liette Charland, et al. *Ce qu'il faut savoir pour renover une maison*. Montréal: Libre Expression, 1982.

LEGG76 Legget, Robert F. *Canals of Canada*. Vancouver: Douglas, David & Charles, 1976.

LEGN79 Legner, Linda, ed. *City House: A Guide to Renovating Older Chicago-Area Houses*. Chicago: City of Chicago/Chicago Review Press, 1979.

LENC82 Lenclos, Jean Philippe, and Dominique Lenclos. *Les couleurs de la France: Maisons et paysages*. Paris: Moniteur, 1982.

LEON73 Leonidoff, Georges, Vianney Guindon, Paul Gagnon. *Comment restaurer une maison traditionnelle*. Québec: Ministère des Affaires culturelles, 1973.

LEST77 Lester, Alfred W. *Hampstead Garden Suburb: The Care and Appreciation of Its Architectural Heritage*. London: Hampstead Garden Suburb Design Study Group, 1977.

LEVI78 Levitt Bernstein Associates. *Supervisor's Guide to Rehabilitation and Conversion*. London: Architectural Press, 1978.

LITC82 Litchfield, Michael W. *Renovation: A Complete Guide*. New York: John Wiley & Sons, 1982.

LITC83 Litchfield, Michael, and Rosmarie Hausherr. *Salvaged Treasures: Designing and Building with Architectural Salvage*. New York: Van Nostrand Reinhold, 1983.

LOCK86 Locke, Peter. *Timber Treatment* (SPAB Information Sheet no. 2). London: Society for the Preservation of Ancient Buildings, 1986.

LOCK86a Locke, Peter. *The Surface Treatment of Timber-Framed Houses* (SPAB Information Sheet no. 3). London: Society for the Preservation of Ancient Buildings, 1986.

LOND84 London, Mark, et Mireille Ostiguy. *Couvertures traditionelles*. Montréal: Héritage Montréal, 1984.

LOND84a London, Mark, et Dinu Bumbaru. *Fenêtres traditionelles*. Montréal: Héritage Montréal, 1984.

LOND84b London, Mark, et Dinu Bumbaru. *Maçonnerie traditionelle*. Montréal: Héritage Montréal, 1984.

LOND85 London, Mark, and Dinu Bumbaru. *Traditional Windows*. Montreal: Heritage Montreal, 1985.

LOND86 London, Mark, et Cecile Baird. *Revêtements traditionnels*. Montréal: Héritage Montréal, 1986.

LONG87 Longstreth, Richard. *The Buildings of Main Street: A Guide to American Commercial Architecture*. Washington, DC: Preservation Press, 1987.

LYNC72 Lynch, Kevin. *What Time is This Place?* Cambridge, MA: MIT Press, 1972.

LYNC76 Lynch, Kevin. *Managing the Sense of a Region*. Cambridge, MA: MIT Press, 1976.

LYNC82 Lynch, Michael F. *How to Care for Religious Properties*. Albany, NY: Preservation League of New York State, 1982.

LYNC82a Lynch, Michael F., and William J. Higgins. *The Maintenance and Repair of Architectural Sandstone*. New York: New York Landmarks Conservancy, 1982.

MACE98 Macey, Frank W. *Specifications in Detail*. London: Spon, 1898.

MACG71 Macgregor, John E. M. *Outward Leaning Walls* (Technical pamphlet 1). London: Society for the Preservation of Ancient Buildings, 1971.

MACG73 Macgregor, John E. M. *Strengthening Timber Floors* (Technical pamphlet 2). London: Society for the Preservation of Ancient Buildings, 1973.

MACR63 Macrae, Marion, and Anthony Adamson. *The Ancestral Roof: Domestic Architecture of Upper Canada*. Toronto: Clarke Irwin, 1963.

MACR75 Macrae, Marion, and Anthony Adamson. *Hallowed Walls: Church Architecture of Upper Canada*. Toronto: Clarke Irwin, 1975.

MACR83 Macrae, Marion, and Anthony Adamson. *Cornerstones of Order: Courthouses and Town Halls of Ontario, 1784-1914*. Toronto: Clarke Irwin, 1983.

MADD85 Maddex, Diane, ed. *All About Old Buildings*. Washington, DC: Preservation Press, 1985.

MADS76 Madsen, Stephan Tschudi. *Restoration and Anti-Restoration: A Study in English Restoration Philosophy*. Oslo: Universitetsforlaget, 1976.

MARK79 Markus, Thomas A., ed. *Building Conversion and Rehabilitation*. London: Butterworths, 1979.

MCAL80 McAllister, Donald M. *Evaluation in Environmental Planning*. Cambridge, MA: MIT Press, 1980.

MCAL84 McAlester, Virginia, and Lee McAlester. *A Field Guide to American Houses*. New York: Alfred A. Knopf, 1984.

MCBR85 McBryde, Isabel, ed. *Who Owns the Past?* Melbourne: Oxford University Press, 1985.

MCCA85 McCann, Michael. *Health Hazards Manual for Artists* (third edition). New York: Nick Lyons Books, 1985.

MCDO80 McDowall, R. W. *Recording Old Houses: A Guide*. London: Council for British Archaeoology, 1980.

MCHU85 McHugh, Patricia. *Toronto Architecture: A City Guide*. Toronto: Mercury Books, 1985.

MCKE70 McKee, Harley J. *Recording Historic Buildings*. Washington, DC: US Department of the Interior (NPS), 1970.

MCPH84 McPhail, Barbara, ed. *BRIC Conservation Guidelines*. Toronto: Ministry of Citizenship and Culture, 1984.

MEAD86 Meadows, Robert E. *Historic Building Façades: A Manual for Inspection and Rehabilitation*. New York: New York Landmarks Conservancy, 1986.

MELV73 Melville, Ian A., and Ian A. Gordon. *The Repair and Maintenance of Houses*. London: Estates Gazette, 1973.

MELV74 Melville, Ian A., Ian A. Gordon, and Anthony Boswood. *Structural Surveys of Dwelling Houses*. London: Estates Gazette, 1974.

MILL77 Miller, Kevin H., ed. *Paint Colour Research and Restoration of Historic Paint*. Ottawa: Association for Preservation Technology, 1977.

MILL78 Miller, Marilyn G. *Straight Lines in Curved Space: Colonization Roads in Eastern Ontario*. Toronto: Ministry of Culture and Recreation, 1978.

MILL80 Mills, Edward D., ed. *Building Maintenance and Preservation*. London: Butterworths, 1980.

MILL86 Miller, Hugh C., Lee H. Nelson, and Emogene A. Bevitt. *Skills Development Plan for Historical Architects in the National Park Service*. Washington, DC: US Department of the Interior (NPS), 1986.

MILL87 Miller, Judith, and Martin Miller. *Period Details: A Sourcebook for House Restoration*. New York: Crown, 1987.

MILN79 Milner, John, Associates. *The Beaufort [South Carolina] Preservation Manual*. West Chester, PA: John Milner Associates, 1979.

MITC82 Mitchell, Harris. *How to Hire a Contractor*. Ottawa: CMHC, 1982.

MONC83 Moncrieff, Anne, and Graham Weaver. *Cleaning* (Science for Conservators, Book 2). London: Crafts Council, 1983.

MOSS87 Moss, Roger W., and Gail Caskey Winkler. *Victorian Exterior Decoration*. New York: Henry Holt, 1987.

MULL81 Mullins, E. J., and T. S. McKnight, eds. *Canadian Woods: Their Properties and Uses* (third edition). Toronto: University of Toronto Press, 1981.

MUNN83 Munn, Harry. *Joinery for Repair and Restoration Contracts*. Eastbourne: Orion, 1983.

MUTH79 Muthesius, Hermann. *The English House* (translation of *Das Englische Haus*. Berlin, 1904/5). London: Granada, 1979.

NASH86 Nash, W.G. *Brickwork Repair and Restoration*. Eastbourne: Attic Books, 1986.

NATC83 National Center for Appropriate Technology. *Moisture and Home Energy Conservation*. Washington, DC: US Department of Energy, 1983.

NATI76 National Trust for Historic Preservation. *Economic Benefits of Preserving Old Buildings*. Washington, DC: Preservation Press, 1976.

NATI76a National Trust for Historic Preservation, et al. *America's Forgotten Architecture*. New York: Pantheon, 1976.

NATI80 *Old & New Architecture: Design Relationship*. Washington, DC: Preservation Press, 1980.

NETH81 Netherlands National Commission for UNESCO. *Conservation of Waterlogged Wood*. The Hague: Ministry of Education and Science, 1981.

NEWC79 Newcomb, Robert M. *Planning the Past: Historical Landscape Resources and Recreation*. Folkestone: Dawson, 1979.

NIBS80 National Institute of Building Sciences. *Guideline on Fire Ratings of Archaic Materials and Assemblies*. Washington, DC: US Dept. of Housing and Urban Development, 1980.

OEHR80 Oehrlein, Mary, L. *Vieux Carré Masonry Maintenance Guidelines*. New Orleans: Vieux Carré Commission, 1980.

OLDH85 *The Old-House Journal Catalog 1986*. Brooklyn: Old-House Journal, 1985.

ONEI71 O'Neil, Isabel. *The Art of the Painted Finish for Furniture and Decoration*. New York: Morrow, 1971.

OXLE83 Oxley, T. A., and E. G. Gobert. *Dampness in Buildings: Diagnosis, Treatment, Instruments*. London: Butterworths, 1983.

PAIN78 Pain, Howard. *The Heritage of Upper Canadian Furniture*. Toronto: Van Nostrand Reinhold, 1978.

PARK79 Parker, Elyse. *A Guide to Heritage Structure Investigations*. Toronto: Ministry of Culture and Recreation, 1979.

PARNnd Parnell, Alan, and David H. Ashford. *Fire Safety in Historic Buildings, Part 1* (Technical pamphlet 6). London: Society for the Preservation of Ancient Buildings, nd.

PARR85 Parry, John, Brian Rhodes, John Windsor. *Parry's Graining and Marbling* (second edition). London: Collins, 1985.

PATT82 Patterson, Robert M. *Manual for the Preparation of "As Found" Drawings*. Victoria: British Columbia Heritage Trust, 1982.

PERC79 Percival, Arthur. *Understanding Our Surroundings*. London: Civic Trust, 1979.

PESK76 Peskin, Sarah. *Guiding Growth and Change*. Boston: Appalachian Mountain Club, 1976.

PETE76 Peterson, Charles E., ed. *Building Early America*. Radnor, PA: Chilton, 1976.

PHIL78 Phillips, Morgan W., and Judith E. Selwyn. *Epoxies for Wood Repairs in Historic Buildings*. Washington, DC: US Department of the Interior (HCRS), 1978.

PICH84 Pichard, Pierre. *Emergency Measures and Damage Assessment After an Earthquake*. Paris: UNESCO, 1984.

PICH84a Pichard, Pierre. *Après un seisme: mésures d'urgence, évaluation des dommages*. Paris: UNESCO, 1984.

POMA87 Pomada, Elizabeth, and Michael Larsen. *Daughters of Painted Ladies*. New York: E.P. Dutton, 1987.

POOR83 Poore, Patricia, and Clem Labine, eds. *The Old-House Journal New Compendium*. Garden City, NY: Doubleday, 1983.

POPP83 Poppeliers, John C., et al. *What Style Is It?* Washington, DC: Preservation Press, 1983.

PORT82 Porter, Tom. *Architectural Color*. New York: Whitney Library of Design, 1982.

POWY29 Powys, A.R. *Repair of Ancient Buildings*. London: Society for the Preservation of Ancient Buildings, 1981.

PRE79 *Pré-voir pour mieux décider*. Paris: Centre de Création Industrielle, 1979.

PRIA76 Priamo, Carol. *Mills of Canada*. Toronto: McGraw-Hill Ryerson, 1976.

PRIA78 Priamo, Carol. *The General Store*. Toronto: McGraw-Hill Ryerson, 1978.

PRIN81 Prince, Arnold. *Carving Wood and Stone*. Englewood Cliffs: Prentice-Hall, 1981.

PRIZ75 Prizeman, John. *Your House: The Outside View*. London: Hutchinson, 1975.

PUIB85 Puiboube, Daniel, ed. *Savoir tout restaurer*. Paris: Denoël, 1985.

PYE78 Pye, David. *The Nature and Aesthetics of Design*. London: Barrie & Jenkins, 1978.

PYKE80 Pyke, Beverley. *The Good Looking House*. Bristol: Redcliffe Press, 1980.

RADF83 Radford, William A. *Old House Measured and Scaled Detail Drawings* (reprint of 1911 edition). New York: Dover, 1983.

RAMS88 "Historic Preservation." Chapter 19 in *Architectural Graphic Standards* (8th edition), edited by Charles G. Ramsey, Harold R. Sleeper, and John R. Hoke, 759-785. New York: John Wiley & Sons, 1988.

RASK84 Rasky, Frank. *Industry in the Wilderness*. Toronto: Dundurn Press, 1984

READ73 *Reader's Digest Complete Do-it-yourself Manual*. Montreal: Reader's Digest Association (Canada), 1973.

READ82 *Reader's Digest Home Improvements Manual*. Montreal: Reader's Digest Association (Canada), 1982.

REAL81 Real Estate Research Corporation. *Economics of Revitalization: A Decisionmaking Guide for Local Officials*. Washington, DC: US Department of the Interior (HCRS), 1981.

REID84 Reid, Esmond. *Understanding Buildings*. Cambridge, MA: MIT Press, 1984.

REIN79 Reiner, Laurence E. *How to Recycle Buildings*. New York: McGraw-Hill, 1979.

REMP80 Rempel, John. *Building with Wood* (revised edition). Toronto: University of Toronto Press, 1980.

RENO85 *Renovation in Westmount / La rénovation à Westmount.* Westmount: Ville de Westmount, 1985.

RENY86 Reny, Claude. *Principes et critères de restauration et d'insertion.* Québec: Commission des biens culturels, 1986.

RESE85 Research and Special Projects Branch. *Planning and Design for Commercial Area Improvements.* Toronto: Ministry of Municipal Affairs and Housing, 1985.

REST86 *The Restoration Directory.* New York: New York Landmarks Conservancy, 1986.

RICHnd Richardson, Douglas,et al. *Architecture in Ontario: A Select Bibliography on Architectural Conservation and the History of Architecture with Special Relevance to the Province of Ontario.* Toronto: Ministry of Culture and Recreation, nd.

RODD83 Roddewig, Richard J. *Preparing a Historic Preservation Ordinance.* Chicago: American Planning Association, 1983.

RODG78 Rodgers, W.R., ed. *Five Studies: Planning for Downtown Conservation.* Toronto: Ministry of Culture and Recreation, 1978.

SAND84 Sandwith, Hermione, and Sheila Stainton. *The National Trust Manual of Housekeeping.* London: Allen Lane, 1984.

SARV81 Sarviel, Ed. *Construction Estimating Reference Data.* Carlsbad, CA: Craftsman Book Co., 1981.

SAUN87 Saunders, Matthew. *The Historic Home Owner's Companion.* London: Batsford, 1987.

SCHO82 Schön, Donald A. *The Reflective Practitioner: How Professionals Think in Action.* New York: Basic Books, 1982.

SCHO85 Schofield, Jane. *Basic Limewash* (SPAB Information Sheet no. 1). London: Society for the Preservation of Ancient Buildings, 1985.

SCOT84 *Scottish Conservation Directory 1985-86.* Edinburgh: Scottish Development Agency, 1984.

SCOT85 *Scottish Architects in Conservation.* Edinburgh: Scottish Development Agency, 1985.

SEDW83 Sedway Cooke Associates. *Retrofit Right.* Oakland, CA: City of Oakland Planning Department, 1983.

SEAL79 Seale, William. *Recreating the Historic House Interior.* Nashville: American Association for State and Local History, 1979.

SEEL85 Seeley, Ivor H. *Building Surveys, Reports and Dilapidations.* London: Macmillan, 1985.

SEYM84 Seymour, John. *The Forgotten Arts.* London: Dorling Kindersley, 1984.

SHAK85 Shakery, Karin, and Robert J. Beckstrom. *Ortho's Home Improvement Encyclopedia.* San Francisco: Chevron Chemical Company, 1985.

SHER75 Sherwood, Gerald E. *New Life for Old Dwellings.* Washington, DC: US Department of Agriculture, 1975.

SHOP86 Shopsin, William C. *Restoring Old Buildings for Contemporary Uses.* New York: Whitney Library of Design, 1986.

SIMP78 *Simple Home Repairs Outside.* Washington, DC: US Department of Agriculture, 1978.

SMIT74 Smith, J. T., and E. M. Yates. *On the Dating of English Houses from External Evidence* (reprint). Faringdon, Berks.: E. W. Classey Ltd., 1974.

SMIT78 Smith, John F. *A Critical Bibliography of Building Conservation.* London: Mansell, 1978.

SMIT84 Smith, Sally W., ed. *How to Replace and Install Doors and Windows.* San Francisco: Chevron Chemical Company, 1984.

SMIT85 Smith, Baird M. *Moisture Problems in Historic Masonry Walls: Diagnosis and Treatment.* Washington, DC: US Department of the Interior (NPS), 1985.

SMITnd Smith, D. Jennings, et al. *Conservation in Essex No. 4: Historic Buildings.* Chelmsford: Essex County Council, nd.

SPAR71 Sparrow, Charles, and David Peace. *Public Inquiries: Presenting the Conservation Case.* London: Council for British Archaeology, 1971.

STAG76 Stagg, William D., and Brian F. Pegg. *Plastering: A Craftsman's Encyclopaedia.* London: Crosby Lockwood Staples, 1976. (also New York: Crown, 1985)

STAH84 Stahl, Frederick A. *A Guide to the Maintenance, Repair, and Alteration of Historic Buildings.* New York: Van Nostrand Reinhold, 1984.

STEN81 Stenning, D. F., P. M. Richards, R. R. Carpenter. *Conservation in Essex No. 5: Shopfronts.* Chelmsford: Essex County Council, 1981.

STEP72 Stephen, George. *Remodeling Old Houses Without Destroying Their Character.* New York: Alfred A. Knopf, 1972.

STEP73 Stephen, George. *Revitalizing Older Houses in Charlestown.* Boston: Boston Redevelopment Authority, 1973.

STIP80 Stipe, Robert E., ed. *New Directions in Rural Preservation.* Washington, DC: US Department of the Interior (HCRS), 1980.

STLOnd St-Louis, Denis. *Fenêtres et portes traditionelles* (Cahier technique No. 1). Québec: Service de l'urbanisme, division du Vieux-Québec et du patrimoine, nd.

STLOnda St-Louis, Denis. *Toitures et corniches traditionelles* (Cahier technique No. 2). Québec: Service de l'urbanisme, division du Vieux-Québec et du patrimoine, nd.

STRA86 Stratton, Arthur. *The Orders of Architecture* (reprint of 1931 edition). London: Studio Editions, 1986.

SYKE84 Sykes, Meredith H. *Manual on Systems of Inventorying Immovable Cultural Property.* Paris: UNESCO, 1984.

SZEK80 Szekely, George, and Dianna Gabay. *A Study of a Community: Staten Island Architecture and Environment .* New York: Staten Island Continuum of Education, 1980.

TAUS86 Tausky, Nancy Z., and Lynne DiStefano. *Victorian Architecture in London and Southwestern Ontario.* Toronto: University of Toronto Press, 1986.

TECH82 Technical Preservation Services (NPS). *Respectful Rehabilitation.* Washington, DC: Preservation Press, 1982.

TECH86 *Technologies for Prehistoric and Historic Preservation.* Washington, DC: Office of Technology Assessment, 1986.

THOM81 Thompson, M. W. *Ruins: Their Preservation and Display.* London: British Museum, 1981.

THOMnd Thomas, Andrew R. *Treatment of Damp in Old Buildings* (Technical pamphlet 8). London: Society for the Preservation of Ancient Buildings, nd.

THOR84 Thornton, Peter. *Authentic Decor: The Domestic Interior, 1620-1920.* New York: Viking, 1984.

THUR83 Thurow, Charles. *Improving Street Climate Through Urban Design.* Chicago: American Planning Association, 1983.

TIMM76 Timmons, Sharon, ed. *Preservation and Conservation: Principles and Practices.* Washington, DC: Preservation Press, 1976

TOPI75 *A Topical Organization of Ontario History.* Toronto: Ontario Ministry of Natural Resources, 1975.

TREA80 *Treatment of Archaeological Properties: A Handbook.* Washington, DC: Advisory Council on Historic Preservation, 1980.

TRIC84 *Tricks of the Trade: Home DIY.* London: Pelham Books, 1984.

TRIL72 Trill, J., and J. T. Bowyer. *Problems in Building Construction.* London: Architectural Press, 1972.

TRIL73 Trill, J., and J. T. Bowyer. *Problems in Building Construction: Tutor's Guide.* London: Architectural Press, 1973.

TUNI86 Tunick, Susan. *Field Guide to Apartment Building Architecture*. New York: Friends of Terra Cotta/New York State, 1986.

UPTO86 Upton, Dell, ed. *America's Architectural Roots: Ethnic Groups That Built America*. Washington, DC: Preservation Press, 1986.

VICT84 *The Victorian Design Book*. Ottawa: Lee Valley Tools, 1984.

VILA81 Vila, Bob. *Bob Vila's This Old House*. New York: E. P. Dutton, 1981.

VONB84 von Baeyer, Edwinna. *Rhetoric and Roses: A History of Canadian Gardening, 1900-1930*. Toronto: Fitzhenry and Whiteside, 1984.

WALK81 Walker, Lester. *American Shelter*. Woodstock, NY: Overlook Press, 1981.

WARL53 Warland, E.G. *Modern Practical Masonry* (second edition). London: Pitman, 1953. [reprinted by the Stone Federation, n.d.]

WARN78 Warner, Raynor M., S. M. Groff, and R. P. Warner. *Business and Preservation*. New York: INFORM, Inc., 1978.

WEAV87 Weaver, Martin E. *Acid Rain vs Canada's Heritage*. Ottawa: Heritage Canada Foundation, 1987.

WEIL82 Weiler, John. *Our Working Past: Conserving Industrial Relics for Recreation and Tourism*. Toronto: John Weiler, 1982.

WEIS82 Weiss, Norman, et al. *Sandstone Restoration Study Report*. New York: New York Landmarks Conservancy, 1982.

WHER82 *Where to Look: A Guide to Preservation Information*. Washington, DC: Advisory Council on Historic Preservation, 1982.

WHIF69 Whiffen, Marcus. *American Architecture Since 1780: A Guide to the Styles*. Cambridge, MA: MIT Press, 1969.

WILL76 Williams, G. B. A. *Chimneys in Old Buildings* (Technical pamphlet 3). London: Society for the Preservation of Ancient Buildings, 1976.

WILL78 Williams, Barrie. *The Underuse of Upper Floors in Historic Town Centres*. York: IAAS, University of York, 1978.

WILL78a Williams, Olga M., ed. *LACACs at work . . .: A Primer of Local Architectural Conservation Advisory Committee Activities in Ontario*. Toronto: Ministry of Culture and Recreation, 1978.

WILL83 Williams, G. B. A. *Pointing Stone and Brick Walling* (Technical pamphlet 5). London: Society for the Preservation of Ancient Buildings, 1983.

WING83 Wing, Charles. *Housewarming with Charlie Wing*. Boston: Little, Brown, 1983.

WOOD83 *Wood Siding - Installing, Finishing, Maintaining*. Washington, DC: US Department of Agriculture, 1983.

WOOD86 *Wood Decay in Houses: How to Prevent and Control It* (revised edition). Washington, DC: US Department of Agriculture, 1986.

WORS69 Worskett, Roy. *The Character of Towns: An Approach to Conservation*. London: Architectural Press, 1969.

WRIG76 Wright, Russell. *A Guide to Delineating Edges of Historic Districts*. Washington, DC: Preservation Press, 1976.

WRIG86 Wright, Adela. *Removing Paint from Old Buildings* (SPAB Information Sheet no. 5). London: Society for the Preservation of Ancient Buildings, 1986.

ZEIS84 Zeisel, John. *Inquiry by Design*. Cambridge: Cambridge University Press, 1984.

Unless credited otherwise, the photographs are by the author (© Mark Fram 1988). Other photographs are used by permission of the photographers. Many of the photographs are from the collection of the Ontario Ministry of Culture and Communications (abbreviated OMCC); these are credited to the individual photographers as much as possible (photographs by the author from the ministry's files are noted as MF/OMCC). Similarly, illustrations held by the Ontario Heritage Foundation are so noted (abbreviated as OHF). Apart from the few locations noted, all photographs are of places and buildings in Ontario.

Drawings are by the author and Scott Kerr, unless credited otherwise. The composite drawings on pages 21, 69, 73 and 191 and portions of other illustrations are based on two properties conserved by the Ontario Heritage Foundation: the Mather-Walls House, Ottawa Street, Keewatin, and the Ontario Heritage Centre (originally the Birkbeck Building), Adelaide Street East, Toronto. Other drawings are adapted from material in the following sources, cited in the bibliography: ASHU83, CHIT80, HERI87a, KITC83, LOND85, MACE98, MCKE70, POOR83 and RADF83.

The verbal illustrations are borrowed for the most part from two books that compile quotations about architecture: KNEV86 and MADD85. The quotation on page 57 is from Alberto Grimoldi, "Architecture as restoration: Notes on restoration in architecture", Lotus International, 57 (1985), 116-127.

front cover: Walton Street, Port Hope.
frontispiece: Ontario Power Generating Station, Niagara Falls.
title page: Parkdale, near Ossington Avenue, Toronto.
1: Temple of the Children of Peace, Sharon.
8: Sussex Drive, Ottawa. *John Weiler/OMCC*
9, top: Corner of Adelaide and Victoria, Toronto.
9, bottom: Corner of Yonge and Queen, Toronto.
12, top: Princess Street, Kingston, early 1860s. *National Archives of Canada, PA62177*
12, middle: Colborne Street, Fenelon Falls, 1903. *National Archives of Canada, C27196*
12, bottom: Highway 11, Latchford.
13: Highway 2, Napanee. *MF/OMCC*
15, top: Lift lock opening, Kirkfield, 1907. *National Archives of Canada, C10956*
15, upper middle: Stone bridge, Pakenham.
15, lower middle: Railway station, Peterborough.
15, bottom: Transmission lines, Queenston.
16, top: Gold Rock, Upper Manitou Lake. *Paul Campbell/OMCC*
16, upper middle: Woodlot, near Peterborough. *MF/OMCC*
16, lower middle: Big Master mine, Upper Manitou Lake. *Paul Campbell/OMCC*
16, bottom: Ball Mill, Baltimore.
17, top: Lennox & Addington County, near Napanee.
17, upper middle: Rideau waterway, near Burritts Rapids.
17, lower middle: Seymour Township, near Campbellford.
17, bottom: Rawdon Township. *MF/OMCC*
18, top: Elementary school, Erin.
18, upper middle: Public library, New Liskeard. *MF/OMCC*
18, lower middle: High Park, Toronto.
18, bottom: Nippissing District court house, North Bay. *MF/OMCC*
19, top: Ontario Psychiatric Hospital, St. Thomas.
19, upper middle: Former Cairns Creamery, Niagara Falls.
19, lower middle: Colborne Street, Fenelon Falls.
19, bottom: Windermere House, Muskoka.
33, top: House, Paris. *Carol Priamo/OMCC*
33, bottom: Barriefield village. *John J.-G. Blumenson/OMCC*
37, top: Way station, Niagara. *OMCC*
37, middle: "The Cone", Port Hope. *Anne M. de Fort-Menares*
37, bottom: Commemorative plaques, Pakenham Bridge.
39: King Street West, Toronto.
43: George Brown House, Toronto.
59: House, Metcalfe Street, Toronto.
72, top: Abandoned brewery, Kingston.
72, middle: Former Victoria College, Cobourg.
72, bottom: Sultan Street, Toronto.
76, top, middle: Former general store, Vivian. *Carol Priamo*
76, bottom left: "Wedding Cake House", Markham. *John J.-G. Blumenson/OMCC*
76, bottom right: "Wedding Cake House", Markham, in context.
78, left: Commercial building, Tweed.
78, right: Former John Street Pumping Station, Toronto.
79, top: Schneider House, Waterloo.
79, bottom: Abandoned railway embankment, near Port Hope.
80: Merrickville. *MF/OMCC*
81, top left: Walton Street, Port Hope.

81, top right: The "Square", Goderich. *OMCC*
81, middle: Bayfield. *OMCC*
82: Mill Street, Elora.
83: Farmhouse, Darlington.
86, top: Wellington County, near Erin.
86, middle: King City. *John J.-G. Blumenson/OMCC*
86, bottom left: Millbrook.
86, bottom right: Newcastle Town Hall, Bowmanville.
87, top: King Street East, Toronto.
87, middle: Gordon Block, Stratford.
87, bottom left: Hazelton Avenue, Toronto.
87, bottom right: St. Clair Avenue West, Toronto.
89, top: Lowther Avenue, Toronto.
89, middle: Sussex Drive, Ottawa. *John Weiler/OMCC*
89, bottom left: Elora Mill, Elora.
89, bottom right: Artpark, Lewiston, New York.
90: Railway station, Gravenhurst. *OMCC*
91, top: Public library, Bracebridge.
91, bottom: Schneider House, Waterloo.
93: Drawing, Mather-Walls House, Keewatin. *OHF*
95, top: Kew Beach, Toronto. *MF/OMCC*
95, middle: Downtown, near Market Square, Kingston. *OMCC*
95, bottom: Legislative Chamber, Queen's Park, Toronto. *MF/OMCC*
99, top, middle: Little Inn, Bayfield. *OMCC*
99, bottom: Drawing, Mather-Walls House, Keewatin. *OHF*
101, top left: Farm, near Fenelon Falls.
101, top right: Mill ruin, Elora.
101, middle: Ball Mill, Baltimore.
102, left: Macaulay House, Picton.
102, right: Power Street, Toronto.
103: Charles Street West, Toronto.
104: Bloor Street West, Toronto.
105, middle: House and garden, Barrie, 1906. *National Archives of Canada, C37498*
105, bottom: House and trees, Bobcaygeon.
106: Hutchison House, Peterborough. *MF/OMCC*
107, middle: Trinity Street, Toronto.
107, bottom left: Osgoode Hall, Toronto.
107, bottom right: Post Office, Millbrook.
108: St. James' Cemetery, Toronto.
109, middle: Upper Grand River valley.
109, bottom left: Windmill ruin, Maitland. *OMCC*
109, bottom right: Guelph. *Carol Priamo/OMCC*
111, all: St. Raphael's ruins, near Williamstown.
112: Drawing, Ontario Heritage Centre. *Spencer R. Higgins/OHF*
113, middle left: Fire hall, Port Hope (demolished).
113, bottom left: Downtown, Perth.
113, right: Former post office, Bracebridge.
115, top: "Villeneuve Castle", Picton (demolished).
115, middle: Summit House, Perth.
117: Elgin Theatre, Toronto. *Gary Beechey/OHF*
118, top: Beverley Street, Toronto.
118, middle: St. Thomas Church, Bracebridge.
118, bottom: Ancaster Mountain Mill, Ancaster. *Carol Priamo*
119, both: St. Thomas Church, Bracebridge.
120, top: Temple of the Children of Peace, Sharon.
120, bottom: Watson's Mill, Manotick. *Carol Priamo*
121, top: Blackfriars Bridge, London. *Carol Priamo/OMCC*
121, bottom: Welland Canal, Thorold.
123: Church, Ameliasburgh.
124: Macaulay House, Picton. *OMCC*
125, top: Anderson House, Stratford.
125, bottom: Mill, Caledonia. *Carol Priamo*
127, top: Former schoolhouse, near Campbellford.
127, middle left: Downtown Galt, Cambridge.
127, middle right: Victoria Hall, Cobourg. *OMCC*

About the author

Mark Fram is an architectural consultant, designer and planner. Widely travelled on this continent and abroad, he has studied and written extensively about the history and planning of buildings and cities, produced plans for several public agencies, and built an accomplished photographic portfolio besides. He holds professional and graduate degrees in architecture and geography from the University of Toronto. He is a director of the Association of Heritage Consultants, and president of the Society for the Study of Architecture in Canada.